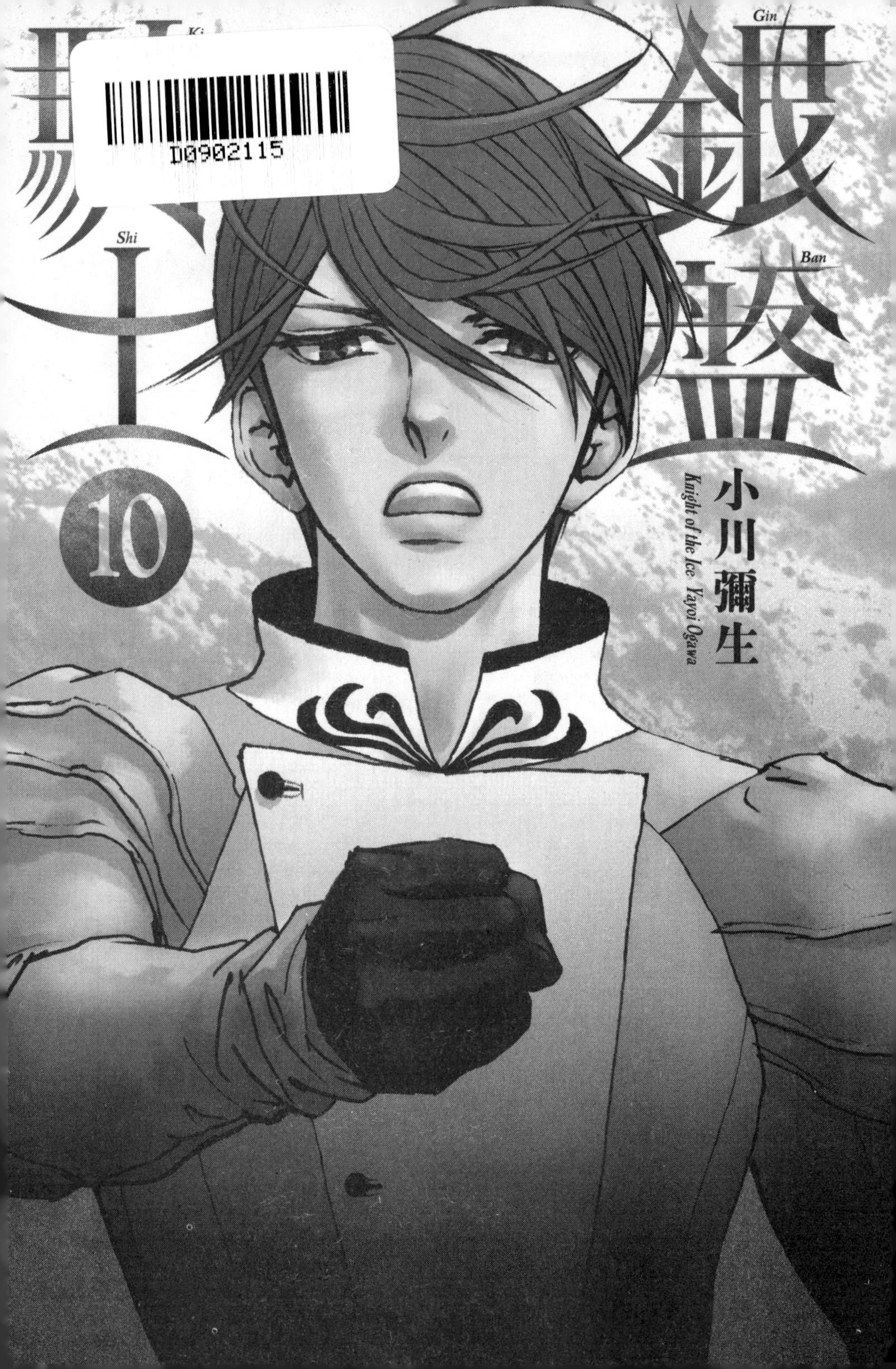
Gin
銀
Ban
盤
Ki
Shi
士
10
小川彌生
Knight of the Ice Yayoi Ogawa

Characters

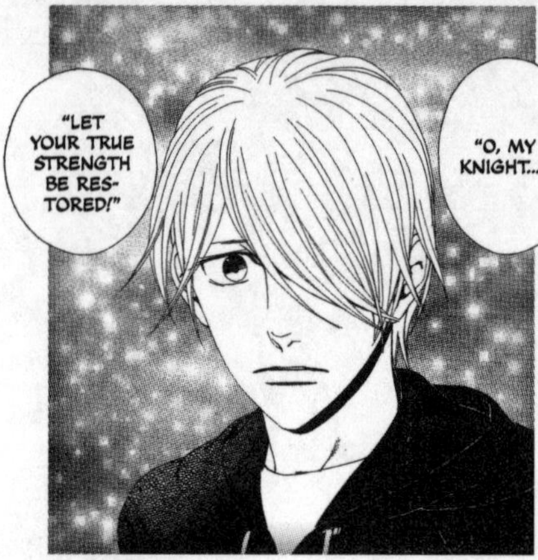
"O, MY KNIGHT..."
"LET YOUR TRUE STRENGTH BE RESTORED!"

Kokoro Kijinami

Japan's top men's figure skater. One of his greatest strengths is the beauty his height lends to his quadruple jumps. He cracks easily under pressure, but he's gotten more consistent since Chitose started reciting their magic spell for him. He's had surgery on his right ankle and is now undergoing physical rehabilitation.

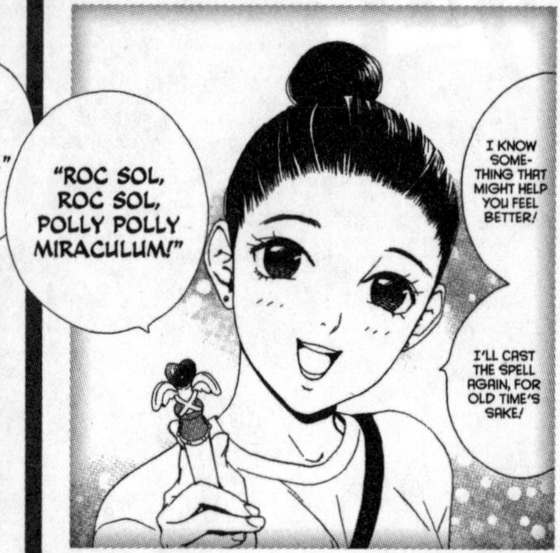
I KNOW SOMETHING THAT MIGHT HELP YOU FEEL BETTER!
I'LL CAST THE SPELL AGAIN, FOR OLD TIME'S SAKE!
"ROC SOL, ROC SOL, POLLY POLLY MIRACULUM!"

Chitose Igari

An editor for the health-and-lifestyle magazine *SASSO.* She's so short that she often gets mistaken for an elementary schooler. She also accompanies Kokoro to competitions and pretends to be his personal trainer. She's been having heart problems and is debating whether to get surgery.

Magical Princess Lady Lala is a magical girl anime that used to air on TV. Chitose and Kokoro loved it, and they often played pretend as the characters.

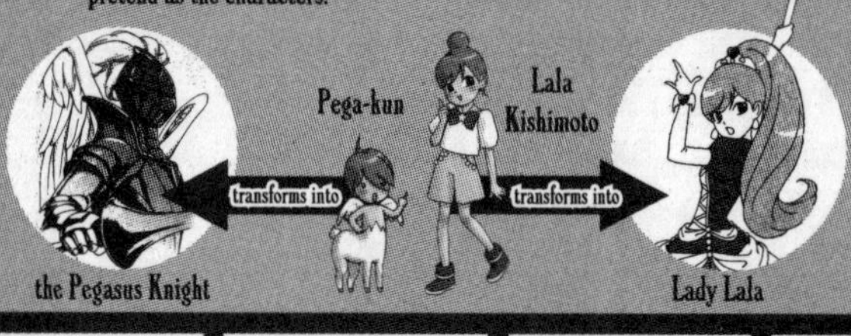
Pega-kun
Lala Kishimoto
transforms into
transforms into
the Pegasus Knight
Lady Lala

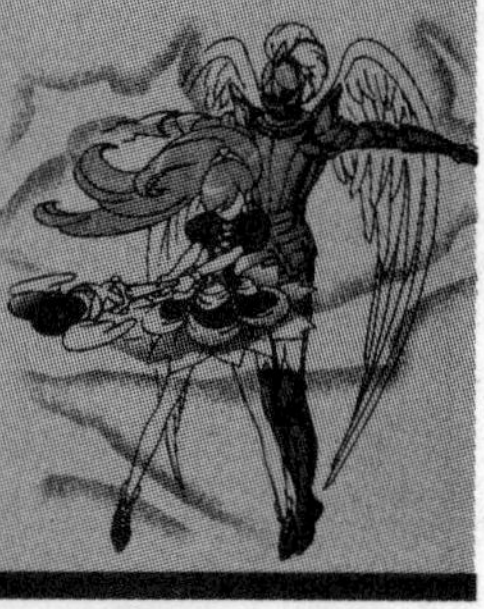

Kokoro's Father

President of the Kijinami Group, a company that runs a number of boutique ryokan.

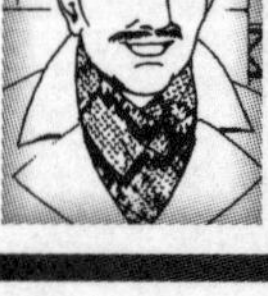

Yayoi Ogata

A manga artist. She went to the same college as Chitose and knows about her relationship with Kokoro.

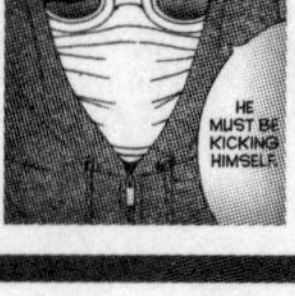
HE MUST BE KICKING HIMSELF.

Reiko Yano

An employee at Kodan Publishing. Until recently, she was married and having an affair with Sawada.

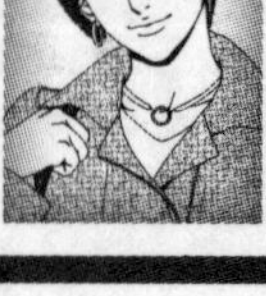

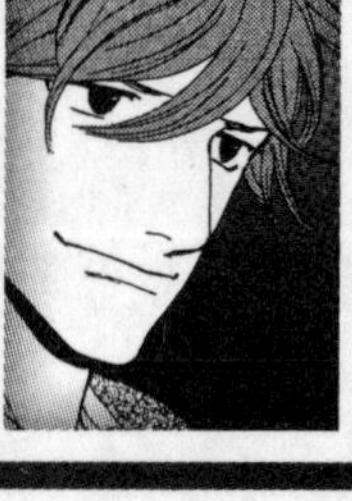

Koichi Sawada

The head of the editorial department for Kodan Publishing's magazine *SASSO.* He's good at his job, but can be somewhat lacking in delicacy...

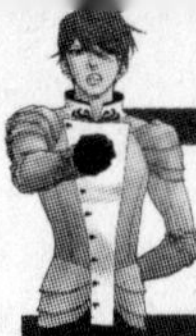

Knight of the Ice

Kokoro's Staff

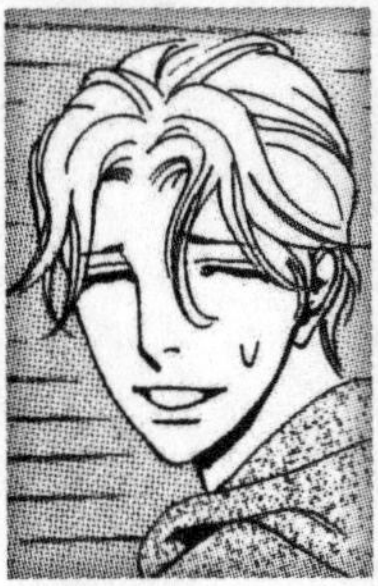

Kenzo Dominic Takiguchi

Kokoro's personal trainer.

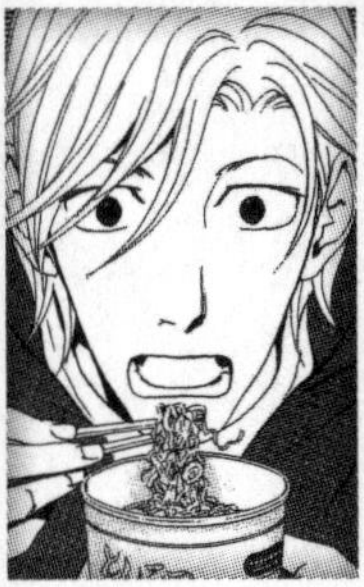

Hikaru Yomota

Kokoro's assistant coach and a former ice dancer.

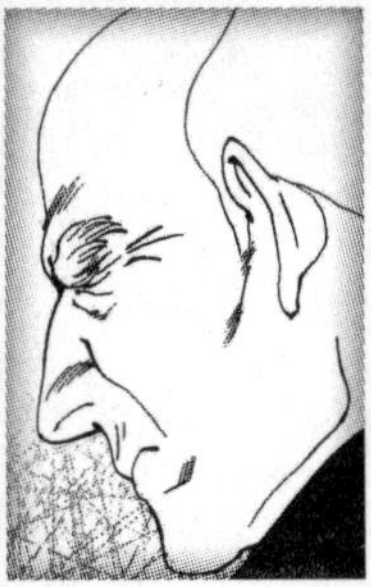

Takejiro Honda

Kokoro's coach and longtime rival of Raito Tamura's grandfather and coach, Masato Tamura.

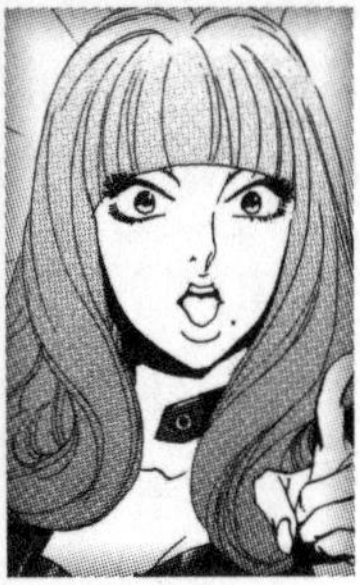

Moriyama

Kokoro's manager. She's not afraid to get a little pushy if that's what it takes to get results.

Kokoro's Rivals

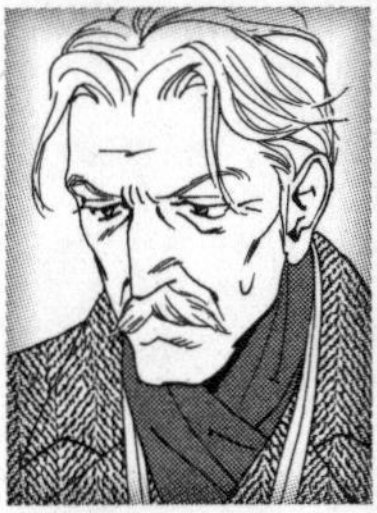

Masato Tamura

Raito Tamura's grandfather and coach.

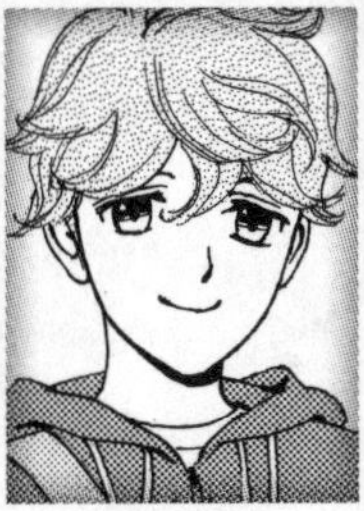

Fuuta Kumano

He can always rely on his speed and his devilish cuteness.

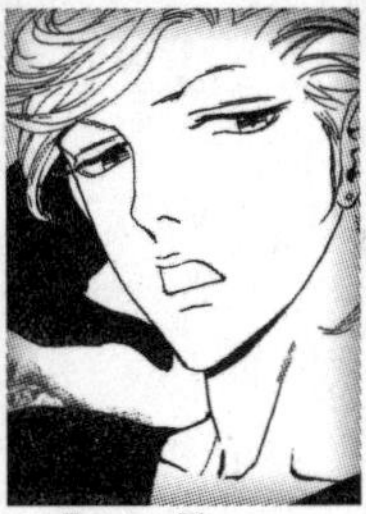

Raito Tamura

He dazzles the crowd with his passion and expressiveness.

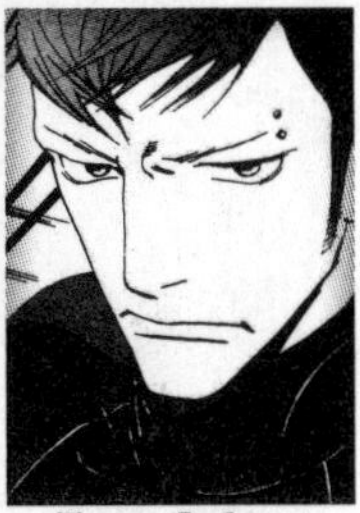

Taiga Aoki

His greatest strength is his ability to land two different quad jumps.

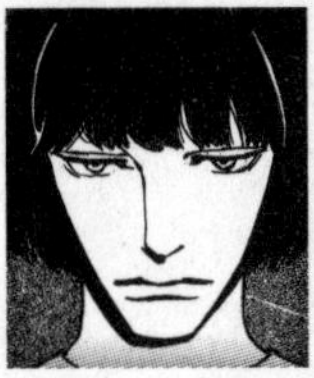

Ilia Sokurov

Russia's young top skater. He's an extreme klutz.

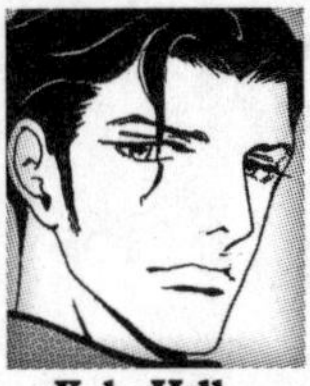

Kyle Miller

An American skater. He and Louis are known together as "KyLou."

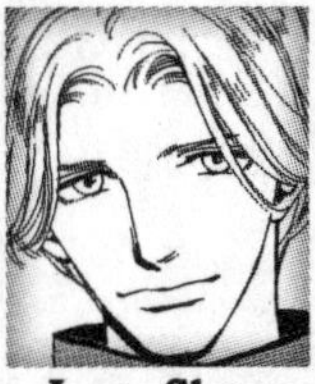

Louis Claire

A Canadian skater. He's a year younger than Kokoro and is the reigning World Champion.

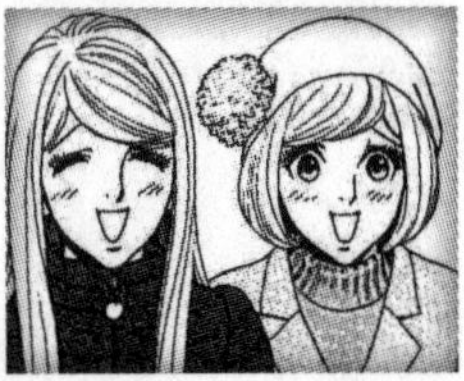

Maria & Anna Kijinami

Kokoro's younger twin sisters. Maria is in a relationship with Taiga.

Contents

Spell 47
Be Brave
006

Spell 48
Thank You
036

Spell 49
I Know You Can Do It
066

Spell 50
Believe in Him
096

Spell 51
The Courage You Gave Me
126

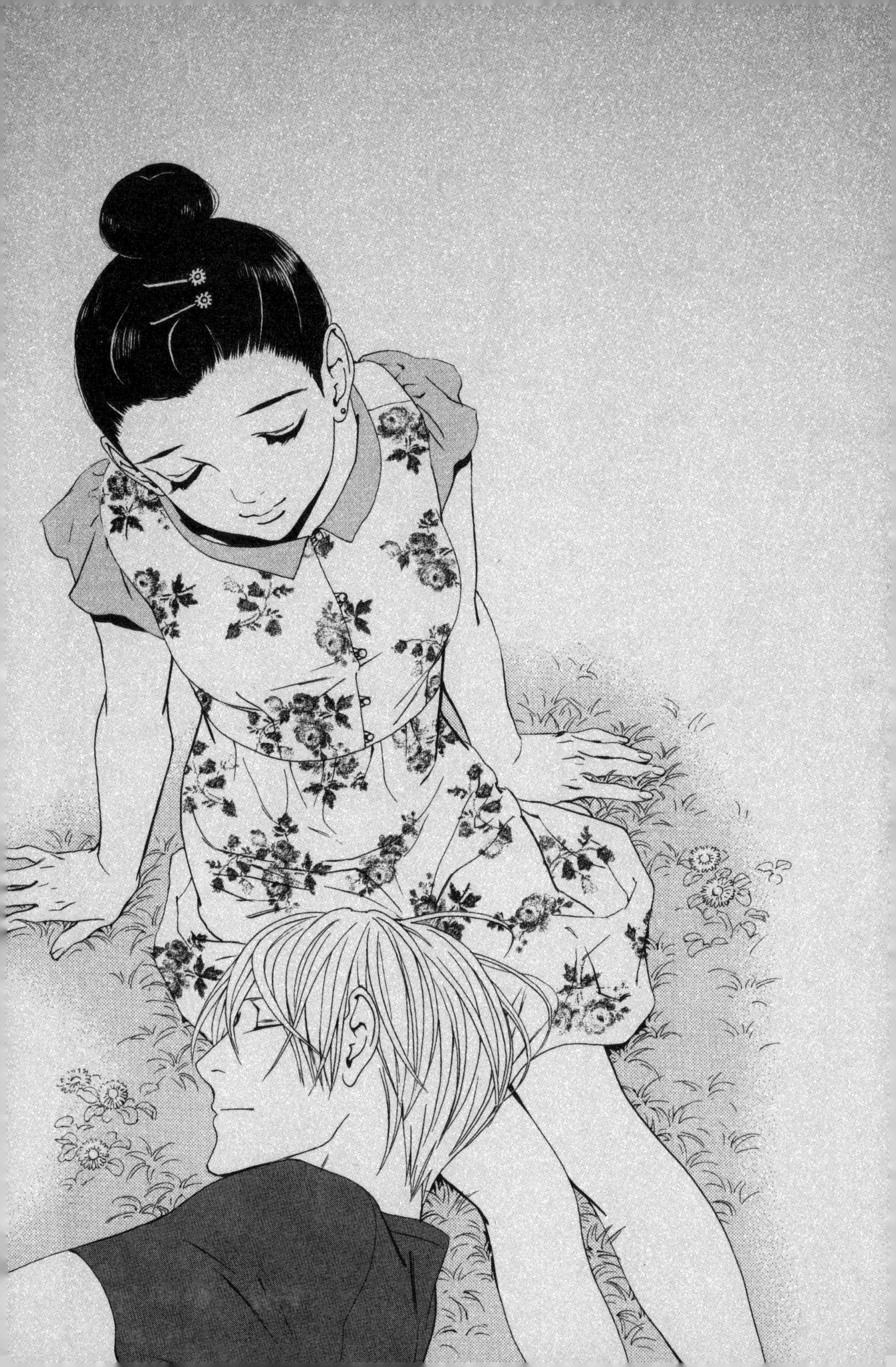

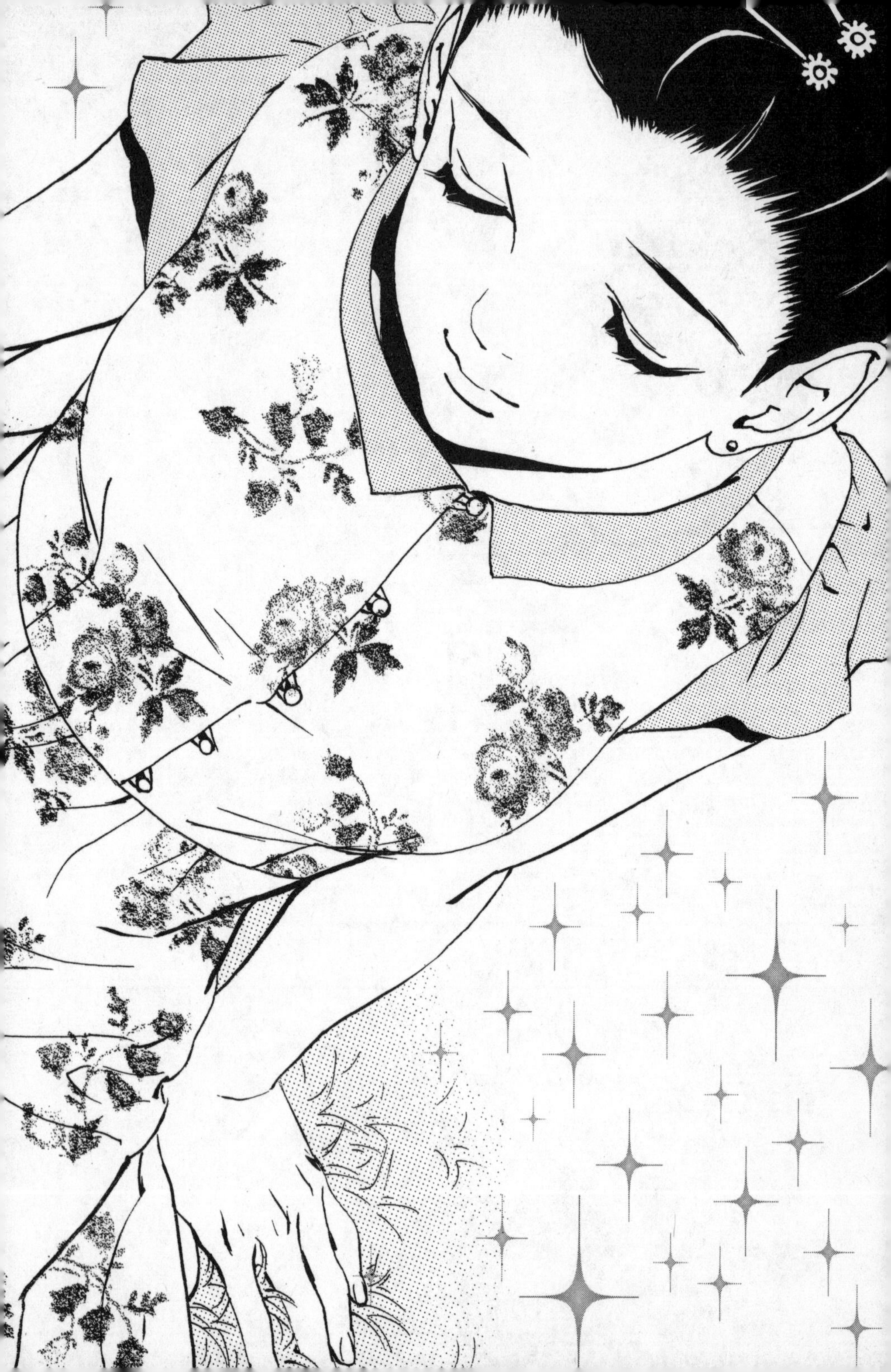

Spell 47
Be Brave

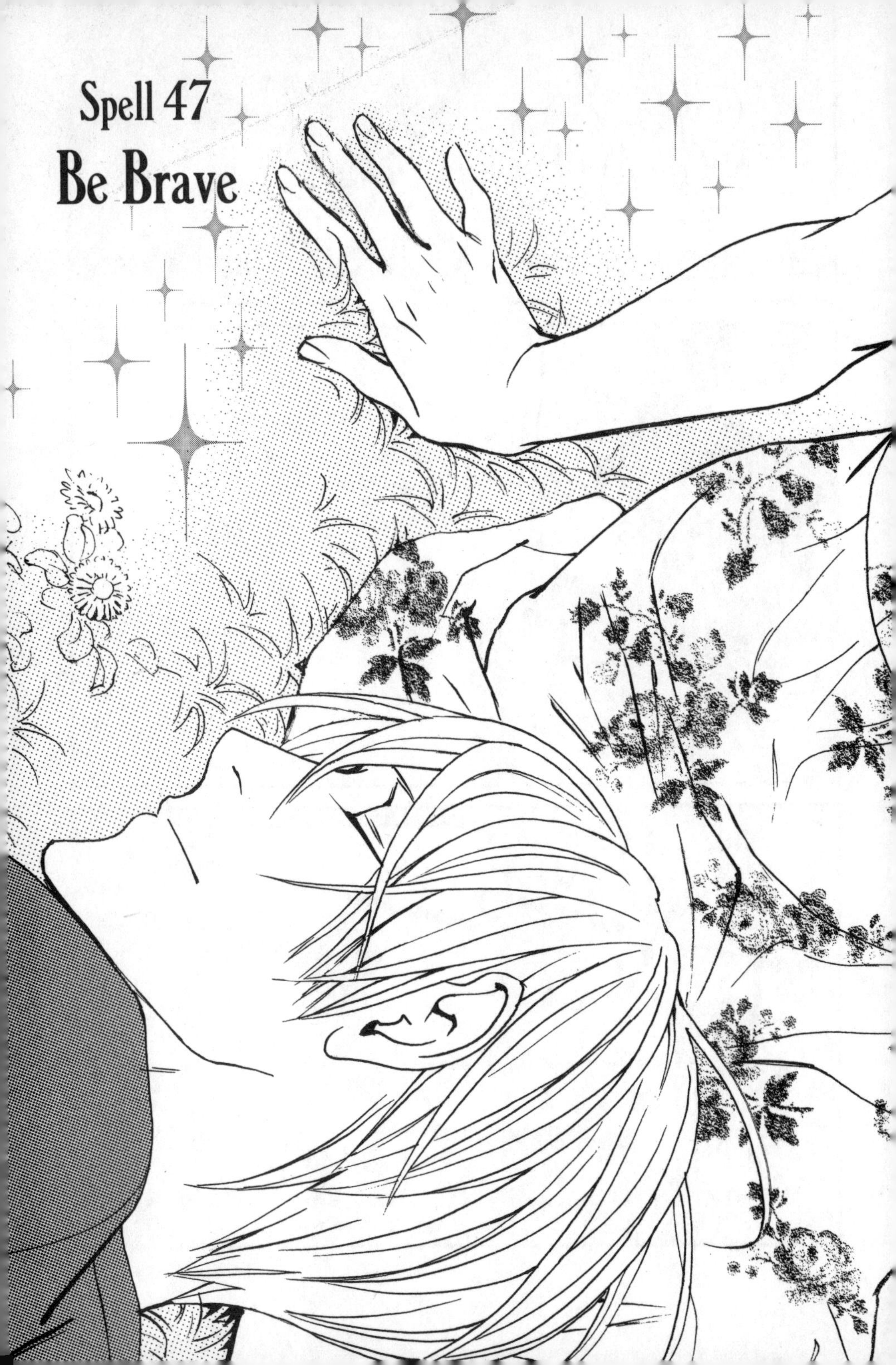

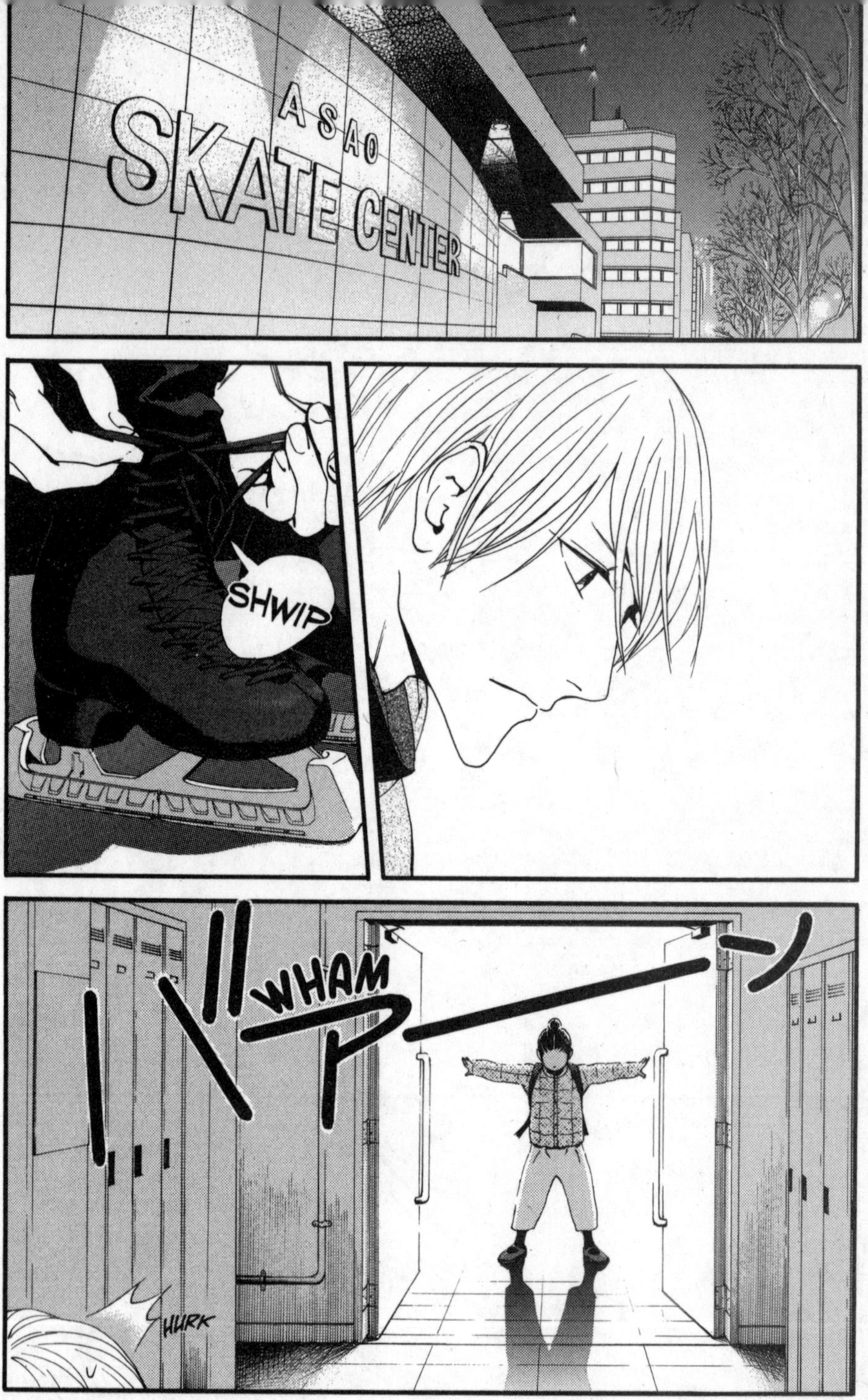
ASAO
SKATE CENTER
SHWIP
WHAM
HURK

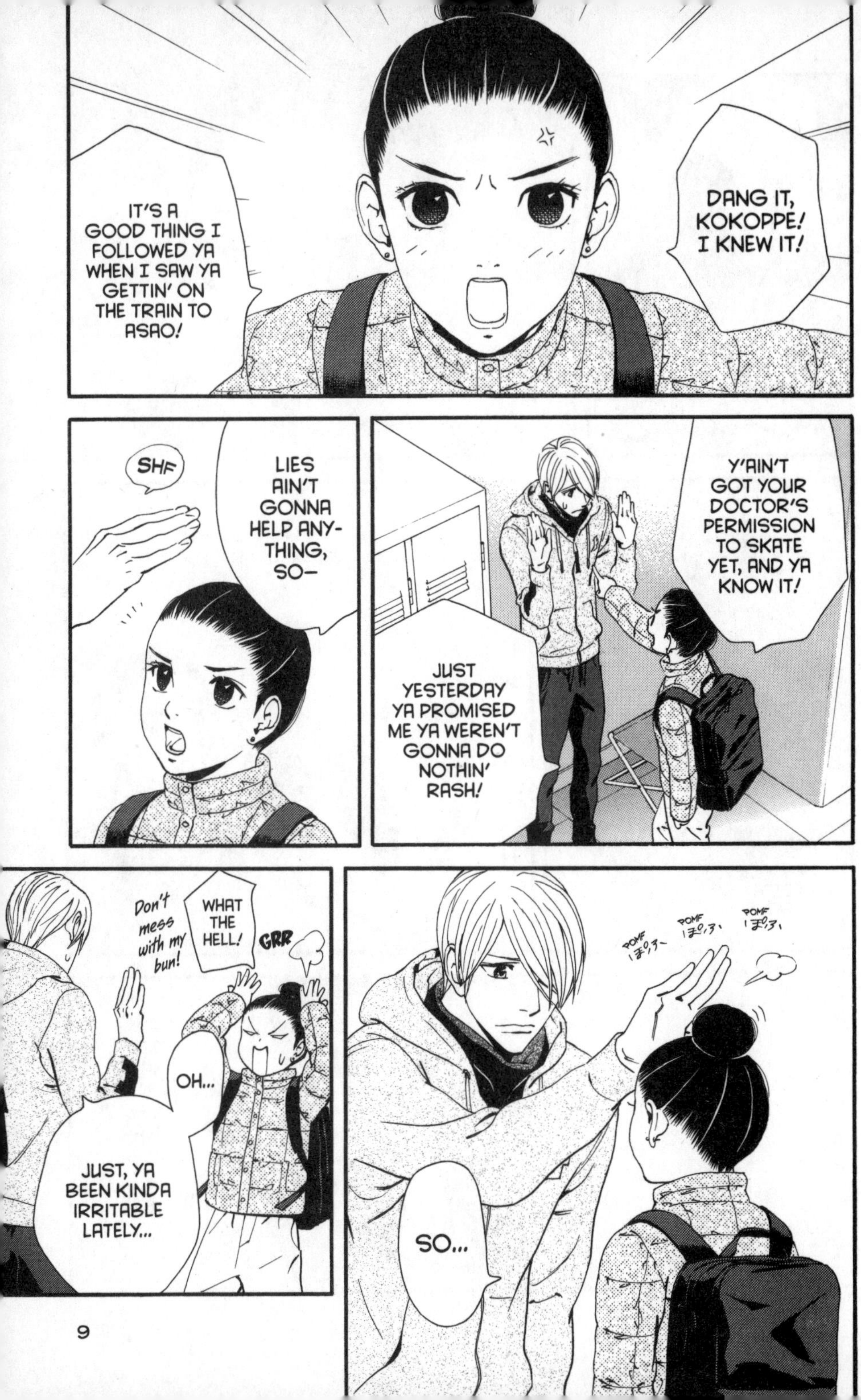
DANG IT, KOKOPPE! I KNEW IT!
IT'S A GOOD THING I FOLLOWED YA WHEN I SAW YA GETTIN' ON THE TRAIN TO ASAO!
Y'AIN'T GOT YOUR DOCTOR'S PERMISSION TO SKATE YET, AND YA KNOW IT!
JUST YESTERDAY YA PROMISED ME YA WEREN'T GONNA DO NOTHIN' RASH!
LIES AIN'T GONNA HELP ANY-THING, SO—
SHF
POMF
POMF
POMF
SO...
WHAT THE HELL!
Don't mess with my bun!
GRR
OH...
JUST, YA BEEN KINDA IRRITABLE LATELY...

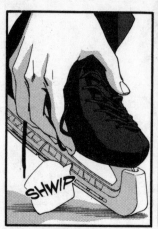

SHWIP

I'M NOT. I JUST...

I'M—

KO-KOPPE?

I'M GONNA WATCH THE OTHERS PRACTICE FOR A BIT.

LOOK.

THEY'RE OFF.

TO BE HONEST ...

SQUEEZE

I'M— I'MA HANG ON TO THESE, YA HEAR?

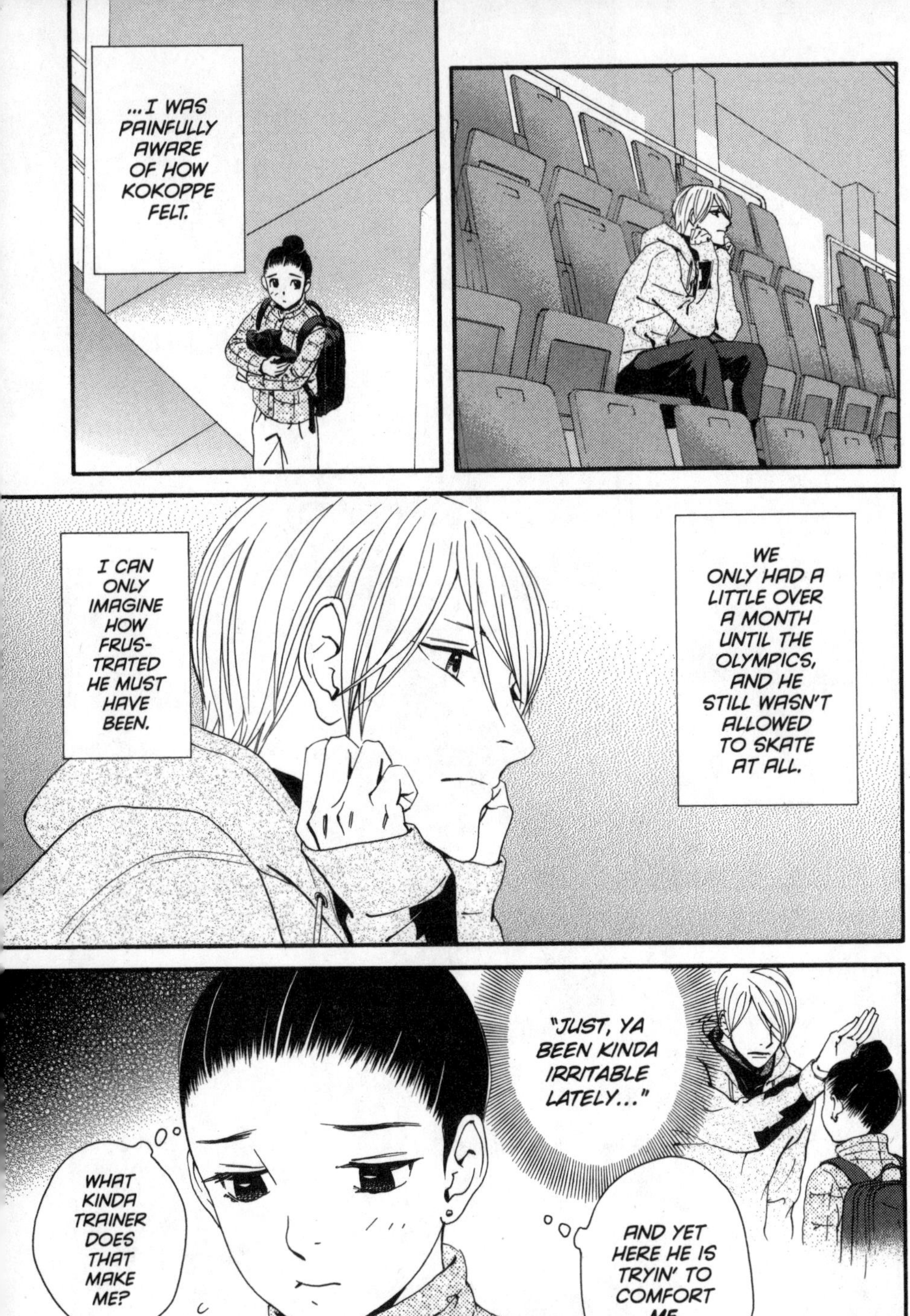
...I WAS PAINFULLY AWARE OF HOW KOKOPPE FELT.
WE ONLY HAD A LITTLE OVER A MONTH UNTIL THE OLYMPICS, AND HE STILL WASN'T ALLOWED TO SKATE AT ALL.
I CAN ONLY IMAGINE HOW FRUS-TRATED HE MUST HAVE BEEN.
"JUST, YA BEEN KINDA IRRITABLE LATELY..."
AND YET HERE HE IS TRYIN' TO COMFORT ME.
WHAT KINDA TRAINER DOES THAT MAKE ME?

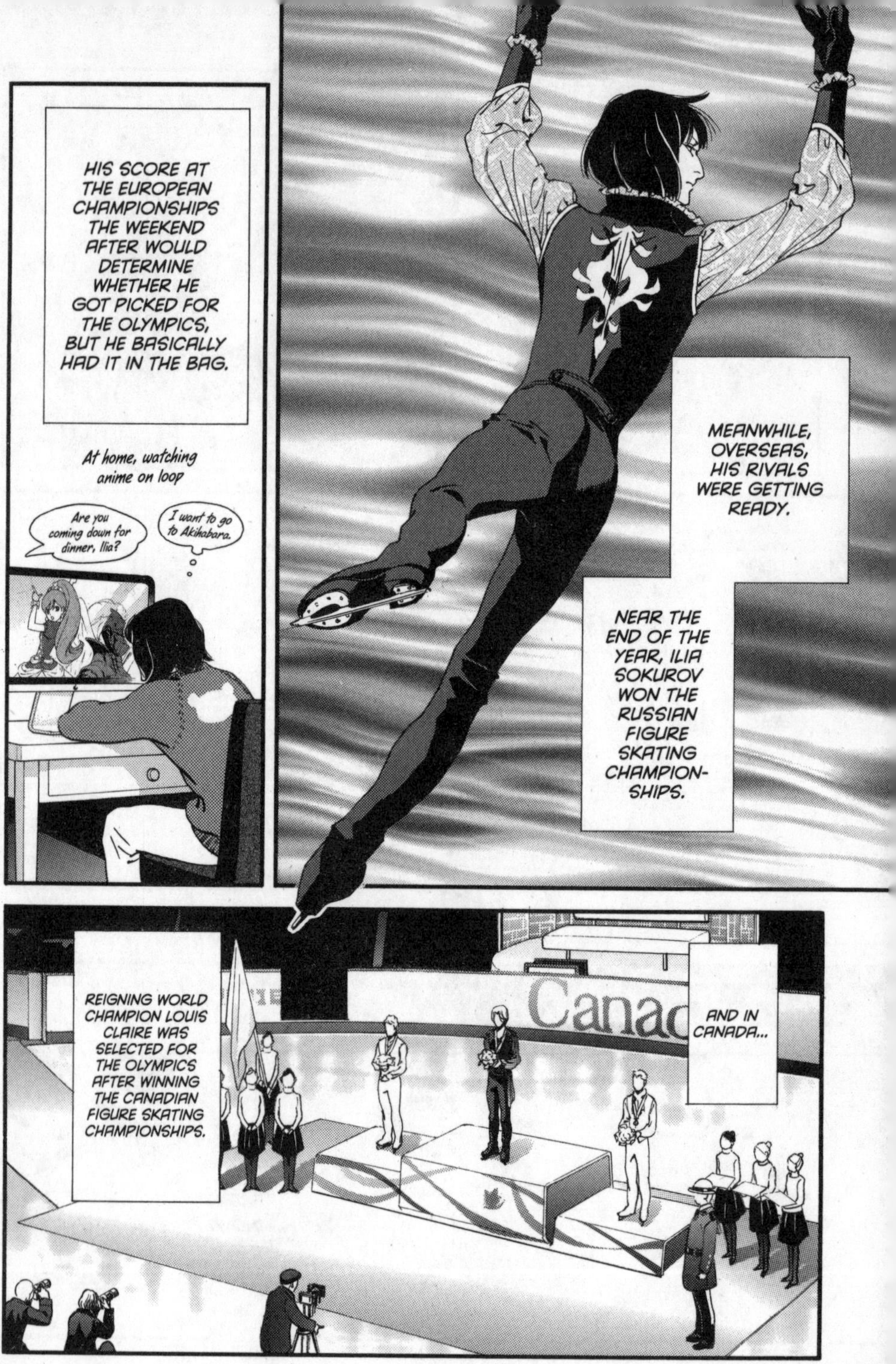
MEANWHILE, OVERSEAS, HIS RIVALS WERE GETTING READY.
NEAR THE END OF THE YEAR, ILIA SOKUROV WON THE RUSSIAN FIGURE SKATING CHAMPION-SHIPS.
HIS SCORE AT THE EUROPEAN CHAMPIONSHIPS THE WEEKEND AFTER WOULD DETERMINE WHETHER HE GOT PICKED FOR THE OLYMPICS, BUT HE BASICALLY HAD IT IN THE BAG.
At home, watching anime on loop
I want to go to Akihabara.
Are you coming down for dinner, Ilia?
AND IN CANADA...
REIGNING WORLD CHAMPION LOUIS CLAIRE WAS SELECTED FOR THE OLYMPICS AFTER WINNING THE CANADIAN FIGURE SKATING CHAMPIONSHIPS.

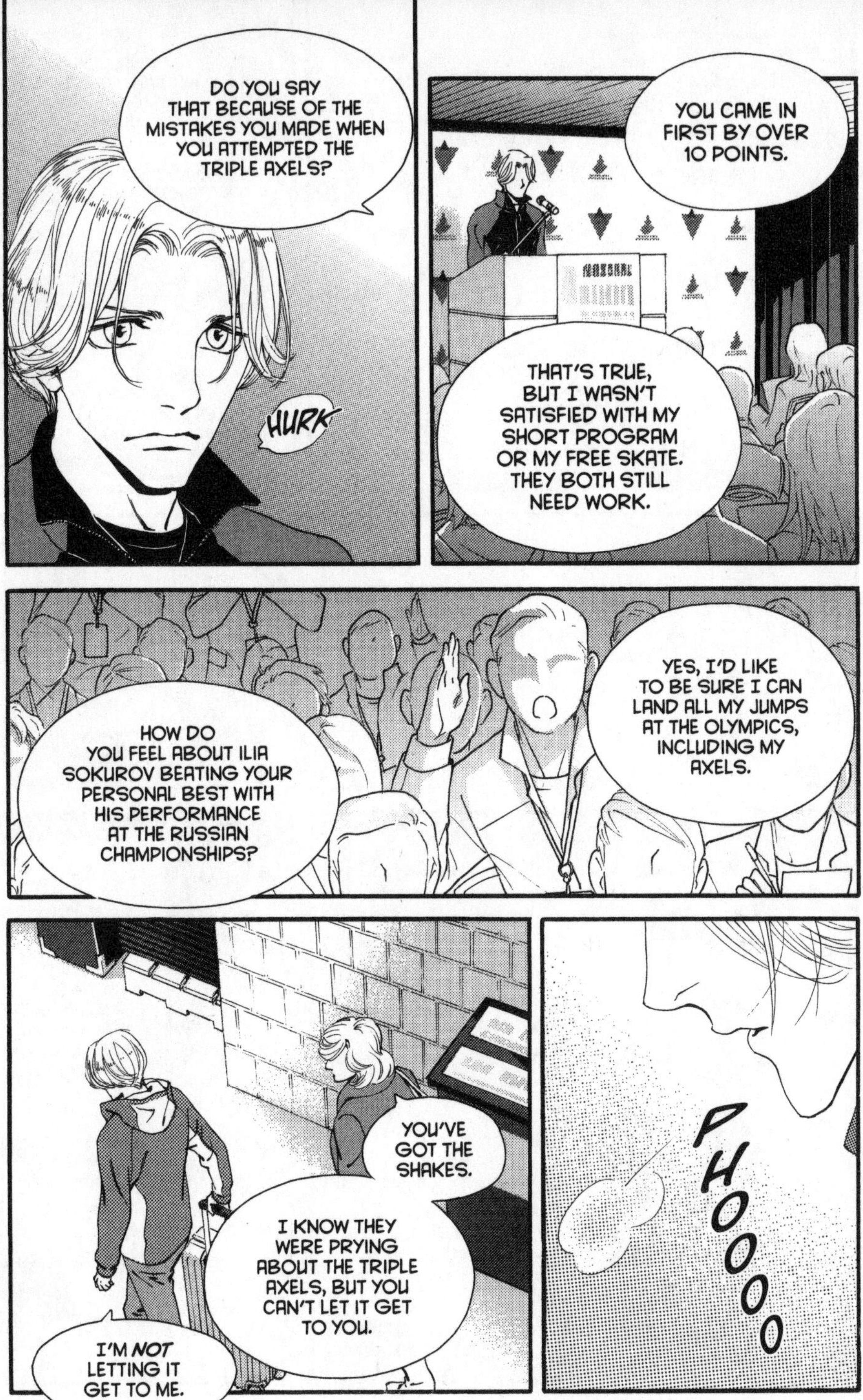
YOU CAME IN FIRST BY OVER 10 POINTS.
THAT'S TRUE, BUT I WASN'T SATISFIED WITH MY SHORT PROGRAM OR MY FREE SKATE. THEY BOTH STILL NEED WORK.
DO YOU SAY THAT BECAUSE OF THE MISTAKES YOU MADE WHEN YOU ATTEMPTED THE TRIPLE AXELS?
HURK
YES, I'D LIKE TO BE SURE I CAN LAND ALL MY JUMPS AT THE OLYMPICS, INCLUDING MY AXELS.
HOW DO YOU FEEL ABOUT ILIA SOKUROV BEATING YOUR PERSONAL BEST WITH HIS PERFORMANCE AT THE RUSSIAN CHAMPIONSHIPS?
PHOOOO
YOU'VE GOT THE SHAKES.
I KNOW THEY WERE PRYING ABOUT THE TRIPLE AXELS, BUT YOU CAN'T LET IT GET TO YOU.
I'M *NOT* LETTING IT GET TO ME.

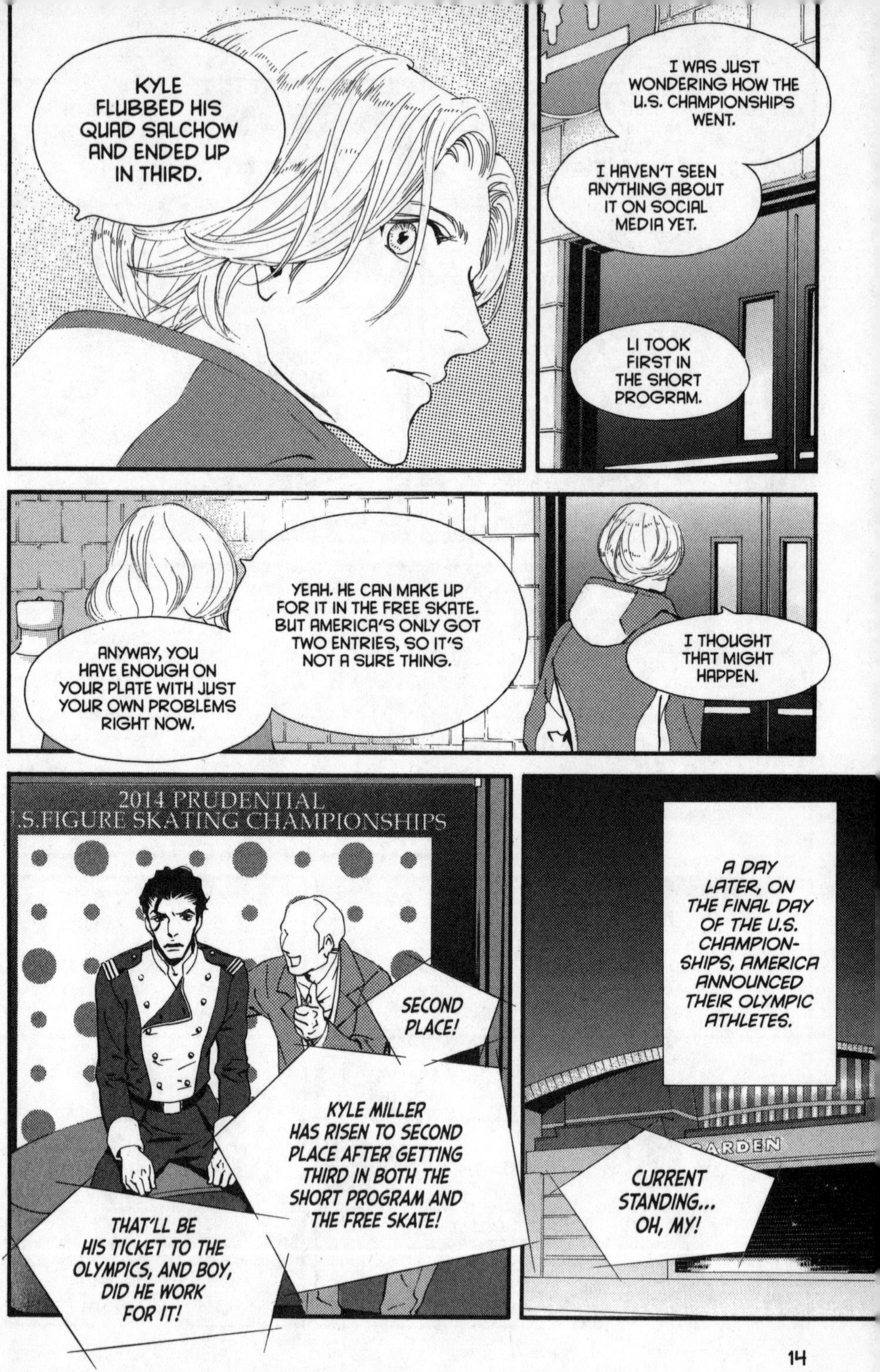
I WAS JUST WONDERING HOW THE U.S. CHAMPIONSHIPS WENT.
I HAVEN'T SEEN ANYTHING ABOUT IT ON SOCIAL MEDIA YET.
LI TOOK FIRST IN THE SHORT PROGRAM.
KYLE FLUBBED HIS QUAD SALCHOW AND ENDED UP IN THIRD.
I THOUGHT THAT MIGHT HAPPEN.
YEAH. HE CAN MAKE UP FOR IT IN THE FREE SKATE. BUT AMERICA'S ONLY GOT TWO ENTRIES, SO IT'S NOT A SURE THING.
ANYWAY, YOU HAVE ENOUGH ON YOUR PLATE WITH JUST YOUR OWN PROBLEMS RIGHT NOW.
A DAY LATER, ON THE FINAL DAY OF THE U.S. CHAMPIONSHIPS, AMERICA ANNOUNCED THEIR OLYMPIC ATHLETES.
CURRENT STANDING... OH, MY!
2014 PRUDENTIAL
S.FIGURE SKATING CHAMPIONSHIPS
SECOND PLACE!
KYLE MILLER HAS RISEN TO SECOND PLACE AFTER GETTING THIRD IN BOTH THE SHORT PROGRAM AND THE FREE SKATE!
THAT'LL BE HIS TICKET TO THE OLYMPICS, AND BOY, DID HE WORK FOR IT!

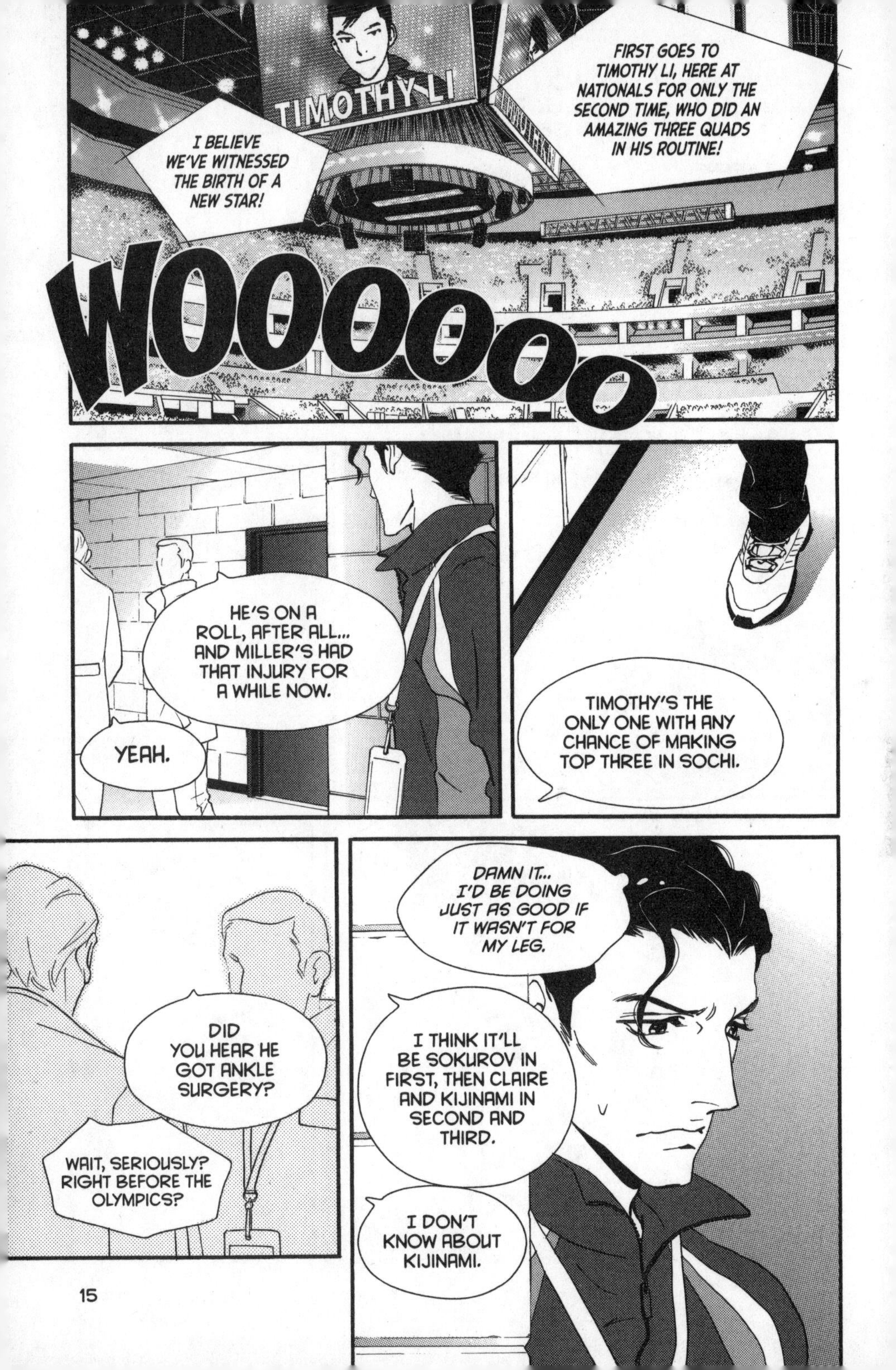
TIMOTHY LI
FIRST GOES TO TIMOTHY LI, HERE AT NATIONALS FOR ONLY THE SECOND TIME, WHO DID AN AMAZING THREE QUADS IN HIS ROUTINE!
I BELIEVE WE'VE WITNESSED THE BIRTH OF A NEW STAR!
WOOOOOO
TIMOTHY'S THE ONLY ONE WITH ANY CHANCE OF MAKING TOP THREE IN SOCHI.
HE'S ON A ROLL, AFTER ALL... AND MILLER'S HAD THAT INJURY FOR A WHILE NOW.
YEAH.
DAMN IT... I'D BE DOING JUST AS GOOD IF IT WASN'T FOR MY LEG.
I THINK IT'LL BE SOKUROV IN FIRST, THEN CLAIRE AND KIJINAMI IN SECOND AND THIRD.
I DON'T KNOW ABOUT KIJINAMI.
DID YOU HEAR HE GOT ANKLE SURGERY?
WAIT, SERIOUSLY? RIGHT BEFORE THE OLYMPICS?

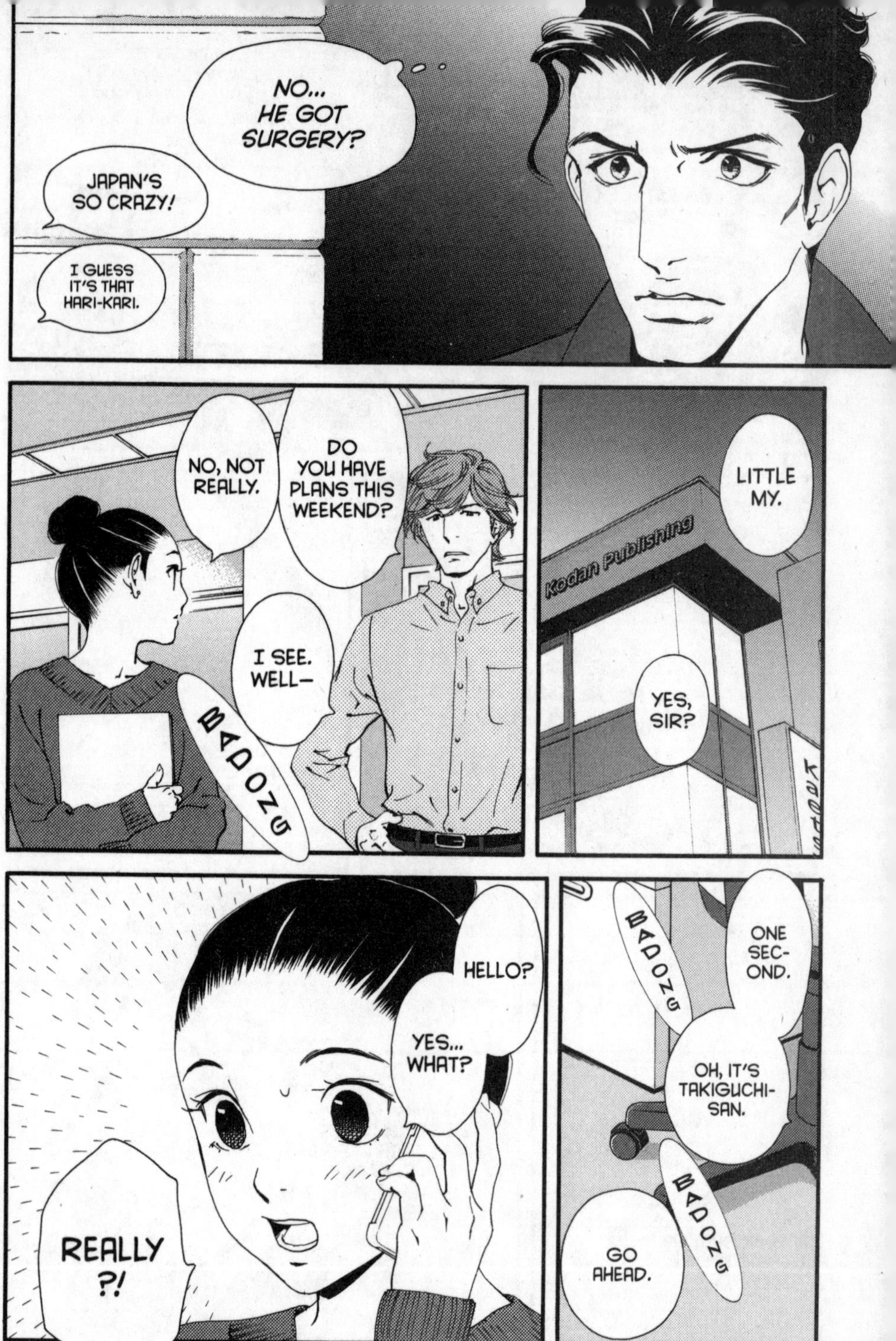
NO... HE GOT SURGERY?
JAPAN'S SO CRAZY!
I GUESS IT'S THAT HARI-KARI.
LITTLE MY.
Kodan Publishing
YES, SIR?
DO YOU HAVE PLANS THIS WEEKEND?
NO, NOT REALLY.
I SEE. WELL—
BADONG
ONE SEC-OND.
BADONG
OH, IT'S TAKIGUCHI-SAN.
BADONG
GO AHEAD.
HELLO?
YES... WHAT?
REALLY ?!

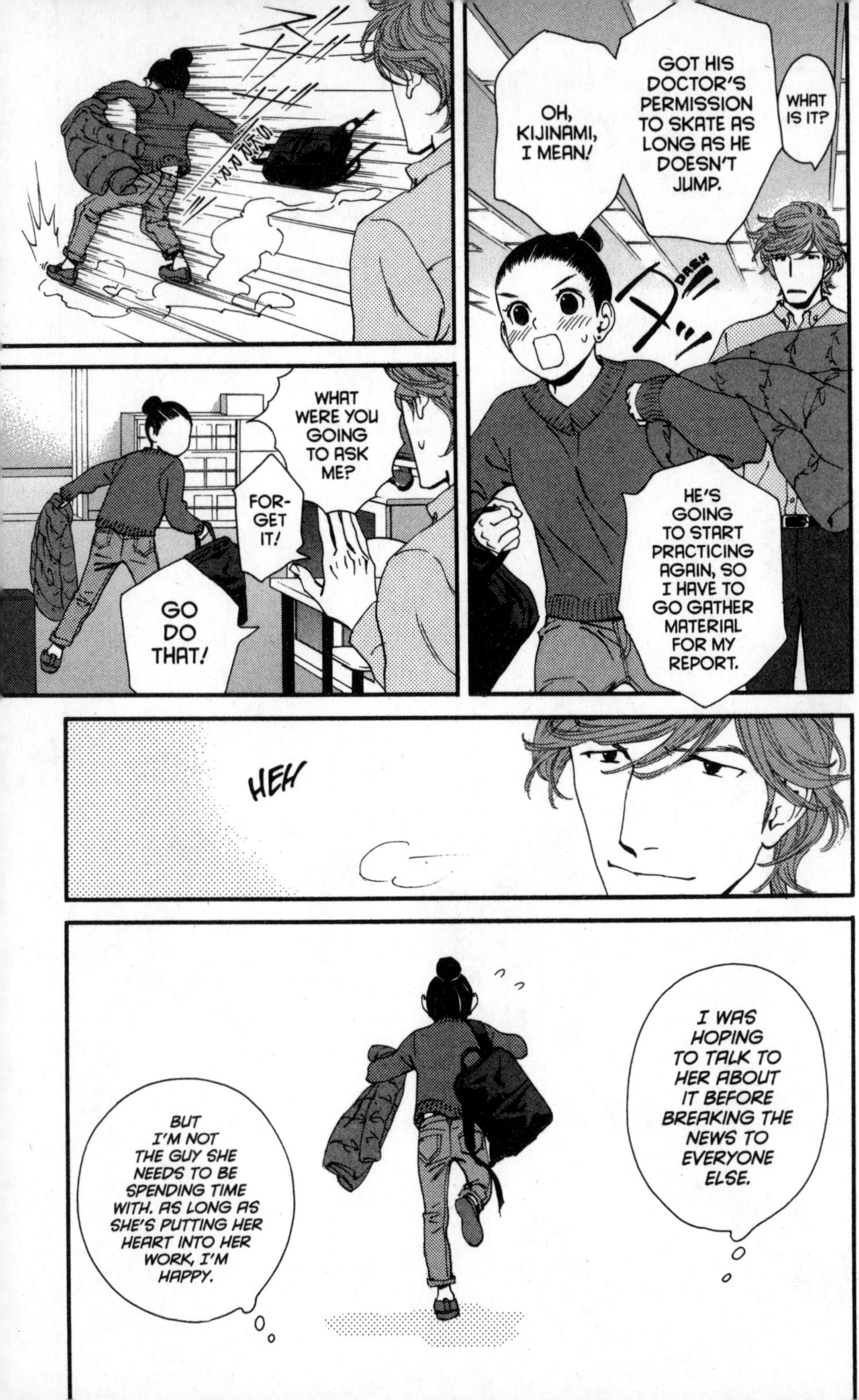
WHAT IS IT?
GOT HIS DOCTOR'S PERMISSION TO SKATE AS LONG AS HE DOESN'T JUMP.
OH, KIJINAMI, I MEAN!
DASH
HE'S GOING TO START PRACTICING AGAIN, SO I HAVE TO GO GATHER MATERIAL FOR MY REPORT.
WHAT WERE YOU GOING TO ASK ME?
FOR-GET IT!
GO DO THAT!
HEH
I WAS HOPING TO TALK TO HER ABOUT IT BEFORE BREAKING THE NEWS TO EVERYONE ELSE.
BUT I'M NOT THE GUY SHE NEEDS TO BE SPENDING TIME WITH. AS LONG AS SHE'S PUTTING HER HEART INTO HER WORK, I'M HAPPY.

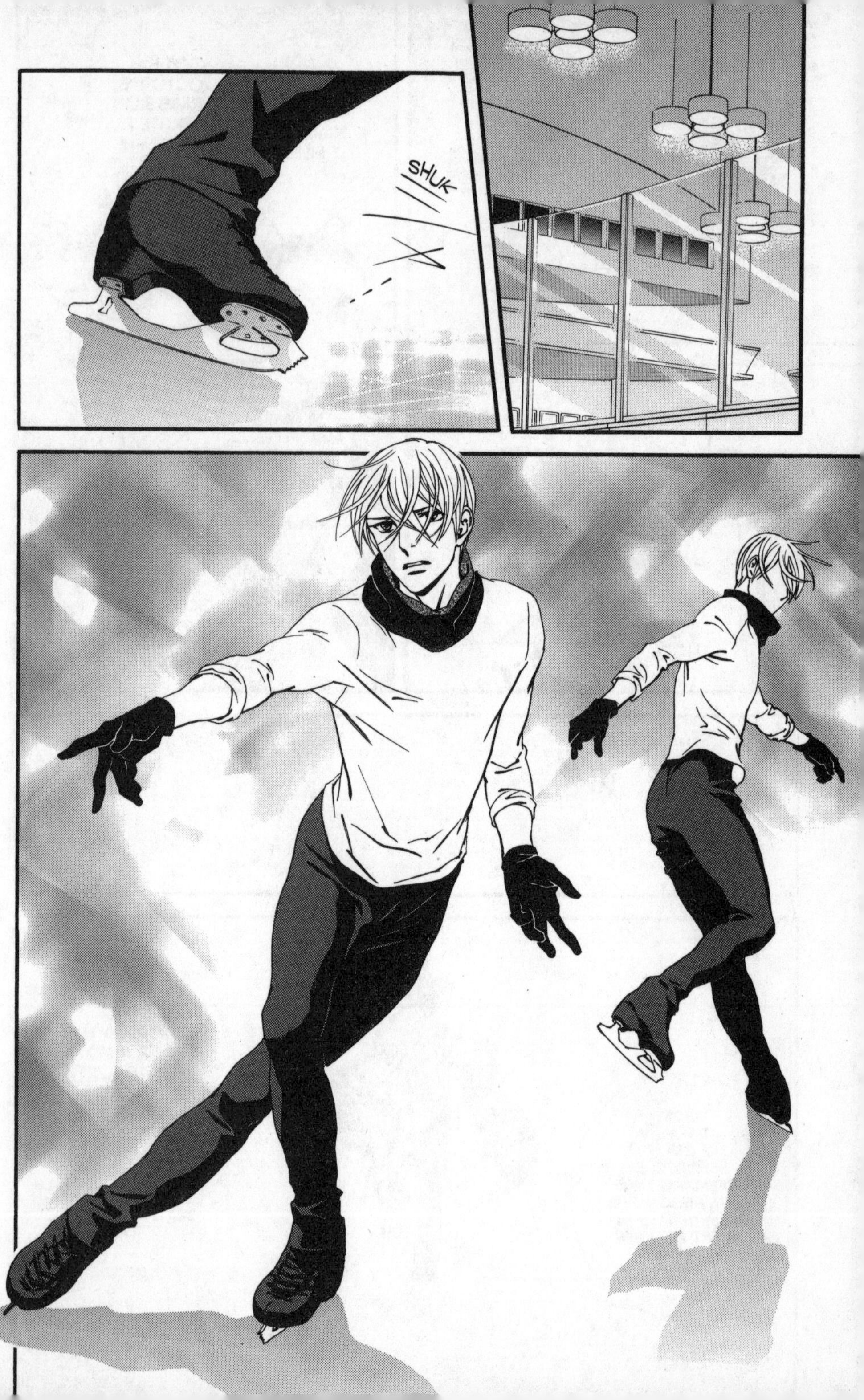
SHUK

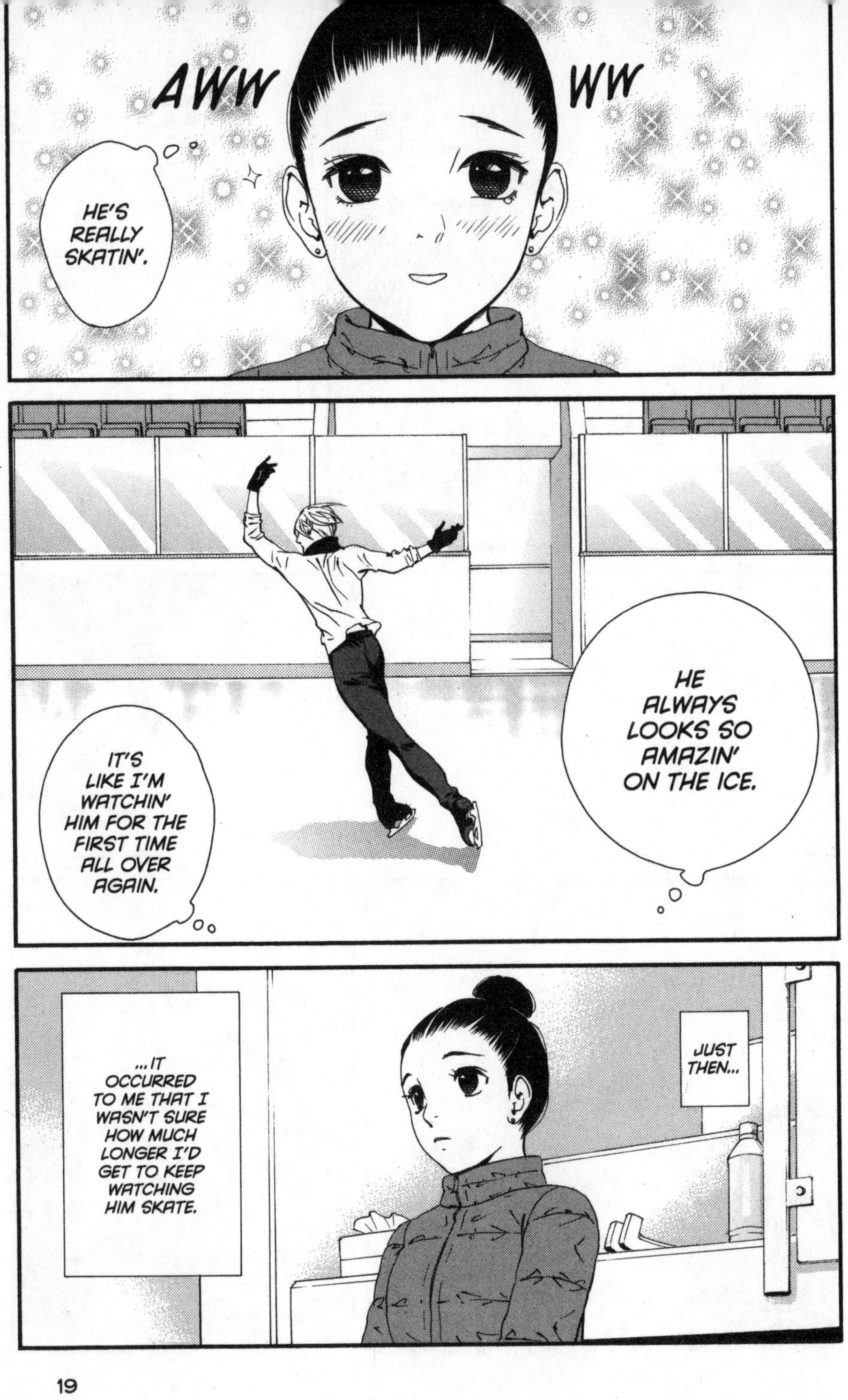
AWWWW
HE'S REALLY SKATIN'.
HE ALWAYS LOOKS SO AMAZIN' ON THE ICE.
IT'S LIKE I'M WATCHIN' HIM FOR THE FIRST TIME ALL OVER AGAIN.
JUST THEN...
...IT OCCURRED TO ME THAT I WASN'T SURE HOW MUCH LONGER I'D GET TO KEEP WATCHING HIM SKATE.

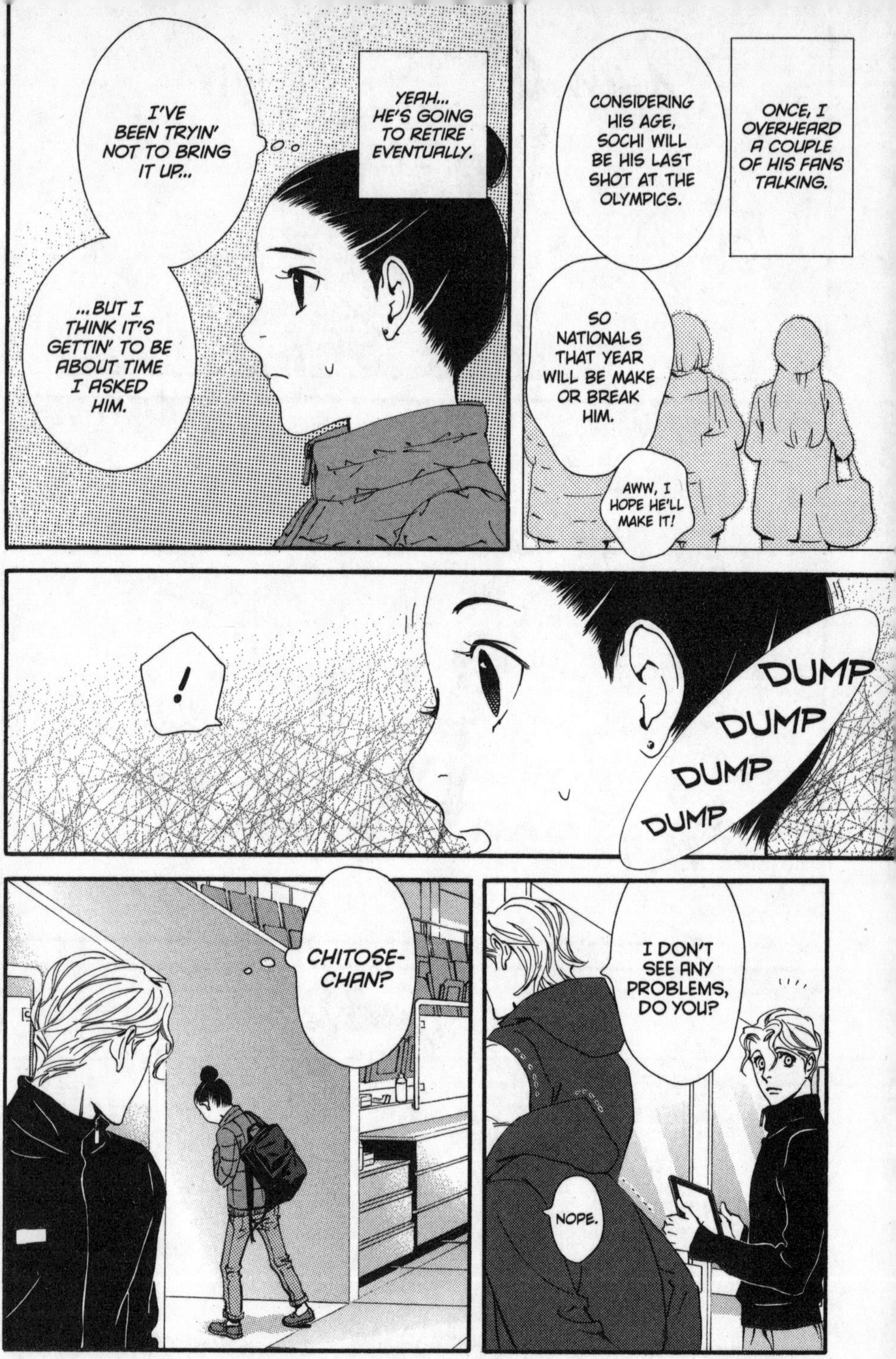
ONCE, I OVERHEARD A COUPLE OF HIS FANS TALKING.
CONSIDERING HIS AGE, SOCHI WILL BE HIS LAST SHOT AT THE OLYMPICS.
SO NATIONALS THAT YEAR WILL BE MAKE OR BREAK HIM.
AWW, I HOPE HE'LL MAKE IT!
YEAH... HE'S GOING TO RETIRE EVENTUALLY.
I'VE BEEN TRYIN' NOT TO BRING IT UP...
...BUT I THINK IT'S GETTIN' TO BE ABOUT TIME I ASKED HIM.
DUMP
DUMP
DUMP
DUMP
!
I DON'T SEE ANY PROBLEMS, DO YOU?
NOPE.
CHITOSE-CHAN?

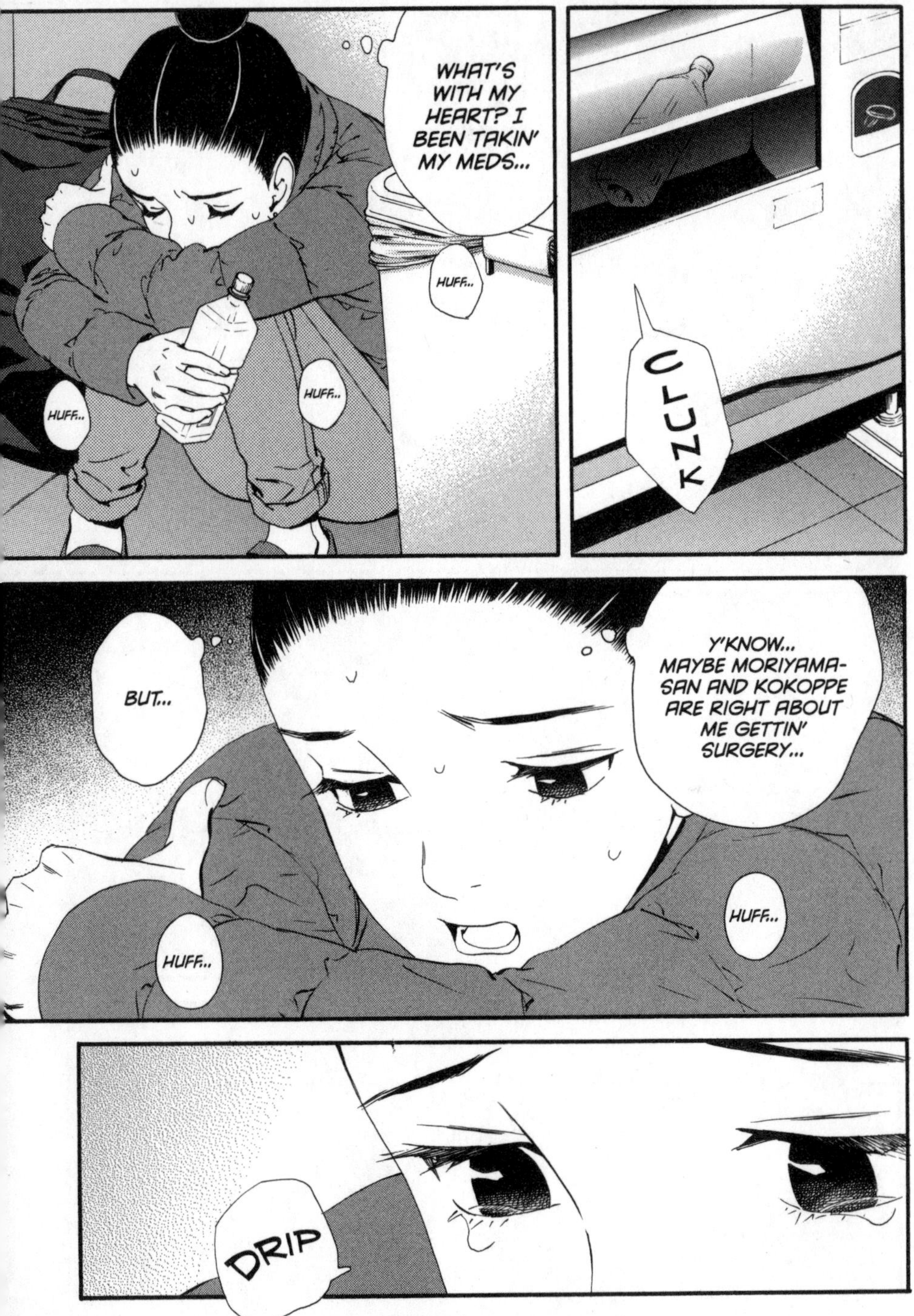
CLUNK
WHAT'S WITH MY HEART? I BEEN TAKIN' MY MEDS...
HUFF...
HUFF...
HUFF...
Y'KNOW... MAYBE MORIYAMA-SAN AND KOKOPPE ARE RIGHT ABOUT ME GETTIN' SURGERY...
BUT...
HUFF...
HUFF...
DRIP

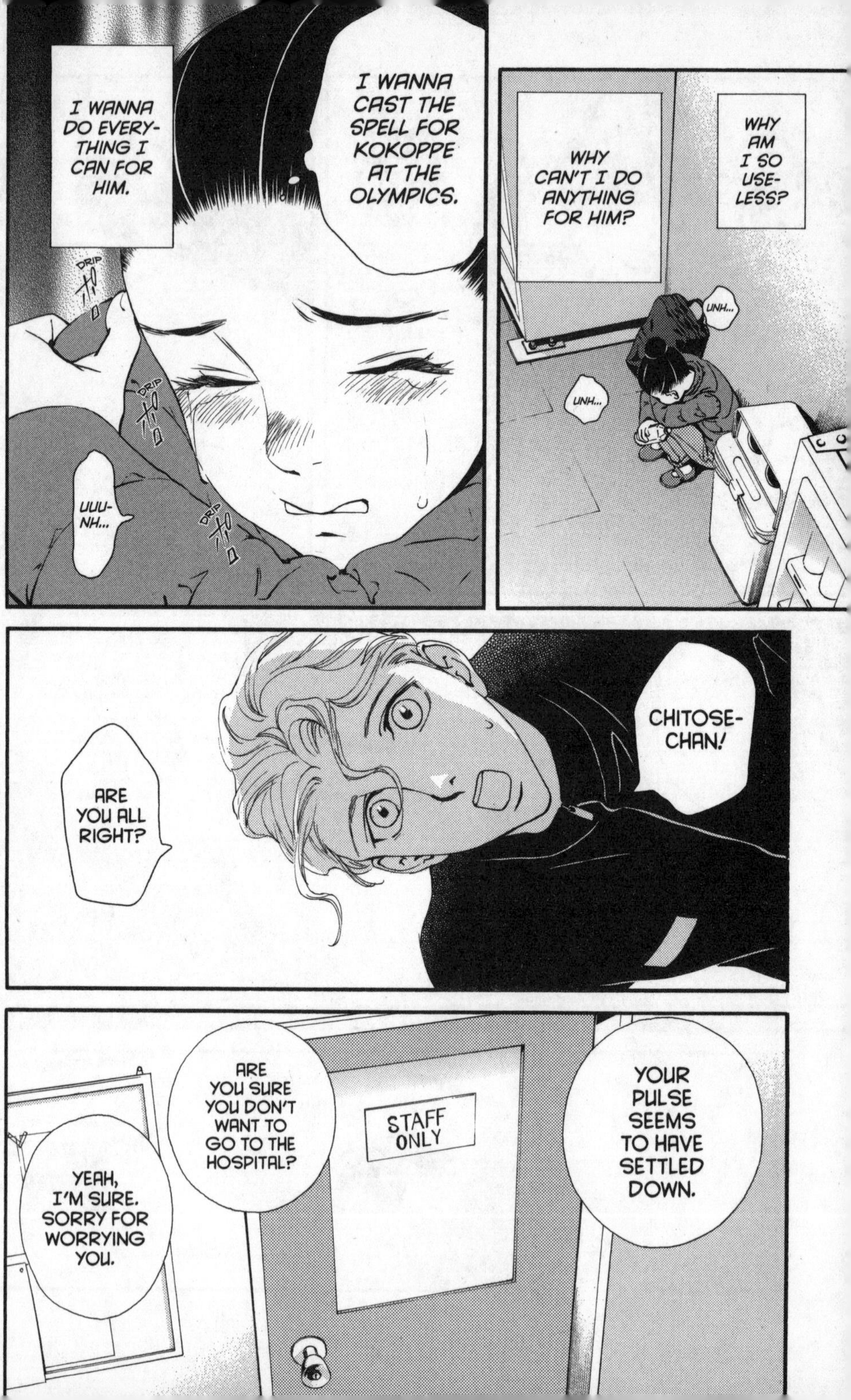
WHY AM I SO USELESS?
WHY CAN'T I DO ANYTHING FOR HIM?
UNH...
UNH...
I WANNA CAST THE SPELL FOR KOKOPPE AT THE OLYMPICS.
I WANNA DO EVERYTHING I CAN FOR HIM.
DRIP
DRIP
DRIP
UUU-NH...
CHITOSE-CHAN!
ARE YOU ALL RIGHT?
YOUR PULSE SEEMS TO HAVE SETTLED DOWN.
STAFF ONLY
ARE YOU SURE YOU DON'T WANT TO GO TO THE HOSPITAL?
YEAH, I'M SURE. SORRY FOR WORRYING YOU.

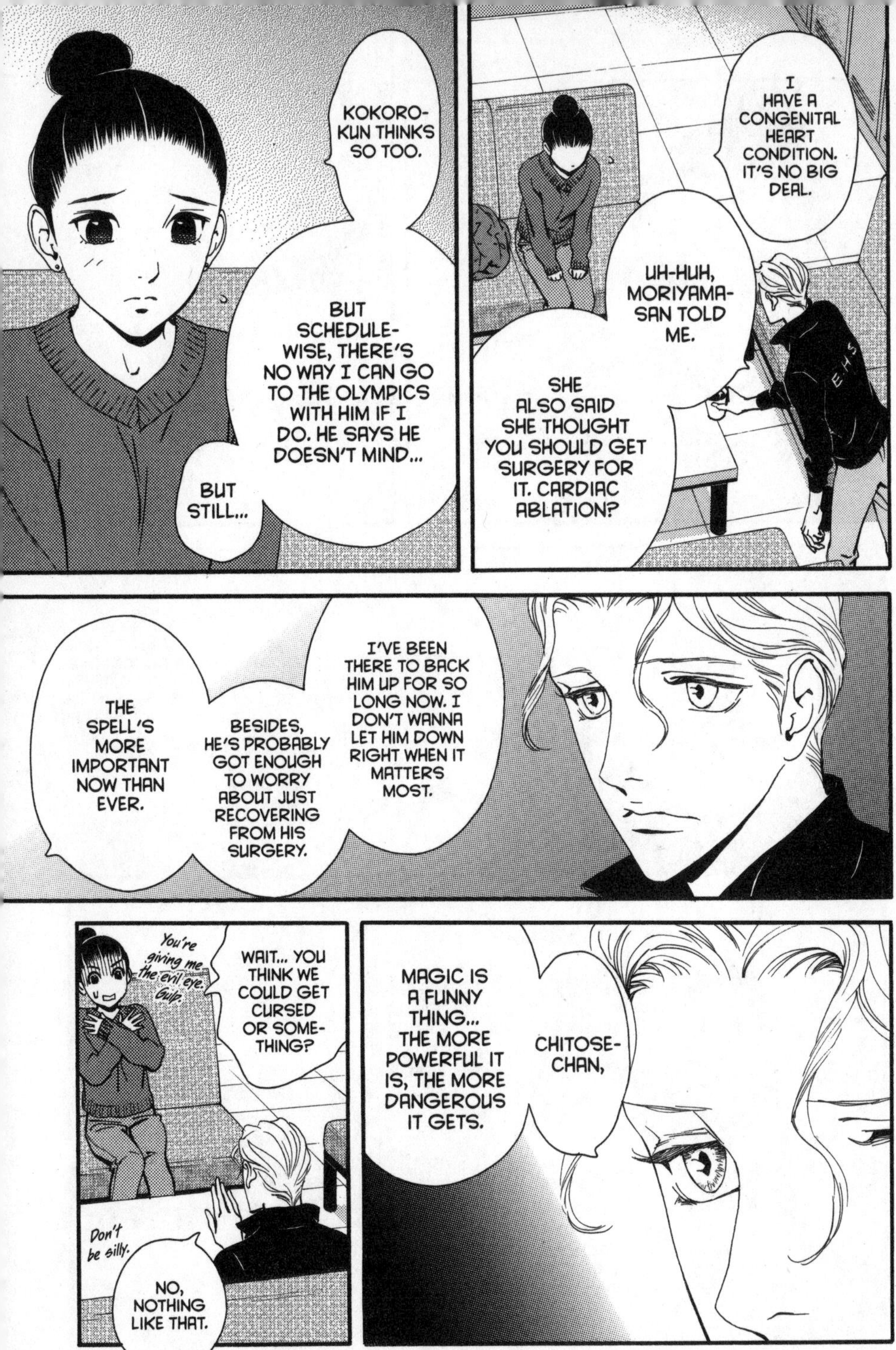
I HAVE A CONGENITAL HEART CONDITION. IT'S NO BIG DEAL.
UH-HUH, MORIYAMA-SAN TOLD ME.
SHE ALSO SAID SHE THOUGHT YOU SHOULD GET SURGERY FOR IT. CARDIAC ABLATION?
KOKORO-KUN THINKS SO TOO.
BUT SCHEDULE-WISE, THERE'S NO WAY I CAN GO TO THE OLYMPICS WITH HIM IF I DO. HE SAYS HE DOESN'T MIND...
BUT STILL...
I'VE BEEN THERE TO BACK HIM UP FOR SO LONG NOW. I DON'T WANNA LET HIM DOWN RIGHT WHEN IT MATTERS MOST.
BESIDES, HE'S PROBABLY GOT ENOUGH TO WORRY ABOUT JUST RECOVERING FROM HIS SURGERY.
THE SPELL'S MORE IMPORTANT NOW THAN EVER.
CHITOSE-CHAN,
MAGIC IS A FUNNY THING... THE MORE POWERFUL IT IS, THE MORE DANGEROUS IT GETS.
WAIT... YOU THINK WE COULD GET CURSED OR SOME-THING?
You're giving me the evil eye. Gulp.
Don't be silly.
NO, NOTHING LIKE THAT.

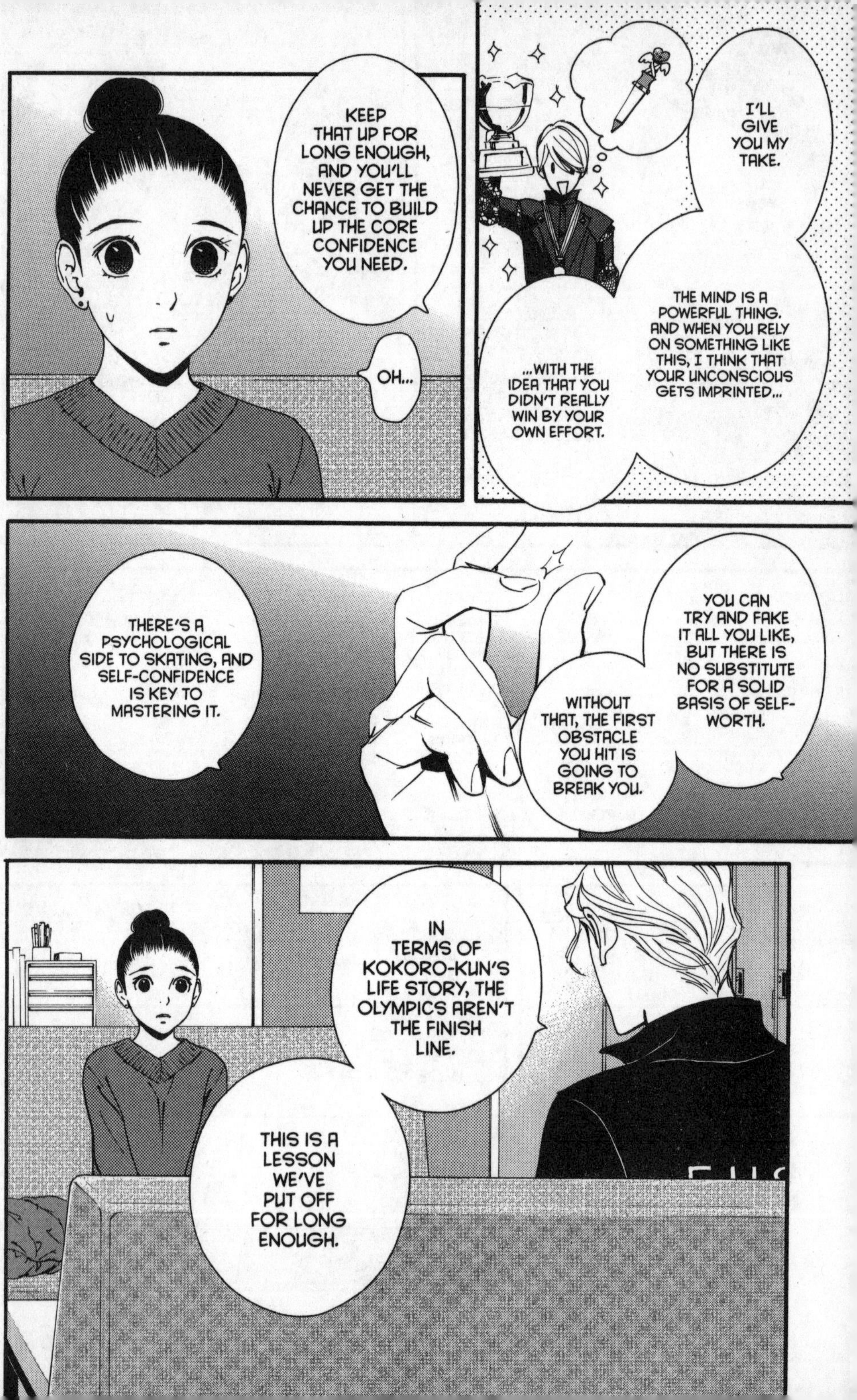
I'LL GIVE YOU MY TAKE.
THE MIND IS A POWERFUL THING. AND WHEN YOU RELY ON SOMETHING LIKE THIS, I THINK THAT YOUR UNCONSCIOUS GETS IMPRINTED...
...WITH THE IDEA THAT YOU DIDN'T REALLY WIN BY YOUR OWN EFFORT.
KEEP THAT UP FOR LONG ENOUGH, AND YOU'LL NEVER GET THE CHANCE TO BUILD UP THE CORE CONFIDENCE YOU NEED.
OH...
YOU CAN TRY AND FAKE IT ALL YOU LIKE, BUT THERE IS NO SUBSTITUTE FOR A SOLID BASIS OF SELF-WORTH.
WITHOUT THAT, THE FIRST OBSTACLE YOU HIT IS GOING TO BREAK YOU.
THERE'S A PSYCHOLOGICAL SIDE TO SKATING, AND SELF-CONFIDENCE IS KEY TO MASTERING IT.
IN TERMS OF KOKORO-KUN'S LIFE STORY, THE OLYMPICS AREN'T THE FINISH LINE.
THIS IS A LESSON WE'VE PUT OFF FOR LONG ENOUGH.

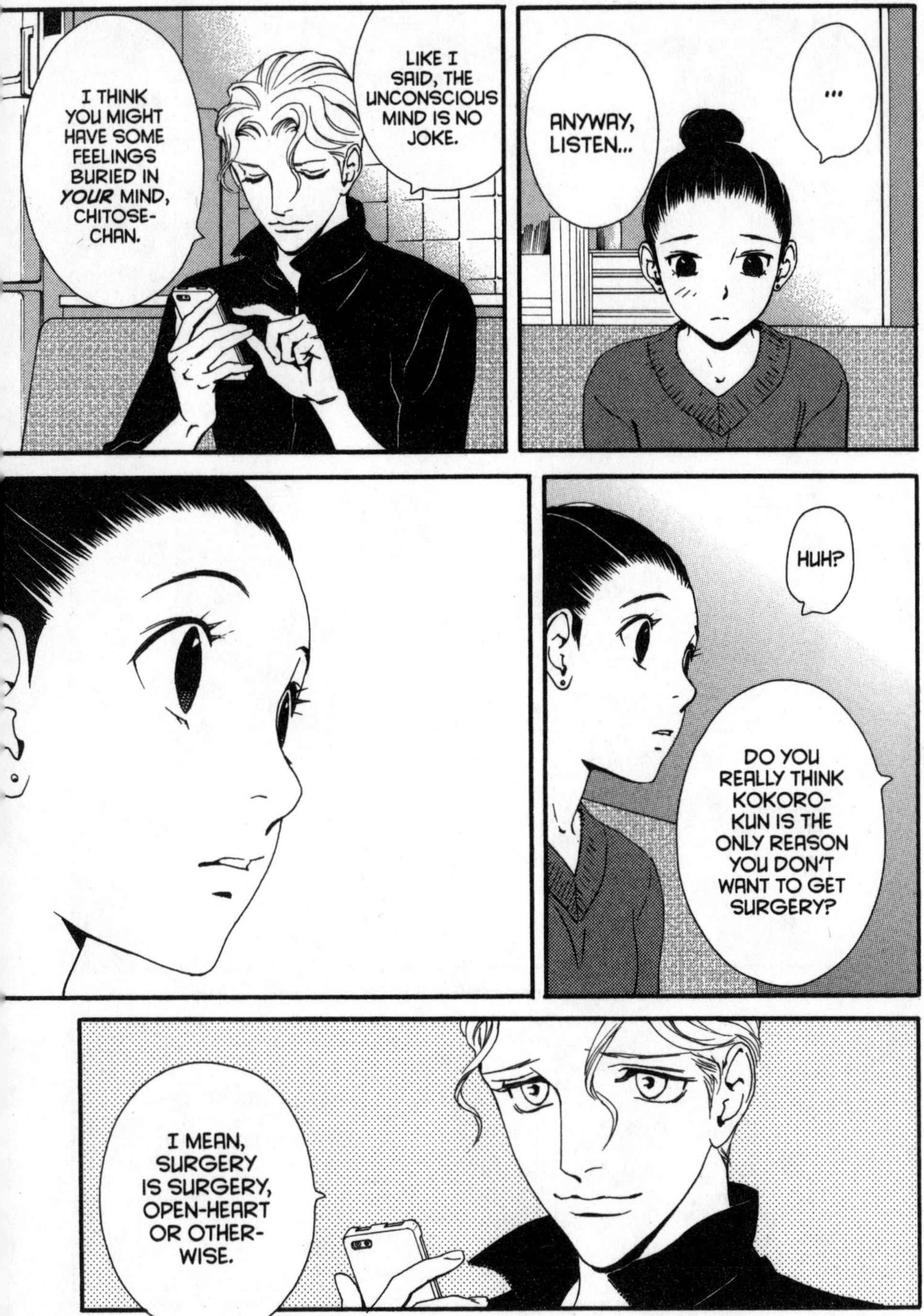
...
ANYWAY, LISTEN...
LIKE I SAID, THE UNCONSCIOUS MIND IS NO JOKE.
I THINK YOU MIGHT HAVE SOME FEELINGS BURIED IN *YOUR* MIND, CHITOSE-CHAN.
HUH?
DO YOU REALLY THINK KOKORO-KUN IS THE ONLY REASON YOU DON'T WANT TO GET SURGERY?
I MEAN, SURGERY IS SURGERY, OPEN-HEART OR OTHER-WISE.

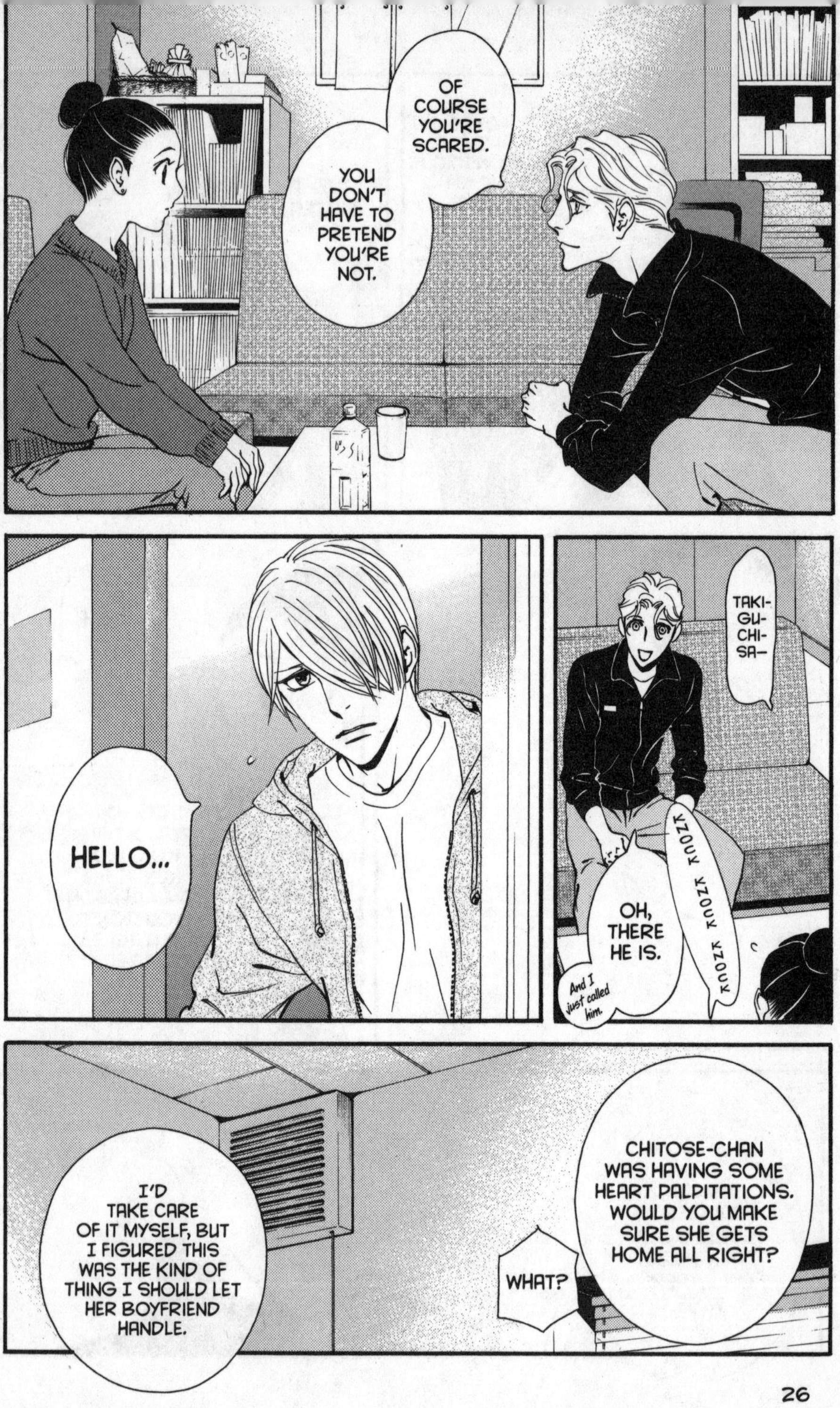
OF COURSE YOU'RE SCARED.
YOU DON'T HAVE TO PRETEND YOU'RE NOT.
TAKI-GU-CHI-SA–
KNOCK KNOCK KNOCK
OH, THERE HE IS.
And I just called him.
HELLO...
CHITOSE-CHAN WAS HAVING SOME HEART PALPITATIONS. WOULD YOU MAKE SURE SHE GETS HOME ALL RIGHT?
WHAT?
I'D TAKE CARE OF IT MYSELF, BUT I FIGURED THIS WAS THE KIND OF THING I SHOULD LET HER BOYFRIEND HANDLE.

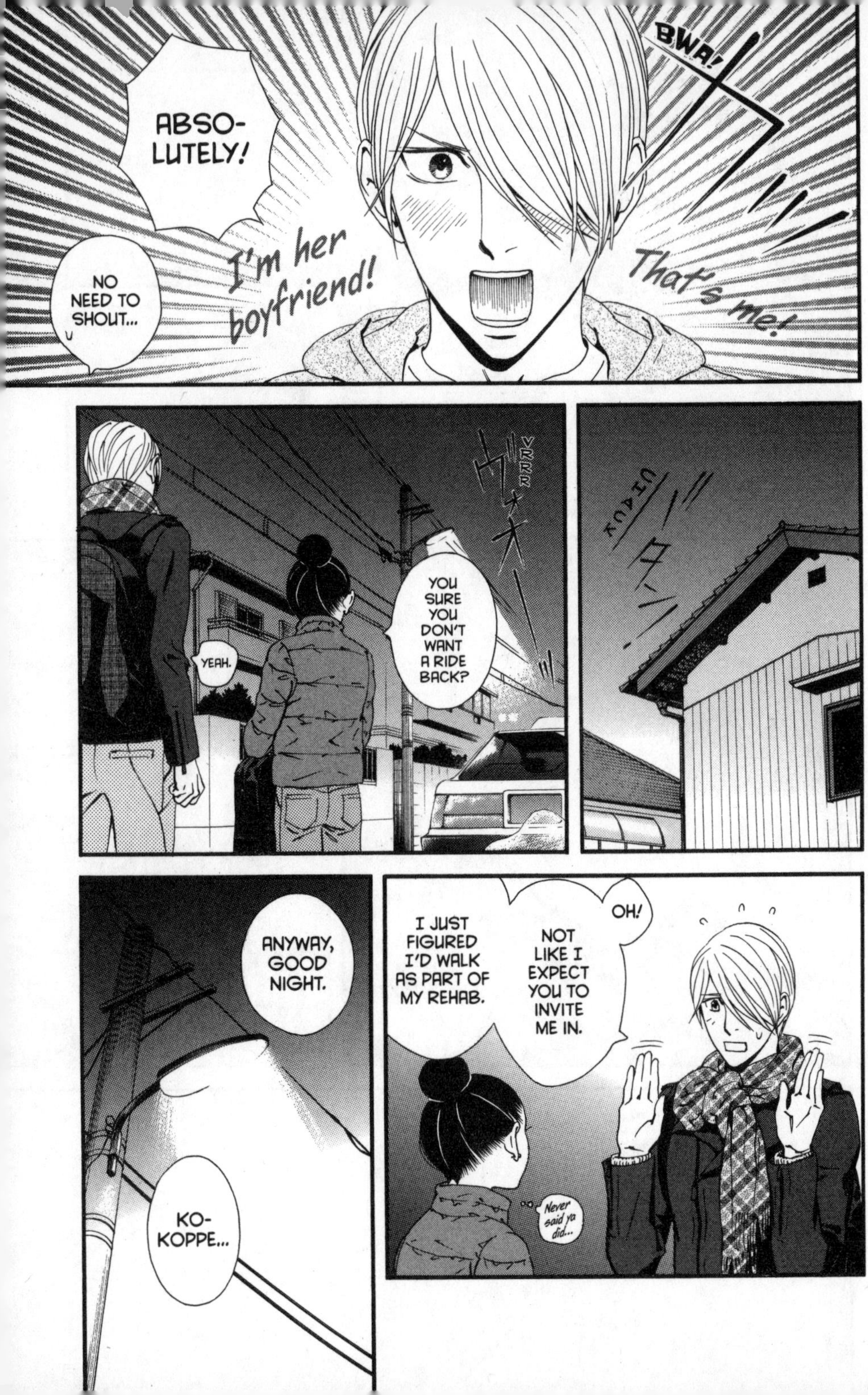
BWA!
That's me!
I'm her boyfriend!
ABSO-LUTELY!
NO NEED TO SHOUT...
UNLOCK
VRRR
YOU SURE YOU DON'T WANT A RIDE BACK?
YEAH.
OH!
NOT LIKE I EXPECT YOU TO INVITE ME IN.
I JUST FIGURED I'D WALK AS PART OF MY REHAB.
Never said ya did...
ANYWAY, GOOD NIGHT.
KO-KOPPE...

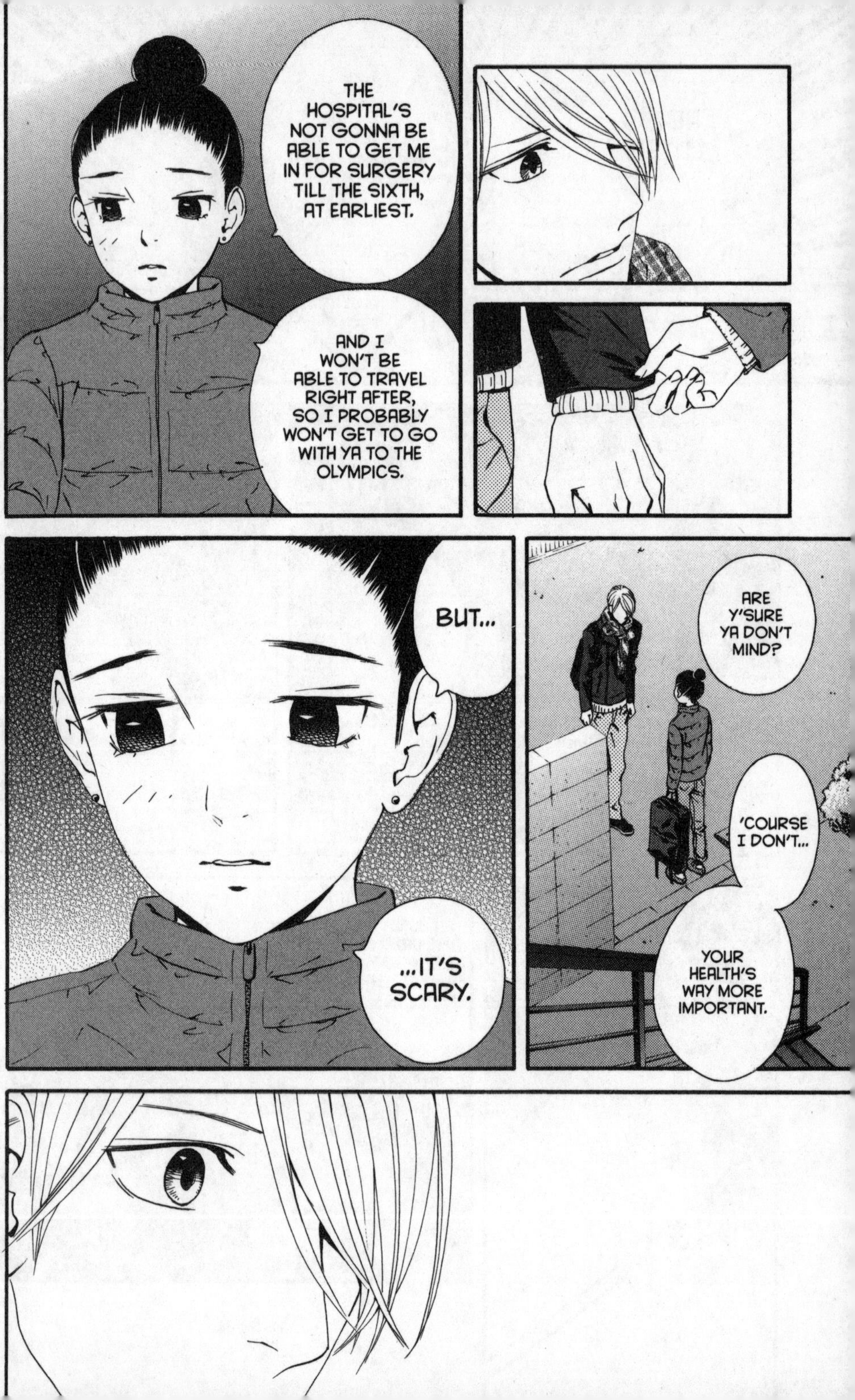
THE HOSPITAL'S NOT GONNA BE ABLE TO GET ME IN FOR SURGERY TILL THE SIXTH, AT EARLIEST.
AND I WON'T BE ABLE TO TRAVEL RIGHT AFTER, SO I PROBABLY WON'T GET TO GO WITH YA TO THE OLYMPICS.
ARE Y'SURE YA DON'T MIND?
'COURSE I DON'T...
YOUR HEALTH'S WAY MORE IMPORTANT.
BUT...
...IT'S SCARY.

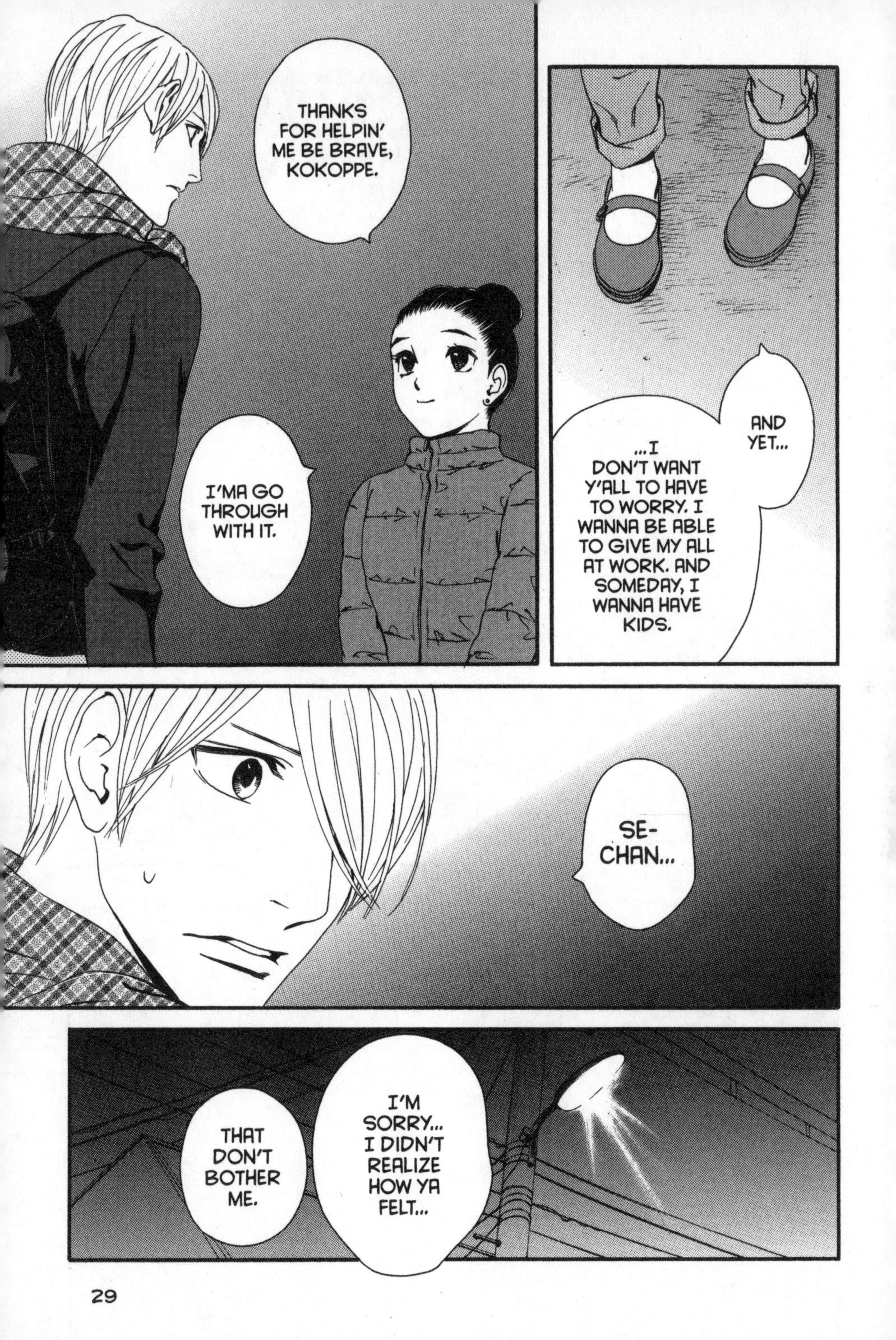
AND YET...
...I DON'T WANT Y'ALL TO HAVE TO WORRY. I WANNA BE ABLE TO GIVE MY ALL AT WORK. AND SOMEDAY, I WANNA HAVE KIDS.
THANKS FOR HELPIN' ME BE BRAVE, KOKOPPE.
I'MA GO THROUGH WITH IT.
SE-CHAN...
I'M SORRY... I DIDN'T REALIZE HOW YA FELT...
THAT DON'T BOTHER ME.

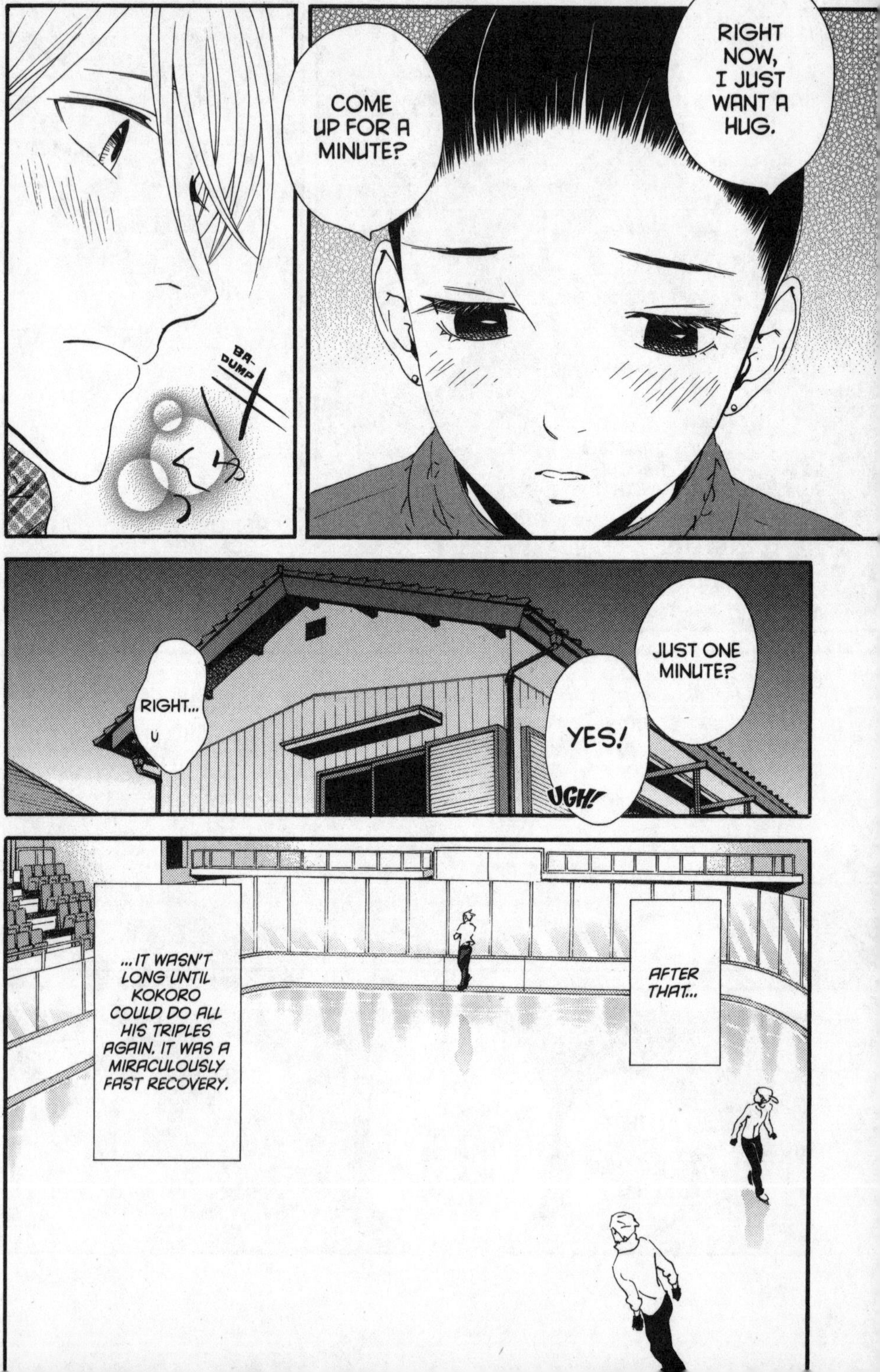
RIGHT NOW, I JUST WANT A HUG.
COME UP FOR A MINUTE?
BA-DUMP
JUST ONE MINUTE?
YES!
UGH!
RIGHT...
AFTER THAT...
...IT WASN'T LONG UNTIL KOKORO COULD DO ALL HIS TRIPLES AGAIN. IT WAS A MIRACULOUSLY FAST RECOVERY.

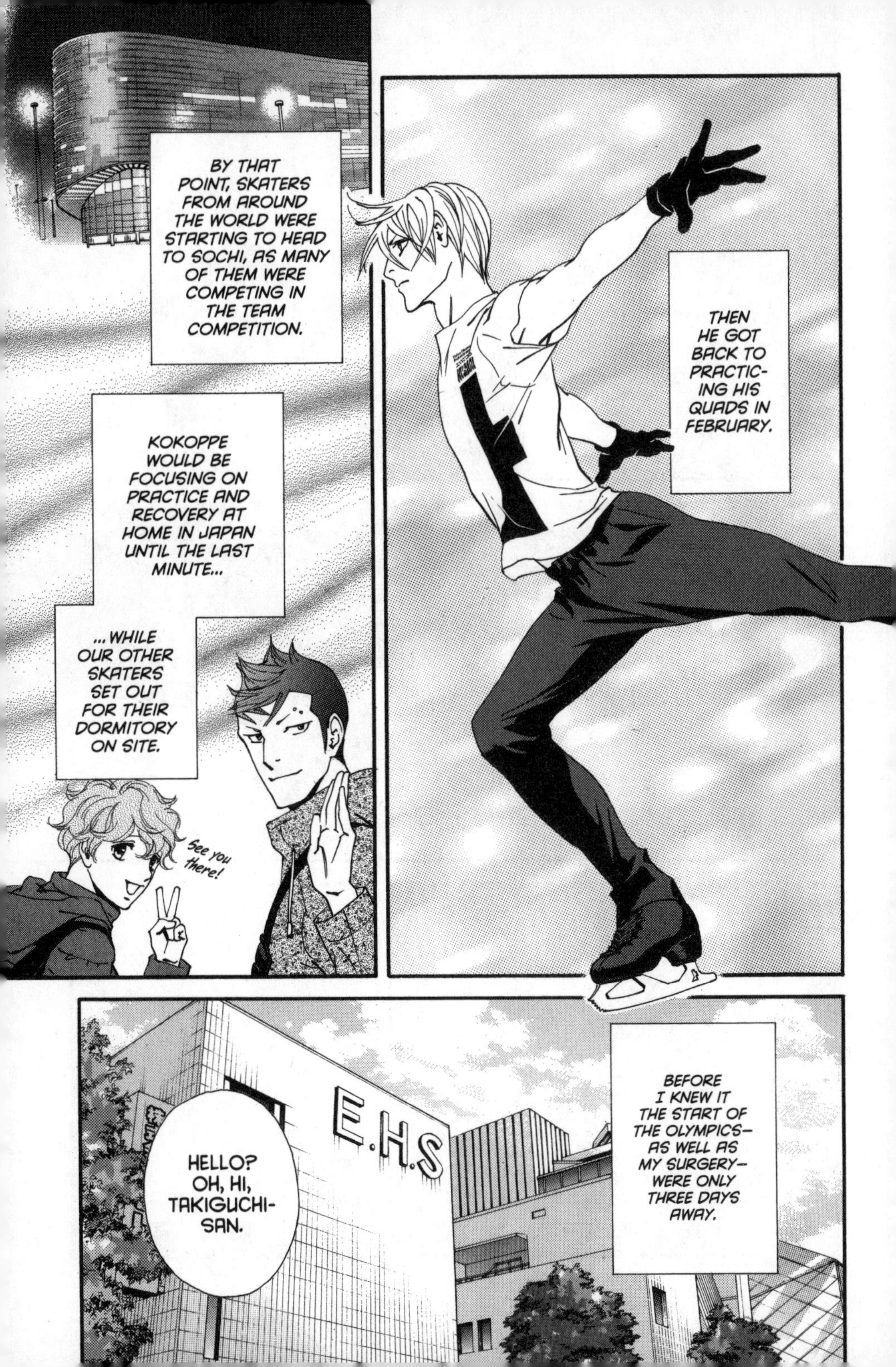
THEN HE GOT BACK TO PRACTIC- ING HIS QUADS IN FEBRUARY.
BY THAT POINT, SKATERS FROM AROUND THE WORLD WERE STARTING TO HEAD TO SOCHI, AS MANY OF THEM WERE COMPETING IN THE TEAM COMPETITION.
KOKOPPE WOULD BE FOCUSING ON PRACTICE AND RECOVERY AT HOME IN JAPAN UNTIL THE LAST MINUTE...
...WHILE OUR OTHER SKATERS SET OUT FOR THEIR DORMITORY ON SITE.
See you there!
BEFORE I KNEW IT THE START OF THE OLYMPICS— AS WELL AS MY SURGERY— WERE ONLY THREE DAYS AWAY.
E.H.S
HELLO? OH, HI, TAKIGUCHI- SAN.

COACH HONDA?!

YOU'RE AT THE HOSPITAL? DON'T TELL ME MEATBALL HEAD—

HUH? IT'S NOT ABOUT HER?

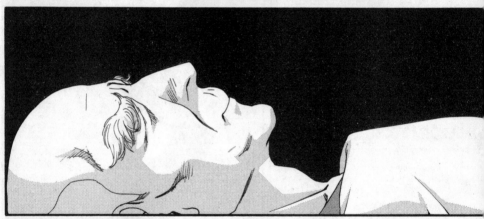

SOB

SOB

SOB

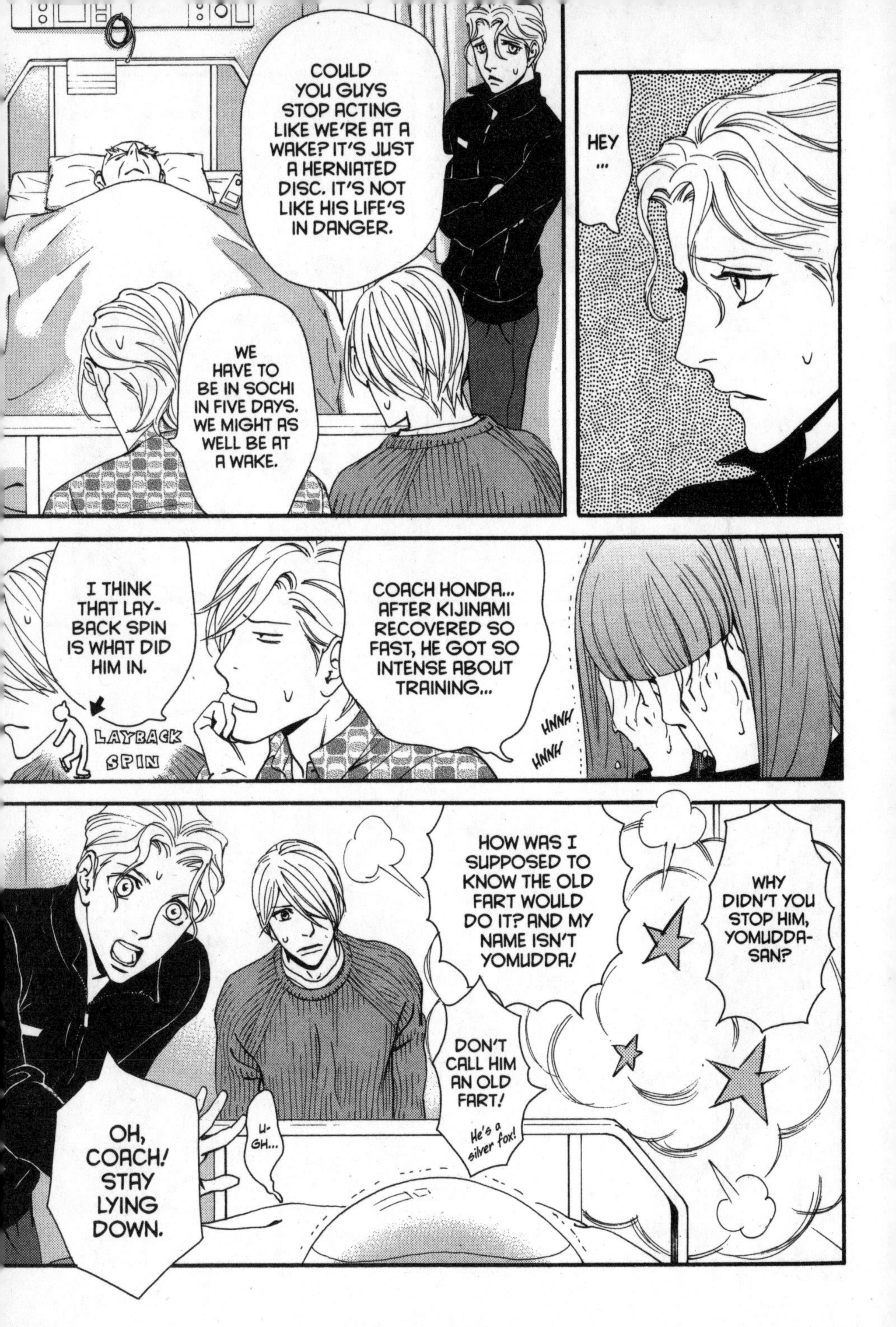
HEY ...
COULD YOU GUYS STOP ACTING LIKE WE'RE AT A WAKE? IT'S JUST A HERNIATED DISC. IT'S NOT LIKE HIS LIFE'S IN DANGER.
WE HAVE TO BE IN SOCHI IN FIVE DAYS. WE MIGHT AS WELL BE AT A WAKE.
HNNH
HNNH
COACH HONDA... AFTER KIJINAMI RECOVERED SO FAST, HE GOT SO INTENSE ABOUT TRAINING...
I THINK THAT LAY-BACK SPIN IS WHAT DID HIM IN.
LAYBACK SPIN
WHY DIDN'T YOU STOP HIM, YOMUDDA-SAN?
HOW WAS I SUPPOSED TO KNOW THE OLD FART WOULD DO IT? AND MY NAME ISN'T YOMUDDA!
DON'T CALL HIM AN OLD FART!
He's a silver fox!
U-GH...
OH, COACH! STAY LYING DOWN.

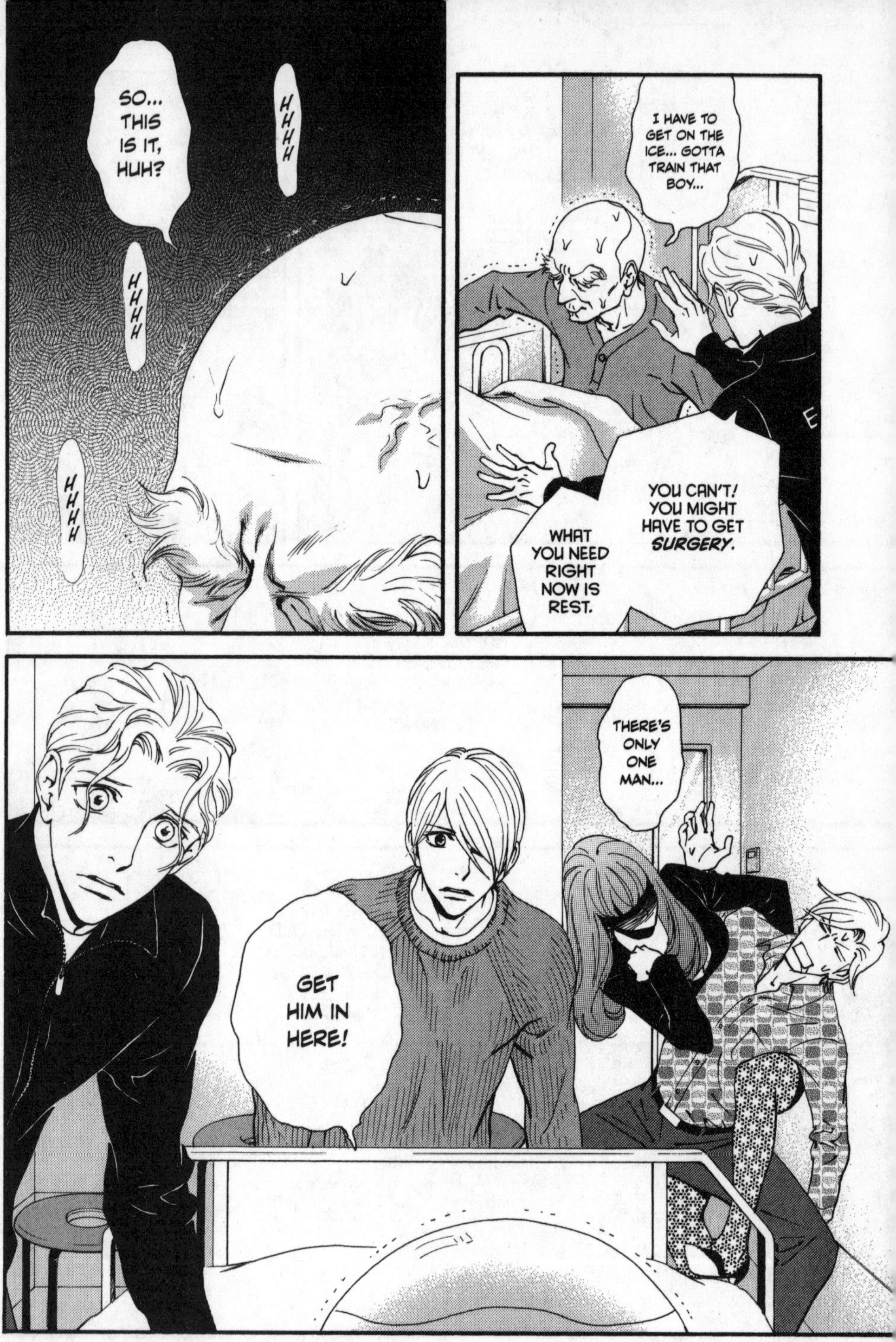
I HAVE TO GET ON THE ICE... GOTTA TRAIN THAT BOY...
YOU CAN'T! YOU MIGHT HAVE TO GET SURGERY.
WHAT YOU NEED RIGHT NOW IS REST.
HHHH
SO... THIS IS IT, HUH?
HHHH
HHHH
THERE'S ONLY ONE MAN...
GET HIM IN HERE!

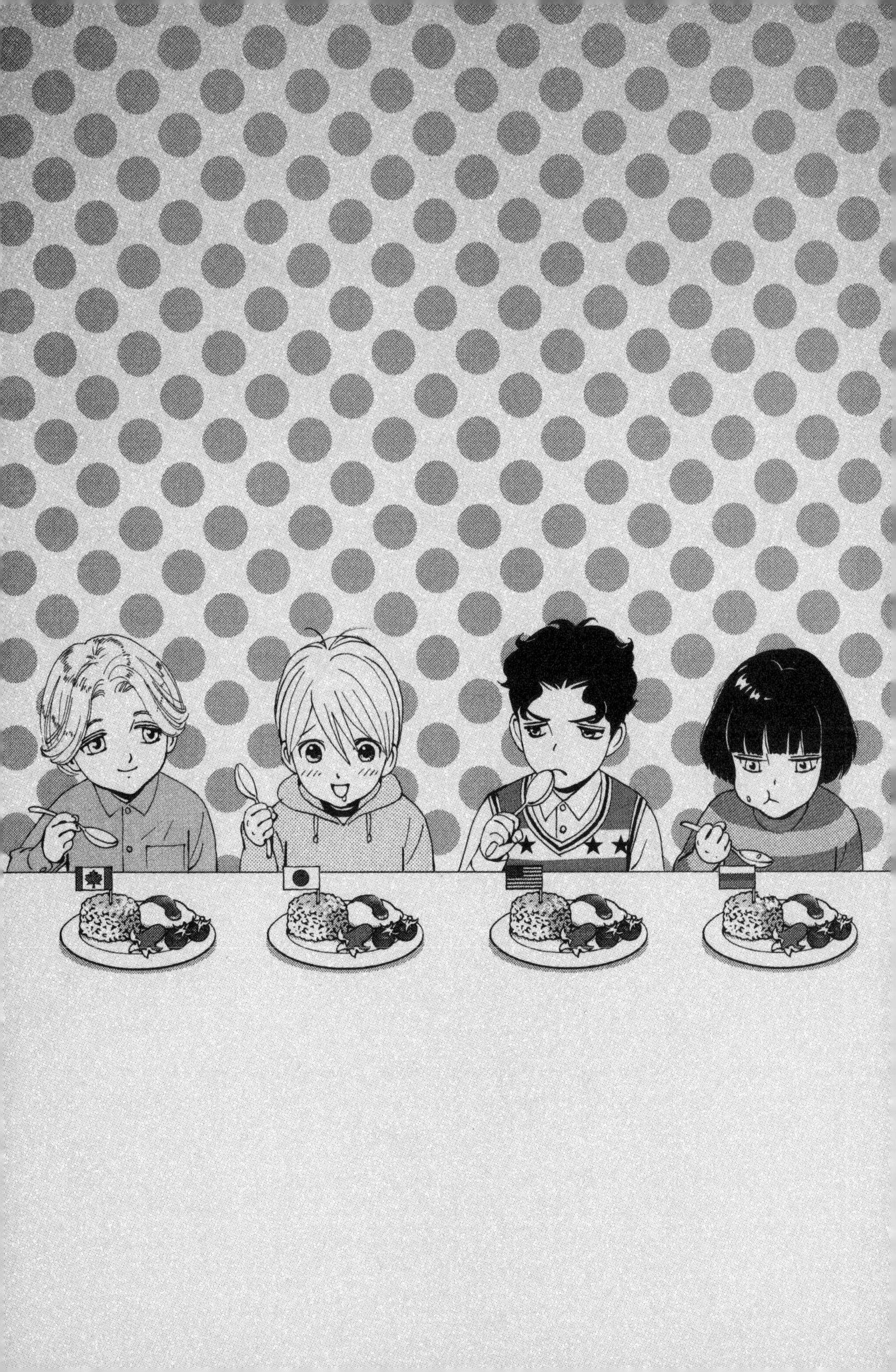

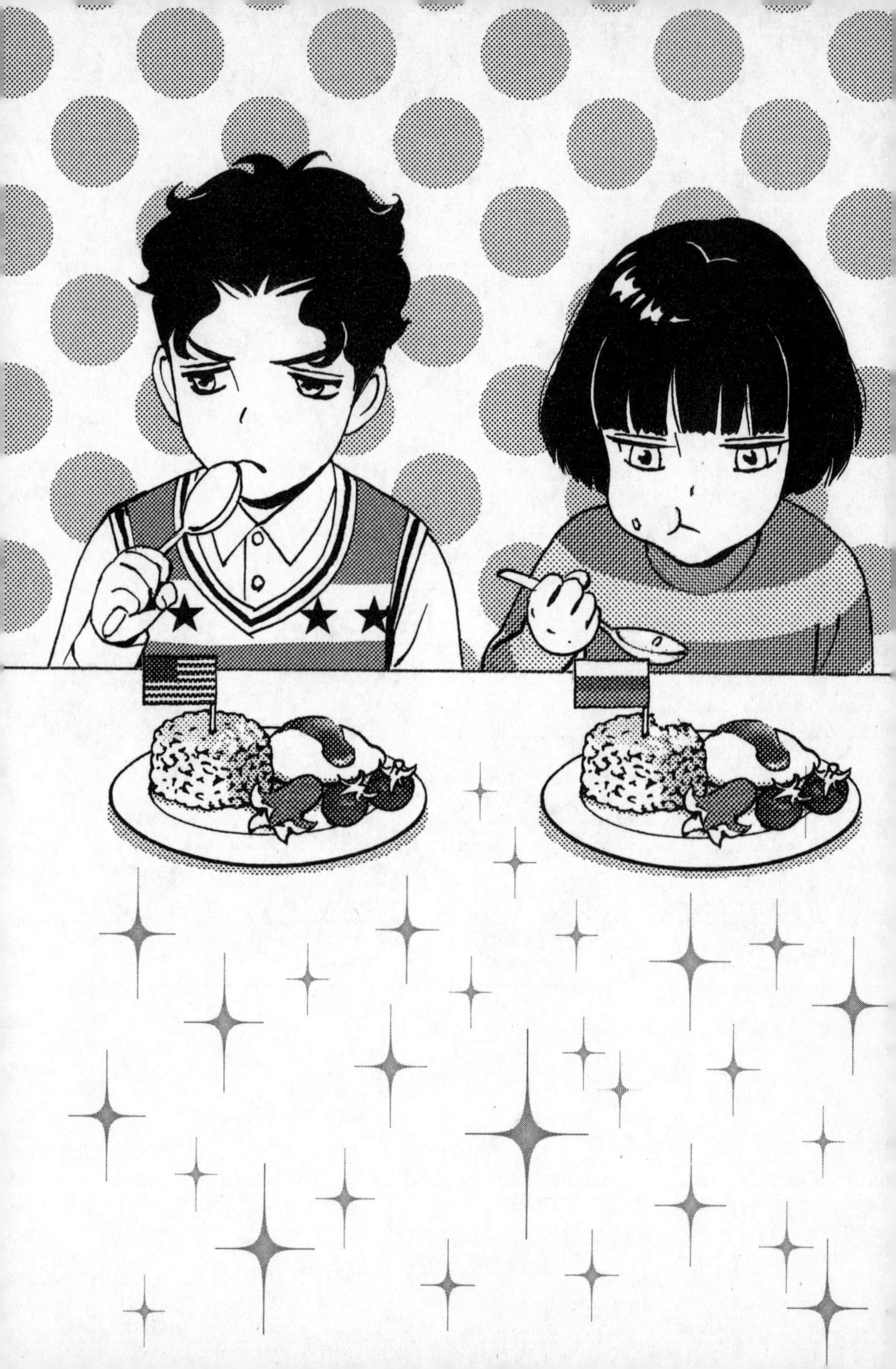

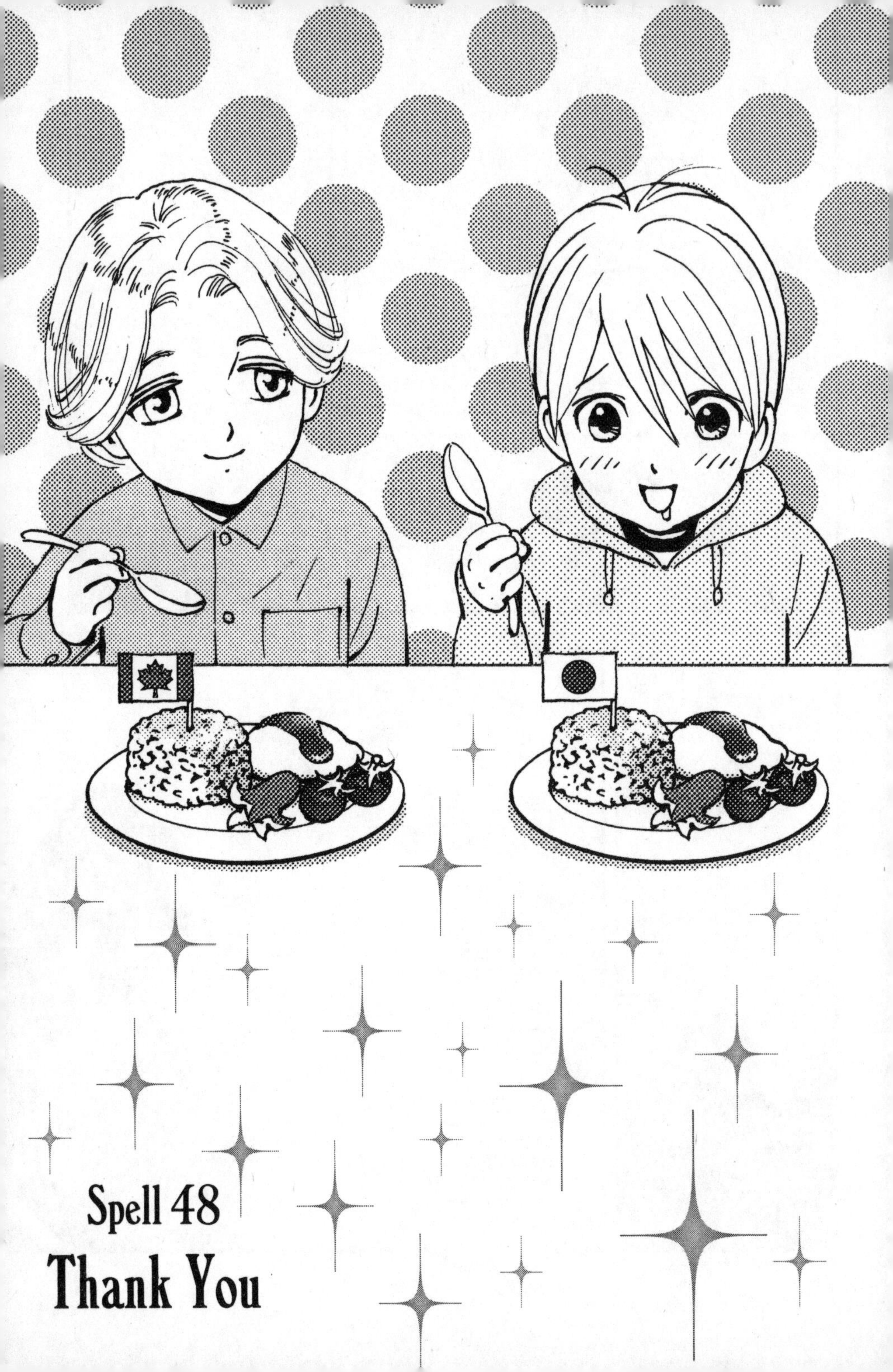

Spell 48

Thank You

YOU MEAN...

WHO WOULD THAT BE?

YOU CAN'T GUESS?

THAT'S RIGHT...

I CAN'T SAY I'M HAPPY ABOUT IT, BUT HE'S THE ONLY ONE I CAN TRUST WITH MY DEAR PUPIL.

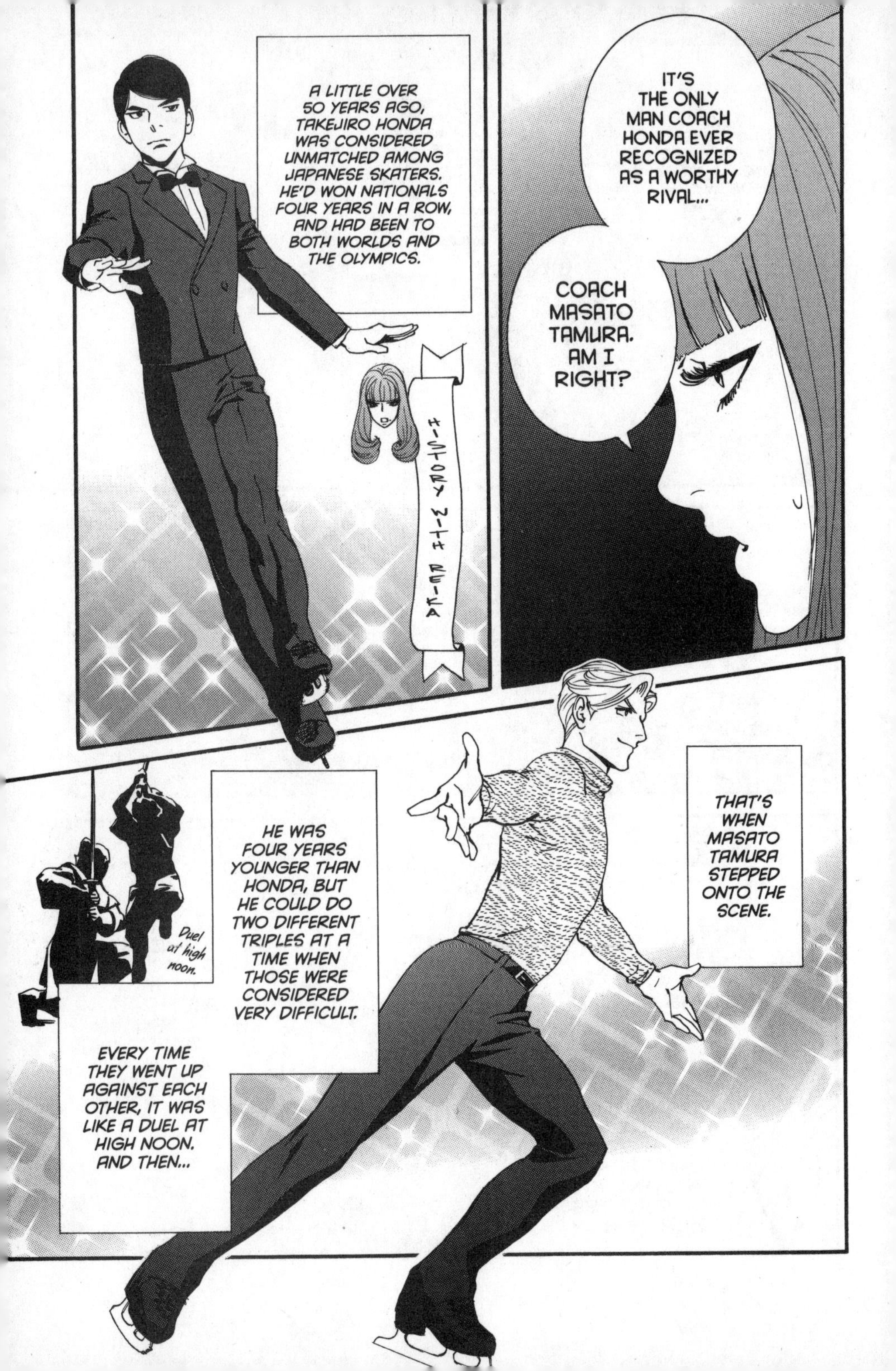

IT'S THE ONLY MAN COACH HONDA EVER RECOGNIZED AS A WORTHY RIVAL...
COACH MASATO TAMURA. AM I RIGHT?
A LITTLE OVER 50 YEARS AGO, TAKEJIRO HONDA WAS CONSIDERED UNMATCHED AMONG JAPANESE SKATERS. HE'D WON NATIONALS FOUR YEARS IN A ROW, AND HAD BEEN TO BOTH WORLDS AND THE OLYMPICS.
HISTORY WITH REIKA
THAT'S WHEN MASATO TAMURA STEPPED ONTO THE SCENE.
HE WAS FOUR YEARS YOUNGER THAN HONDA, BUT HE COULD DO TWO DIFFERENT TRIPLES AT A TIME WHEN THOSE WERE CONSIDERED VERY DIFFICULT.
Duel at high noon.
EVERY TIME THEY WENT UP AGAINST EACH OTHER, IT WAS LIKE A DUEL AT HIGH NOON. AND THEN...

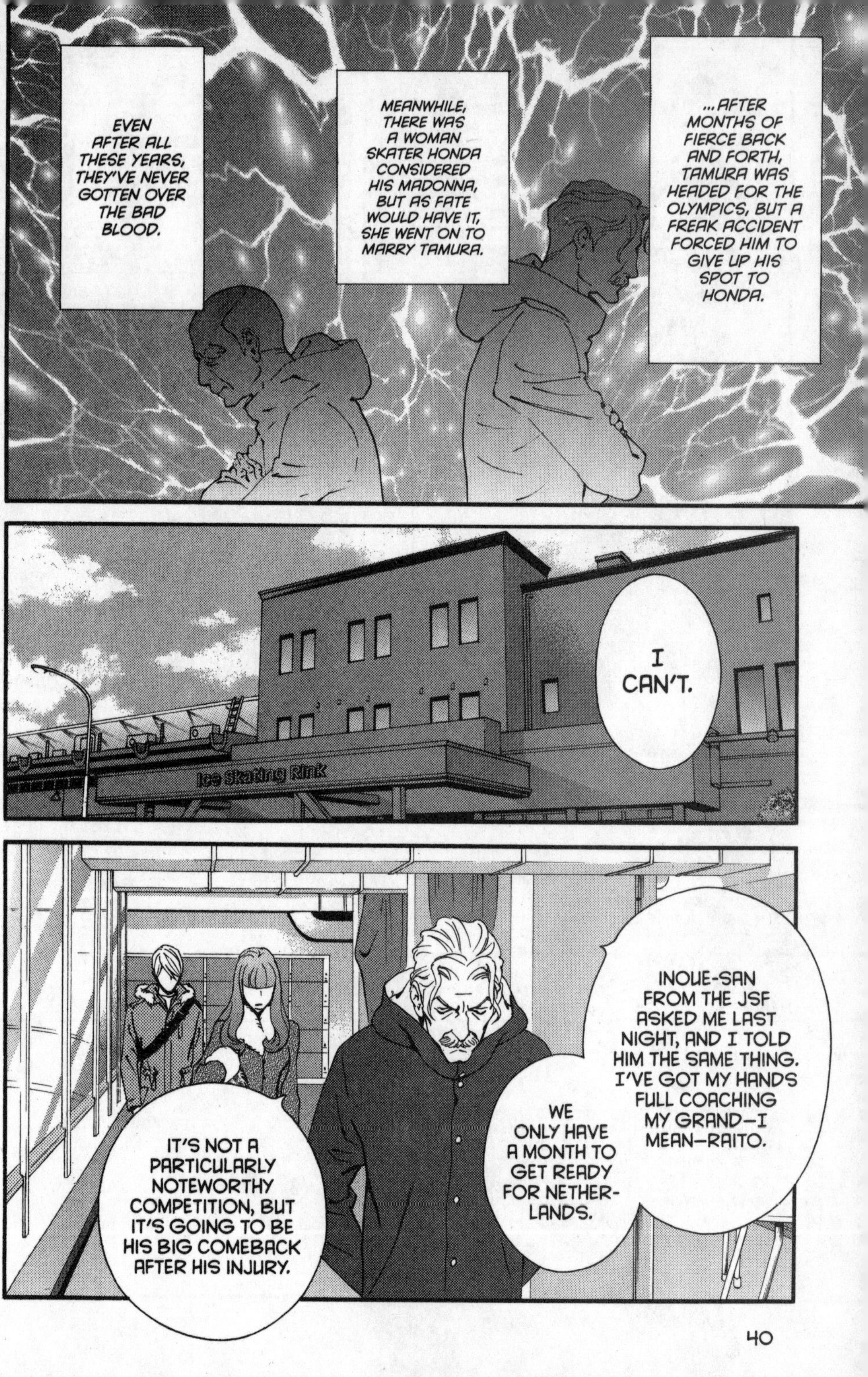
...AFTER MONTHS OF FIERCE BACK AND FORTH, TAMURA WAS HEADED FOR THE OLYMPICS, BUT A FREAK ACCIDENT FORCED HIM TO GIVE UP HIS SPOT TO HONDA.
MEANWHILE, THERE WAS A WOMAN SKATER HONDA CONSIDERED HIS MADONNA, BUT AS FATE WOULD HAVE IT, SHE WENT ON TO MARRY TAMURA.
EVEN AFTER ALL THESE YEARS, THEY'VE NEVER GOTTEN OVER THE BAD BLOOD.
I CAN'T.
Ice Skating Rink
INOUE-SAN FROM THE JSF ASKED ME LAST NIGHT, AND I TOLD HIM THE SAME THING. I'VE GOT MY HANDS FULL COACHING MY GRAND—I MEAN—RAITO.
WE ONLY HAVE A MONTH TO GET READY FOR NETHER-LANDS.
IT'S NOT A PARTICULARLY NOTEWORTHY COMPETITION, BUT IT'S GOING TO BE HIS BIG COMEBACK AFTER HIS INJURY.

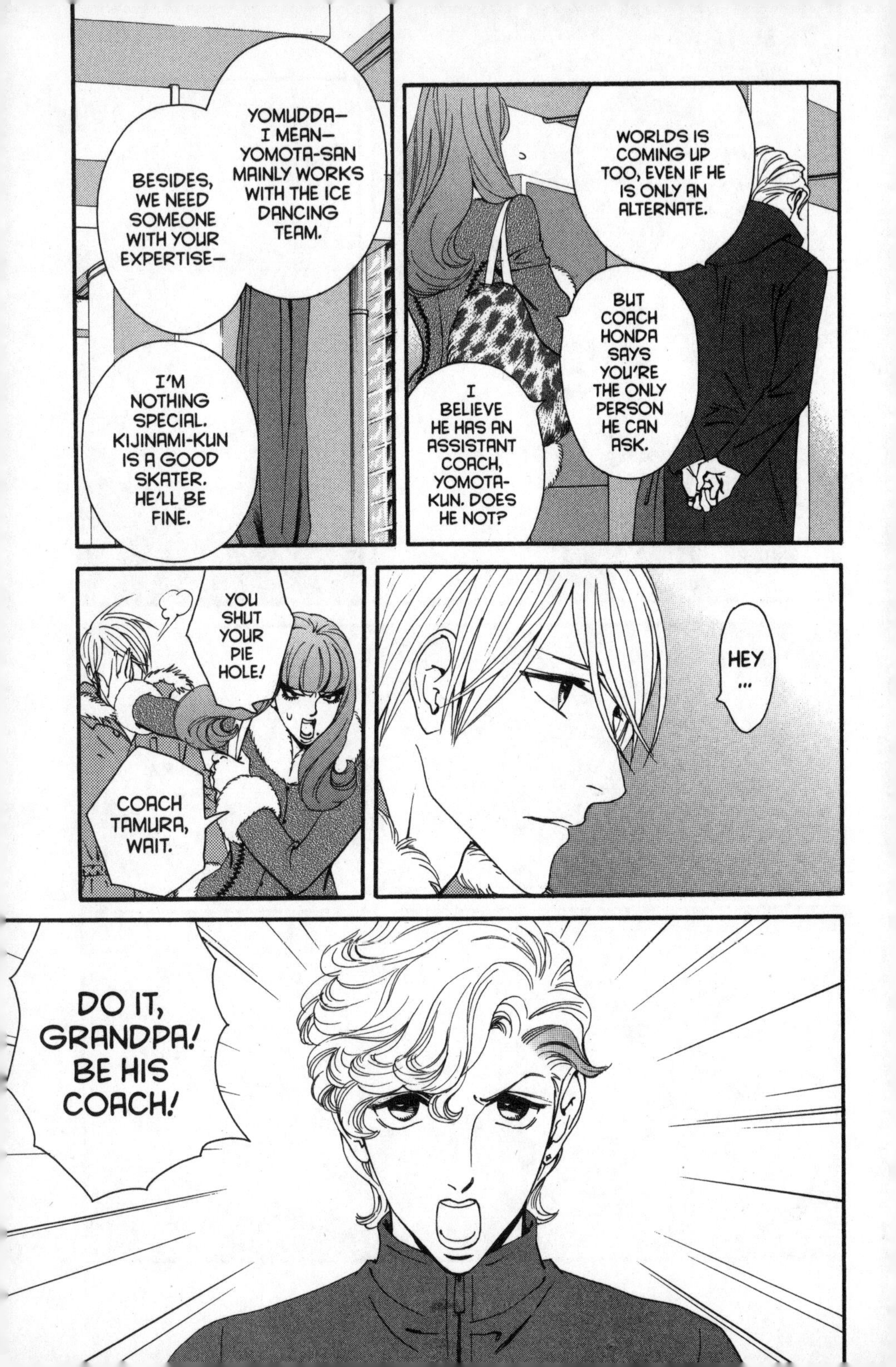
WORLDS IS COMING UP TOO, EVEN IF HE IS ONLY AN ALTERNATE.
BUT COACH HONDA SAYS YOU'RE THE ONLY PERSON HE CAN ASK.
I BELIEVE HE HAS AN ASSISTANT COACH, YOMOTA-KUN. DOES HE NOT?
YOMUDDA— I MEAN— YOMOTA-SAN MAINLY WORKS WITH THE ICE DANCING TEAM.
BESIDES, WE NEED SOMEONE WITH YOUR EXPERTISE—
I'M NOTHING SPECIAL. KIJINAMI-KUN IS A GOOD SKATER. HE'LL BE FINE.
HEY ...
YOU SHUT YOUR PIE HOLE!
COACH TAMURA, WAIT.
DO IT, GRANDPA! BE HIS COACH!

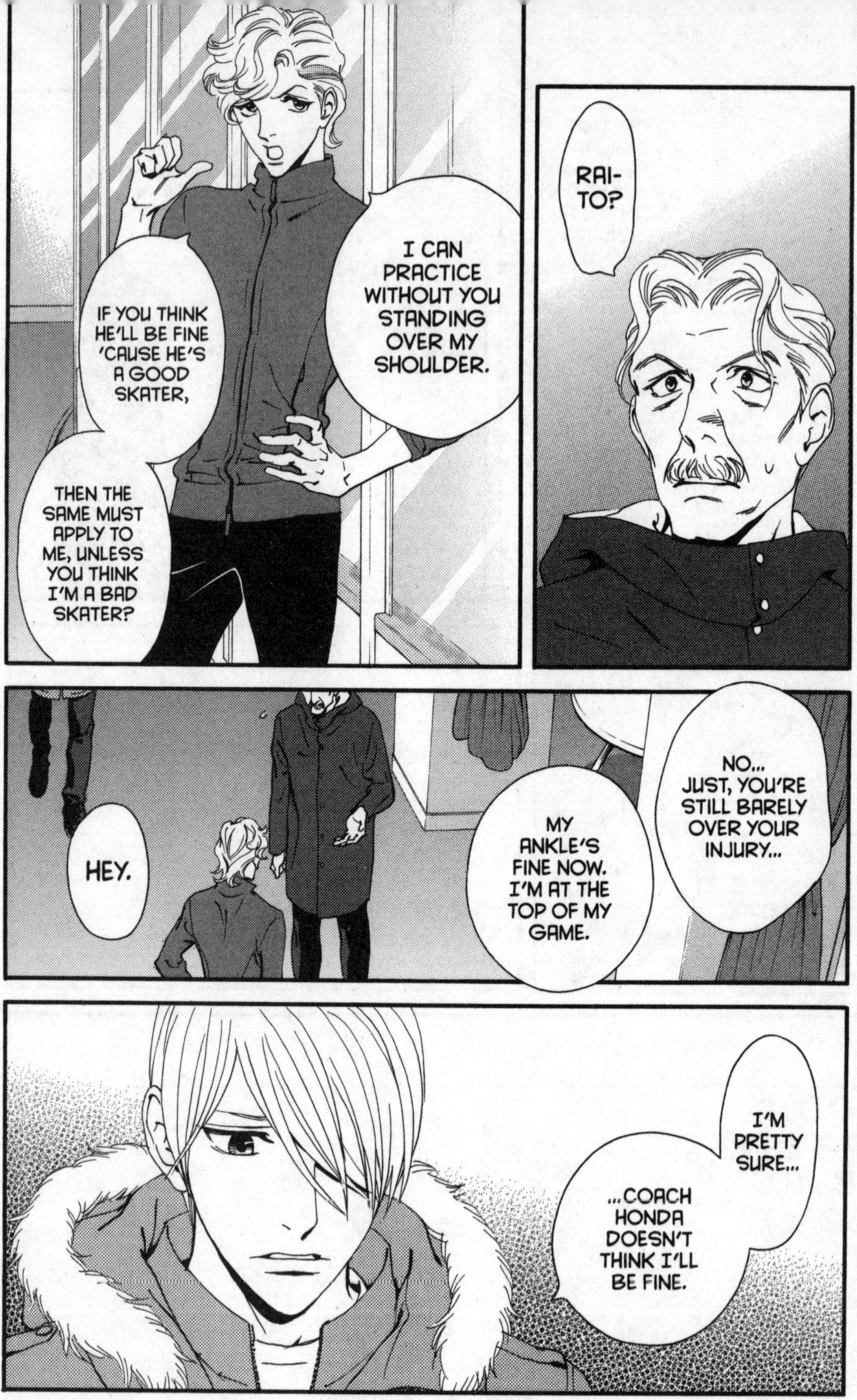
RAI-TO?
I CAN PRACTICE WITHOUT YOU STANDING OVER MY SHOULDER.
IF YOU THINK HE'LL BE FINE 'CAUSE HE'S A GOOD SKATER,
THEN THE SAME MUST APPLY TO ME, UNLESS YOU THINK I'M A BAD SKATER?
NO... JUST, YOU'RE STILL BARELY OVER YOUR INJURY...
MY ANKLE'S FINE NOW. I'M AT THE TOP OF MY GAME.
HEY.
I'M PRETTY SURE...
...COACH HONDA DOESN'T THINK I'LL BE FINE.

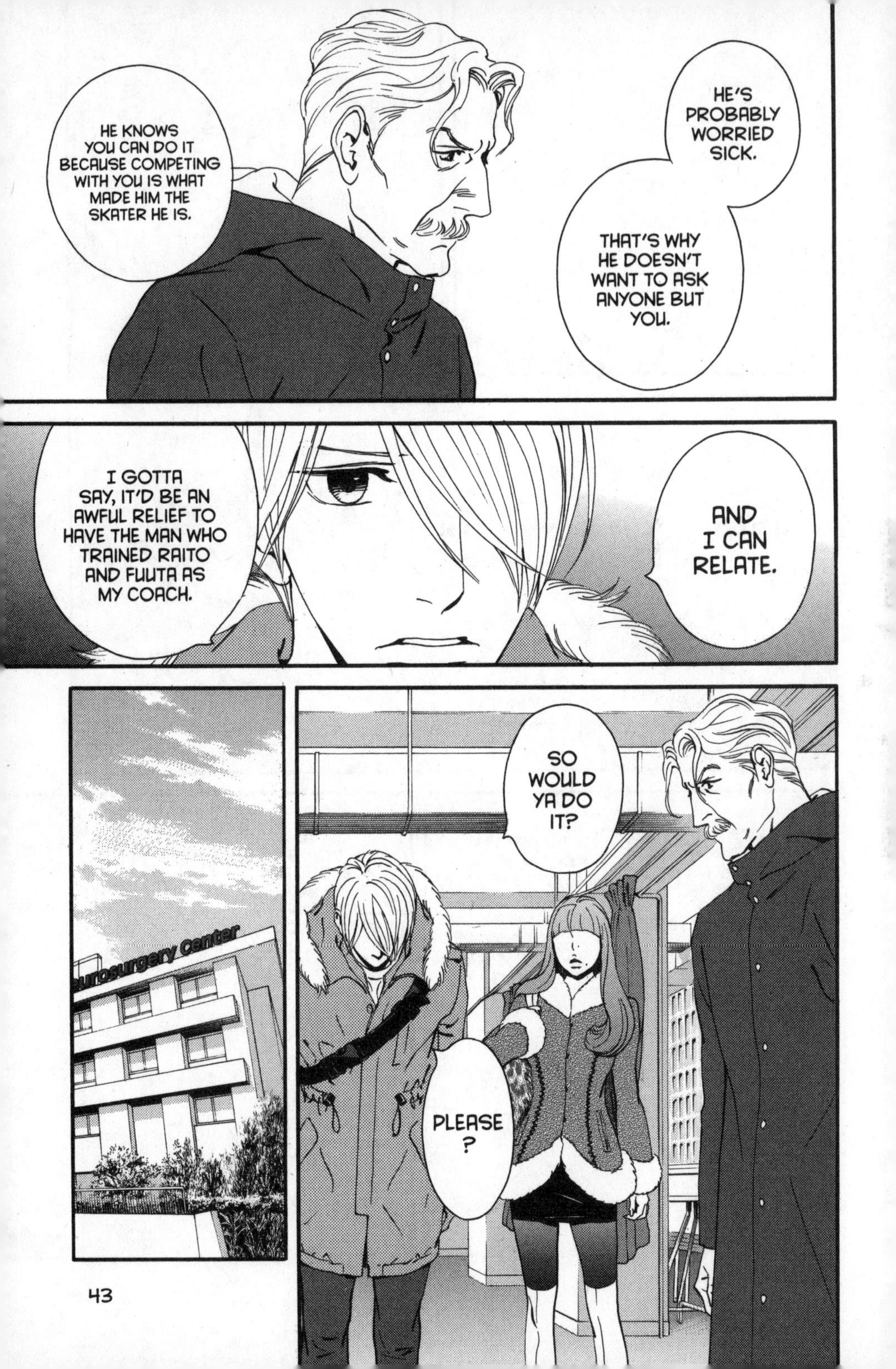
HE'S PROBABLY WORRIED SICK.
THAT'S WHY HE DOESN'T WANT TO ASK ANYONE BUT YOU.
HE KNOWS YOU CAN DO IT BECAUSE COMPETING WITH YOU IS WHAT MADE HIM THE SKATER HE IS.
AND I CAN RELATE.
I GOTTA SAY, IT'D BE AN AWFUL RELIEF TO HAVE THE MAN WHO TRAINED RAITO AND FUUTA AS MY COACH.
SO WOULD YA DO IT?
PLEASE?
eurosurgery Center

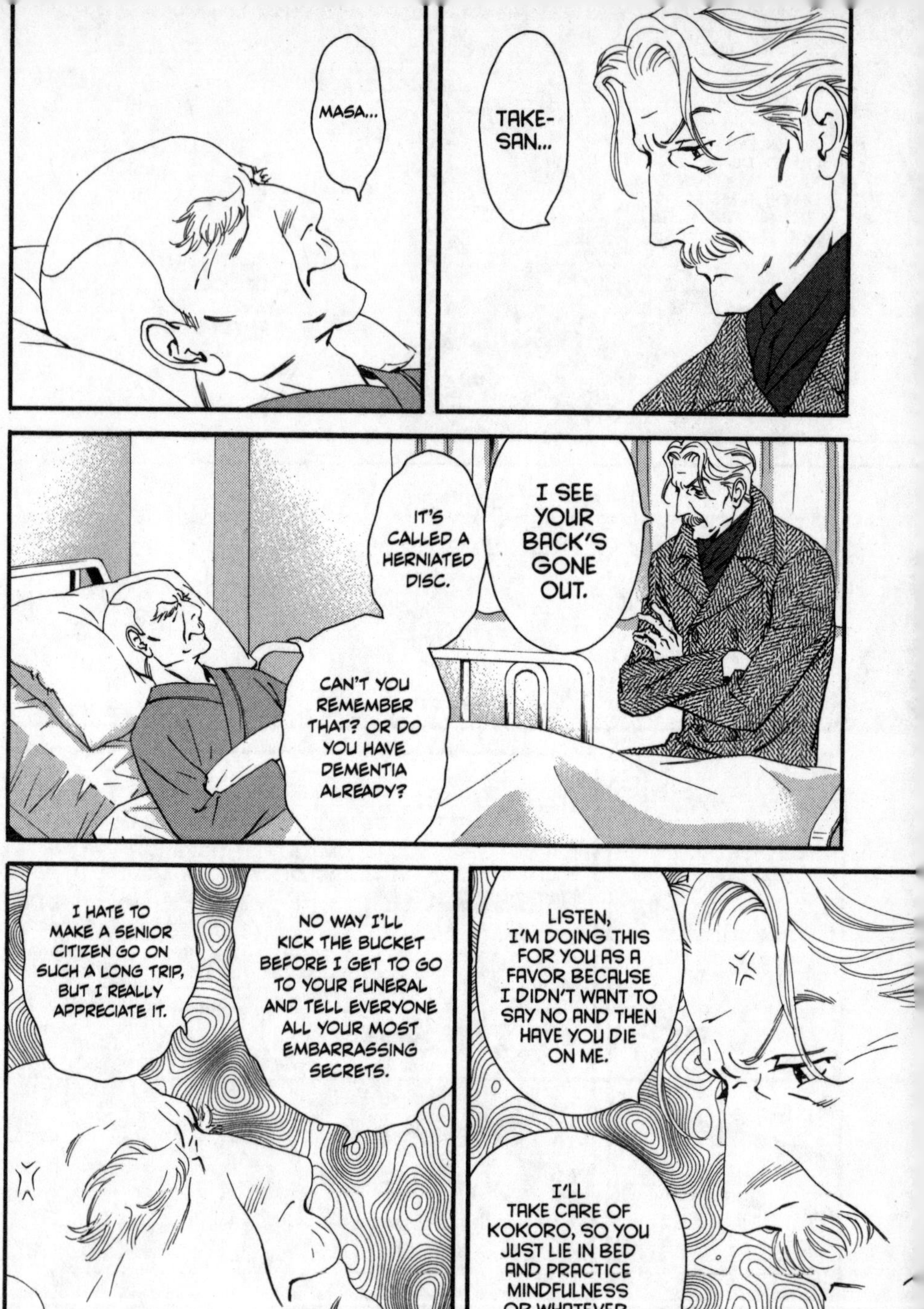
TAKE-SAN...
MASA...
I SEE YOUR BACK'S GONE OUT.
IT'S CALLED A HERNIATED DISC.
CAN'T YOU REMEMBER THAT? OR DO YOU HAVE DEMENTIA ALREADY?
LISTEN, I'M DOING THIS FOR YOU AS A FAVOR BECAUSE I DIDN'T WANT TO SAY NO AND THEN HAVE YOU DIE ON ME.
I'LL TAKE CARE OF KOKORO, SO YOU JUST LIE IN BED AND PRACTICE MINDFULNESS OR WHATEVER, OLD MAN.
NO WAY I'LL KICK THE BUCKET BEFORE I GET TO GO TO YOUR FUNERAL AND TELL EVERYONE ALL YOUR MOST EMBARRASSING SECRETS.
I HATE TO MAKE A SENIOR CITIZEN GO ON SUCH A LONG TRIP, BUT I REALLY APPRECIATE IT.

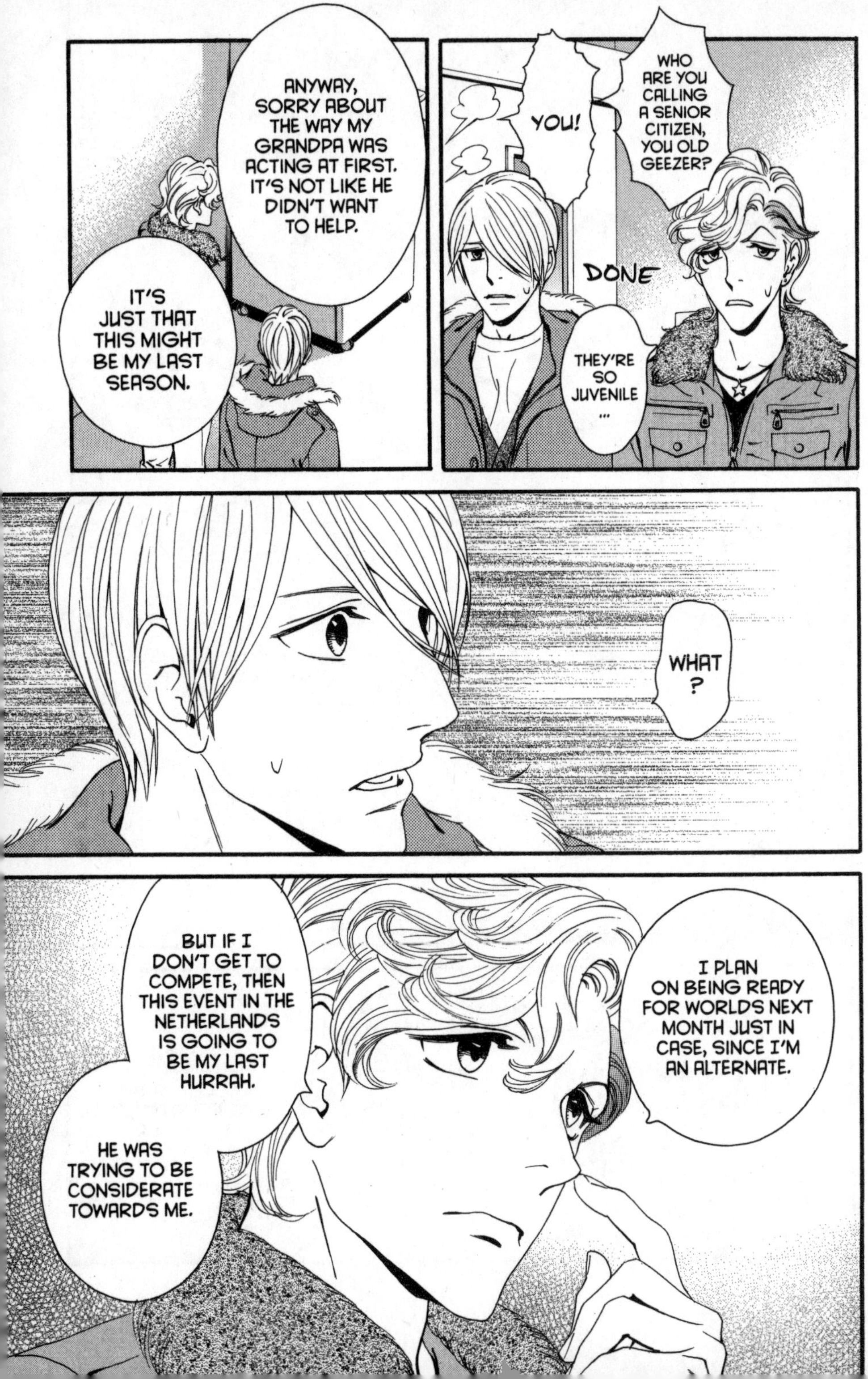
WHO ARE YOU CALLING A SENIOR CITIZEN, YOU OLD GEEZER?
YOU!
DONE
THEY'RE SO JUVENILE ...
ANYWAY, SORRY ABOUT THE WAY MY GRANDPA WAS ACTING AT FIRST. IT'S NOT LIKE HE DIDN'T WANT TO HELP.
IT'S JUST THAT THIS MIGHT BE MY LAST SEASON.
WHAT?
I PLAN ON BEING READY FOR WORLDS NEXT MONTH JUST IN CASE, SINCE I'M AN ALTERNATE.
BUT IF I DON'T GET TO COMPETE, THEN THIS EVENT IN THE NETHERLANDS IS GOING TO BE MY LAST HURRAH.
HE WAS TRYING TO BE CONSIDERATE TOWARDS ME.

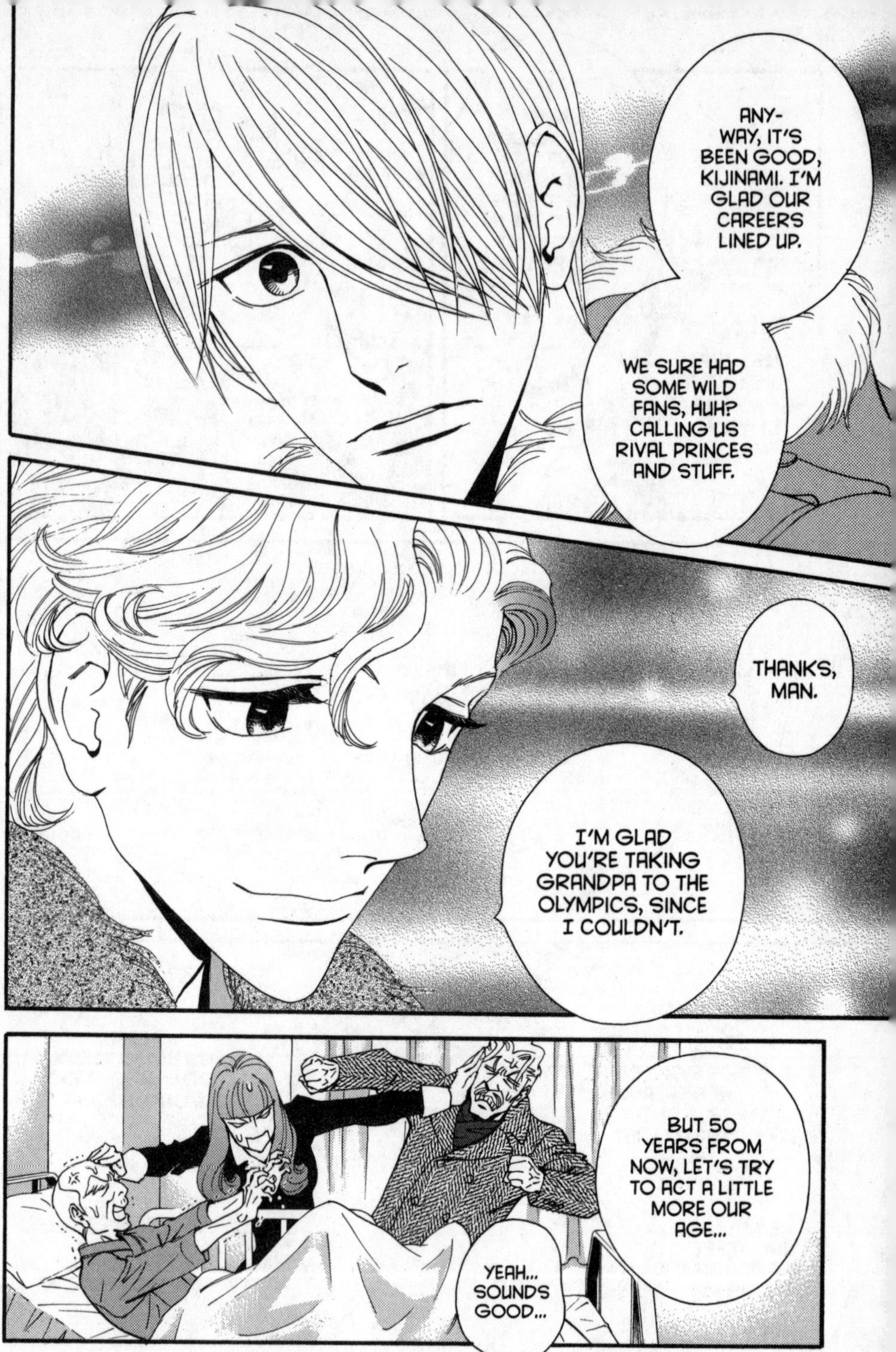
ANY-WAY, IT'S BEEN GOOD, KIJINAMI. I'M GLAD OUR CAREERS LINED UP.
WE SURE HAD SOME WILD FANS, HUH? CALLING US RIVAL PRINCES AND STUFF.
THANKS, MAN.
I'M GLAD YOU'RE TAKING GRANDPA TO THE OLYMPICS, SINCE I COULDN'T.
BUT 50 YEARS FROM NOW, LET'S TRY TO ACT A LITTLE MORE OUR AGE...
YEAH... SOUNDS GOOD...

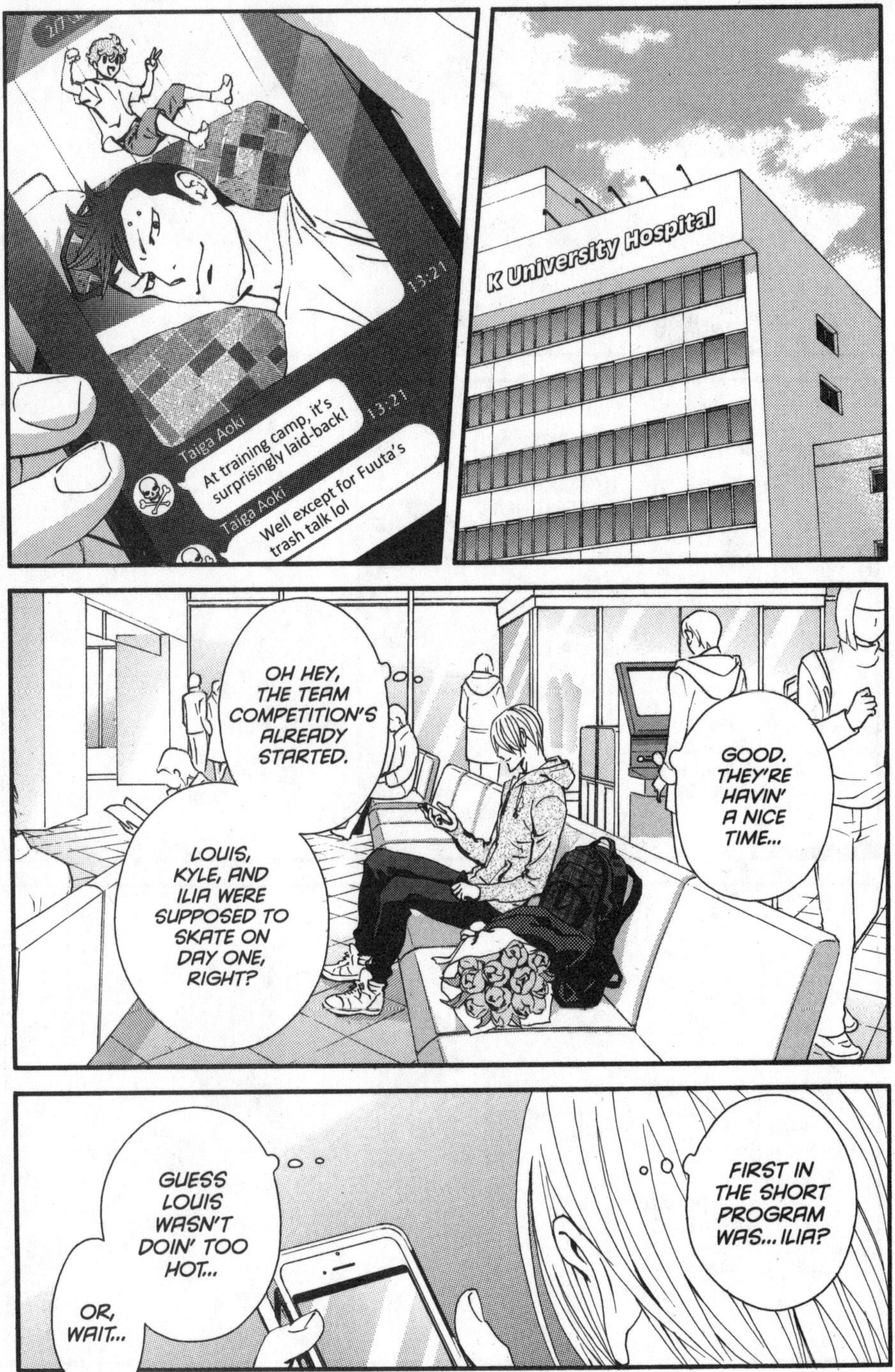
K University Hospital
Taiga Aoki
At training camp, it's surprisingly laid-back!
13:21
Taiga Aoki
Well except for Fuuta's trash talk lol
GOOD. THEY'RE HAVIN' A NICE TIME...
OH HEY, THE TEAM COMPETITION'S ALREADY STARTED.
LOUIS, KYLE, AND ILIA WERE SUPPOSED TO SKATE ON DAY ONE, RIGHT?
FIRST IN THE SHORT PROGRAM WAS... ILIA?
GUESS LOUIS WASN'T DOIN' TOO HOT...
OR, WAIT...

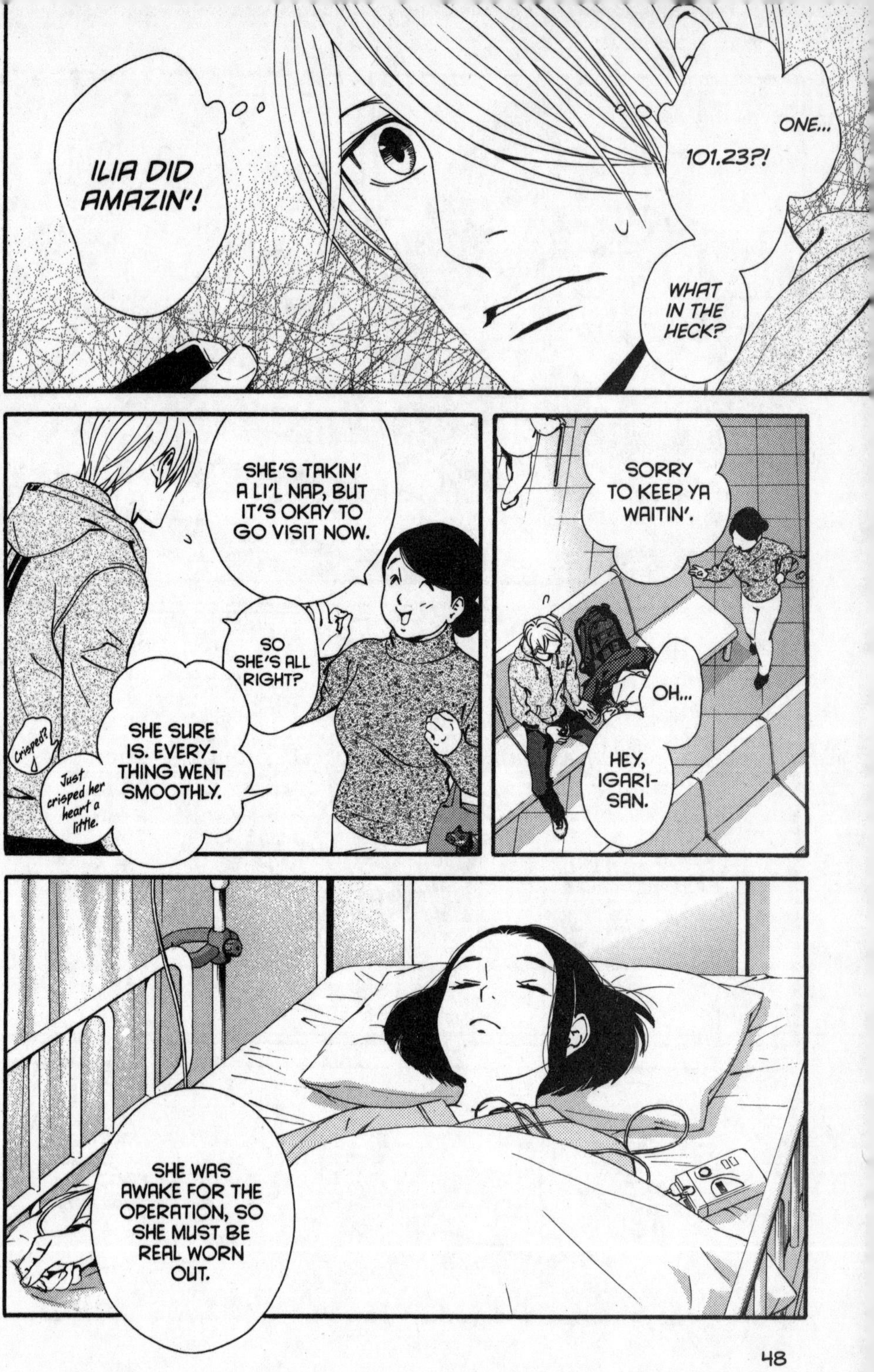
ONE... 101.23?!
WHAT IN THE HECK?
ILIA DID AMAZIN'!
SORRY TO KEEP YA WAITIN'.
OH...
HEY, IGARI-SAN.
SHE'S TAKIN' A LI'L NAP, BUT IT'S OKAY TO GO VISIT NOW.
SO SHE'S ALL RIGHT?
SHE SURE IS. EVERY-THING WENT SMOOTHLY.
Just crisped her heart a little.
Crisped?
SHE WAS AWAKE FOR THE OPERATION, SO SHE MUST BE REAL WORN OUT.

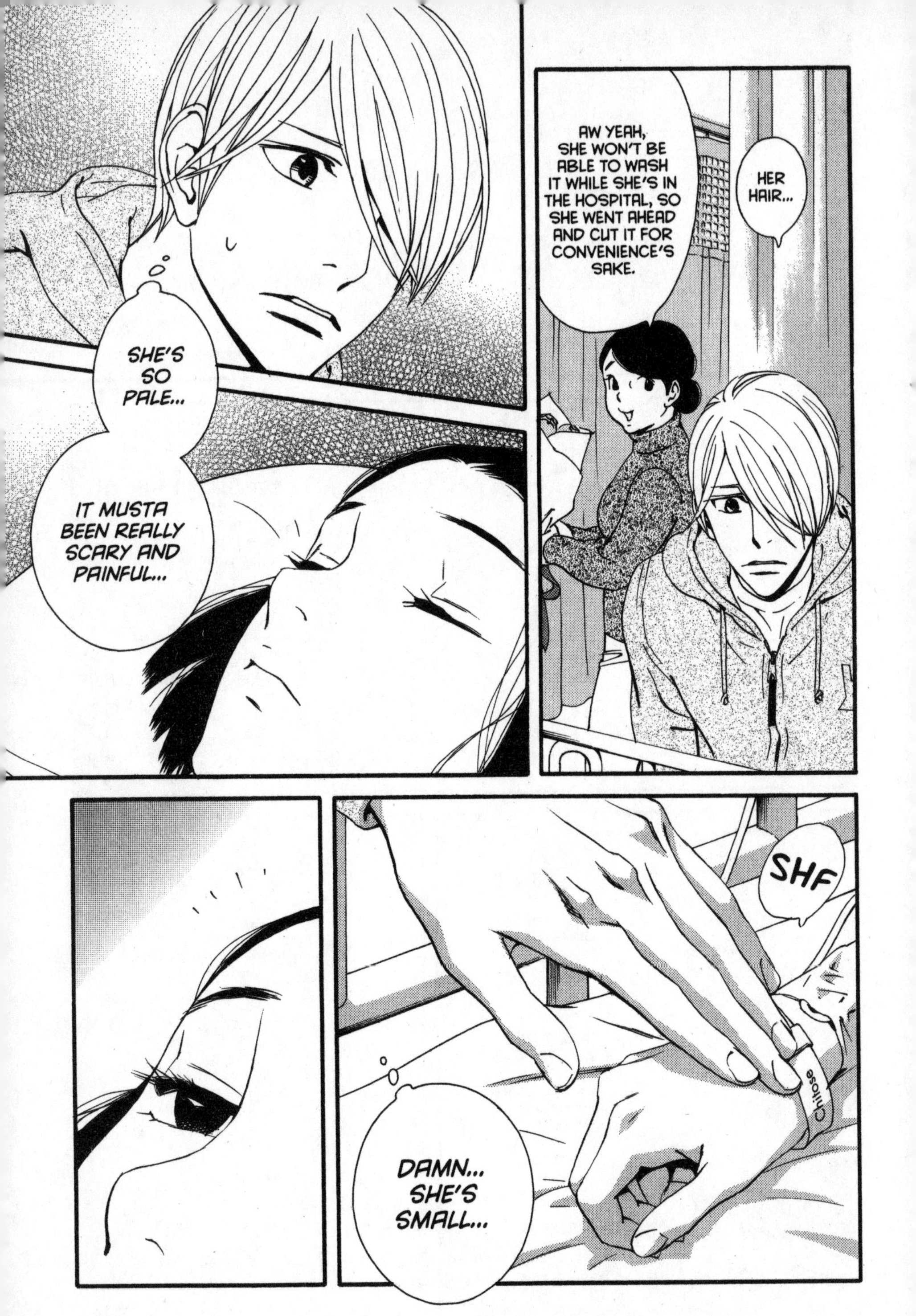
HER HAIR...
AW YEAH, SHE WON'T BE ABLE TO WASH IT WHILE SHE'S IN THE HOSPITAL, SO SHE WENT AHEAD AND CUT IT FOR CONVENIENCE'S SAKE.
SHE'S SO PALE...
IT MUSTA BEEN REALLY SCARY AND PAINFUL...
SHF
Chitose
DAMN... SHE'S SMALL...

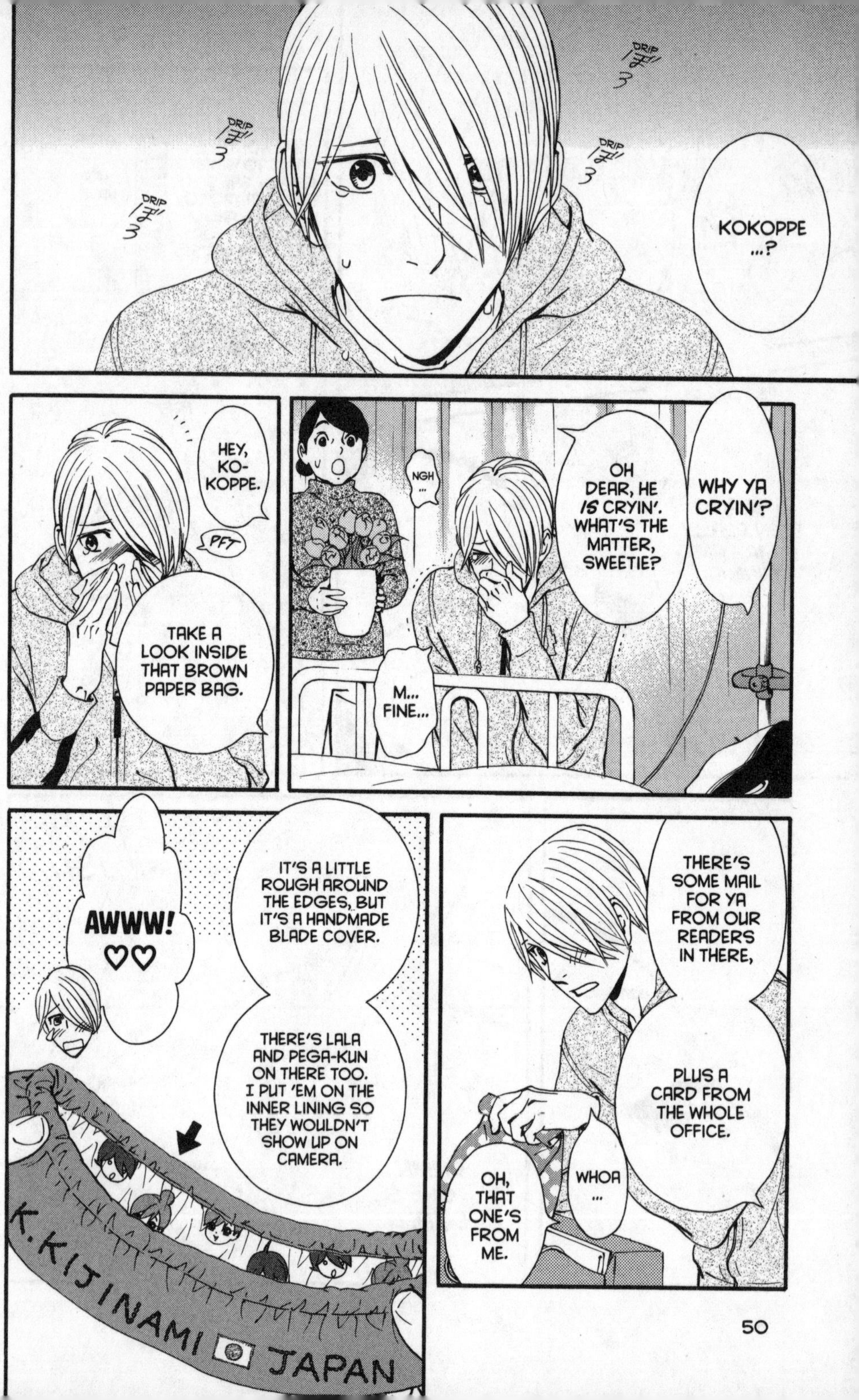
DRIP
DRIP
DRIP
DRIP
KOKOPPE ...?
WHY YA CRYIN'?
OH DEAR, HE *IS* CRYIN'. WHAT'S THE MATTER, SWEETIE?
NGH ...
M... FINE...
HEY, KO-KOPPE.
PFT
TAKE A LOOK INSIDE THAT BROWN PAPER BAG.
THERE'S SOME MAIL FOR YA FROM OUR READERS IN THERE,
PLUS A CARD FROM THE WHOLE OFFICE.
WHOA ...
OH, THAT ONE'S FROM ME.
IT'S A LITTLE ROUGH AROUND THE EDGES, BUT IT'S A HANDMADE BLADE COVER.
THERE'S LALA AND PEGA-KUN ON THERE TOO. I PUT 'EM ON THE INNER LINING SO THEY WOULDN'T SHOW UP ON CAMERA.
AWWW! ♡♡
K.KIJINAMI JAPAN

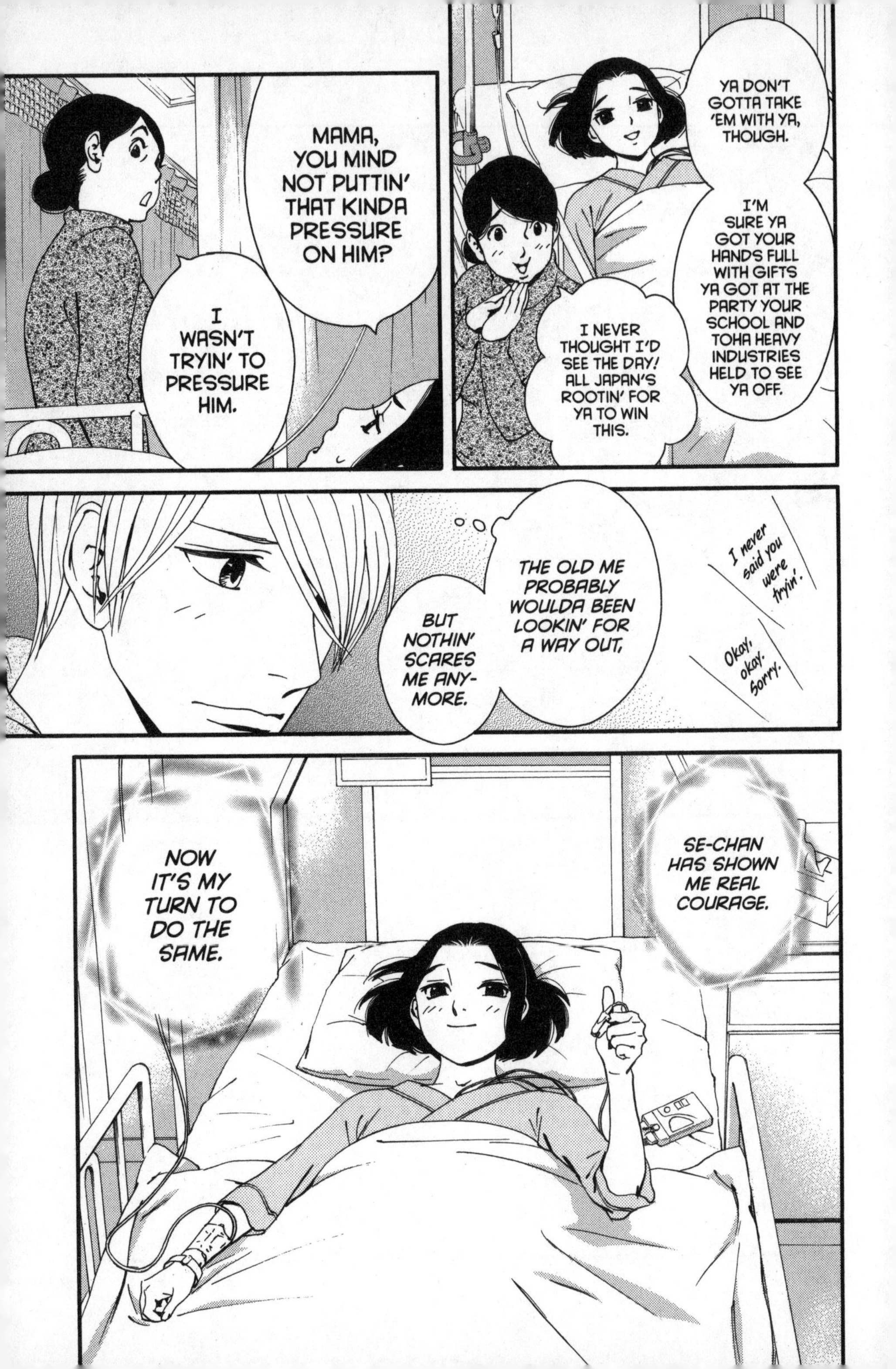
YA DON'T GOTTA TAKE 'EM WITH YA, THOUGH.
I'M SURE YA GOT YOUR HANDS FULL WITH GIFTS YA GOT AT THE PARTY YOUR SCHOOL AND TOHA HEAVY INDUSTRIES HELD TO SEE YA OFF.
I NEVER THOUGHT I'D SEE THE DAY! ALL JAPAN'S ROOTIN' FOR YA TO WIN THIS.
MAMA, YOU MIND NOT PUTTIN' THAT KINDA PRESSURE ON HIM?
I WASN'T TRYIN' TO PRESSURE HIM.
I never said you were tryin'.
Okay, okay. Sorry.
THE OLD ME PROBABLY WOULDA BEEN LOOKIN' FOR A WAY OUT,
BUT NOTHIN' SCARES ME ANY-MORE.
SE-CHAN HAS SHOWN ME REAL COURAGE.
NOW IT'S MY TURN TO DO THE SAME.

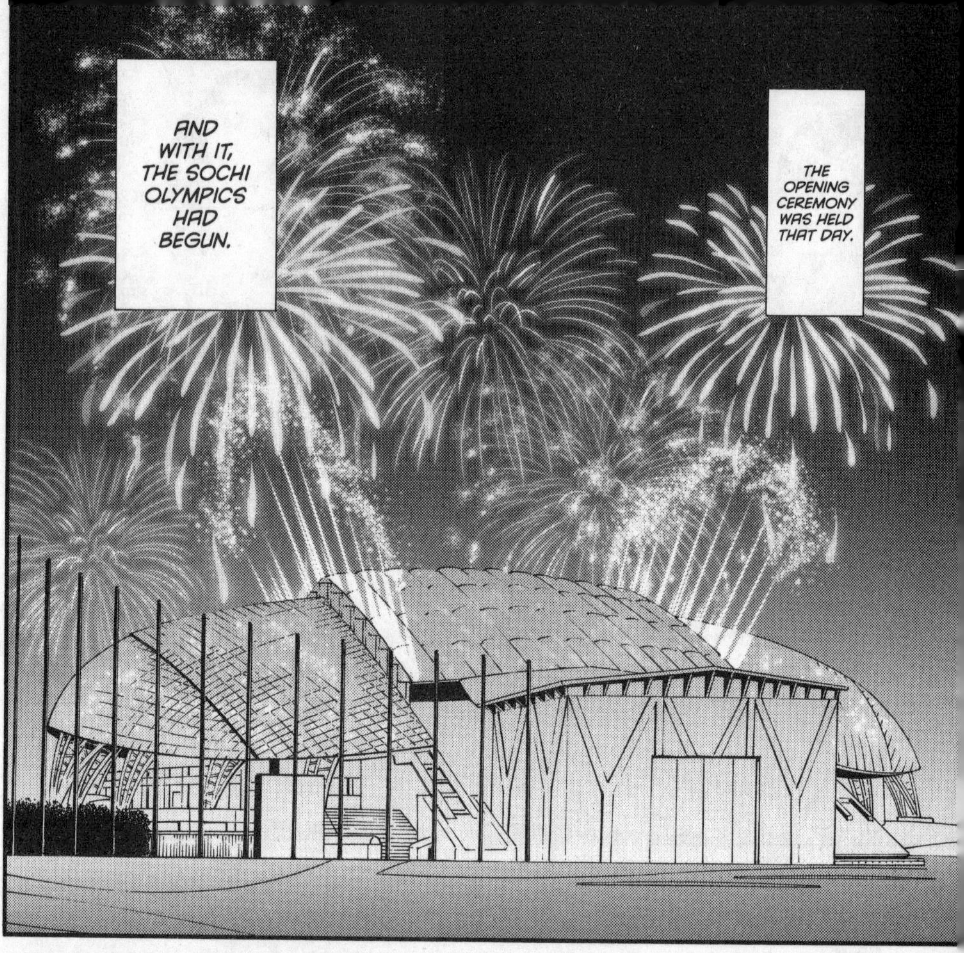
THE OPENING CEREMONY WAS HELD THAT DAY.
AND WITH IT, THE SOCHI OLYMPICS HAD BEGUN.

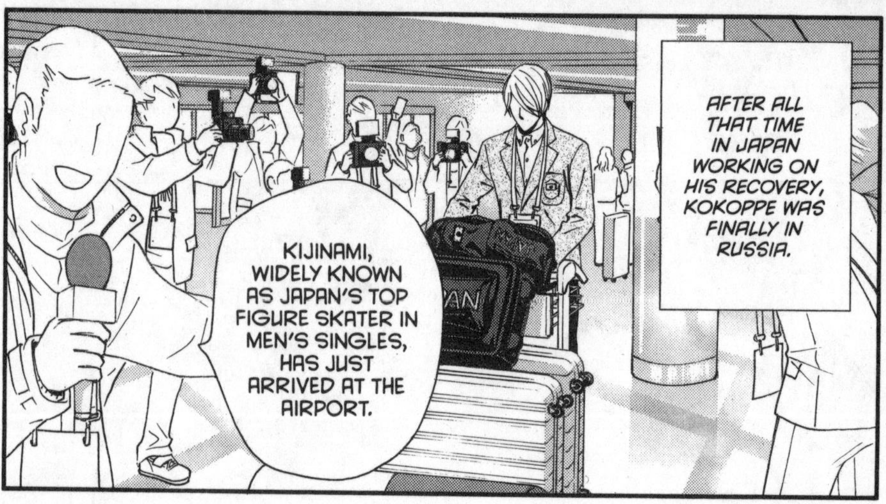
AFTER ALL THAT TIME IN JAPAN WORKING ON HIS RECOVERY, KOKOPPE WAS FINALLY IN RUSSIA.
KIJINAMI, WIDELY KNOWN AS JAPAN'S TOP FIGURE SKATER IN MEN'S SINGLES, HAS JUST ARRIVED AT THE AIRPORT.

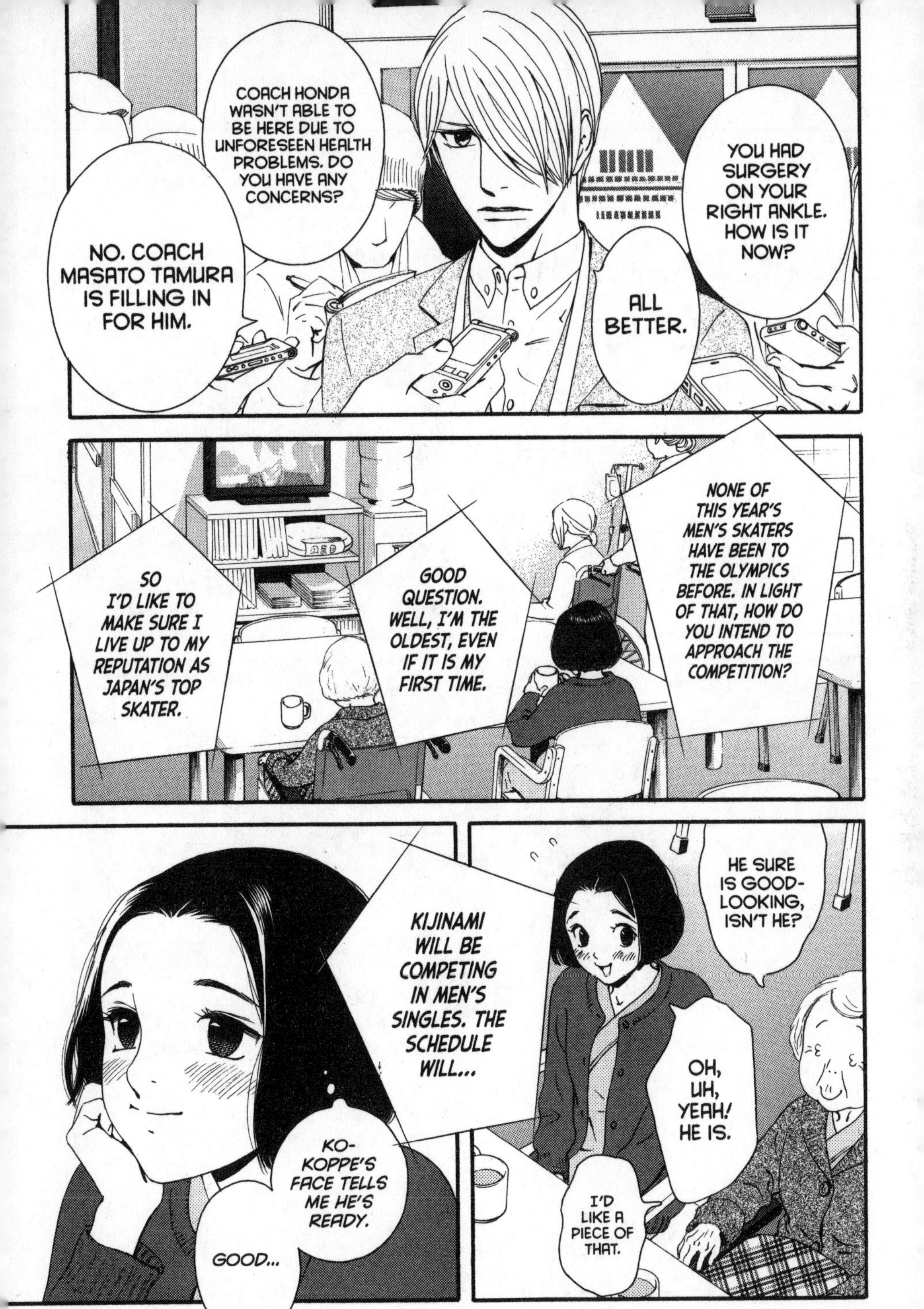
YOU HAD SURGERY ON YOUR RIGHT ANKLE. HOW IS IT NOW?
ALL BETTER.
COACH HONDA WASN'T ABLE TO BE HERE DUE TO UNFORESEEN HEALTH PROBLEMS. DO YOU HAVE ANY CONCERNS?
NO. COACH MASATO TAMURA IS FILLING IN FOR HIM.
NONE OF THIS YEAR'S MEN'S SKATERS HAVE BEEN TO THE OLYMPICS BEFORE. IN LIGHT OF THAT, HOW DO YOU INTEND TO APPROACH THE COMPETITION?
GOOD QUESTION. WELL, I'M THE OLDEST, EVEN IF IT IS MY FIRST TIME.
SO I'D LIKE TO MAKE SURE I LIVE UP TO MY REPUTATION AS JAPAN'S TOP SKATER.
HE SURE IS GOOD-LOOKING, ISN'T HE?
OH, UH, YEAH! HE IS.
I'D LIKE A PIECE OF THAT.
KIJINAMI WILL BE COMPETING IN MEN'S SINGLES. THE SCHEDULE WILL...
KO-KOPPE'S FACE TELLS ME HE'S READY.
GOOD...

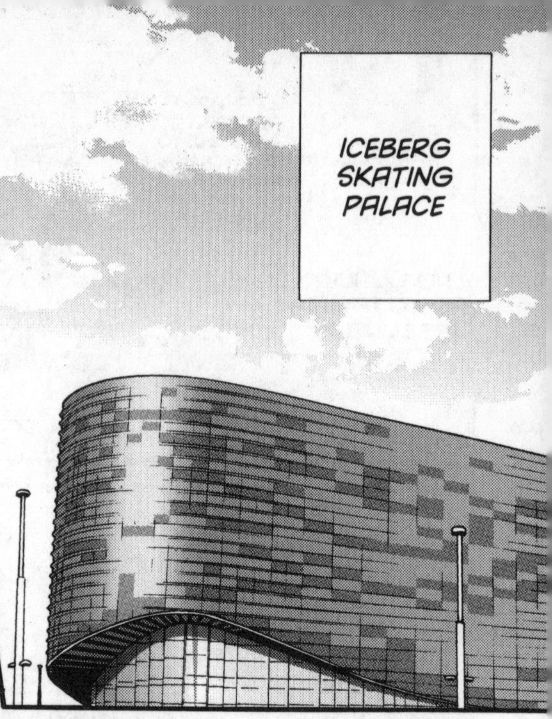
ICEBERG
SKATING
PALACE

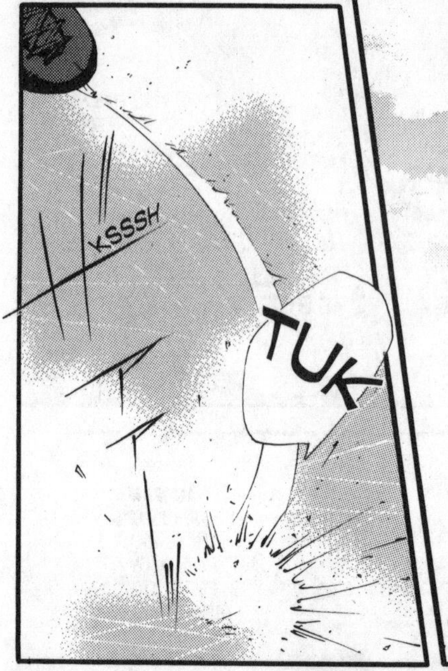
KSSSH
TUK

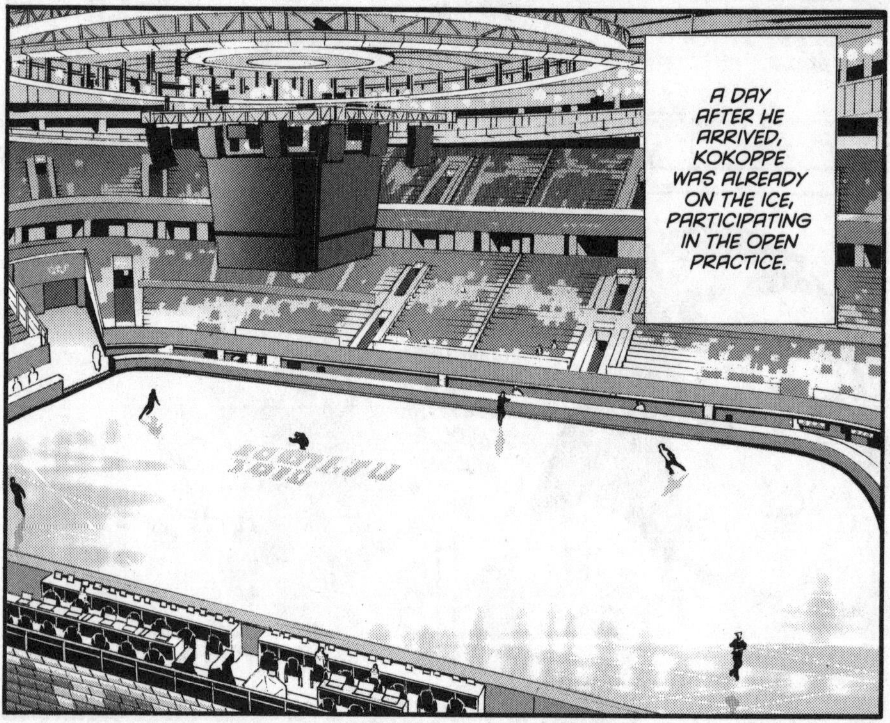
A DAY
AFTER HE
ARRIVED,
KOKOPPE
WAS ALREADY
ON THE ICE,
PARTICIPATING
IN THE OPEN
PRACTICE.

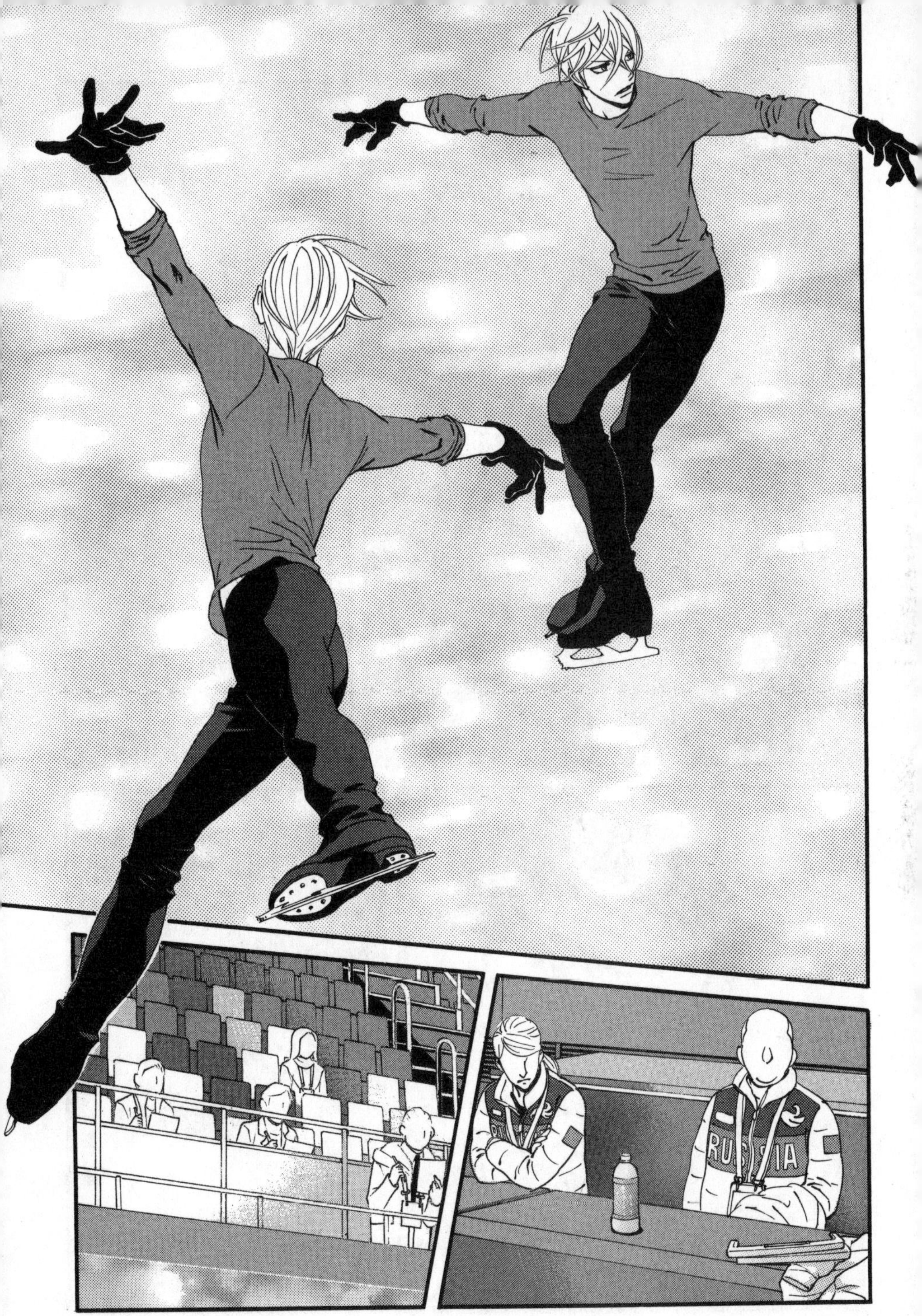

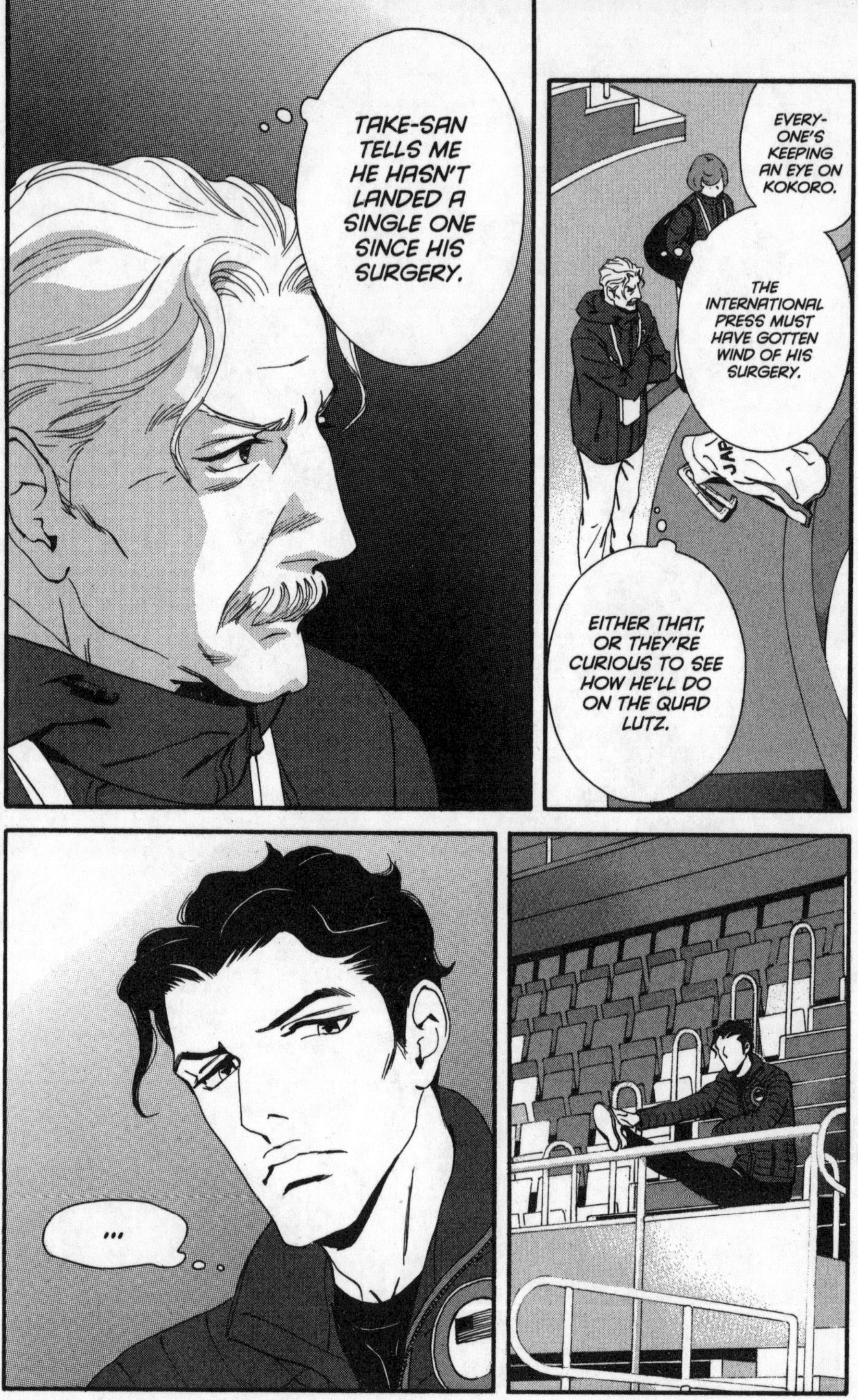
EVERY-ONE'S KEEPING AN EYE ON KOKORO.
THE INTERNATIONAL PRESS MUST HAVE GOTTEN WIND OF HIS SURGERY.
EITHER THAT, OR THEY'RE CURIOUS TO SEE HOW HE'LL DO ON THE QUAD LUTZ.
TAKE-SAN TELLS ME HE HASN'T LANDED A SINGLE ONE SINCE HIS SURGERY.
...

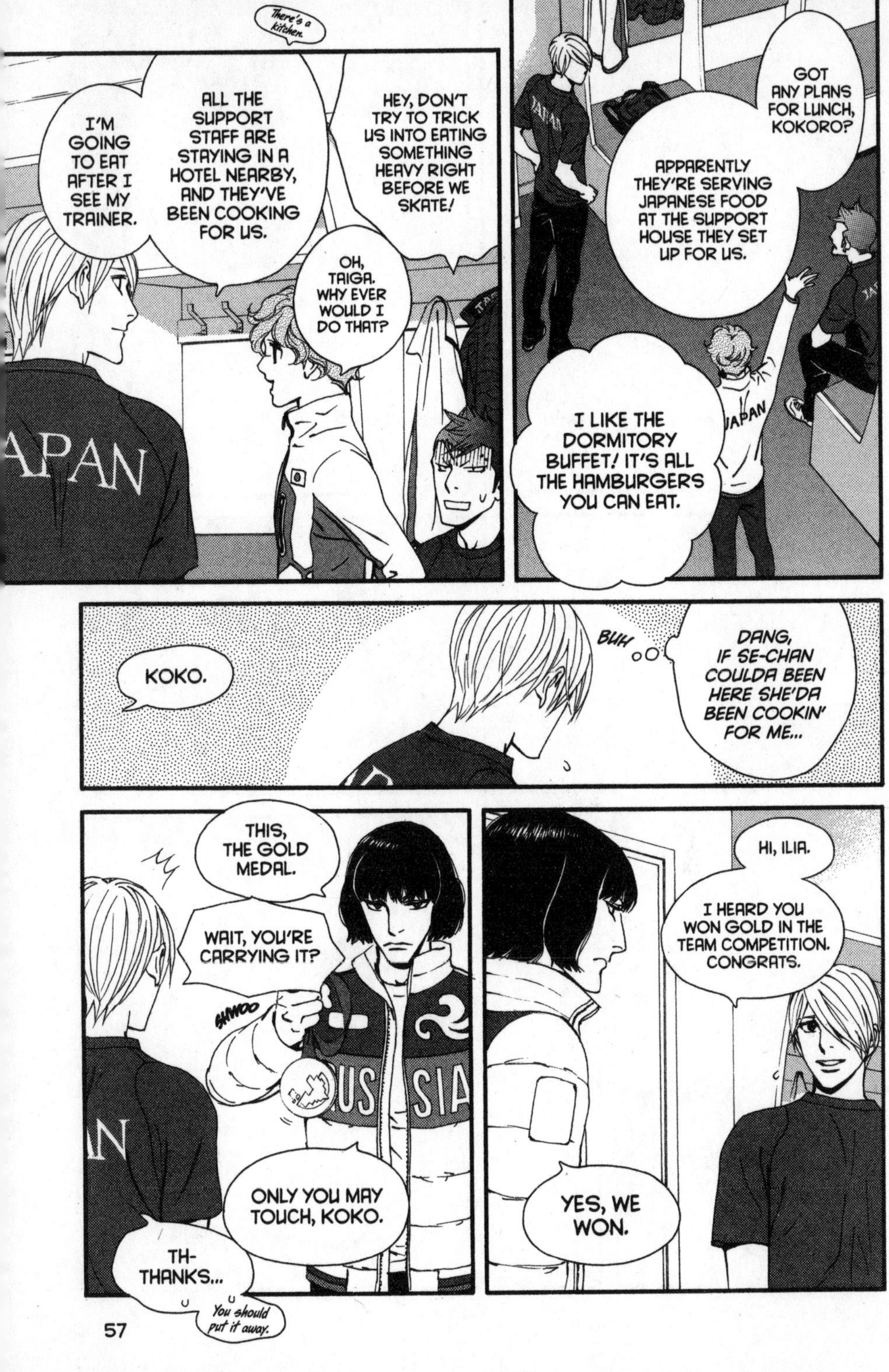

GOT ANY PLANS FOR LUNCH, KOKORO?
APPARENTLY THEY'RE SERVING JAPANESE FOOD AT THE SUPPORT HOUSE THEY SET UP FOR US.
I LIKE THE DORMITORY BUFFET! IT'S ALL THE HAMBURGERS YOU CAN EAT.
There's a kitchen.
ALL THE SUPPORT STAFF ARE STAYING IN A HOTEL NEARBY, AND THEY'VE BEEN COOKING FOR US.
HEY, DON'T TRY TO TRICK US INTO EATING SOMETHING HEAVY RIGHT BEFORE WE SKATE!
OH, TAIGA. WHY EVER WOULD I DO THAT?
I'M GOING TO EAT AFTER I SEE MY TRAINER.
DANG, IF SE-CHAN COULDA BEEN HERE SHE'DA BEEN COOKIN' FOR ME...
BUH
KOKO.
HI, ILIA.
I HEARD YOU WON GOLD IN THE TEAM COMPETITION. CONGRATS.
YES, WE WON.
THIS, THE GOLD MEDAL.
WAIT, YOU'RE CARRYING IT?
SHWOO
ONLY YOU MAY TOUCH, KOKO.
TH- THANKS...
You should put it away.

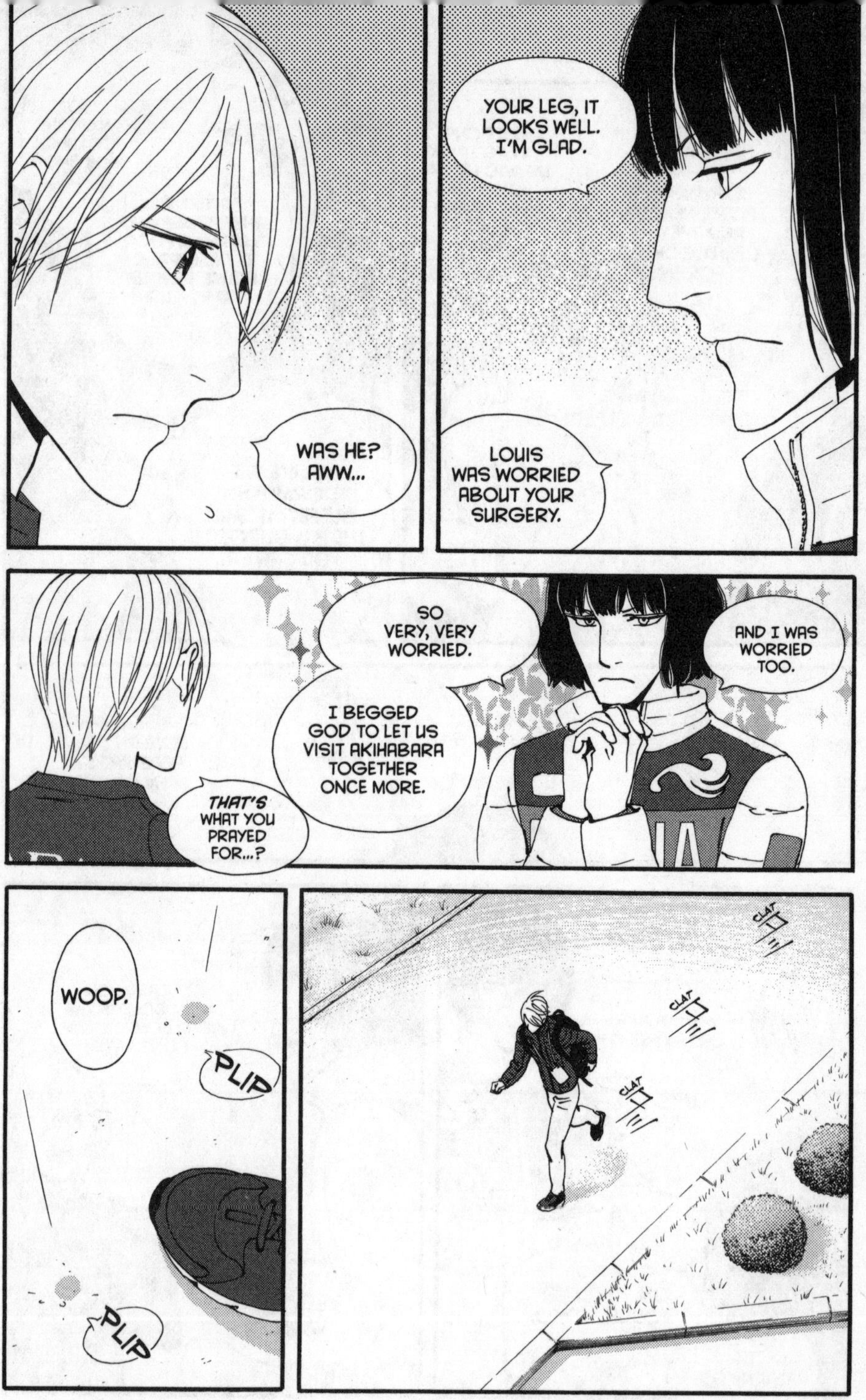
YOUR LEG, IT LOOKS WELL. I'M GLAD.
LOUIS WAS WORRIED ABOUT YOUR SURGERY.
WAS HE? AWW...
AND I WAS WORRIED TOO.
SO VERY, VERY WORRIED.
I BEGGED GOD TO LET US VISIT AKIHABARA TOGETHER ONCE MORE.
THAT'S WHAT YOU PRAYED FOR...?
CLAT
CLAT
CLAT
WOOP.
PLIP
PLIP

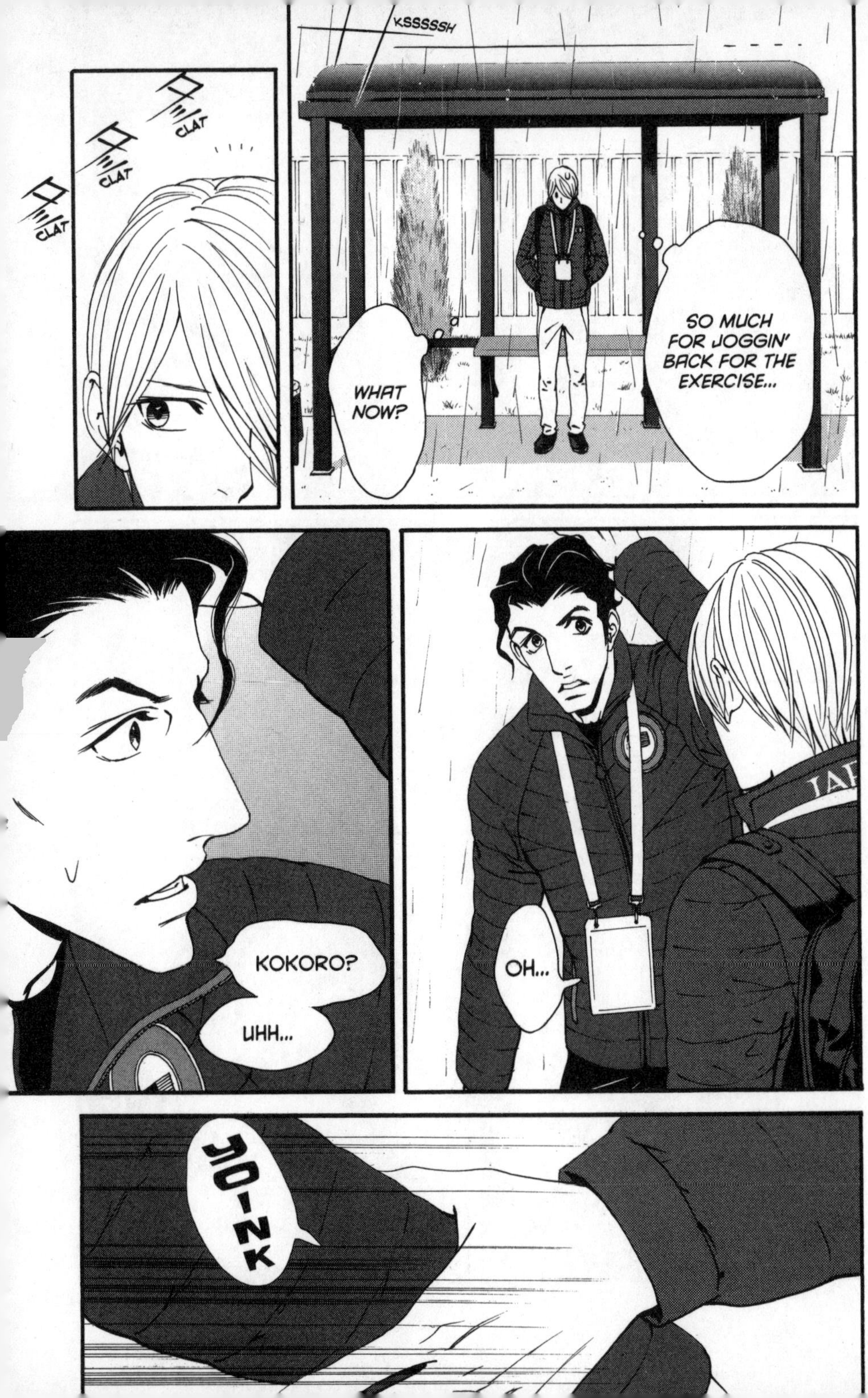
KSSSSSH
SO MUCH FOR JOGGIN' BACK FOR THE EXERCISE...
WHAT NOW?
CLAT
CLAT
CLAT
OH...
KOKORO?
UHH...
JOINK

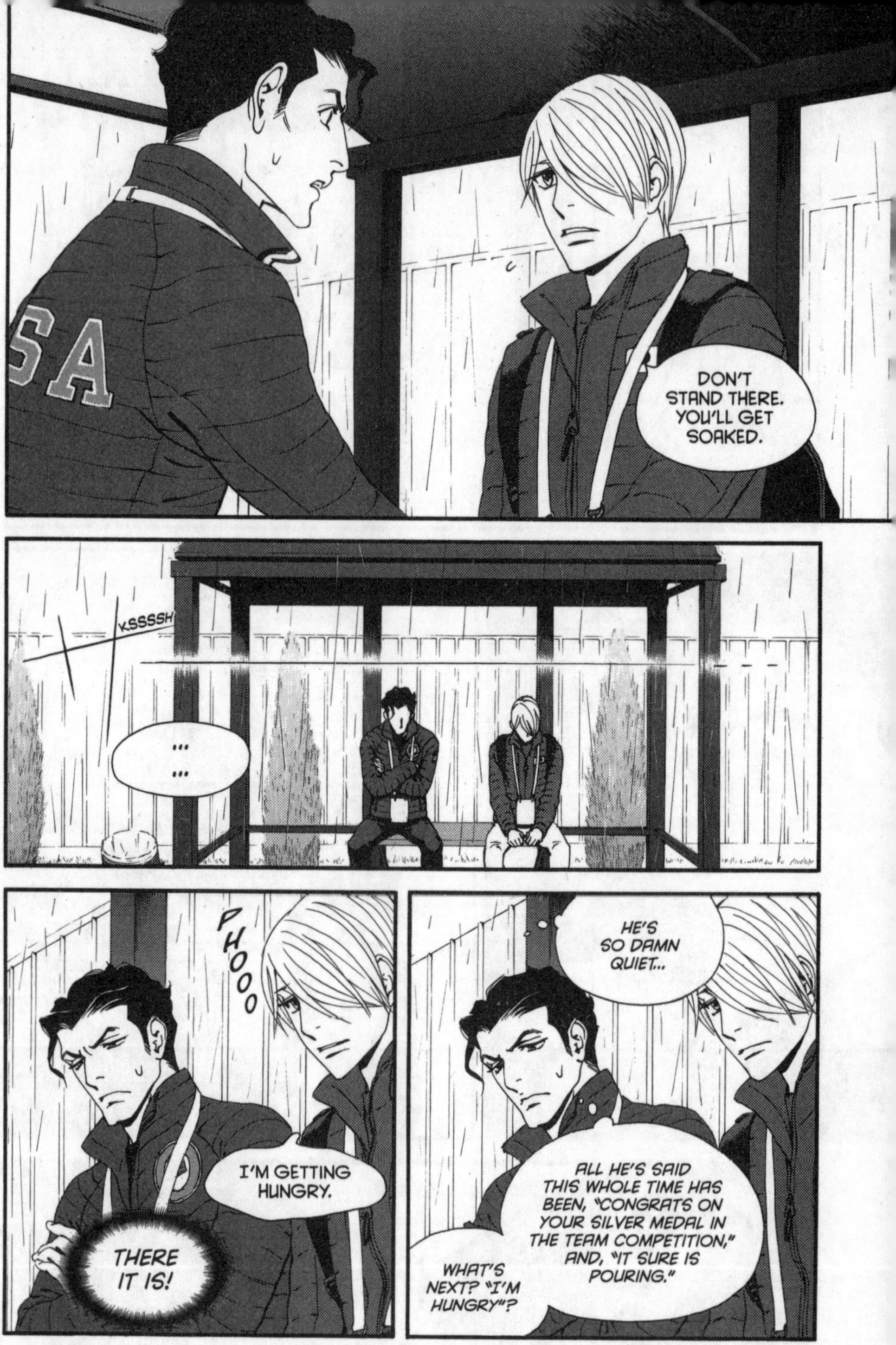
DON'T STAND THERE. YOU'LL GET SOAKED.
KSSSSH
...
...
HE'S SO DAMN QUIET...
ALL HE'S SAID THIS WHOLE TIME HAS BEEN, "CONGRATS ON YOUR SILVER MEDAL IN THE TEAM COMPETITION," AND, "IT SURE IS POURING."
WHAT'S NEXT? "I'M HUNGRY"?
PHOOO
I'M GETTING HUNGRY.
THERE IT IS!

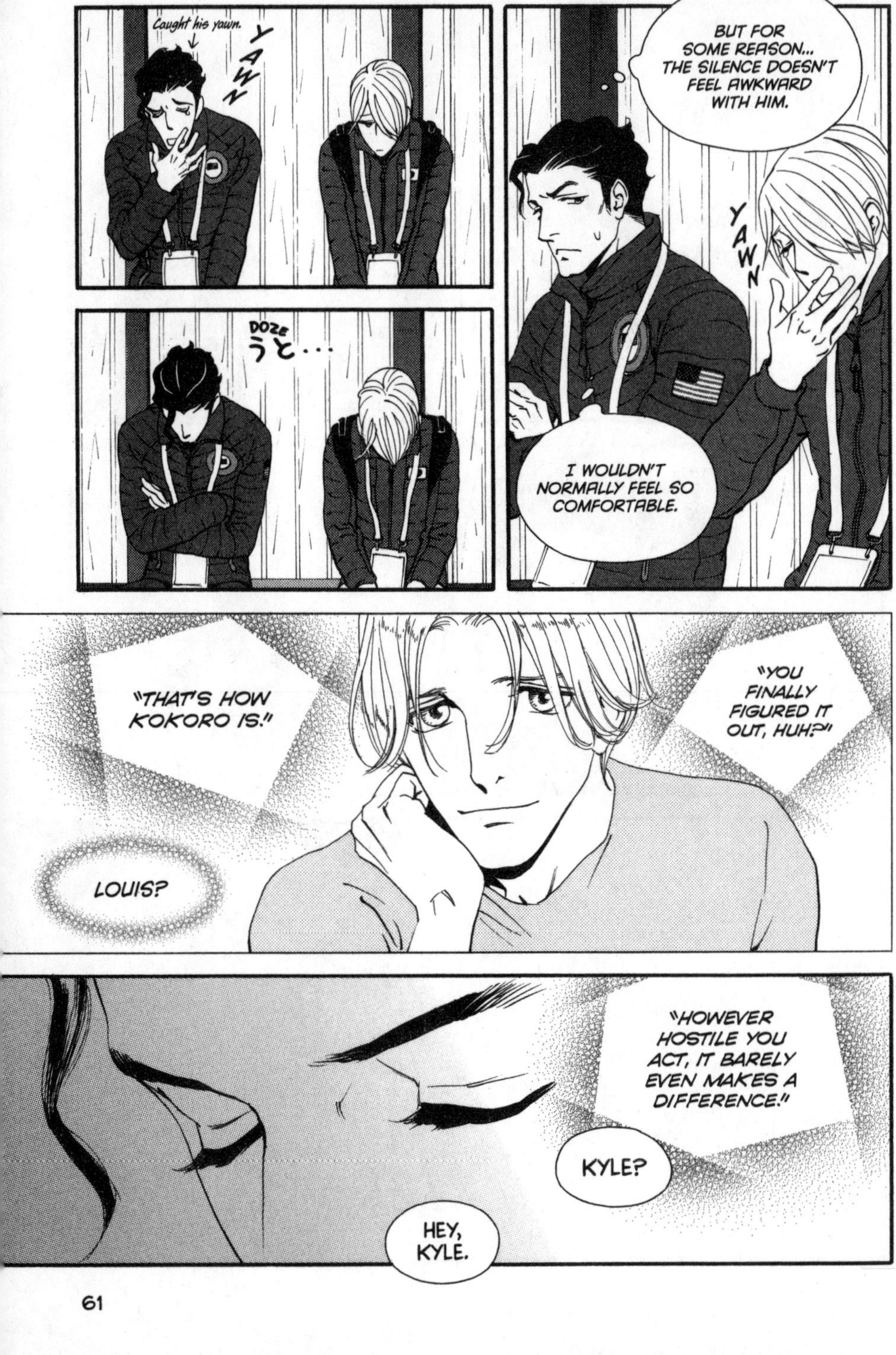
BUT FOR SOME REASON... THE SILENCE DOESN'T FEEL AWKWARD WITH HIM.
YAWN
I WOULDN'T NORMALLY FEEL SO COMFORTABLE.
Caught his yawn.
YAWN
DOZE
うと・・・
"YOU FINALLY FIGURED IT OUT, HUH?"
"THAT'S HOW KOKORO IS."
LOUIS?
"HOWEVER HOSTILE YOU ACT, IT BARELY EVEN MAKES A DIFFERENCE."
KYLE?
HEY, KYLE.

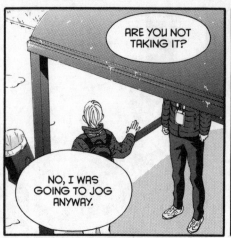

HUH?!
THE RAIN STOPPED,
AND THE BUS IS ALMOST HERE.
ARE YOU NOT TAKING IT?
NO, I WAS GOING TO JOG ANYWAY.
KOKORO!
THANK YOU!

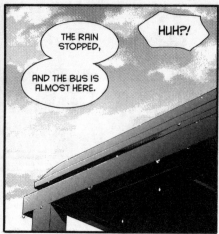

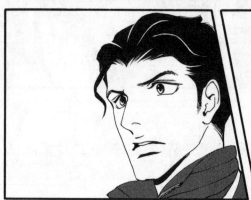

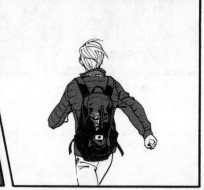

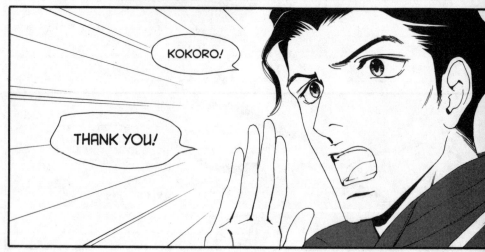

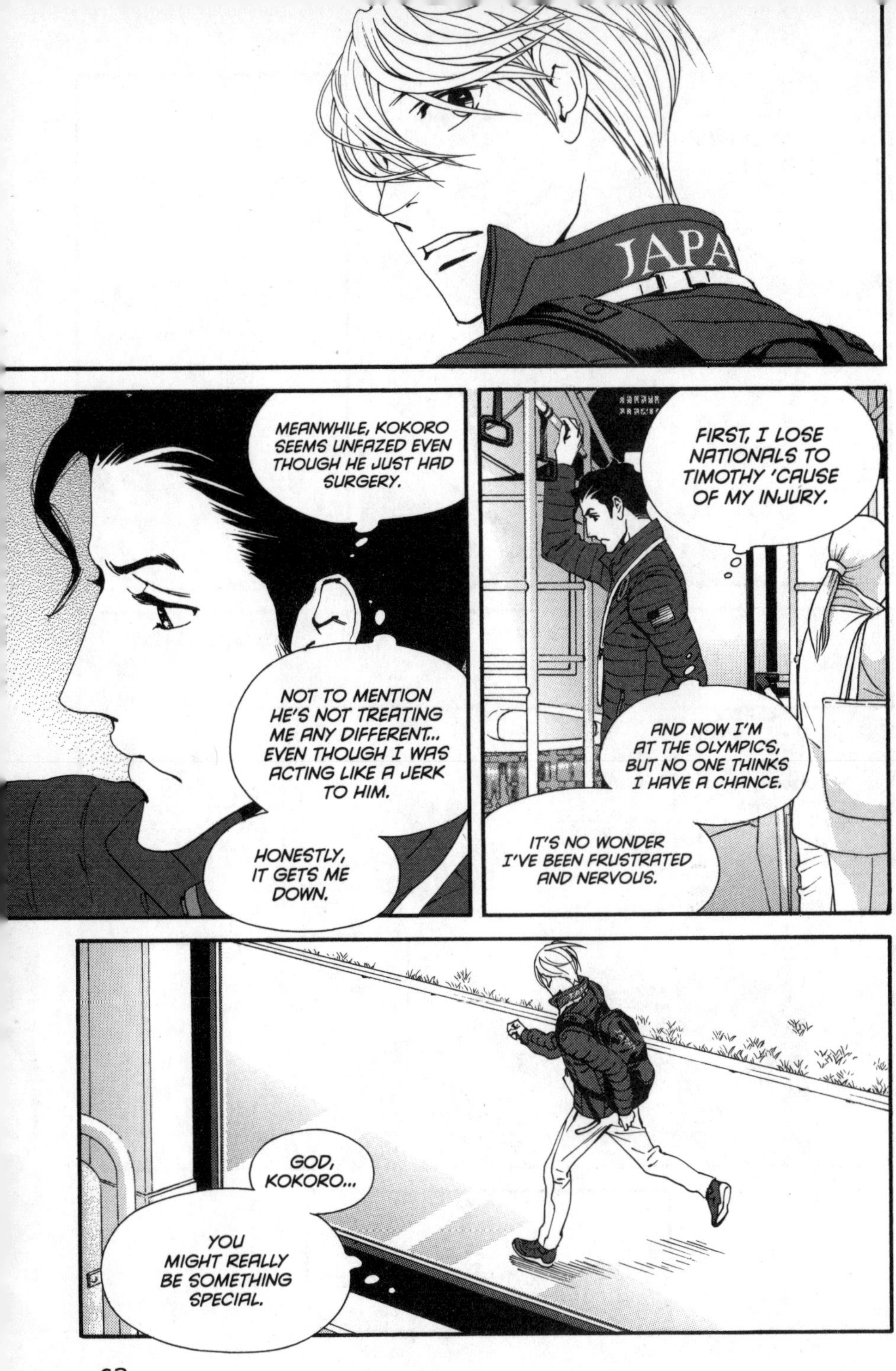
JAPA
FIRST, I LOSE NATIONALS TO TIMOTHY 'CAUSE OF MY INJURY.
AND NOW I'M AT THE OLYMPICS, BUT NO ONE THINKS I HAVE A CHANCE.
IT'S NO WONDER I'VE BEEN FRUSTRATED AND NERVOUS.
MEANWHILE, KOKORO SEEMS UNFAZED EVEN THOUGH HE JUST HAD SURGERY.
NOT TO MENTION HE'S NOT TREATING ME ANY DIFFERENT... EVEN THOUGH I WAS ACTING LIKE A JERK TO HIM.
HONESTLY, IT GETS ME DOWN.
GOD, KOKORO...
YOU MIGHT REALLY BE SOMETHING SPECIAL.

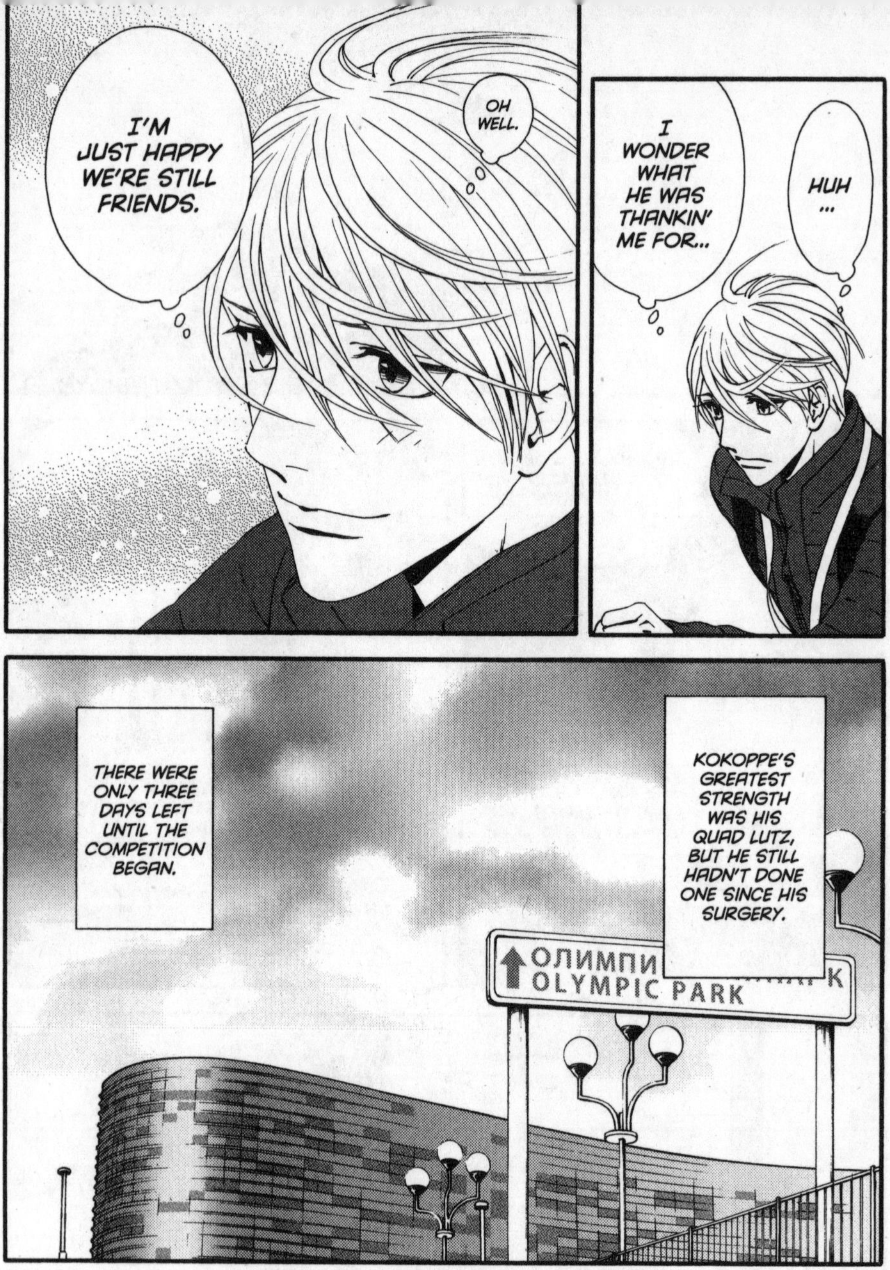
HUH ...
I WONDER WHAT HE WAS THANKIN' ME FOR..
OH WELL.
I'M JUST HAPPY WE'RE STILL FRIENDS.
KOKOPPE'S GREATEST STRENGTH WAS HIS QUAD LUTZ, BUT HE STILL HADN'T DONE ONE SINCE HIS SURGERY.
OLYMPIC PARK
THERE WERE ONLY THREE DAYS LEFT UNTIL THE COMPETITION BEGAN.
SINCE WHEN DOES HONDA MAKE RULERS? AND WHAT IS ONE DOING IN MY BAG?
NINJA

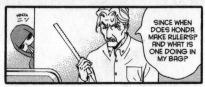

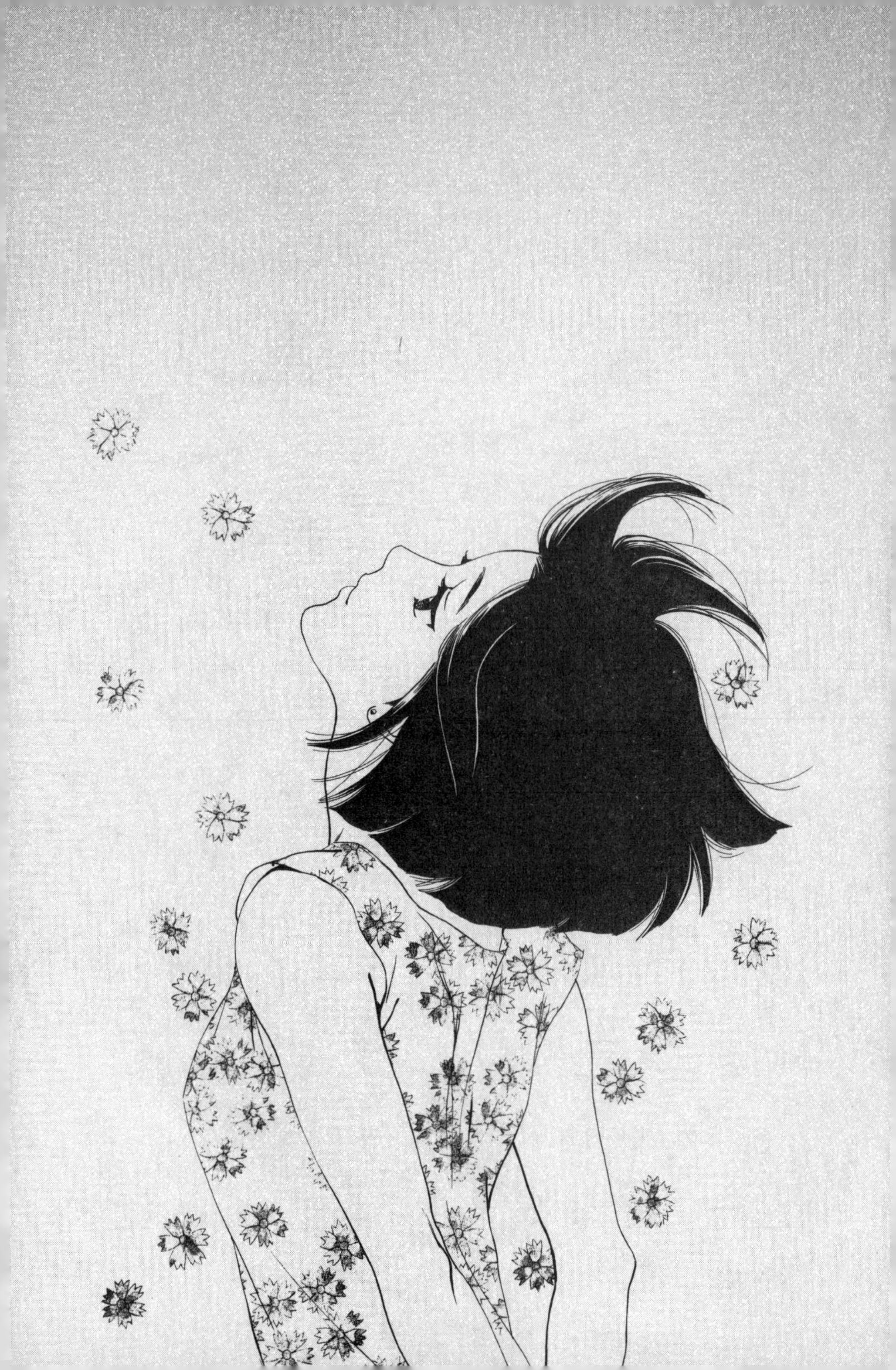

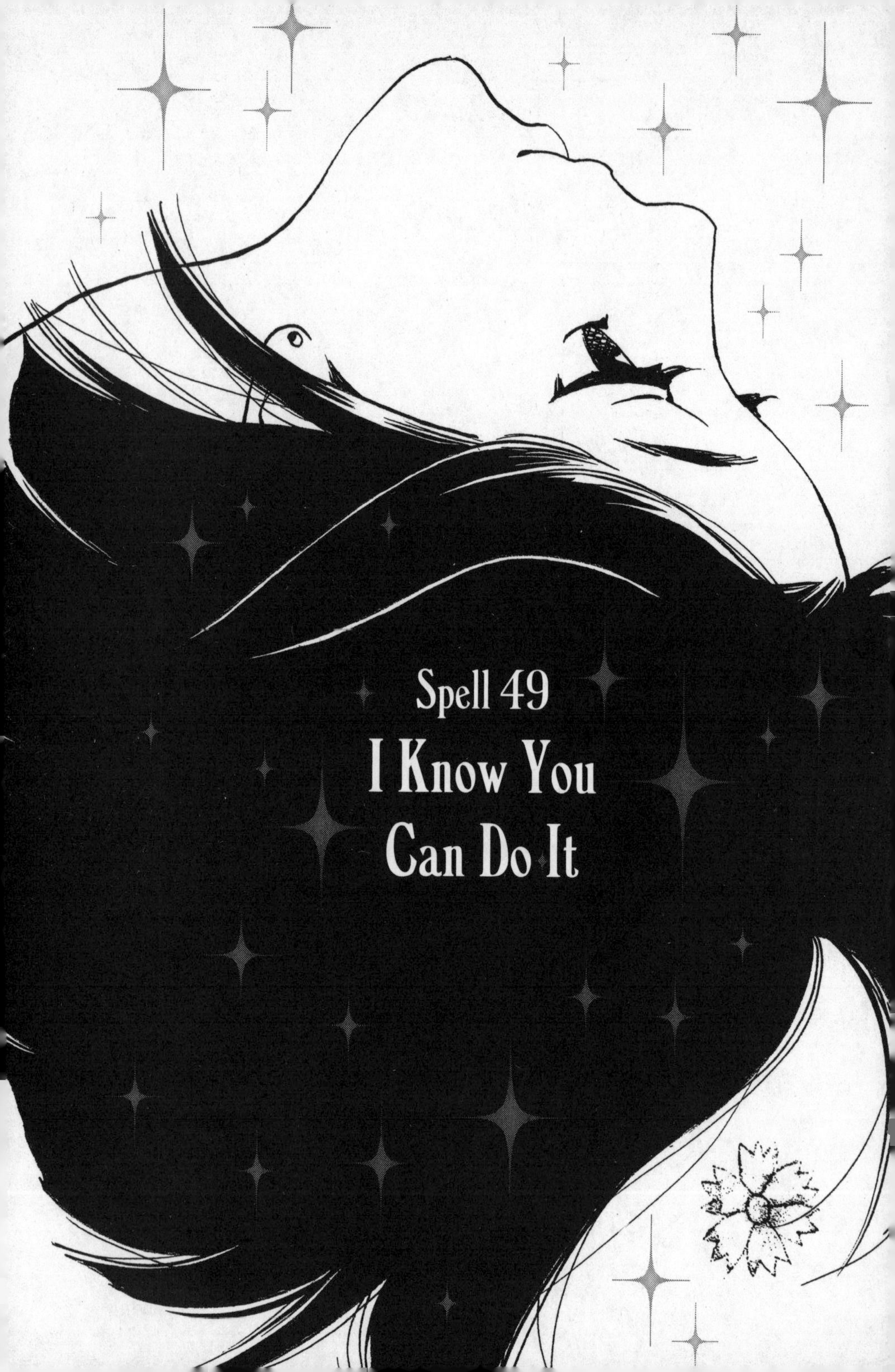
Spell 49
I Know You Can Do It

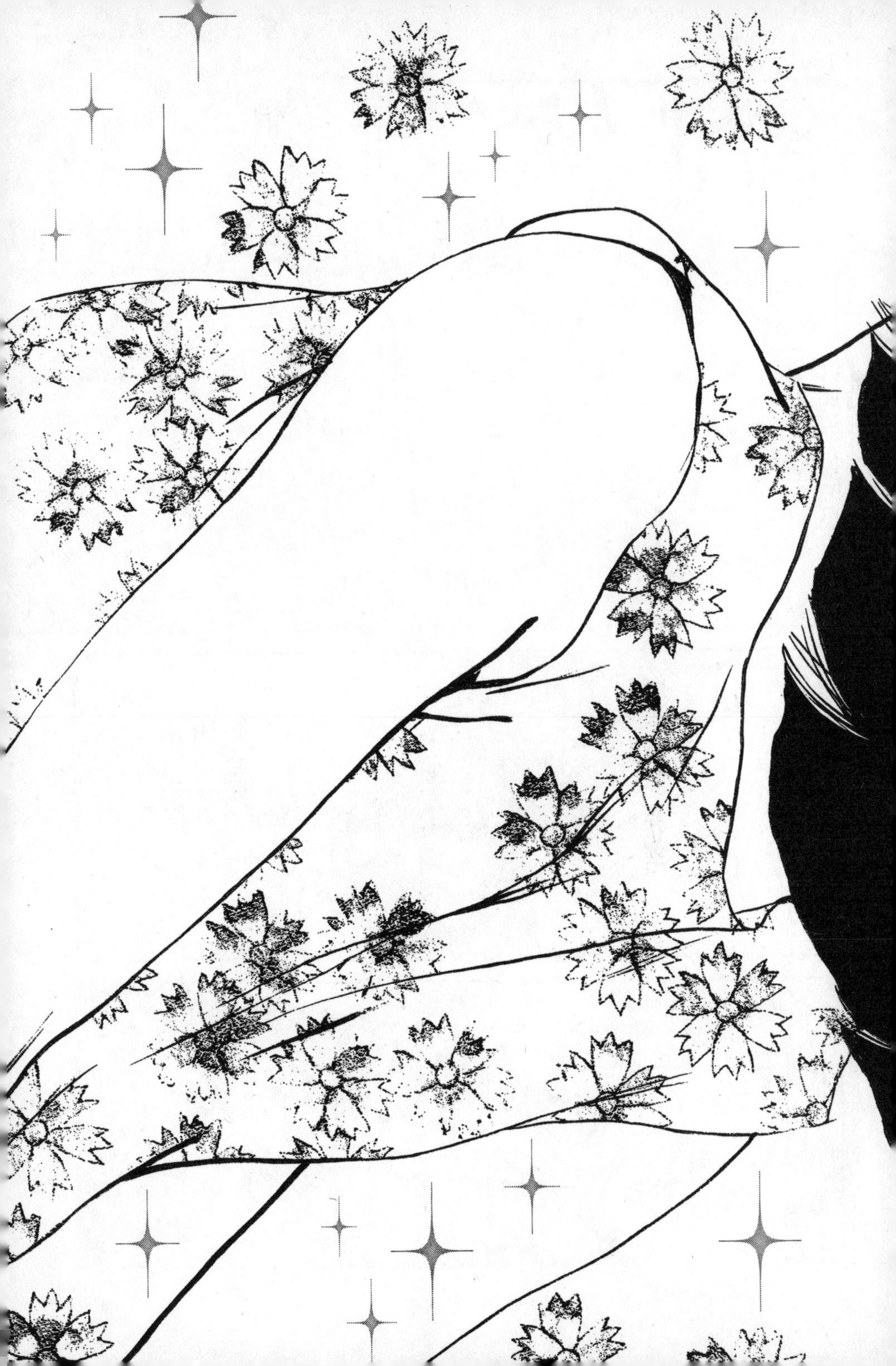

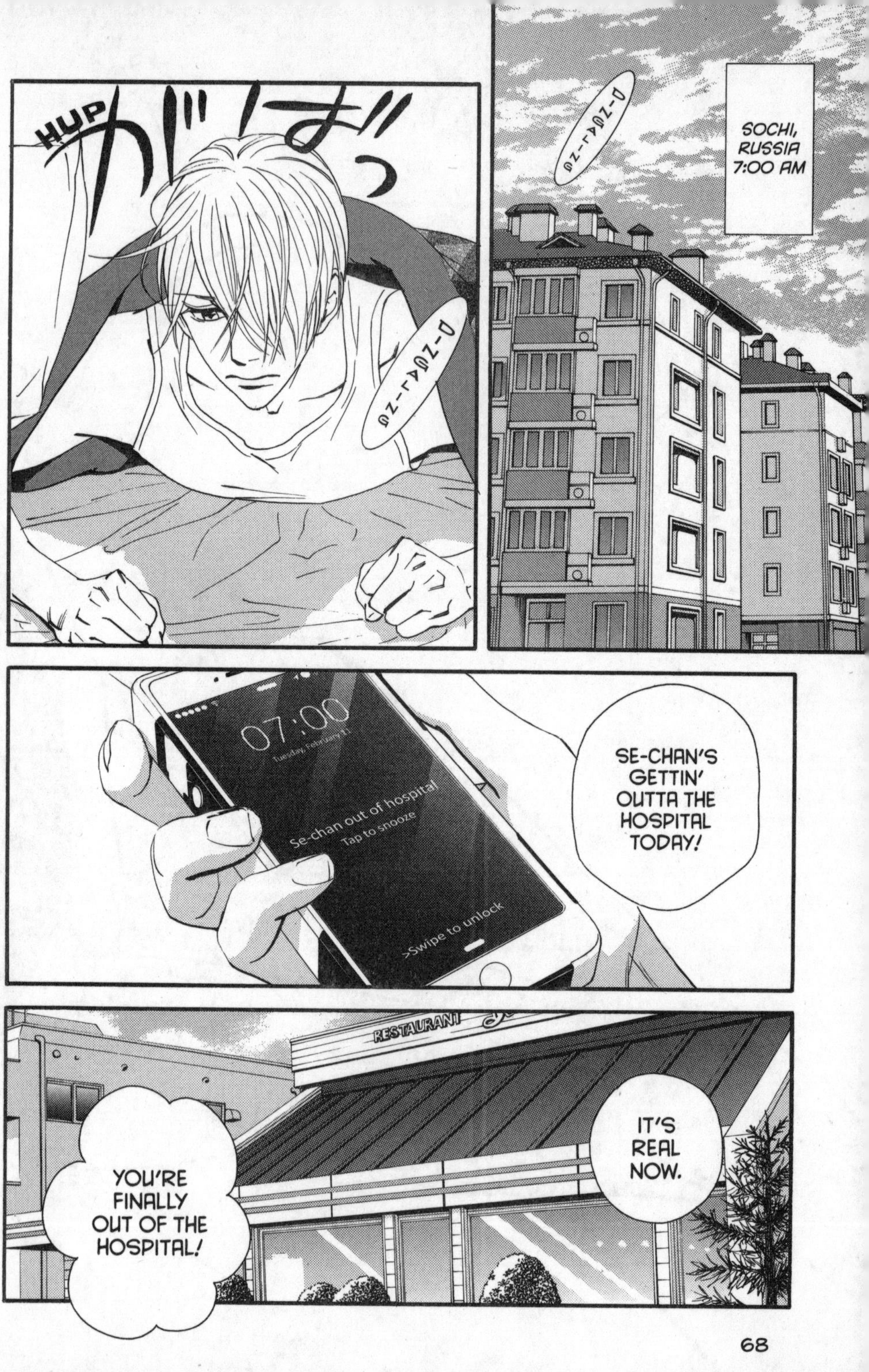
SOCHI, RUSSIA 7:00 AM
HUP
がばっ
07:00
Tuesday, February 11
Se-chan out of hospital
Tap to snooze
>Swipe to unlock
SE-CHAN'S GETTIN' OUTTA THE HOSPITAL TODAY!
RESTAURANT
IT'S REAL NOW.
YOU'RE FINALLY OUT OF THE HOSPITAL!

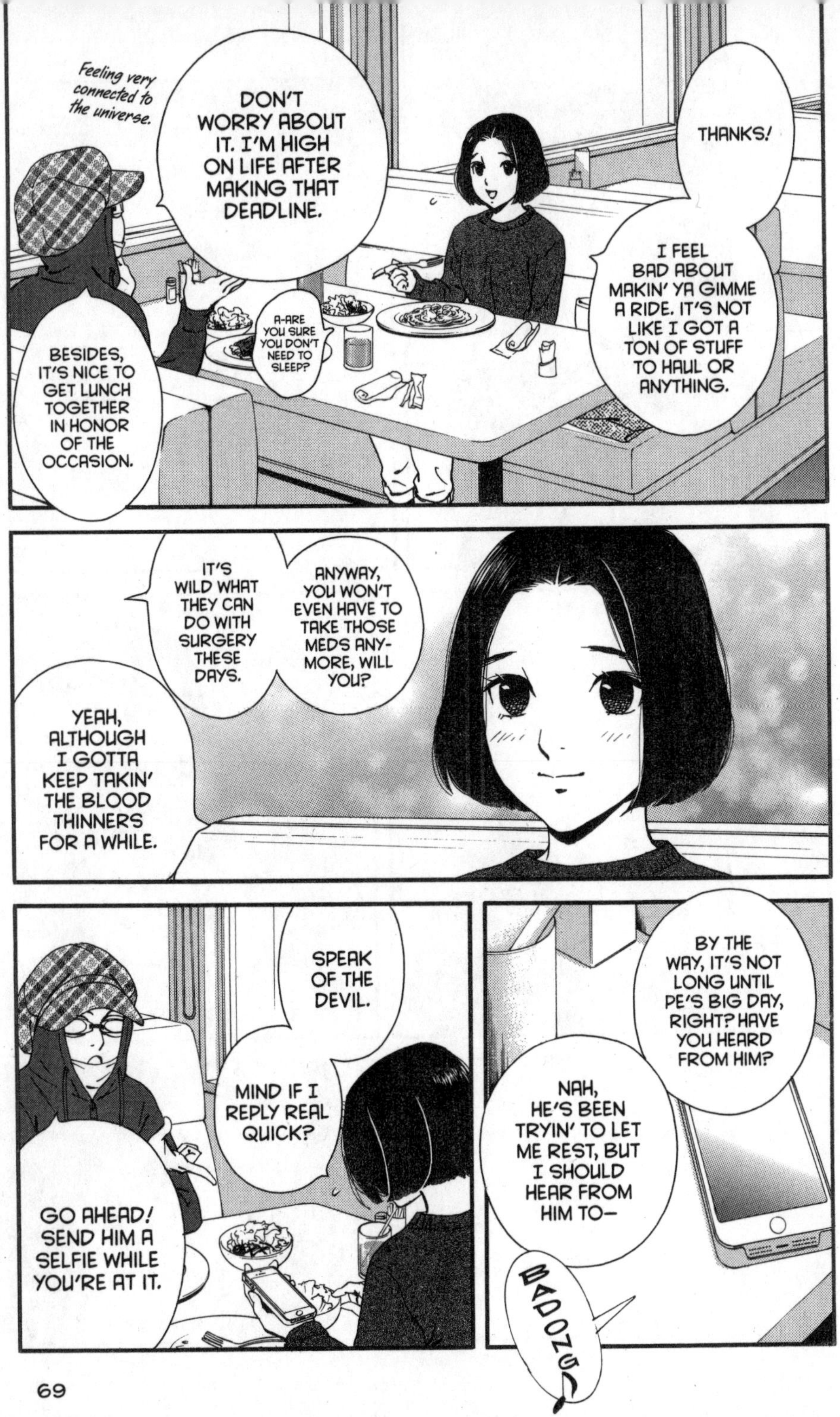
THANKS!
I FEEL BAD ABOUT MAKIN' YA GIMME A RIDE. IT'S NOT LIKE I GOT A TON OF STUFF TO HAUL OR ANYTHING.
DON'T WORRY ABOUT IT. I'M HIGH ON LIFE AFTER MAKING THAT DEADLINE.
Feeling very connected to the universe.
A-ARE YOU SURE YOU DON'T NEED TO SLEEP?
BESIDES, IT'S NICE TO GET LUNCH TOGETHER IN HONOR OF THE OCCASION.
ANYWAY, YOU WON'T EVEN HAVE TO TAKE THOSE MEDS ANY-MORE, WILL YOU?
IT'S WILD WHAT THEY CAN DO WITH SURGERY THESE DAYS.
YEAH, ALTHOUGH I GOTTA KEEP TAKIN' THE BLOOD THINNERS FOR A WHILE.
BY THE WAY, IT'S NOT LONG UNTIL PE'S BIG DAY, RIGHT? HAVE YOU HEARD FROM HIM?
NAH, HE'S BEEN TRYIN' TO LET ME REST, BUT I SHOULD HEAR FROM HIM TO—
BADONG♪
SPEAK OF THE DEVIL.
MIND IF I REPLY REAL QUICK?
GO AHEAD! SEND HIM A SELFIE WHILE YOU'RE AT IT.

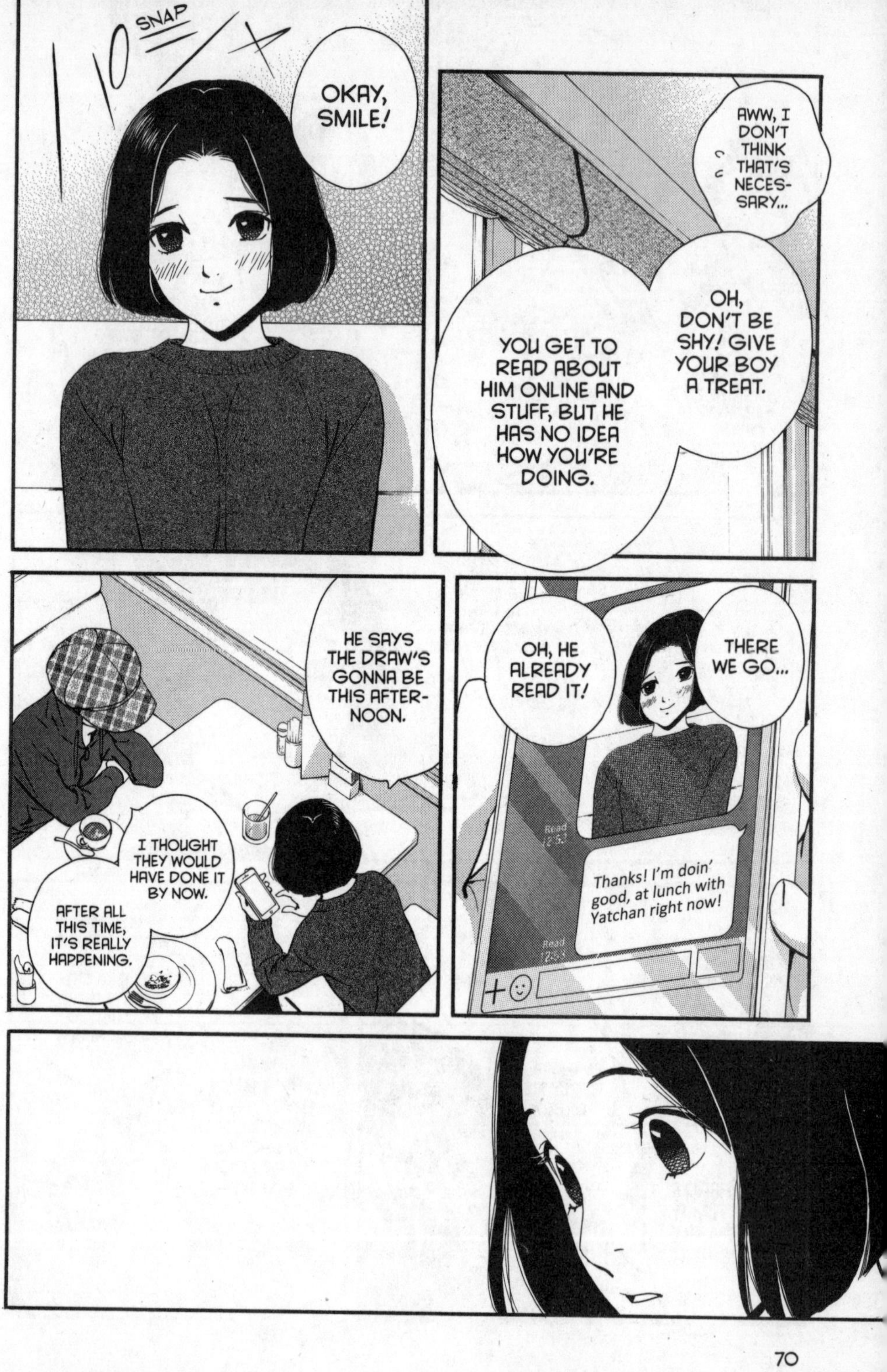
AWW, I DON'T THINK THAT'S NECES-SARY...
OH, DON'T BE SHY! GIVE YOUR BOY A TREAT.
YOU GET TO READ ABOUT HIM ONLINE AND STUFF, BUT HE HAS NO IDEA HOW YOU'RE DOING.
SNAP
OKAY, SMILE!
THERE WE GO...
OH, HE ALREADY READ IT!
Thanks! I'm doin' good, at lunch with Yatchan right now!
HE SAYS THE DRAW'S GONNA BE THIS AFTER-NOON.
I THOUGHT THEY WOULD HAVE DONE IT BY NOW.
AFTER ALL THIS TIME, IT'S REALLY HAPPENING.

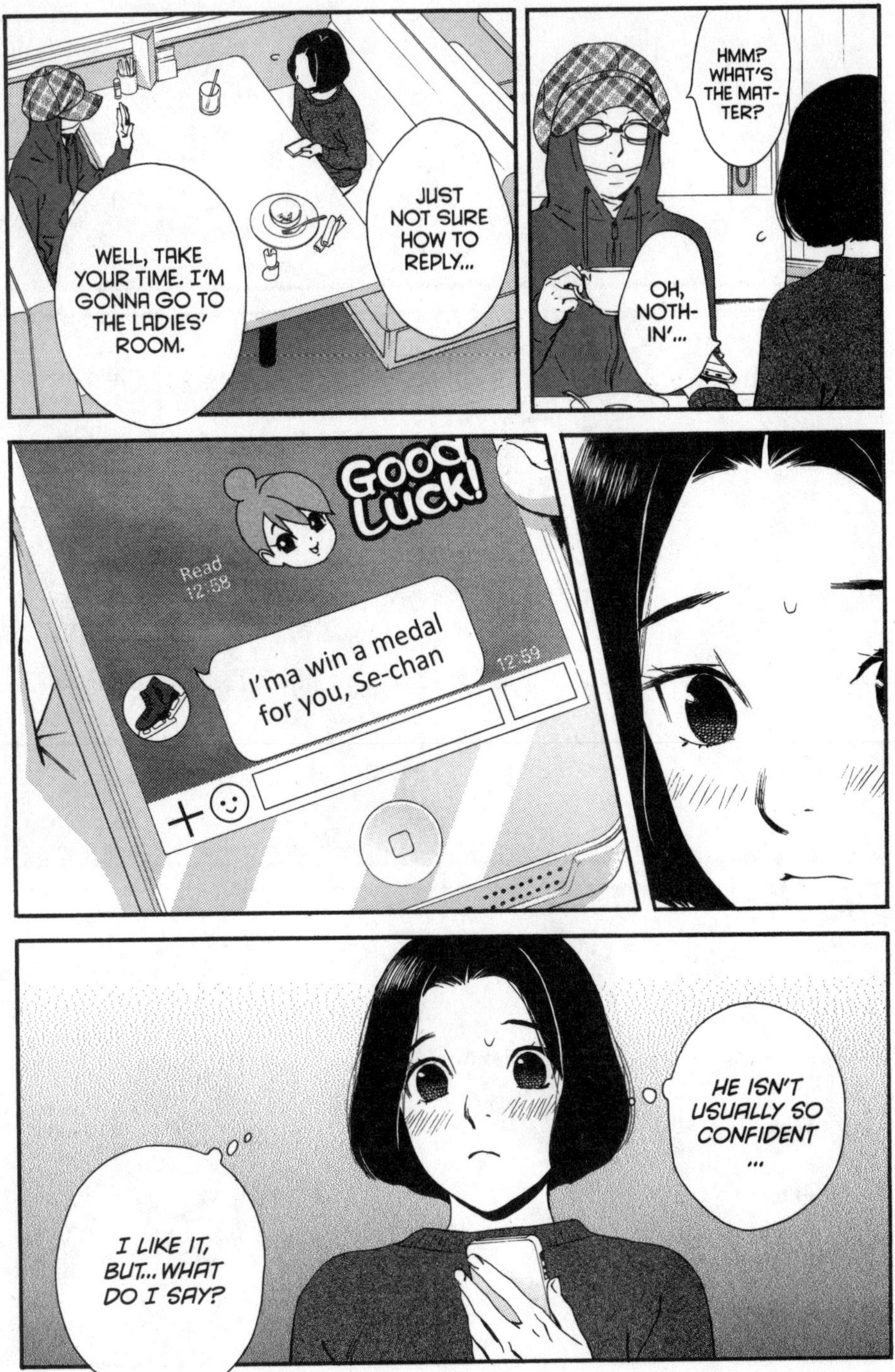
HMM? WHAT'S THE MATTER?
OH, NOTHIN'...
JUST NOT SURE HOW TO REPLY...
WELL, TAKE YOUR TIME. I'M GONNA GO TO THE LADIES' ROOM.
Good Luck!
Read 12:58
I'ma win a medal for you, Se-chan
12:59
HE ISN'T USUALLY SO CONFIDENT...
I LIKE IT, BUT...WHAT DO I SAY?

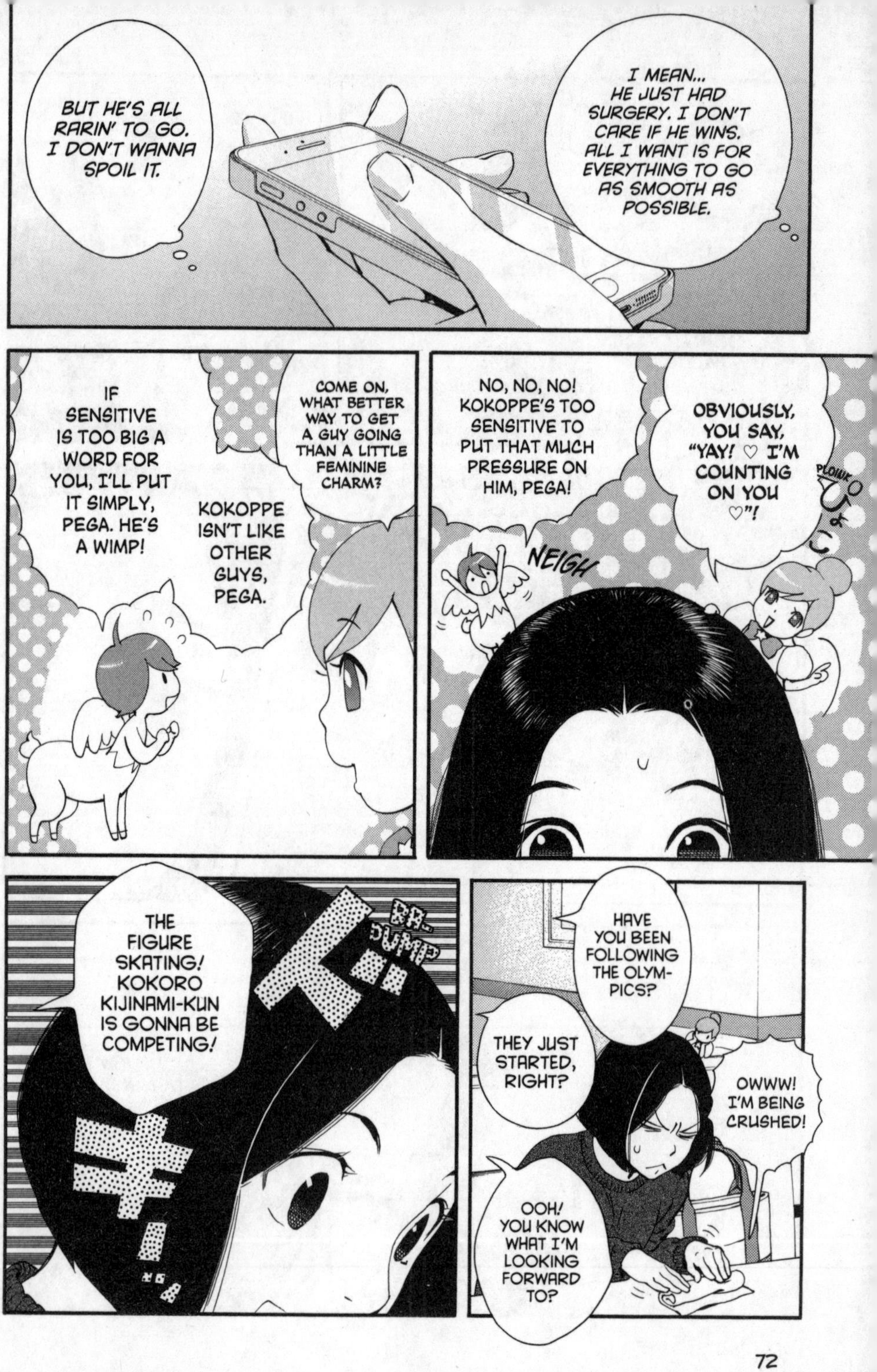
I MEAN... HE JUST HAD SURGERY. I DON'T CARE IF HE WINS. ALL I WANT IS FOR EVERYTHING TO GO AS SMOOTH AS POSSIBLE.
BUT HE'S ALL RARIN' TO GO. I DON'T WANNA SPOIL IT.
OBVIOUSLY, YOU SAY, "YAY! ♡ I'M COUNTING ON YOU ♡"!
PLOINK
NO, NO, NO! KOKOPPE'S TOO SENSITIVE TO PUT THAT MUCH PRESSURE ON HIM, PEGA!
NEIGH
COME ON, WHAT BETTER WAY TO GET A GUY GOING THAN A LITTLE FEMININE CHARM?
IF SENSITIVE IS TOO BIG A WORD FOR YOU, I'LL PUT IT SIMPLY, PEGA. HE'S A WIMP!
KOKOPPE ISN'T LIKE OTHER GUYS, PEGA.
HAVE YOU BEEN FOLLOWING THE OLYM-PICS?
THEY JUST STARTED, RIGHT?
OWWW! I'M BEING CRUSHED!
OOH! YOU KNOW WHAT I'M LOOKING FORWARD TO?
BA-DUMP
THE FIGURE SKATING! KOKORO KIJINAMI-KUN IS GONNA BE COMPETING!

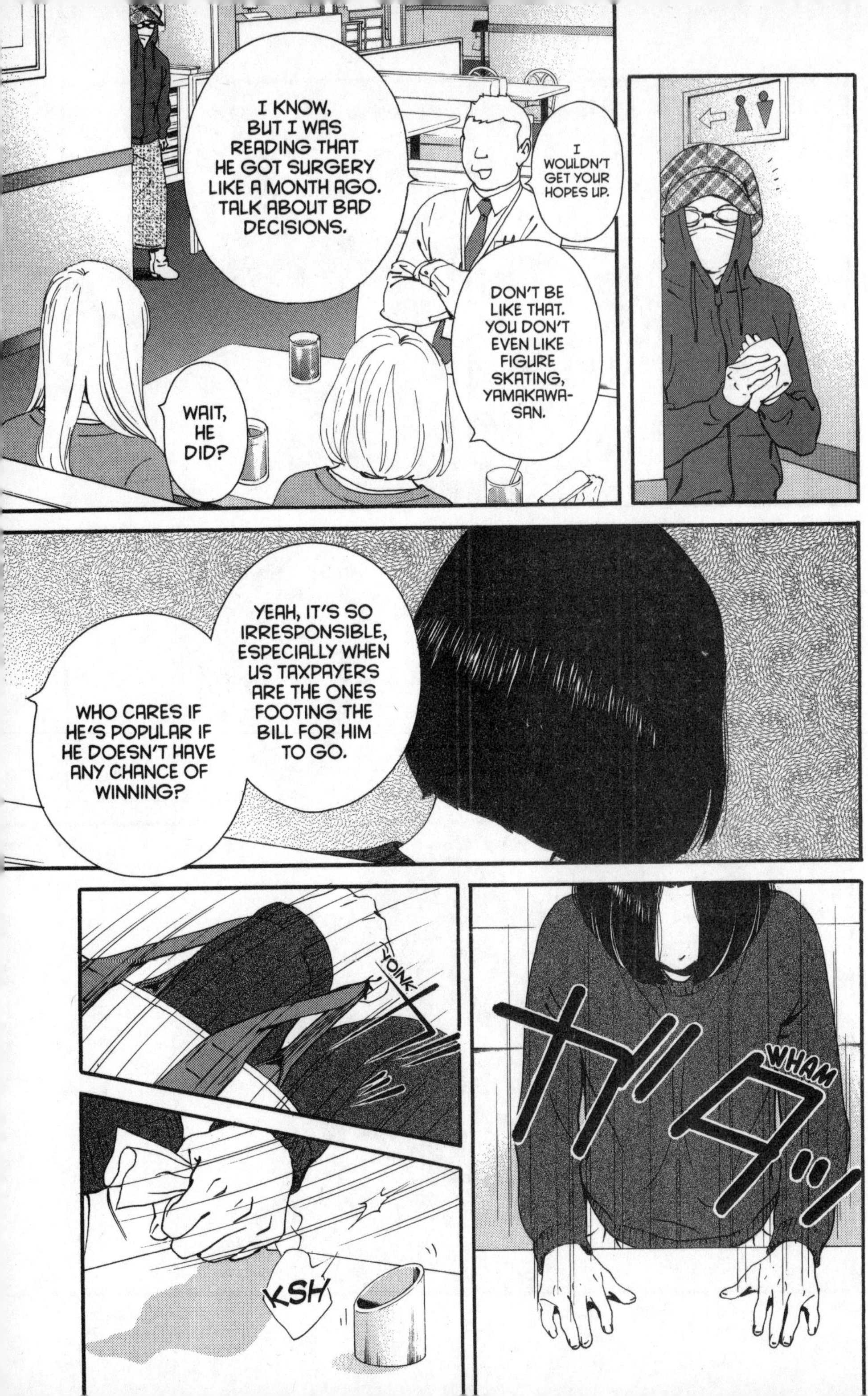
I WOULDN'T GET YOUR HOPES UP.
I KNOW, BUT I WAS READING THAT HE GOT SURGERY LIKE A MONTH AGO. TALK ABOUT BAD DECISIONS.
DON'T BE LIKE THAT. YOU DON'T EVEN LIKE FIGURE SKATING, YAMAKAWA-SAN.
WAIT, HE DID?
YEAH, IT'S SO IRRESPONSIBLE, ESPECIALLY WHEN US TAXPAYERS ARE THE ONES FOOTING THE BILL FOR HIM TO GO.
WHO CARES IF HE'S POPULAR IF HE DOESN'T HAVE ANY CHANCE OF WINNING?
カタッ!
WHAM
YOINK
KSH

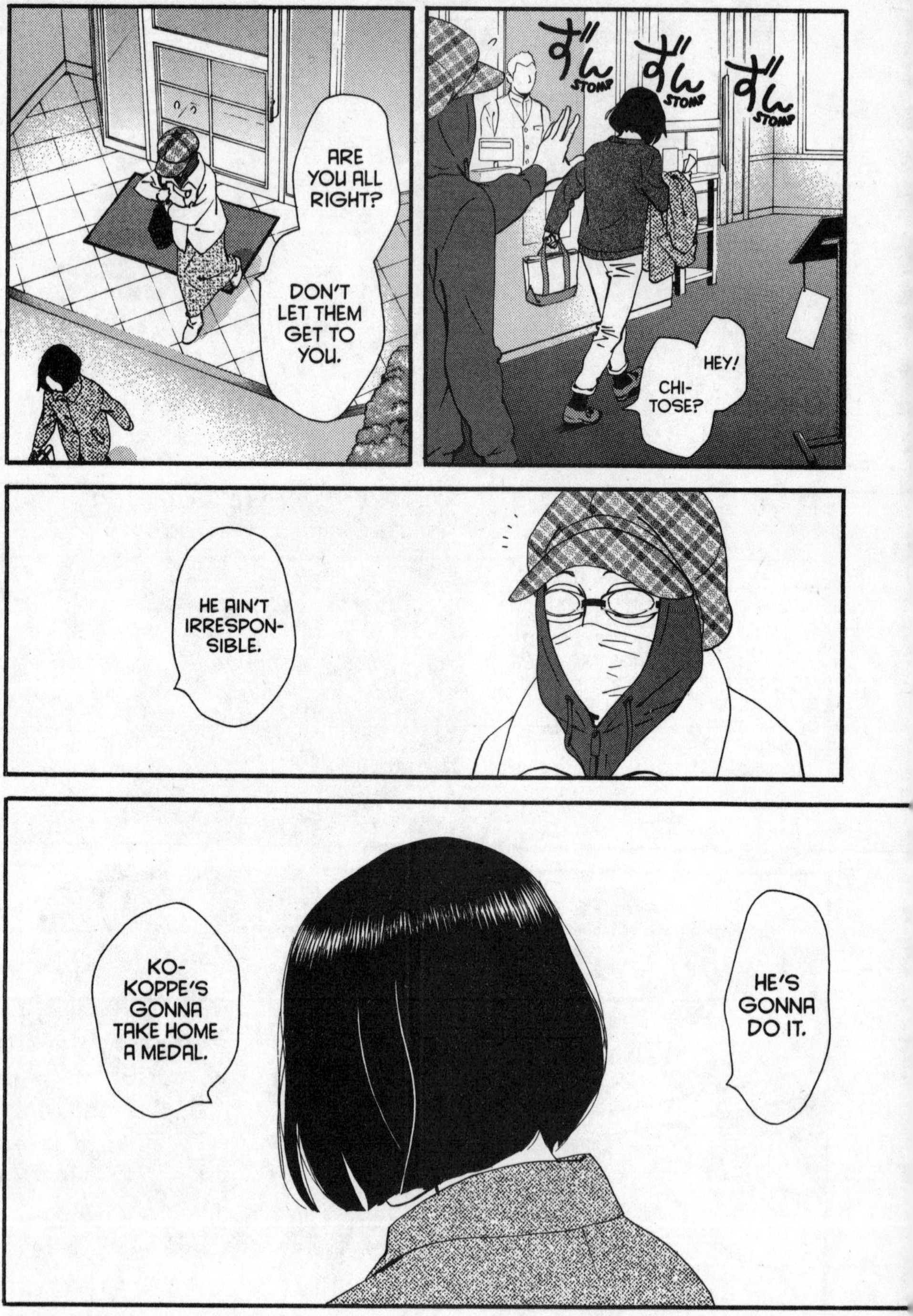
ずん STOMP
ずん STOMP
ずん STOMP
HEY! CHI-TOSE?
ARE YOU ALL RIGHT?
DON'T LET THEM GET TO YOU.
HE AIN'T IRRESPON-SIBLE.
HE'S GONNA DO IT.
KO-KOPPE'S GONNA TAKE HOME A MEDAL.

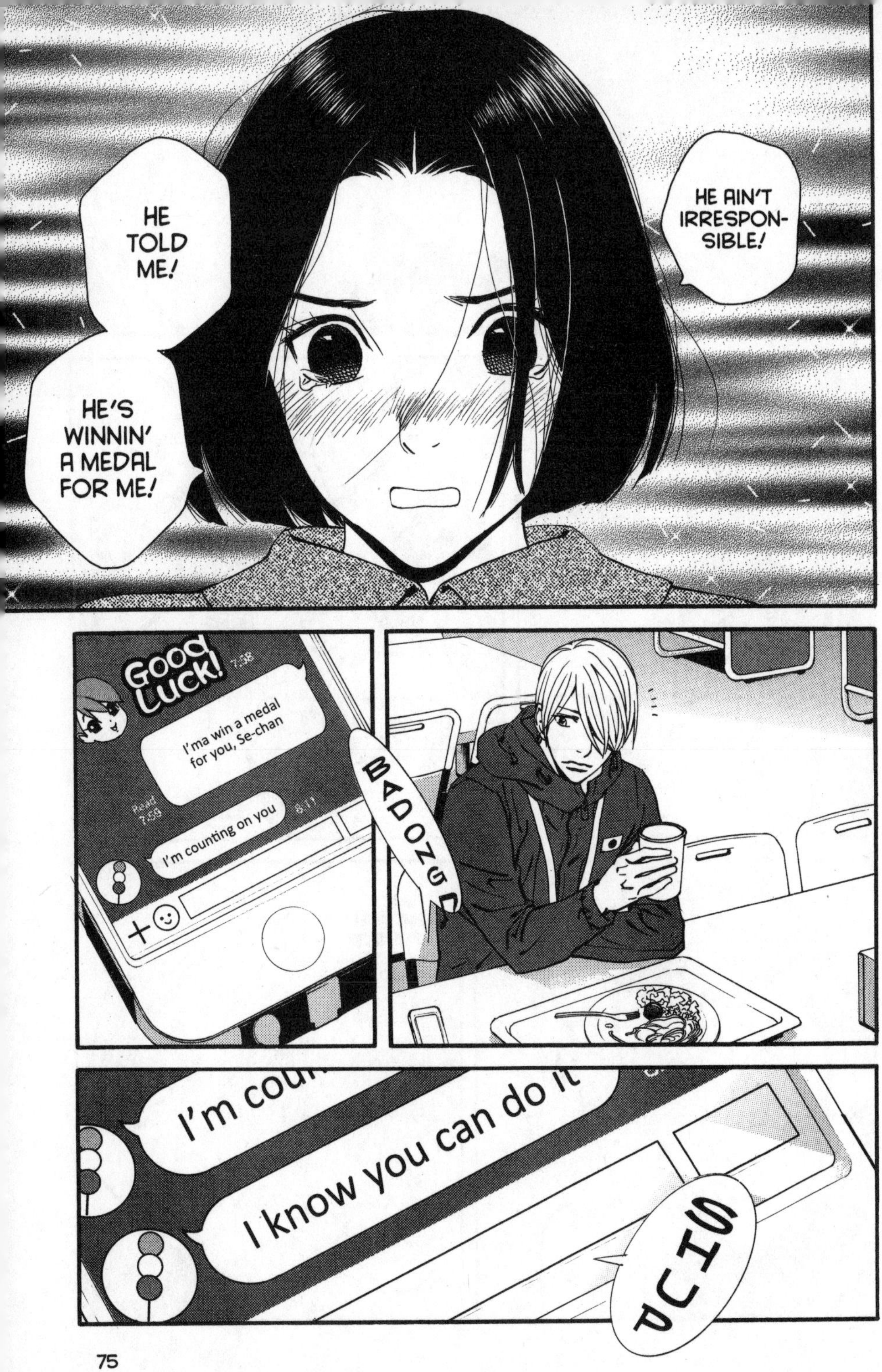
HE AIN'T IRRESPONSIBLE!
HE TOLD ME!
HE'S WINNIN' A MEDAL FOR ME!
BADONG
GOOD LUCK!
7:58
I'ma win a medal for you, Se-chan
Read 7:59
I'm counting on you
8:11
I'm coun
I know you can do it
SIP

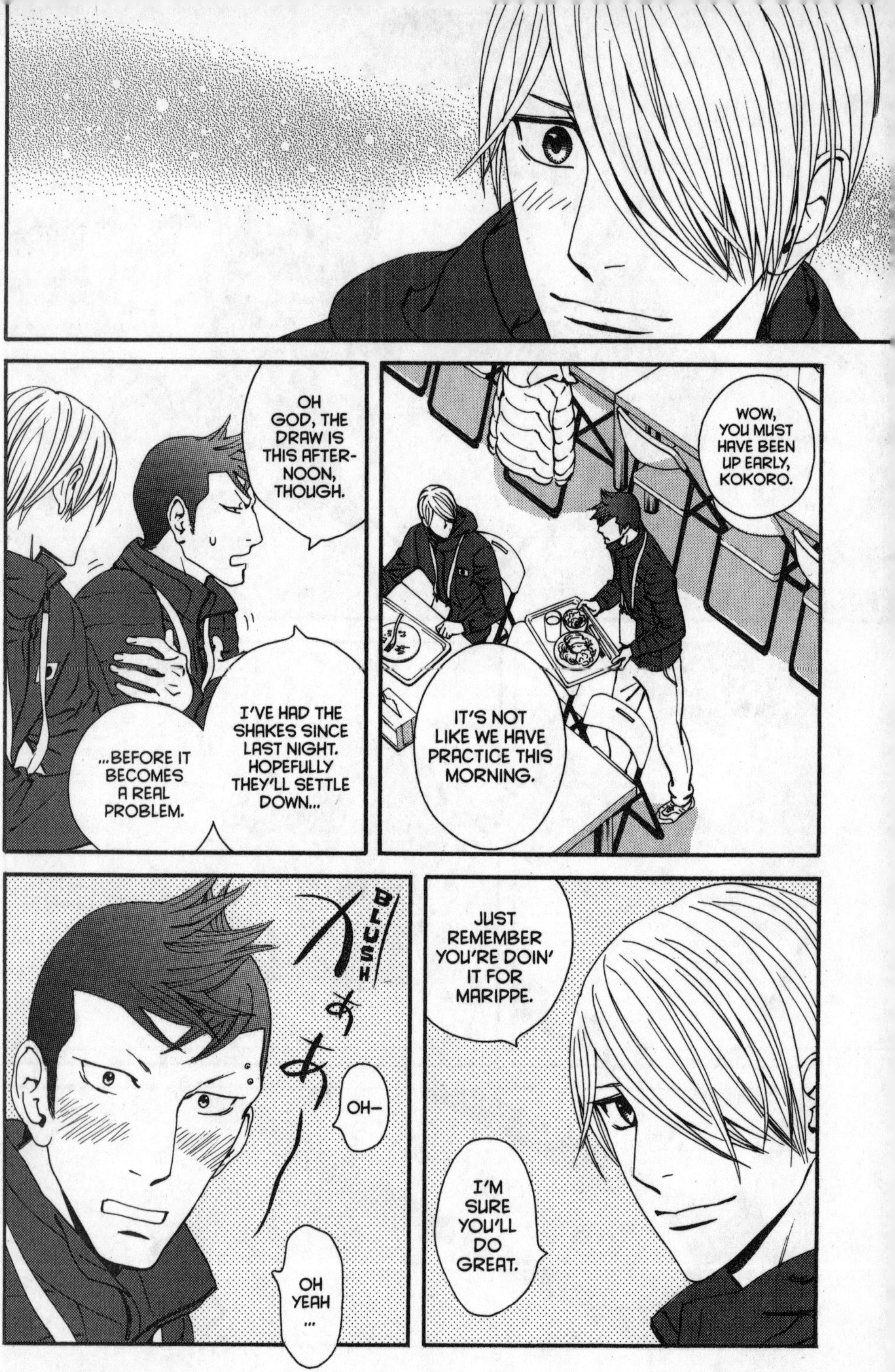
WOW, YOU MUST HAVE BEEN UP EARLY, KOKORO.
IT'S NOT LIKE WE HAVE PRACTICE THIS MORNING.
OH GOD, THE DRAW IS THIS AFTER-NOON, THOUGH.
I'VE HAD THE SHAKES SINCE LAST NIGHT. HOPEFULLY THEY'LL SETTLE DOWN...
...BEFORE IT BECOMES A REAL PROBLEM.
JUST REMEMBER YOU'RE DOIN' IT FOR MARIPPE.
I'M SURE YOU'LL DO GREAT.
BLUSH
OH—
OH YEAH ...

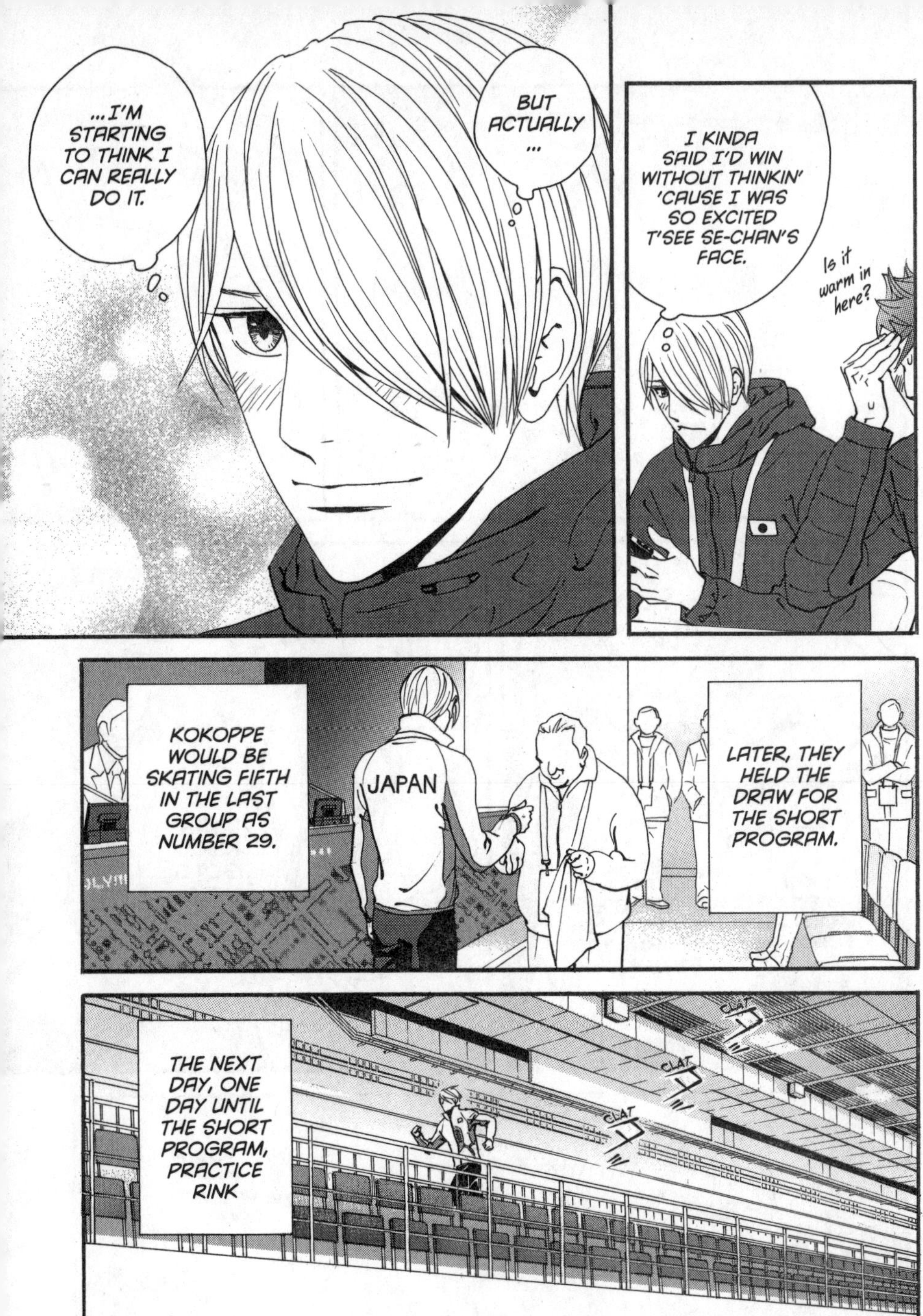
I KINDA SAID I'D WIN WITHOUT THINKIN' 'CAUSE I WAS SO EXCITED T'SEE SE-CHAN'S FACE.
Is it warm in here?
BUT ACTUALLY ...
...I'M STARTING TO THINK I CAN REALLY DO IT.
LATER, THEY HELD THE DRAW FOR THE SHORT PROGRAM.
JAPAN
KOKOPPE WOULD BE SKATING FIFTH IN THE LAST GROUP AS NUMBER 29.
CLAT
CLAT
CLAT
THE NEXT DAY, ONE DAY UNTIL THE SHORT PROGRAM, PRACTICE RINK

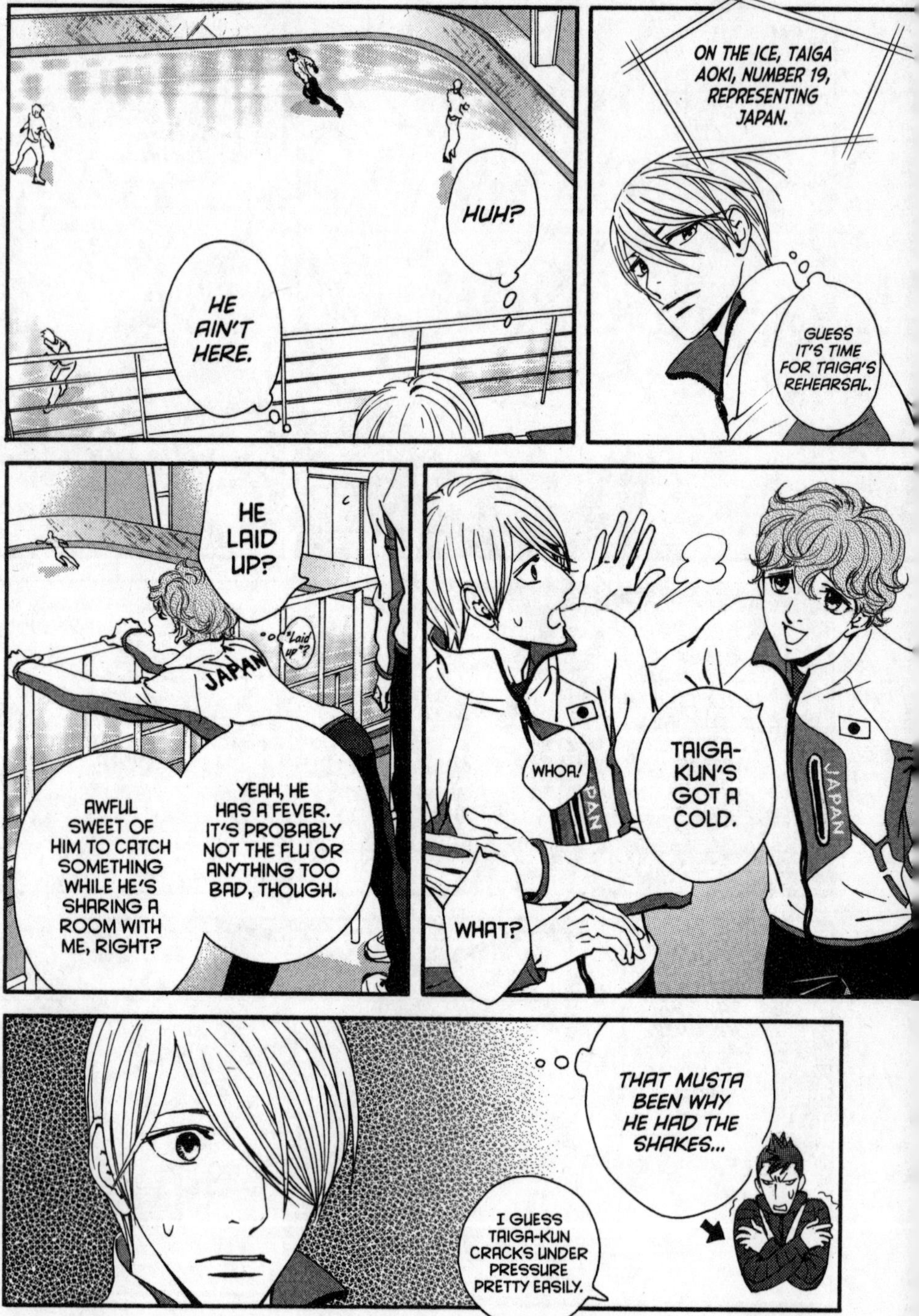
ON THE ICE, TAIGA AOKI, NUMBER 19, REPRESENTING JAPAN.
GUESS IT'S TIME FOR TAIGA'S REHEARSAL.
HUH?
HE AIN'T HERE.
TAIGA-KUN'S GOT A COLD.
WHOA!
WHAT?
HE LAID UP?
"Laid up"?
YEAH, HE HAS A FEVER. IT'S PROBABLY NOT THE FLU OR ANYTHING TOO BAD, THOUGH.
AWFUL SWEET OF HIM TO CATCH SOMETHING WHILE HE'S SHARING A ROOM WITH ME, RIGHT?
THAT MUSTA BEEN WHY HE HAD THE SHAKES...
I GUESS TAIGA-KUN CRACKS UNDER PRESSURE PRETTY EASILY.

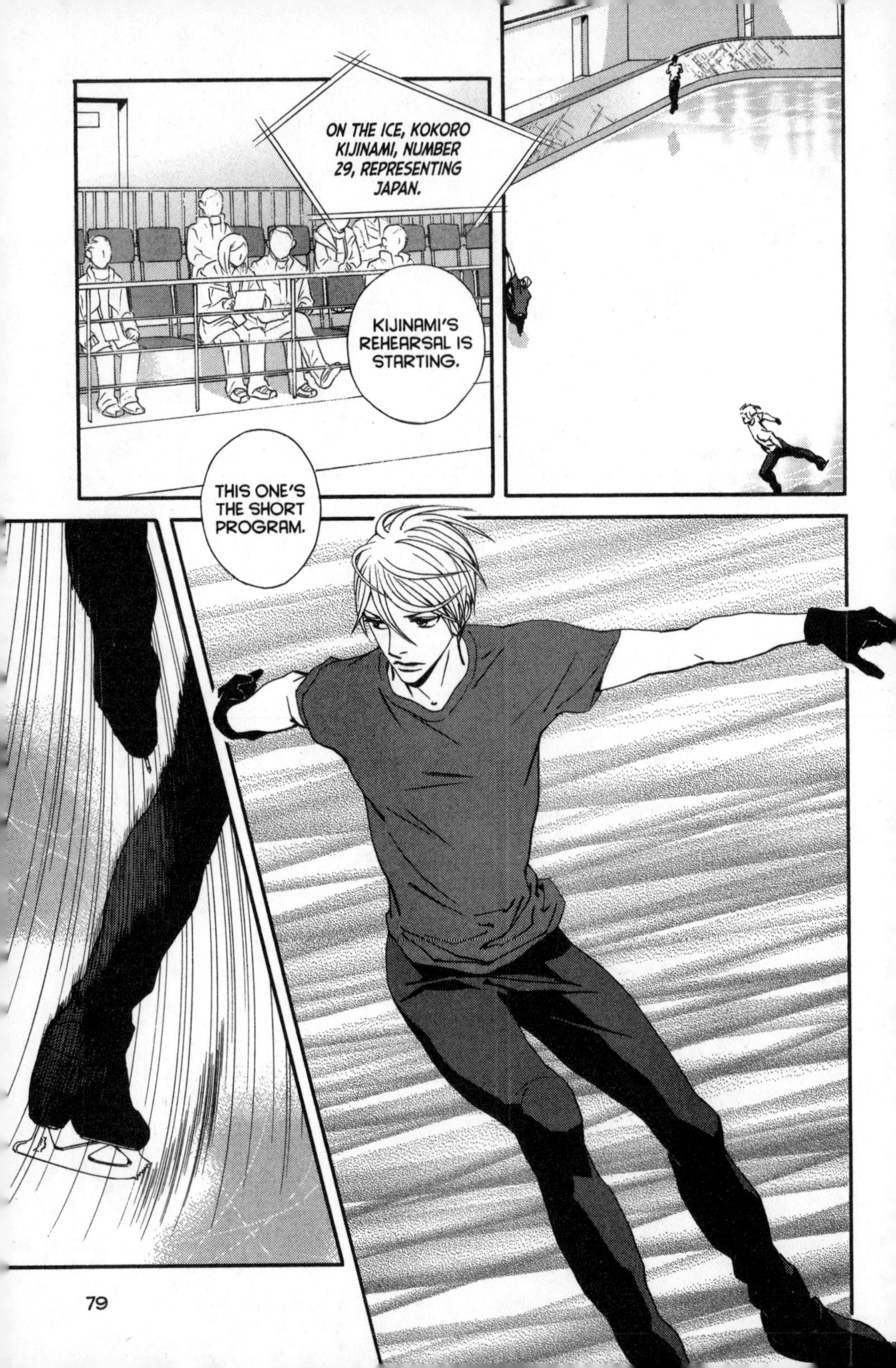
ON THE ICE, KOKORO KIJINAMI, NUMBER 29, REPRESENTING JAPAN.
KIJINAMI'S REHEARSAL IS STARTING.
THIS ONE'S THE SHORT PROGRAM.

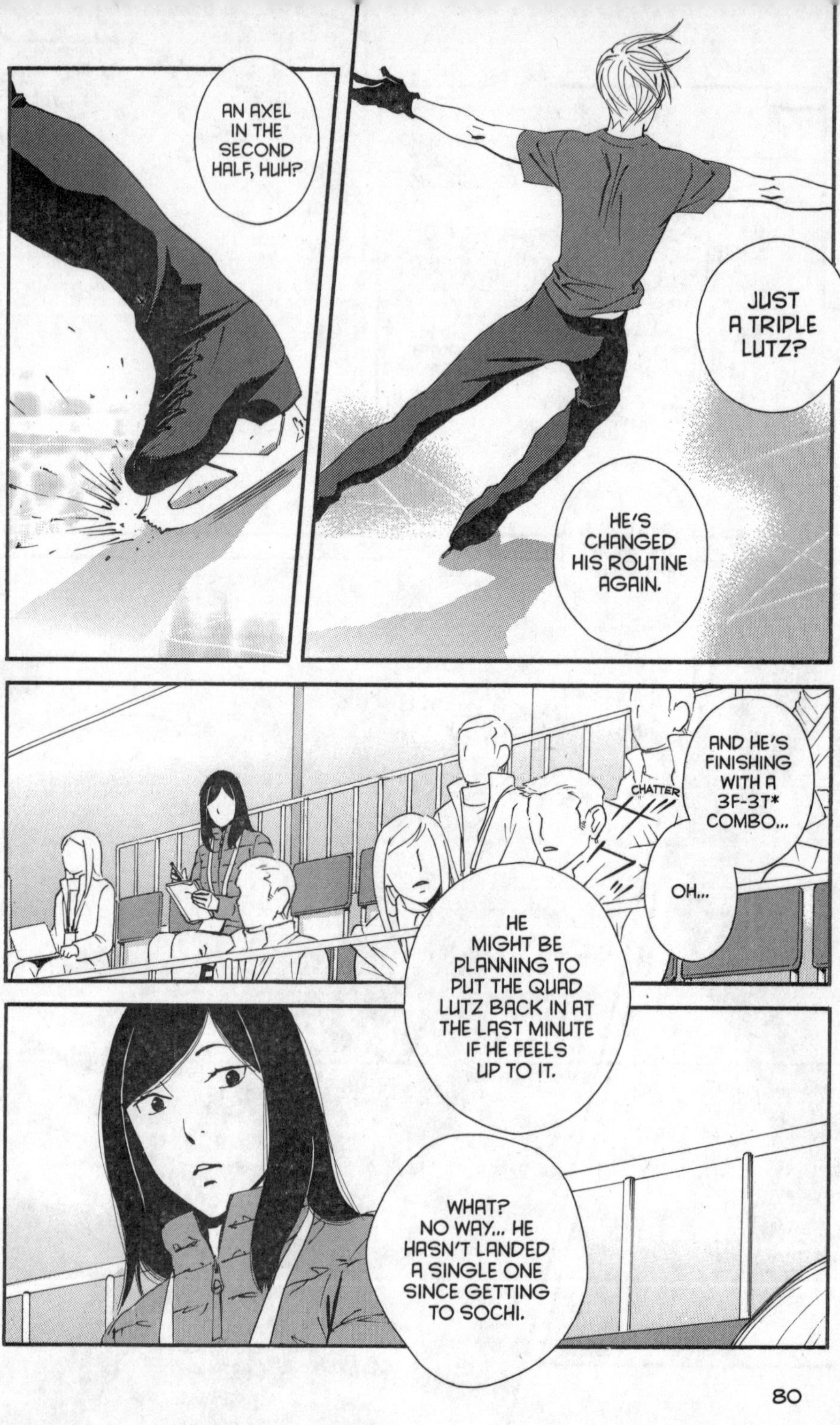
JUST A TRIPLE LUTZ?
HE'S CHANGED HIS ROUTINE AGAIN.
AN AXEL IN THE SECOND HALF, HUH?
AND HE'S FINISHING WITH A 3F-3T* COMBO...
CHATTER
OH...
HE MIGHT BE PLANNING TO PUT THE QUAD LUTZ BACK IN AT THE LAST MINUTE IF HE FEELS UP TO IT.
WHAT? NO WAY... HE HASN'T LANDED A SINGLE ONE SINCE GETTING TO SOCHI.

*TRIPLE FLIP-TRIPLE TOE LOOP

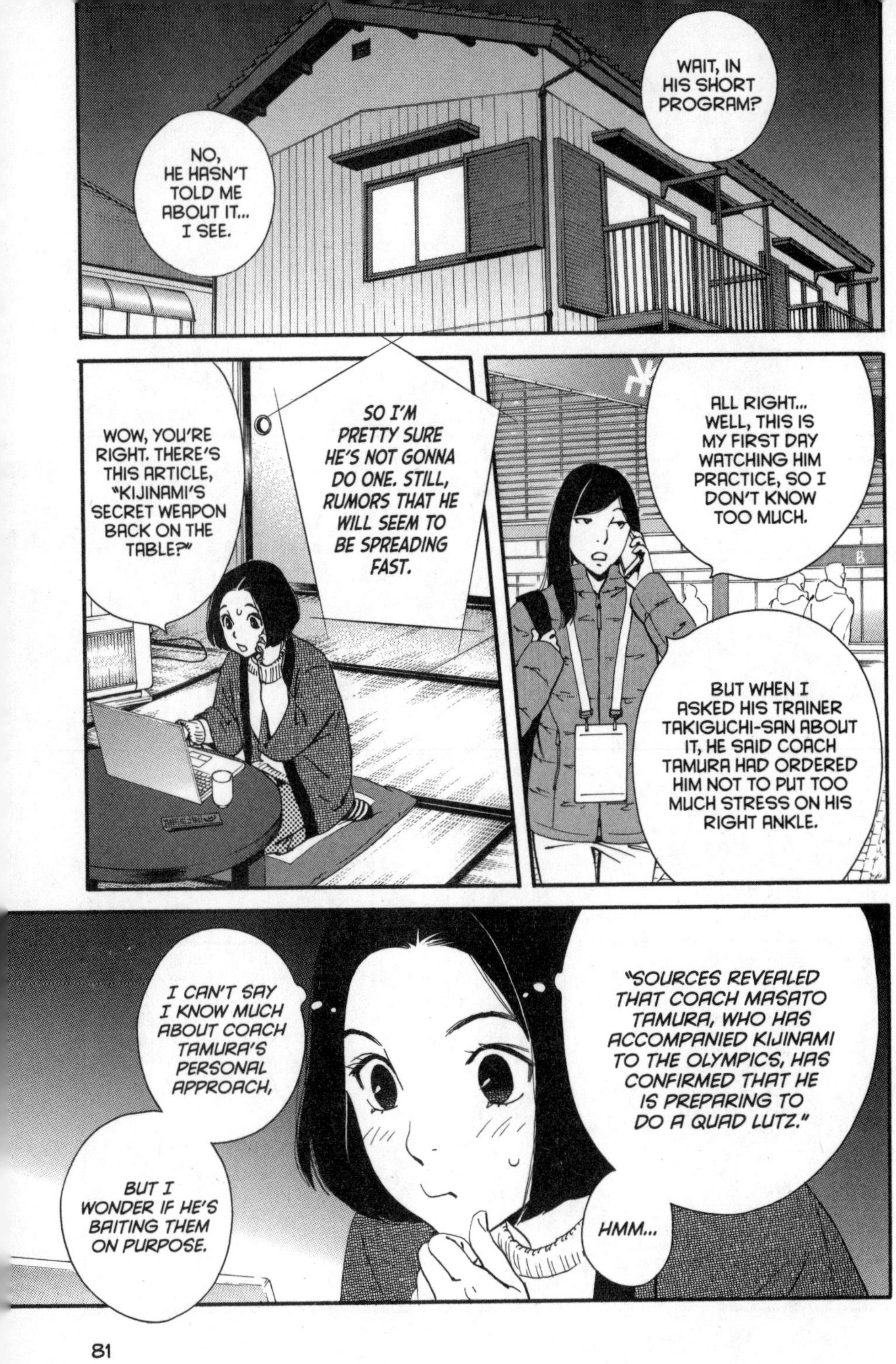

WAIT, IN HIS SHORT PROGRAM?
NO, HE HASN'T TOLD ME ABOUT IT... I SEE.
ALL RIGHT... WELL, THIS IS MY FIRST DAY WATCHING HIM PRACTICE, SO I DON'T KNOW TOO MUCH.
BUT WHEN I ASKED HIS TRAINER TAKIGUCHI-SAN ABOUT IT, HE SAID COACH TAMURA HAD ORDERED HIM NOT TO PUT TOO MUCH STRESS ON HIS RIGHT ANKLE.
SO I'M PRETTY SURE HE'S NOT GONNA DO ONE. STILL, RUMORS THAT HE WILL SEEM TO BE SPREADING FAST.
WOW, YOU'RE RIGHT. THERE'S THIS ARTICLE, "KIJINAMI'S SECRET WEAPON BACK ON THE TABLE?"
"SOURCES REVEALED THAT COACH MASATO TAMURA, WHO HAS ACCOMPANIED KIJINAMI TO THE OLYMPICS, HAS CONFIRMED THAT HE IS PREPARING TO DO A QUAD LUTZ."
HMM...
I CAN'T SAY I KNOW MUCH ABOUT COACH TAMURA'S PERSONAL APPROACH,
BUT I WONDER IF HE'S BAITING THEM ON PURPOSE.

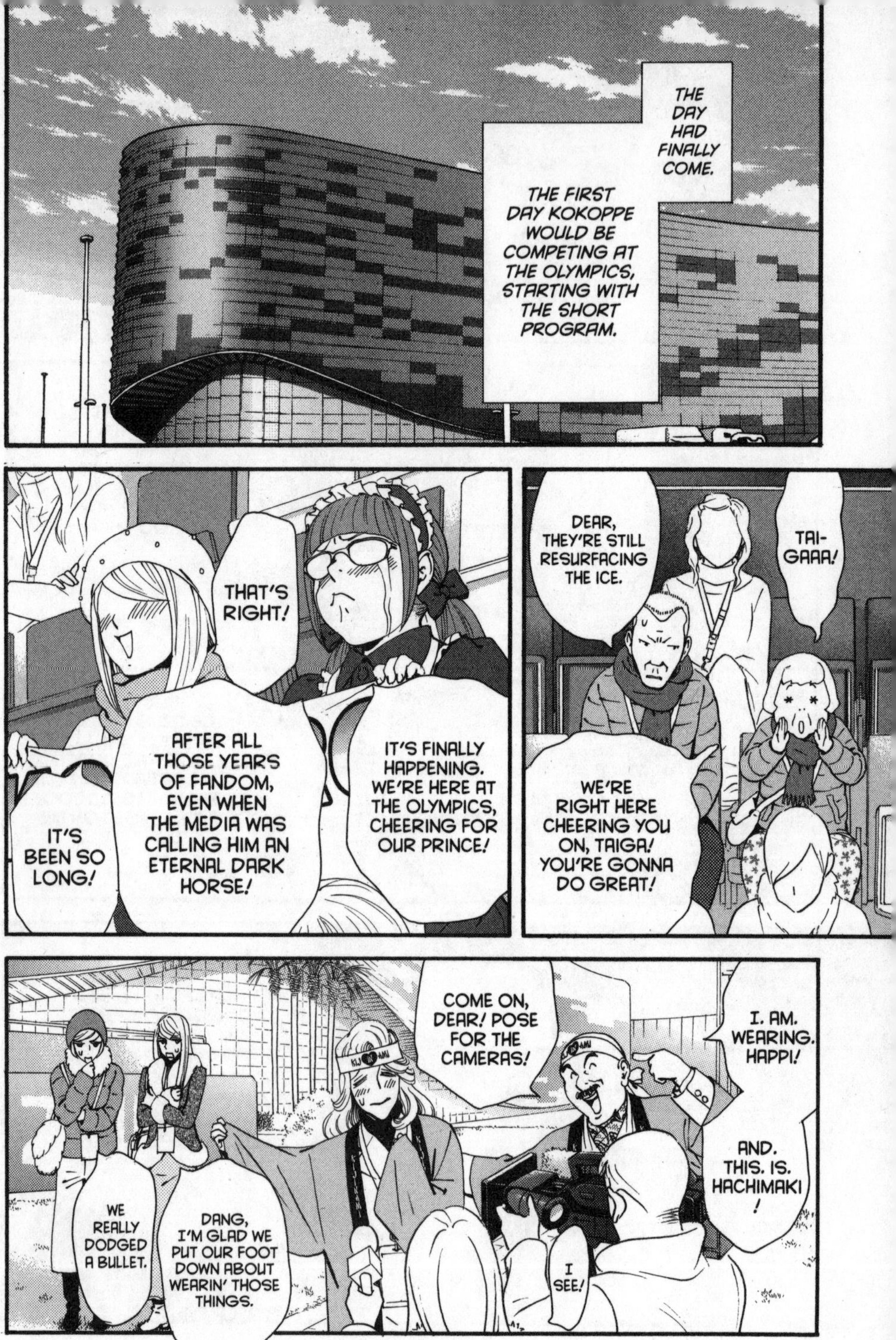
THE DAY HAD FINALLY COME.
THE FIRST DAY KOKOPPE WOULD BE COMPETING AT THE OLYMPICS, STARTING WITH THE SHORT PROGRAM.
TAI-GAAA!
DEAR, THEY'RE STILL RESURFACING THE ICE.
WE'RE RIGHT HERE CHEERING YOU ON, TAIGA! YOU'RE GONNA DO GREAT!
THAT'S RIGHT!
IT'S FINALLY HAPPENING. WE'RE HERE AT THE OLYMPICS, CHEERING FOR OUR PRINCE!
AFTER ALL THOSE YEARS OF FANDOM, EVEN WHEN THE MEDIA WAS CALLING HIM AN ETERNAL DARK HORSE!
IT'S BEEN SO LONG!
I. AM. WEARING. HAPPI!
AND. THIS. IS. HACHIMAKI!
COME ON, DEAR! POSE FOR THE CAMERAS!
I SEE!
DANG, I'M GLAD WE PUT OUR FOOT DOWN ABOUT WEARIN' THOSE THINGS.
WE REALLY DODGED A BULLET.

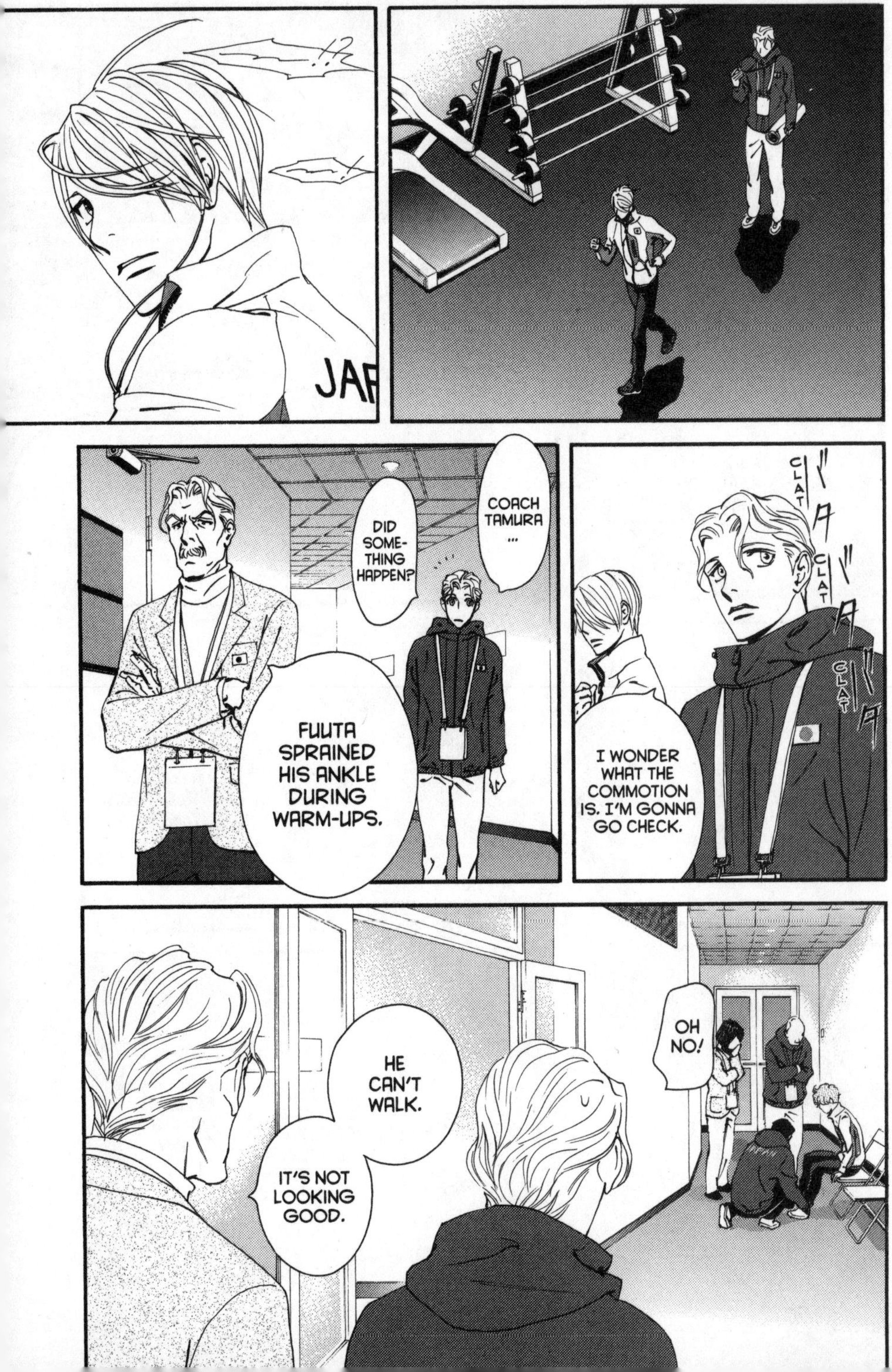
!?
JAP
CLAT CLAT CLAT
I WONDER WHAT THE COMMOTION IS. I'M GONNA GO CHECK.
COACH TAMURA ...
DID SOME-THING HAPPEN?
FUUTA SPRAINED HIS ANKLE DURING WARM-UPS.
OH NO!
HE CAN'T WALK.
IT'S NOT LOOKING GOOD.

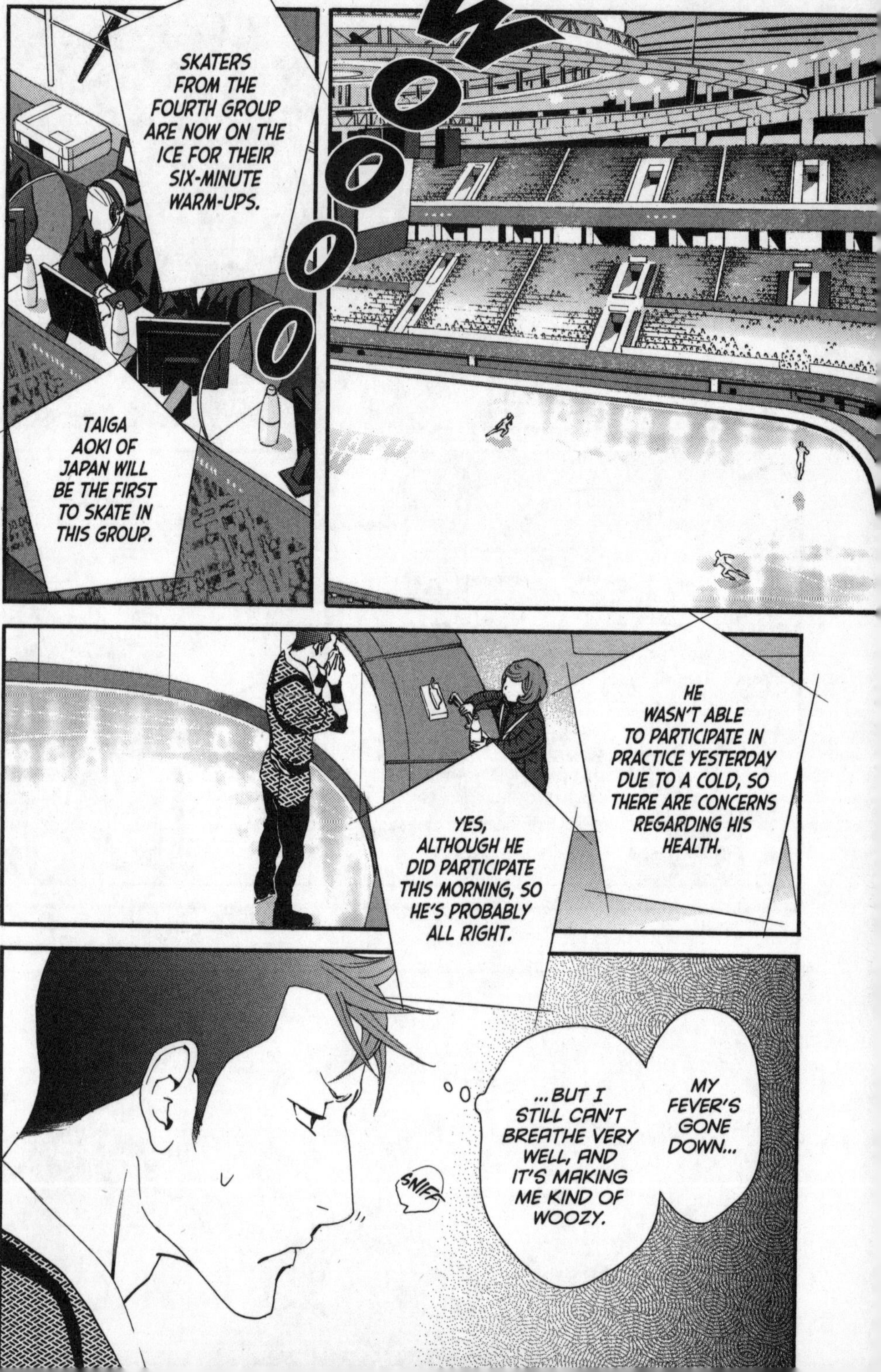
WOOOOO
SKATERS FROM THE FOURTH GROUP ARE NOW ON THE ICE FOR THEIR SIX-MINUTE WARM-UPS.
TAIGA AOKI OF JAPAN WILL BE THE FIRST TO SKATE IN THIS GROUP.
HE WASN'T ABLE TO PARTICIPATE IN PRACTICE YESTERDAY DUE TO A COLD, SO THERE ARE CONCERNS REGARDING HIS HEALTH.
YES, ALTHOUGH HE DID PARTICIPATE THIS MORNING, SO HE'S PROBABLY ALL RIGHT.
MY FEVER'S GONE DOWN...
...BUT I STILL CAN'T BREATHE VERY WELL, AND IT'S MAKING ME KIND OF WOOZY.
SNIFF

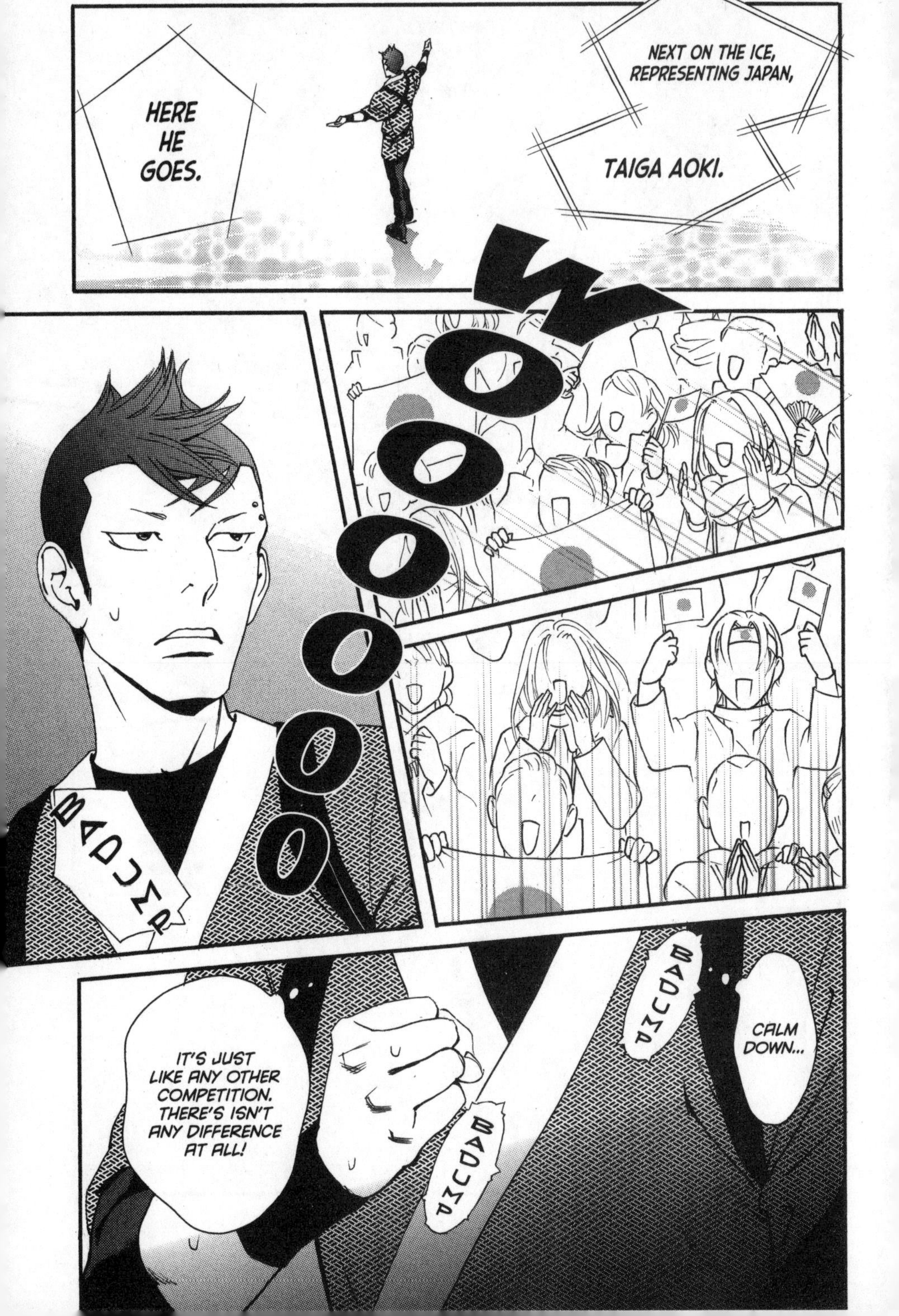
NEXT ON THE ICE, REPRESENTING JAPAN,
TAIGA AOKI.
HERE HE GOES.
WOOOOOO
CALM DOWN...
BADUMP
BADUMP
IT'S JUST LIKE ANY OTHER COMPETITION. THERE'S ISN'T ANY DIFFERENCE AT ALL!

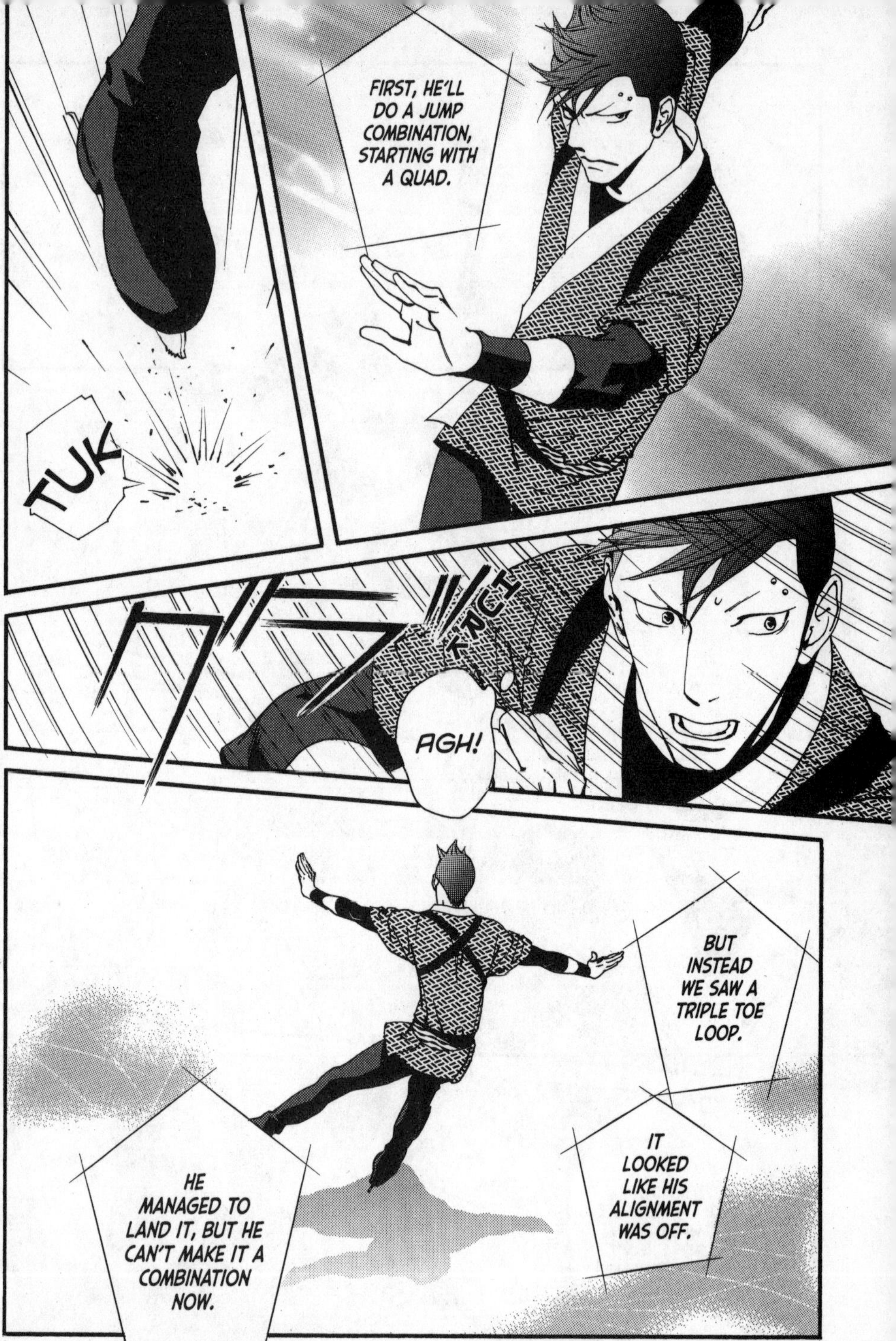
FIRST, HE'LL DO A JUMP COMBINATION, STARTING WITH A QUAD.
TUK
KRCH
AGH!
グラ
BUT INSTEAD WE SAW A TRIPLE TOE LOOP.
IT LOOKED LIKE HIS ALIGNMENT WAS OFF.
HE MANAGED TO LAND IT, BUT HE CAN'T MAKE IT A COMBINATION NOW.

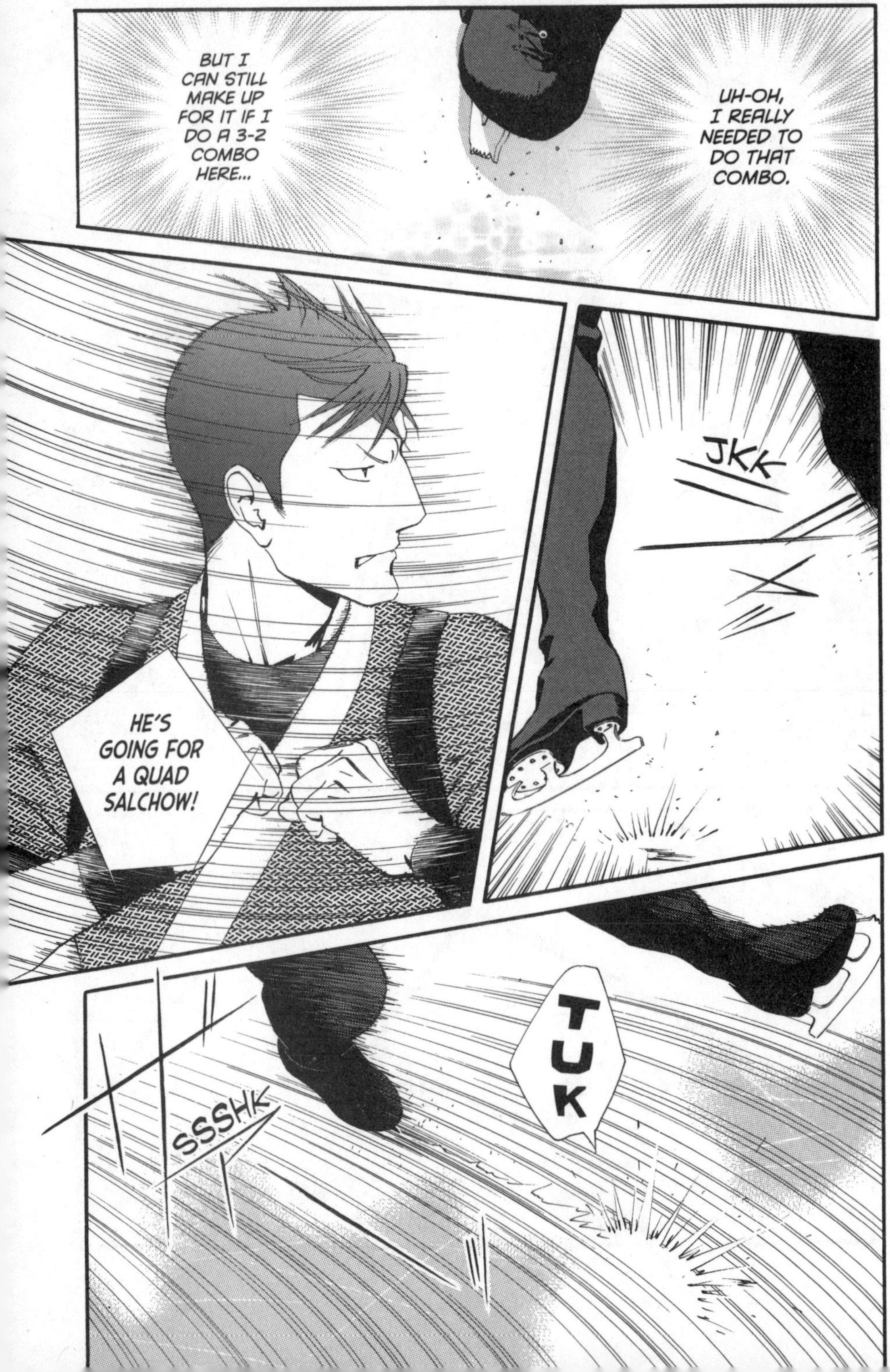
UH-OH, I REALLY NEEDED TO DO THAT COMBO.
BUT I CAN STILL MAKE UP FOR IT IF I DO A 3-2 COMBO HERE...
JKK
HE'S GOING FOR A QUAD SALCHOW!
TUK
SSSHK

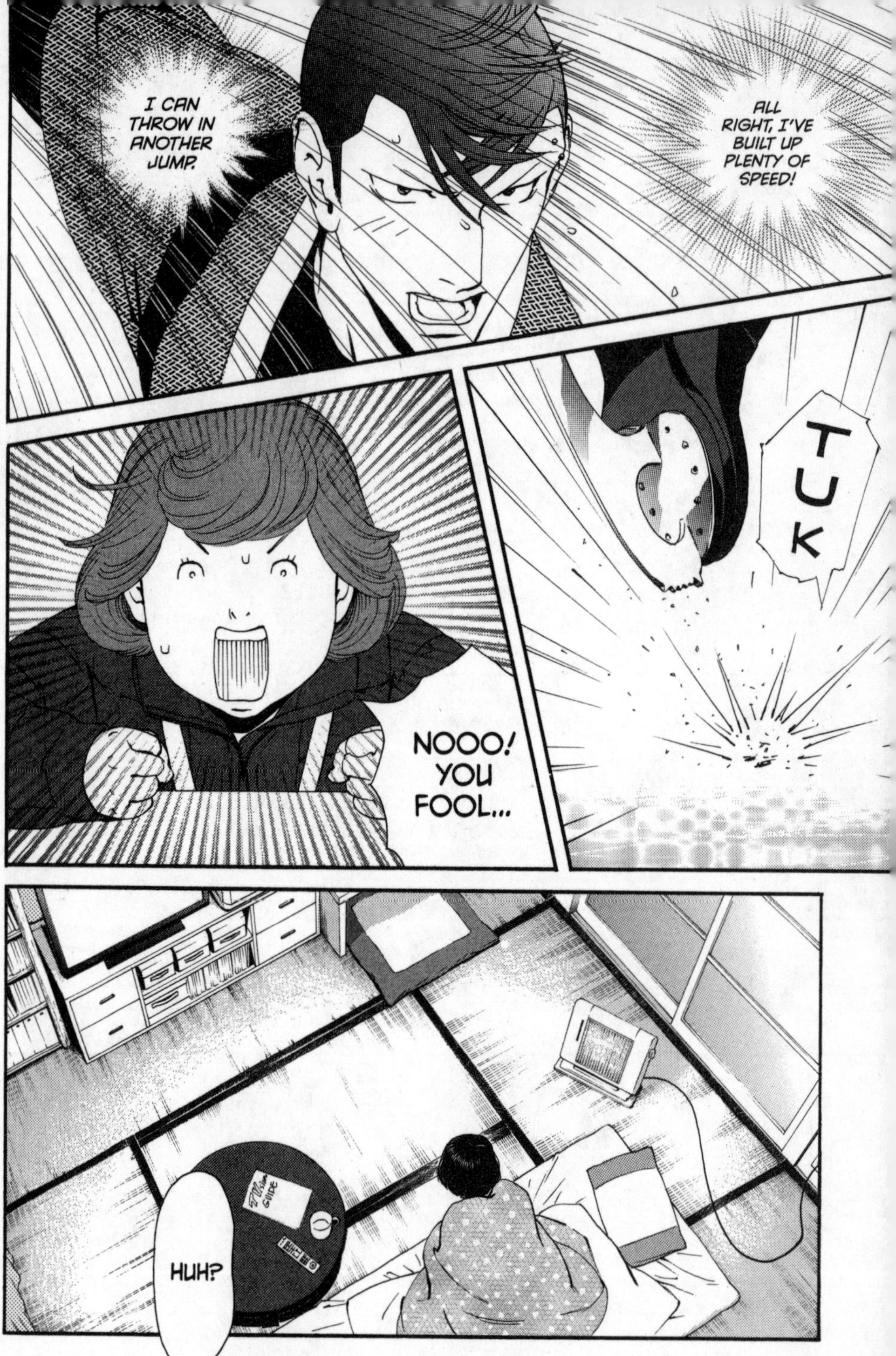
ALL RIGHT, I'VE BUILT UP PLENTY OF SPEED!
I CAN THROW IN ANOTHER JUMP.
TUK
NOOO! YOU FOOL...
HUH?

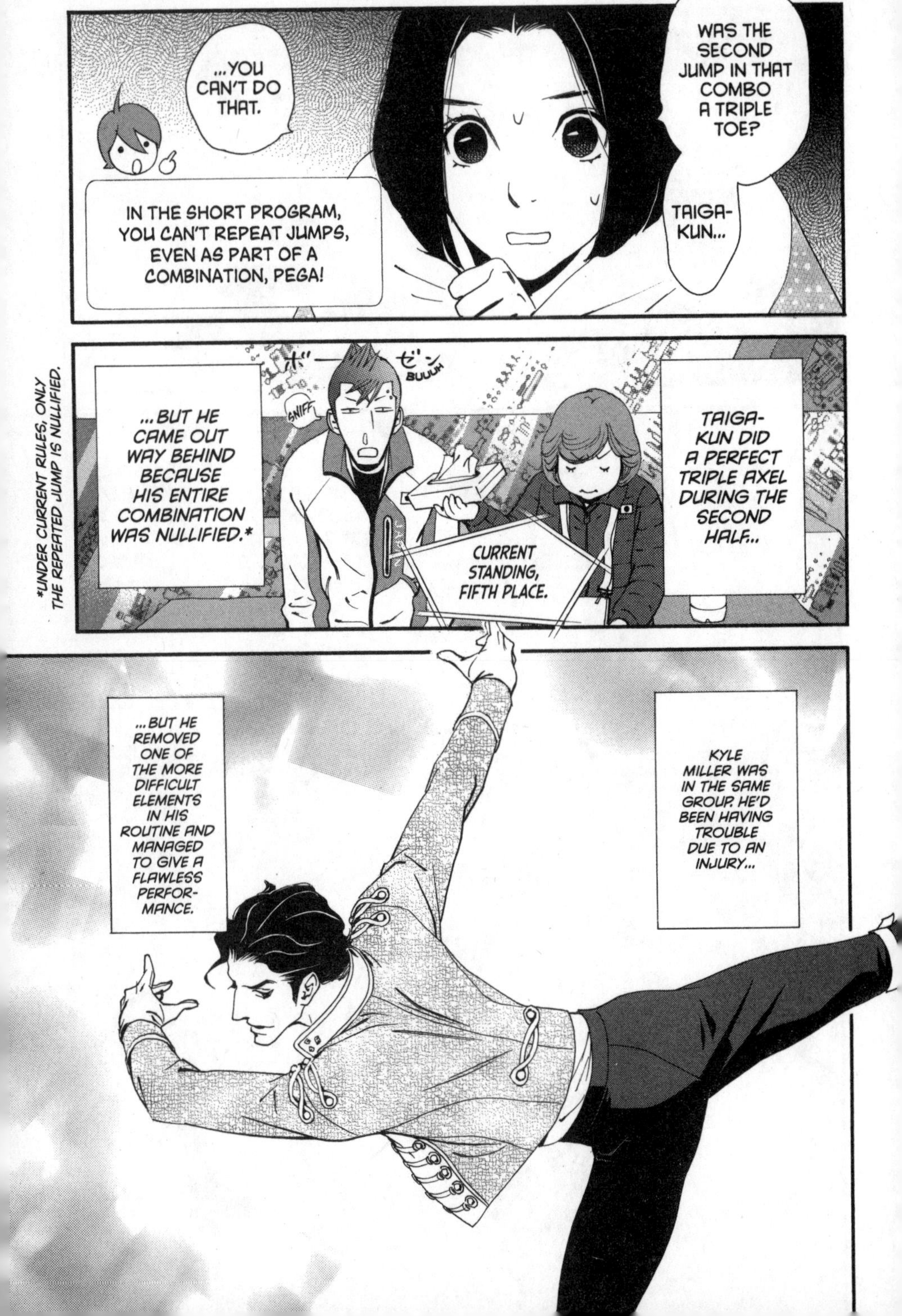
WAS THE SECOND JUMP IN THAT COMBO A TRIPLE TOE?
TAIGA-KUN...
...YOU CAN'T DO THAT.
IN THE SHORT PROGRAM, YOU CAN'T REPEAT JUMPS, EVEN AS PART OF A COMBINATION, PEGA!
TAIGA-KUN DID A PERFECT TRIPLE AXEL DURING THE SECOND HALF...
ボーゼン
BUUUH
CURRENT STANDING, FIFTH PLACE.
SNIFF
...BUT HE CAME OUT WAY BEHIND BECAUSE HIS ENTIRE COMBINATION WAS NULLIFIED.*
KYLE MILLER WAS IN THE SAME GROUP. HE'D BEEN HAVING TROUBLE DUE TO AN INJURY...
...BUT HE REMOVED ONE OF THE MORE DIFFICULT ELEMENTS IN HIS ROUTINE AND MANAGED TO GIVE A FLAWLESS PERFORMANCE.

*UNDER CURRENT RULES, ONLY THE REPEATED JUMP IS NULLIFIED.

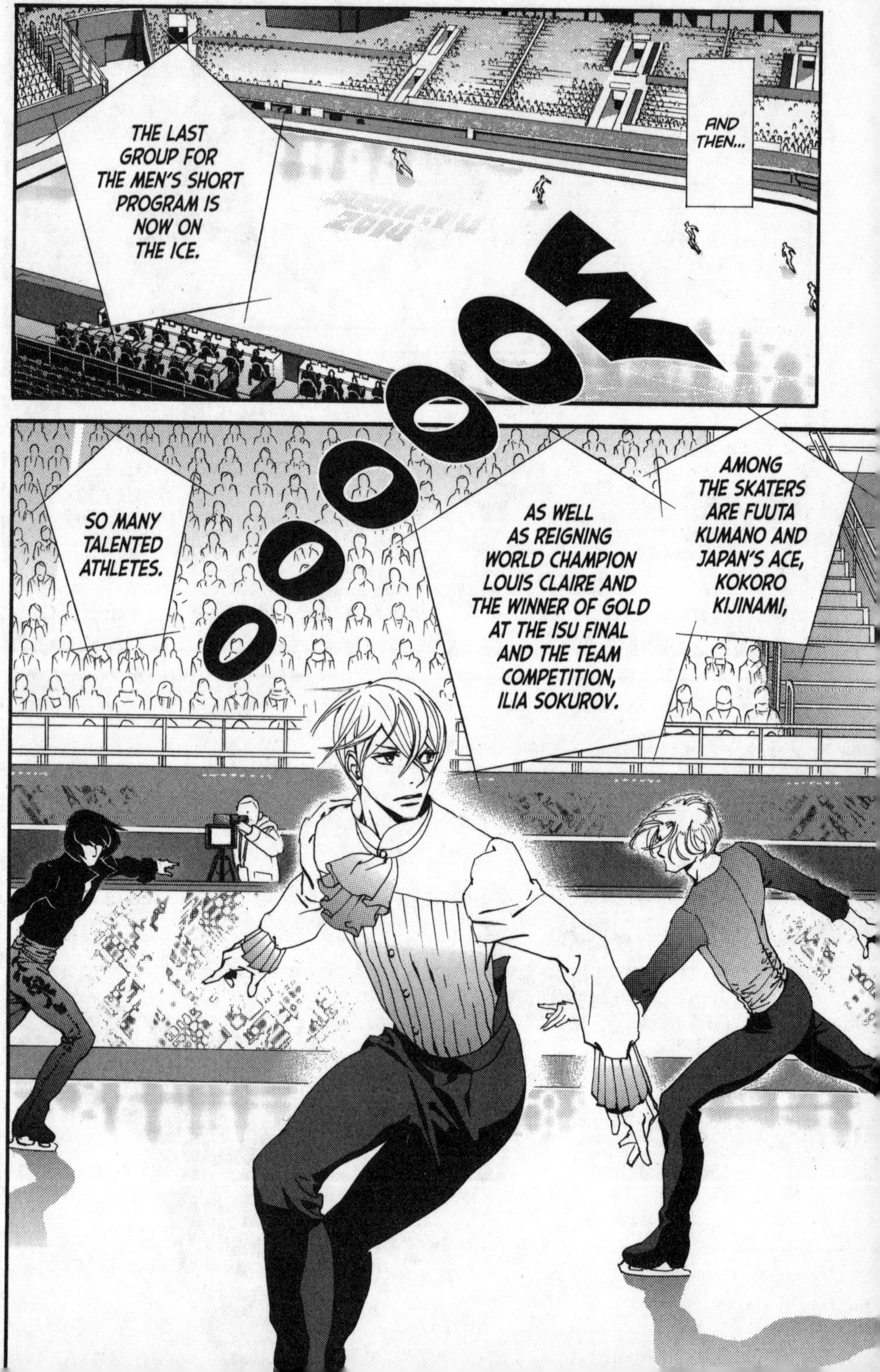
AND THEN...
THE LAST GROUP FOR THE MEN'S SHORT PROGRAM IS NOW ON THE ICE.
WOOOOOOO
AMONG THE SKATERS ARE FUUTA KUMANO AND JAPAN'S ACE, KOKORO KIJINAMI,
AS WELL AS REIGNING WORLD CHAMPION LOUIS CLAIRE AND THE WINNER OF GOLD AT THE ISU FINAL AND THE TEAM COMPETITION, ILIA SOKUROV.
SO MANY TALENTED ATHLETES.

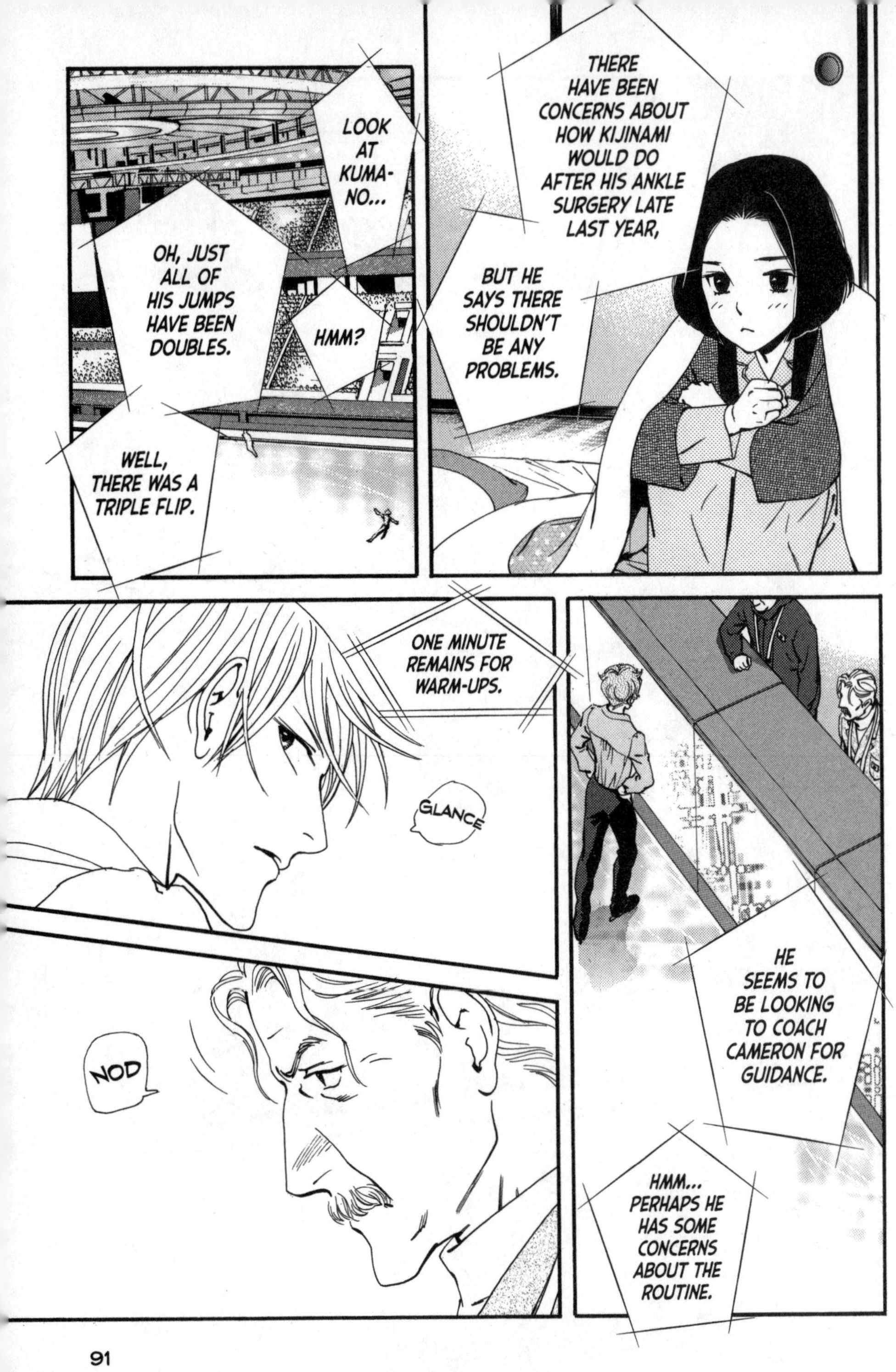
THERE HAVE BEEN CONCERNS ABOUT HOW KIJINAMI WOULD DO AFTER HIS ANKLE SURGERY LATE LAST YEAR,
BUT HE SAYS THERE SHOULDN'T BE ANY PROBLEMS.
LOOK AT KUMA-NO...
HMM?
OH, JUST ALL OF HIS JUMPS HAVE BEEN DOUBLES.
WELL, THERE WAS A TRIPLE FLIP.
HE SEEMS TO BE LOOKING TO COACH CAMERON FOR GUIDANCE.
HMM... PERHAPS HE HAS SOME CONCERNS ABOUT THE ROUTINE.
ONE MINUTE REMAINS FOR WARM-UPS.
GLANCE
NOD

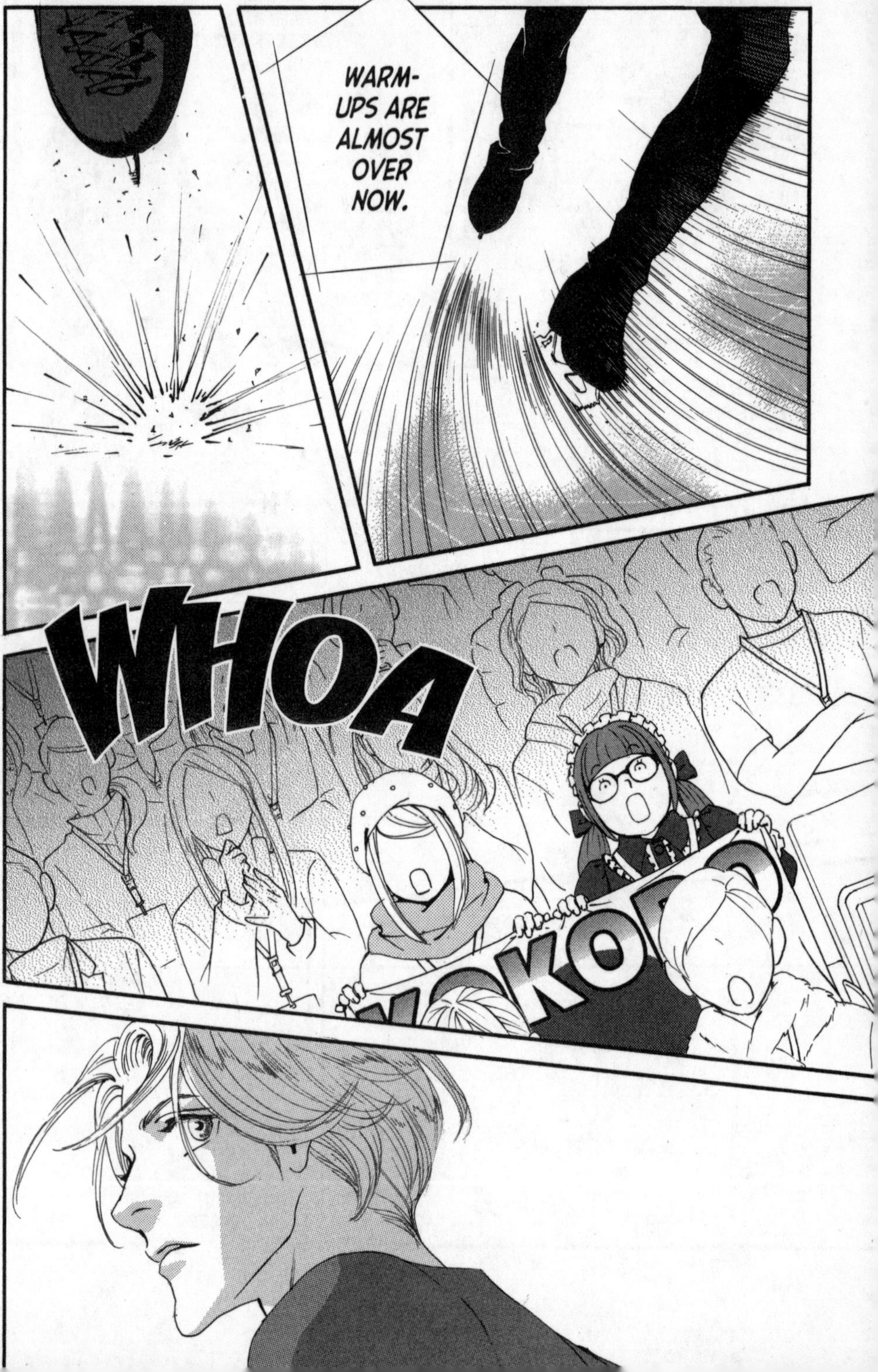
WARM-UPS ARE ALMOST OVER NOW.
WHOA

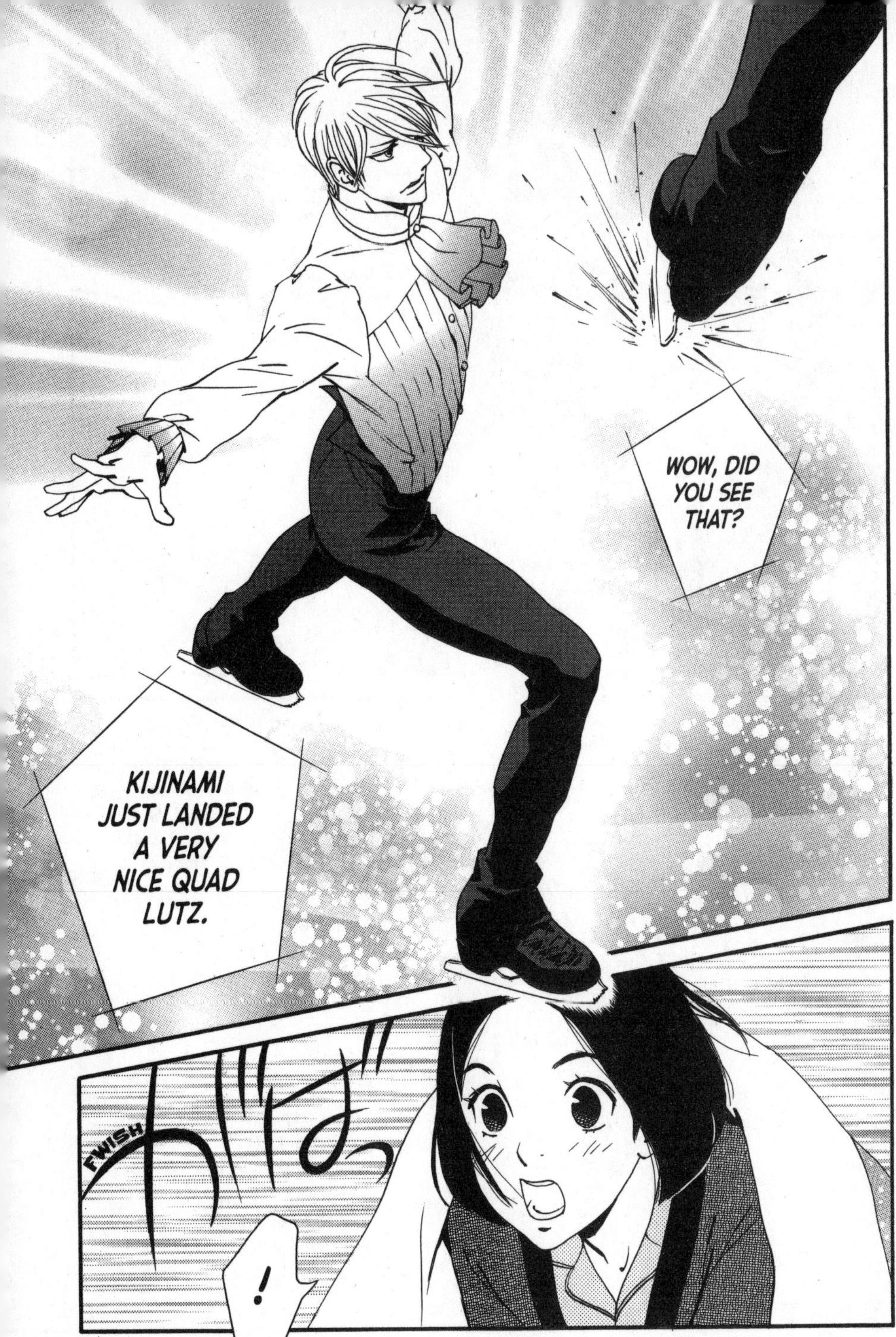
WOW, DID YOU SEE THAT?
KIJINAMI JUST LANDED A VERY NICE QUAD LUTZ.
FWISH
!

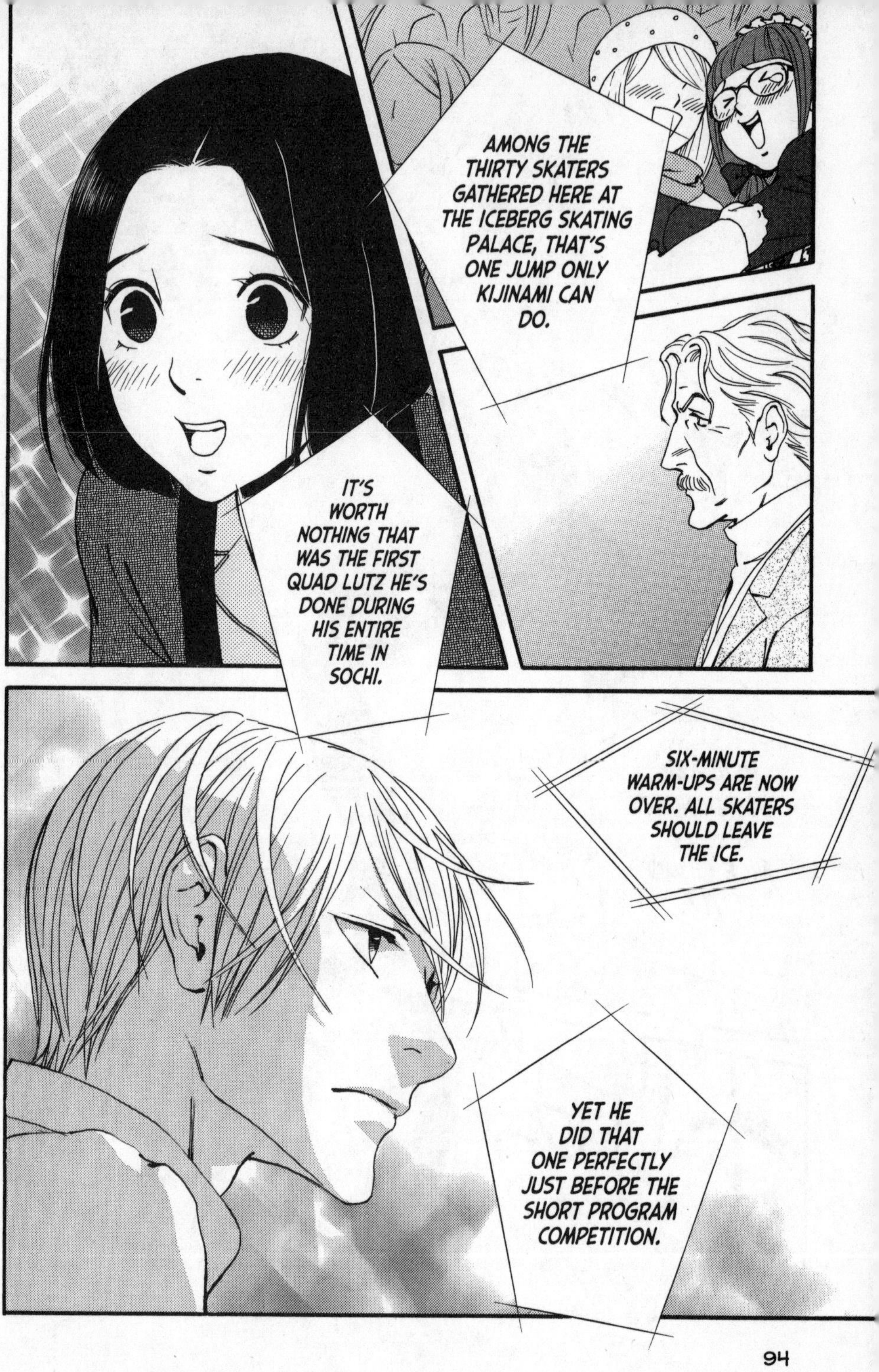
AMONG THE THIRTY SKATERS GATHERED HERE AT THE ICEBERG SKATING PALACE, THAT'S ONE JUMP ONLY KIJINAMI CAN DO.
IT'S WORTH NOTHING THAT WAS THE FIRST QUAD LUTZ HE'S DONE DURING HIS ENTIRE TIME IN SOCHI.
SIX-MINUTE WARM-UPS ARE NOW OVER. ALL SKATERS SHOULD LEAVE THE ICE.
YET HE DID THAT ONE PERFECTLY JUST BEFORE THE SHORT PROGRAM COMPETITION.

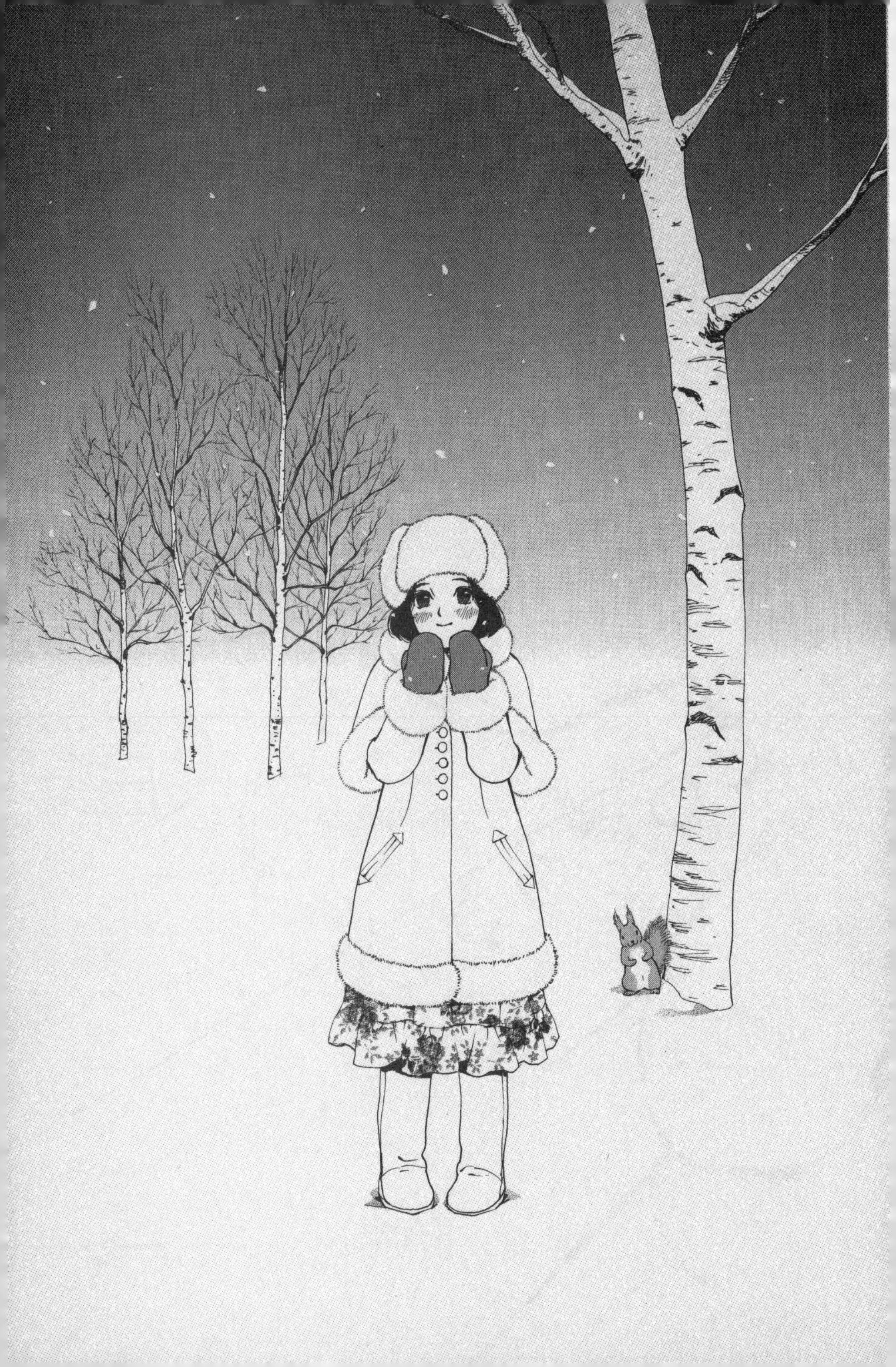

Spell 50
Believe in Him

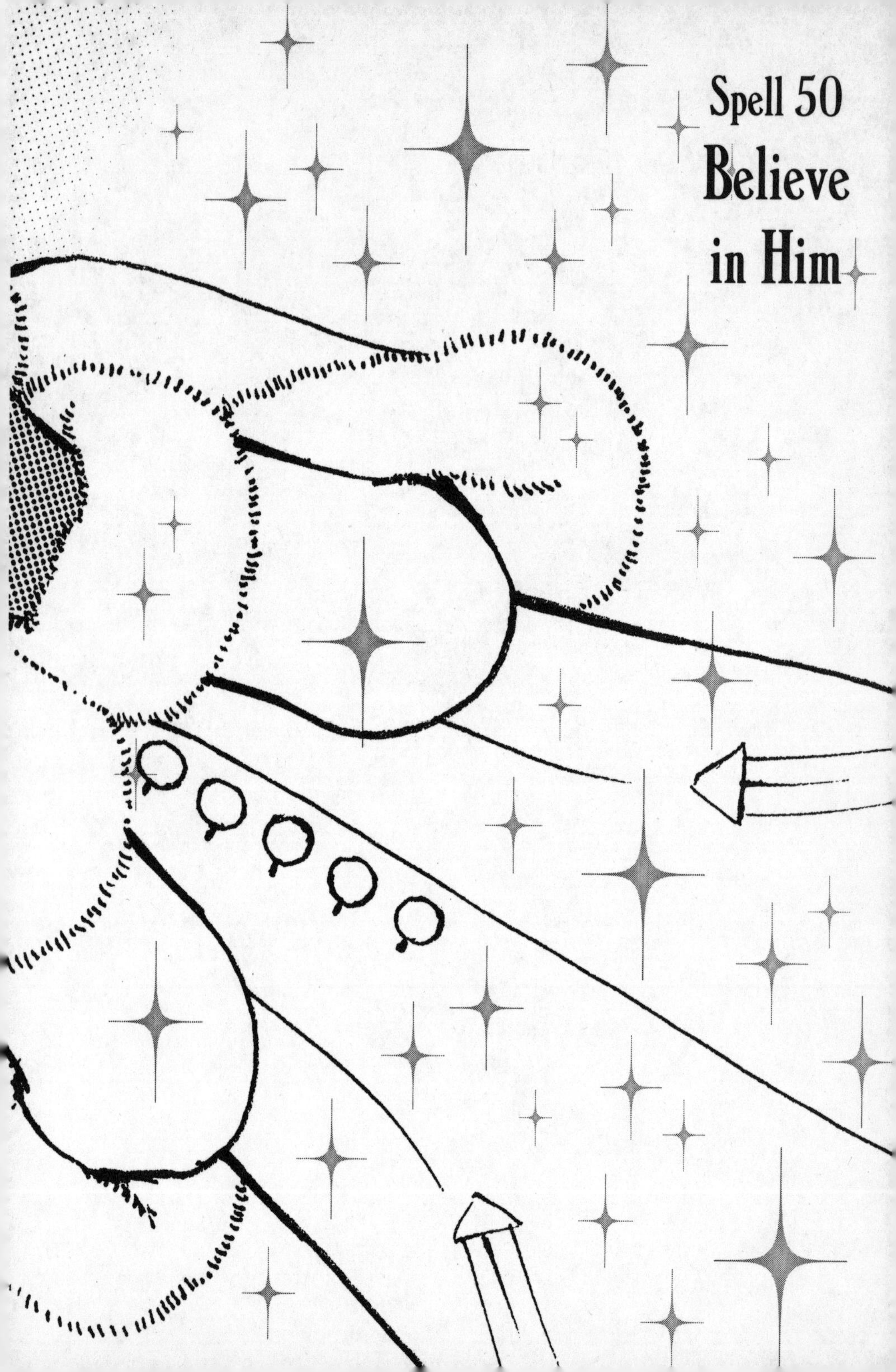

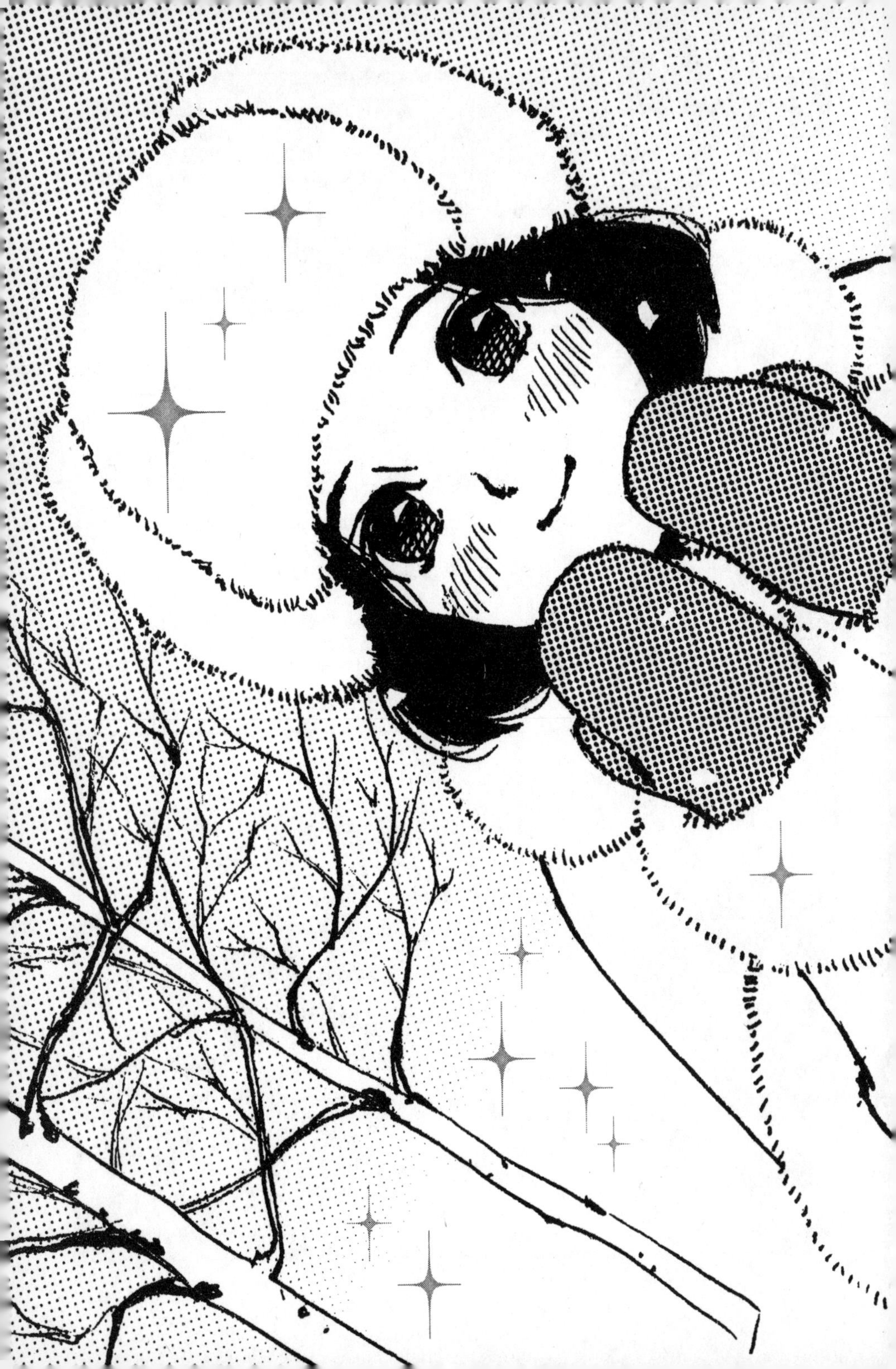

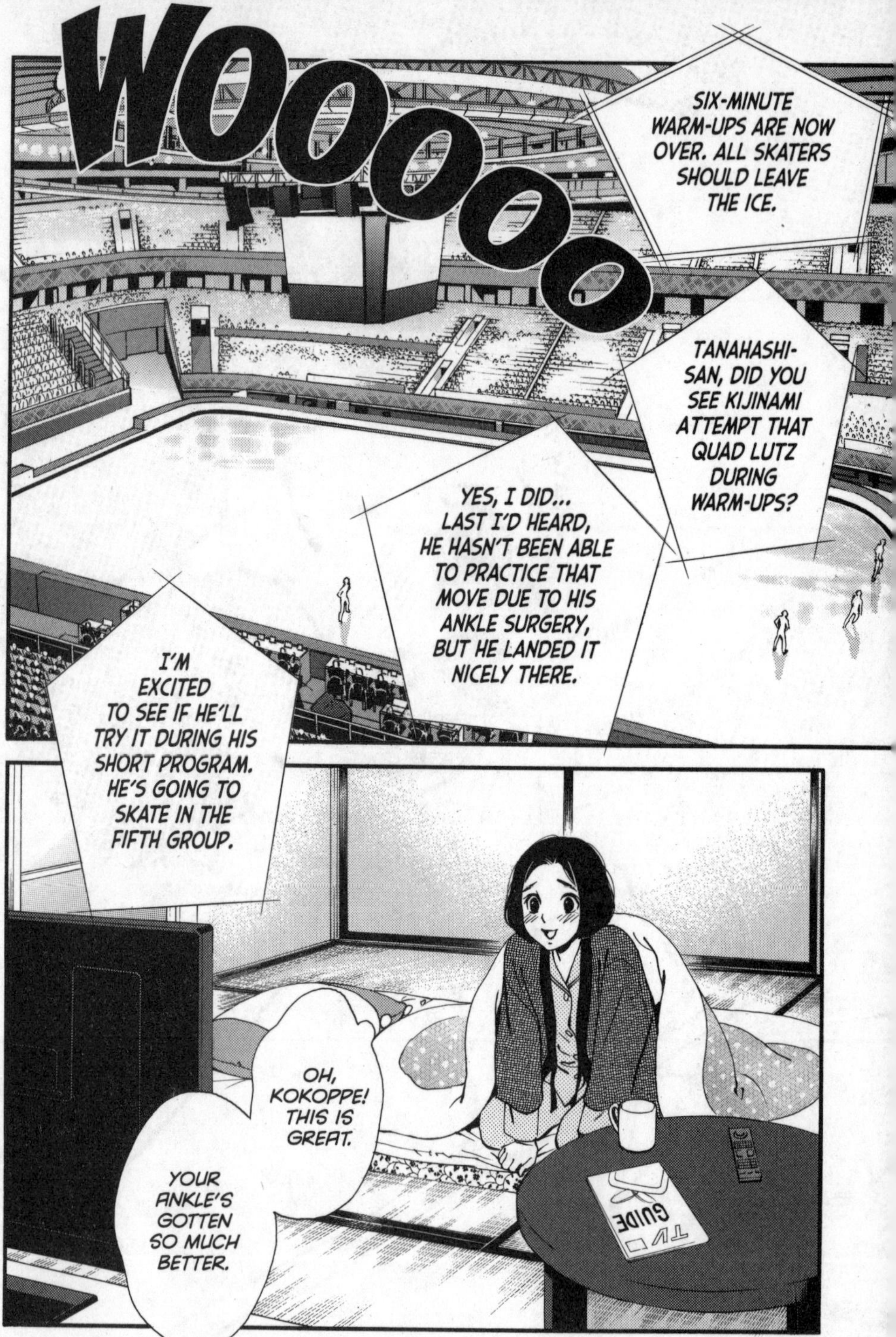
WOOOOOO
SIX-MINUTE WARM-UPS ARE NOW OVER. ALL SKATERS SHOULD LEAVE THE ICE.
TANAHASHI-SAN, DID YOU SEE KIJINAMI ATTEMPT THAT QUAD LUTZ DURING WARM-UPS?
YES, I DID... LAST I'D HEARD, HE HASN'T BEEN ABLE TO PRACTICE THAT MOVE DUE TO HIS ANKLE SURGERY, BUT HE LANDED IT NICELY THERE.
I'M EXCITED TO SEE IF HE'LL TRY IT DURING HIS SHORT PROGRAM. HE'S GOING TO SKATE IN THE FIFTH GROUP.
OH, KOKOPPE! THIS IS GREAT.
YOUR ANKLE'S GOTTEN SO MUCH BETTER.
TV GUIDE

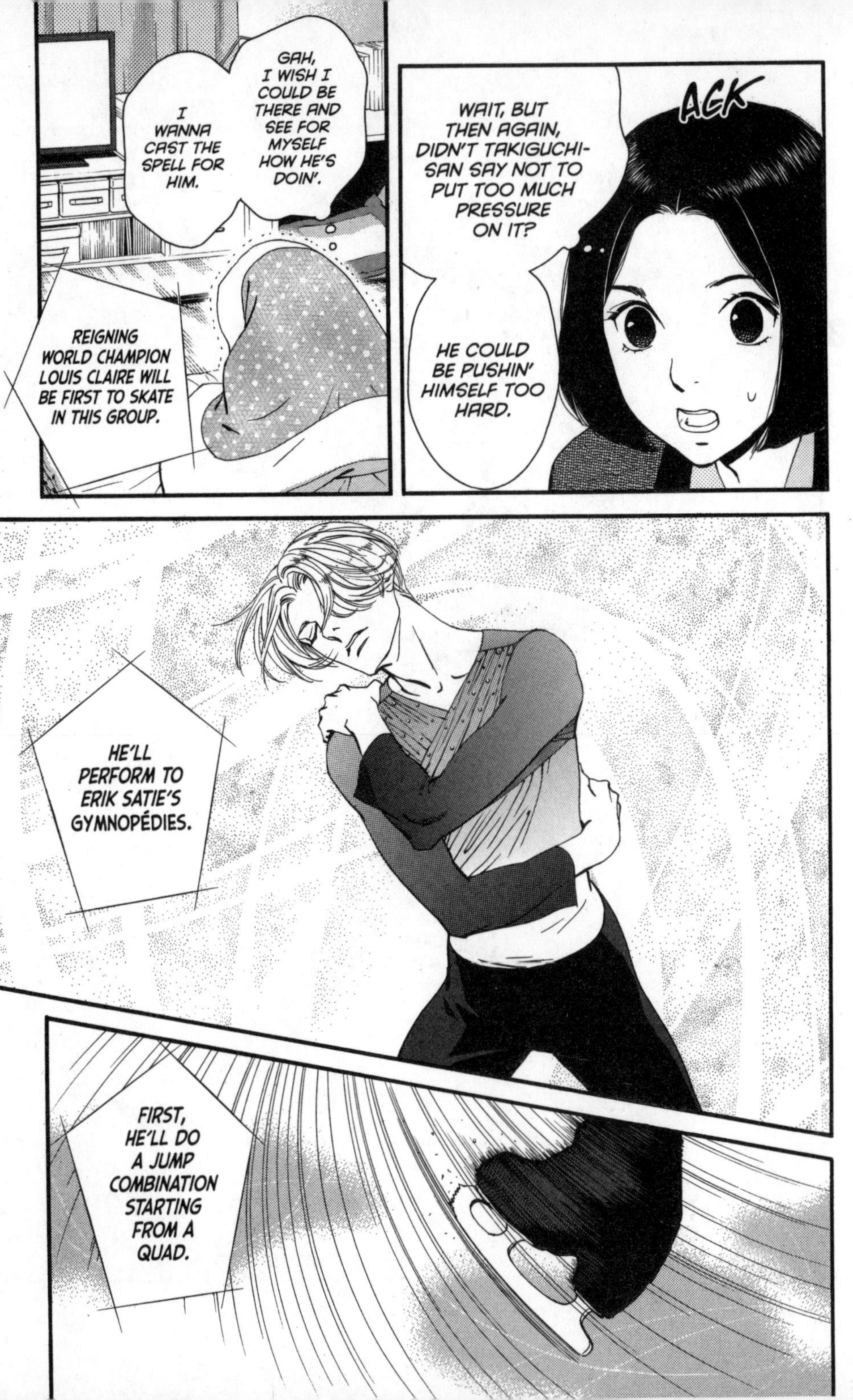
ACK
WAIT, BUT THEN AGAIN, DIDN'T TAKIGUCHI-SAN SAY NOT TO PUT TOO MUCH PRESSURE ON IT?
HE COULD BE PUSHIN' HIMSELF TOO HARD.
GAH, I WISH I COULD BE THERE AND SEE FOR MYSELF HOW HE'S DOIN'.
I WANNA CAST THE SPELL FOR HIM.
REIGNING WORLD CHAMPION LOUIS CLAIRE WILL BE FIRST TO SKATE IN THIS GROUP.
HE'LL PERFORM TO ERIK SATIE'S GYMNOPÉDIES.
FIRST, HE'LL DO A JUMP COMBINATION STARTING FROM A QUAD.

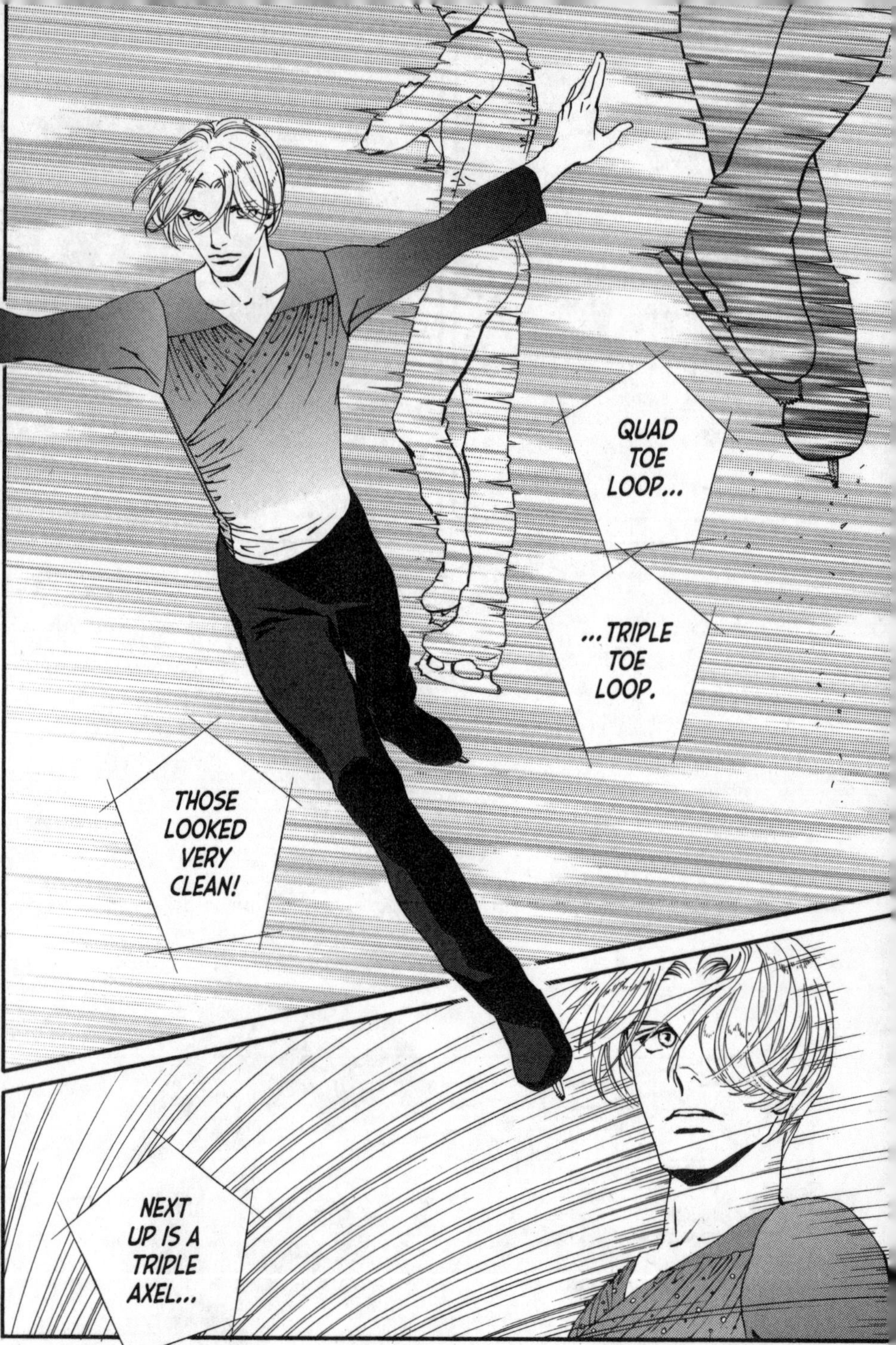
QUAD TOE LOOP...
...TRIPLE TOE LOOP.
THOSE LOOKED VERY CLEAN!
NEXT UP IS A TRIPLE AXEL...

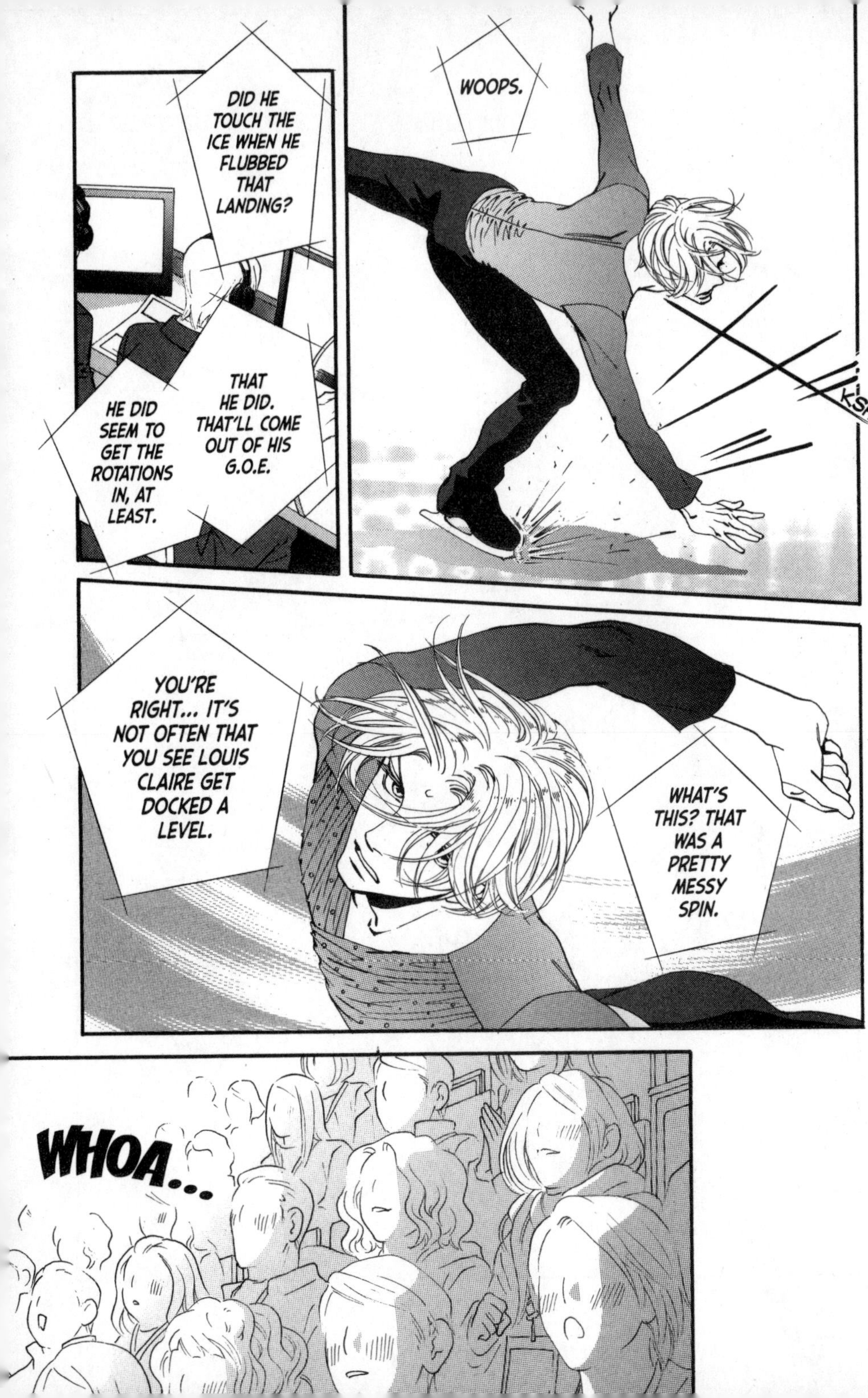
WOOPS.
KSH
DID HE TOUCH THE ICE WHEN HE FLUBBED THAT LANDING?
THAT HE DID. THAT'LL COME OUT OF HIS G.O.E.
HE DID SEEM TO GET THE ROTATIONS IN, AT LEAST.
WHAT'S THIS? THAT WAS A PRETTY MESSY SPIN.
YOU'RE RIGHT... IT'S NOT OFTEN THAT YOU SEE LOUIS CLAIRE GET DOCKED A LEVEL.
WHOA...

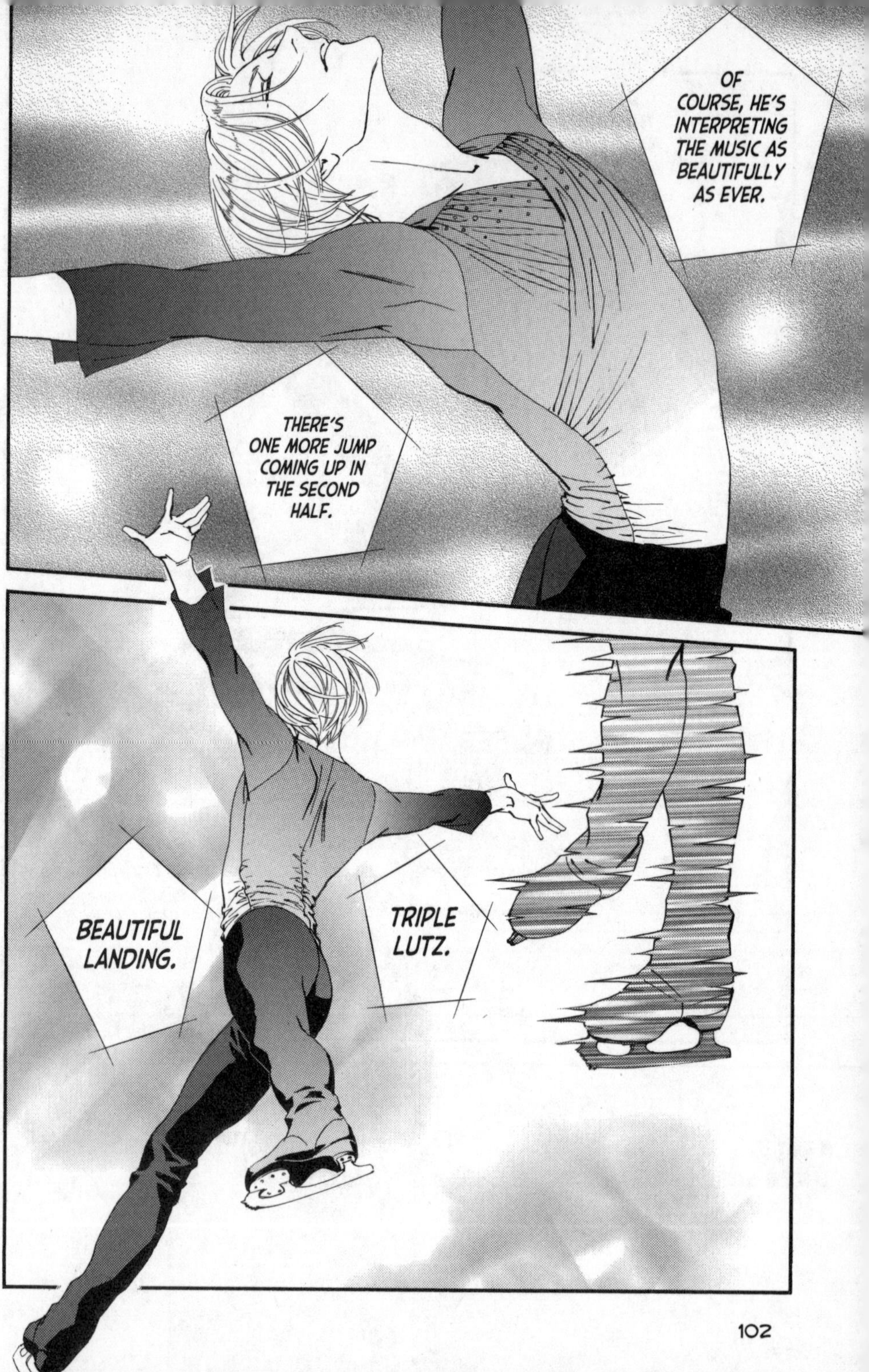
OF COURSE, HE'S INTERPRETING THE MUSIC AS BEAUTIFULLY AS EVER.
THERE'S ONE MORE JUMP COMING UP IN THE SECOND HALF.
TRIPLE LUTZ.
BEAUTIFUL LANDING.

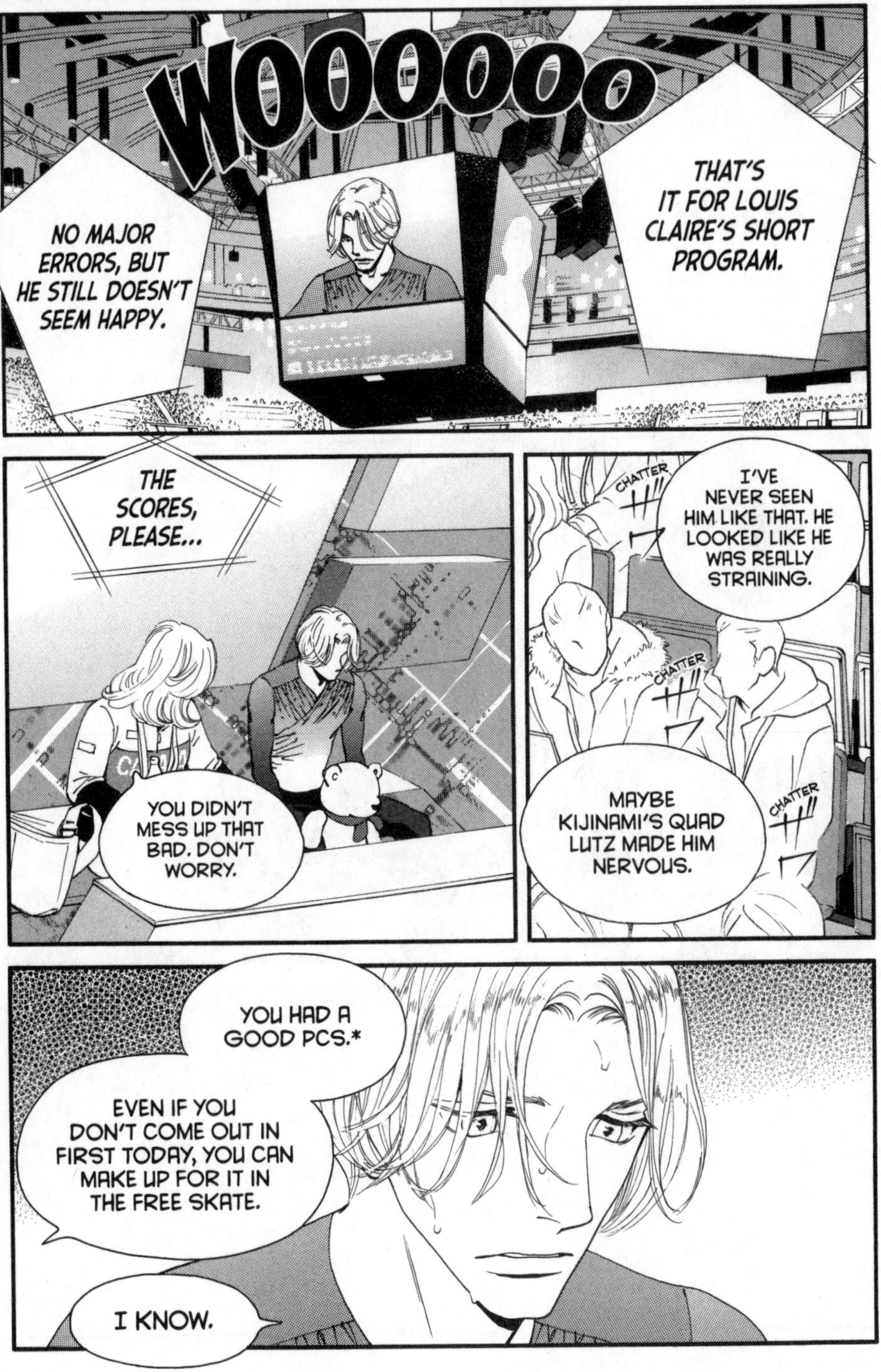
THAT'S IT FOR LOUIS CLAIRE'S SHORT PROGRAM.
WOOOOOO
NO MAJOR ERRORS, BUT HE STILL DOESN'T SEEM HAPPY.
CHATTER
I'VE NEVER SEEN HIM LIKE THAT. HE LOOKED LIKE HE WAS REALLY STRAINING.
CHATTER
MAYBE KIJINAMI'S QUAD LUTZ MADE HIM NERVOUS.
CHATTER
THE SCORES, PLEASE...
YOU DIDN'T MESS UP THAT BAD. DON'T WORRY.
YOU HAD A GOOD PCS.*
EVEN IF YOU DON'T COME OUT IN FIRST TODAY, YOU CAN MAKE UP FOR IT IN THE FREE SKATE.
I KNOW.

*PROGRAM COMPONENTS SCORE.

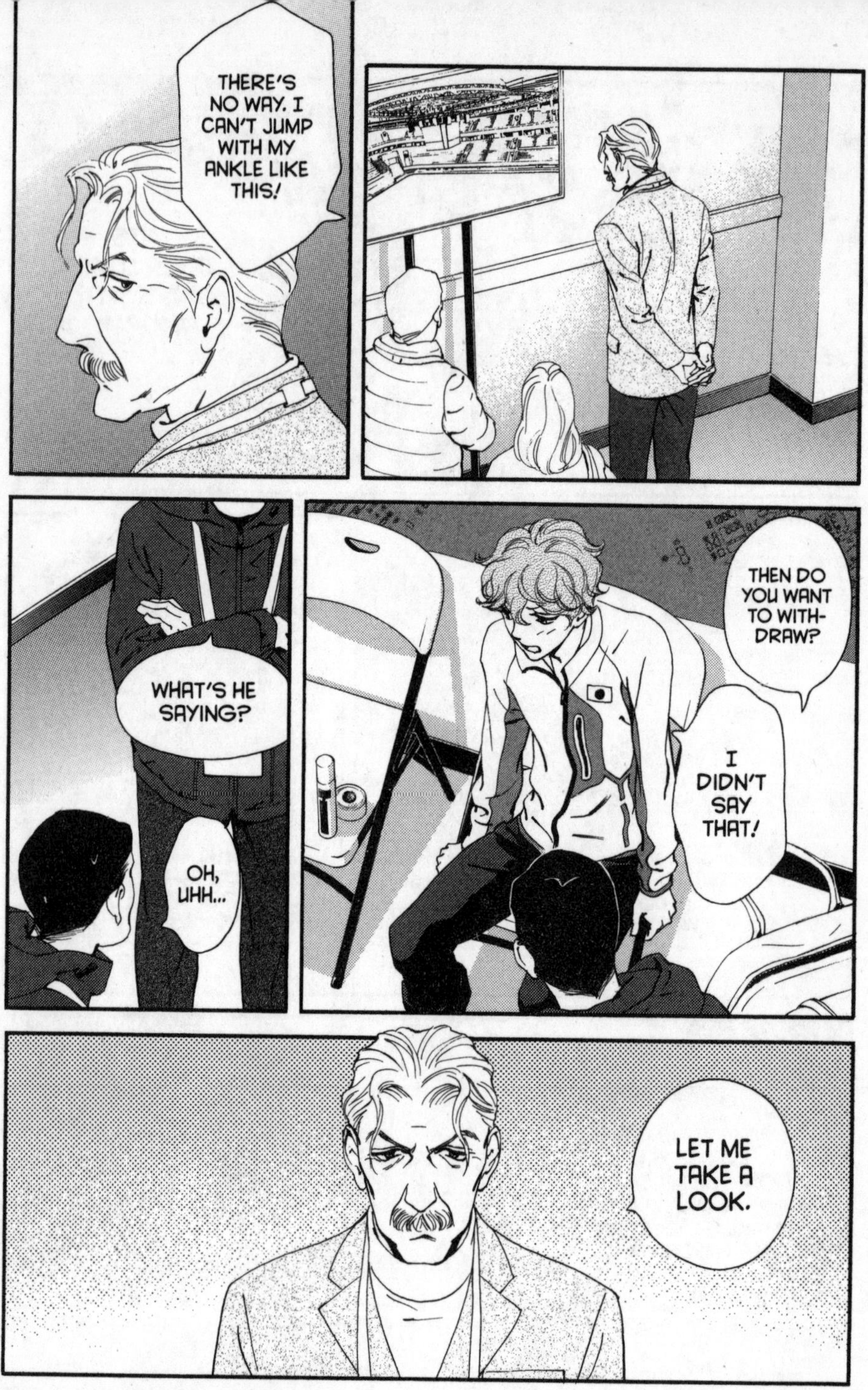
THERE'S NO WAY. I CAN'T JUMP WITH MY ANKLE LIKE THIS!
THEN DO YOU WANT TO WITH-DRAW?
I DIDN'T SAY THAT!
WHAT'S HE SAYING?
OH, UHH...
LET ME TAKE A LOOK.

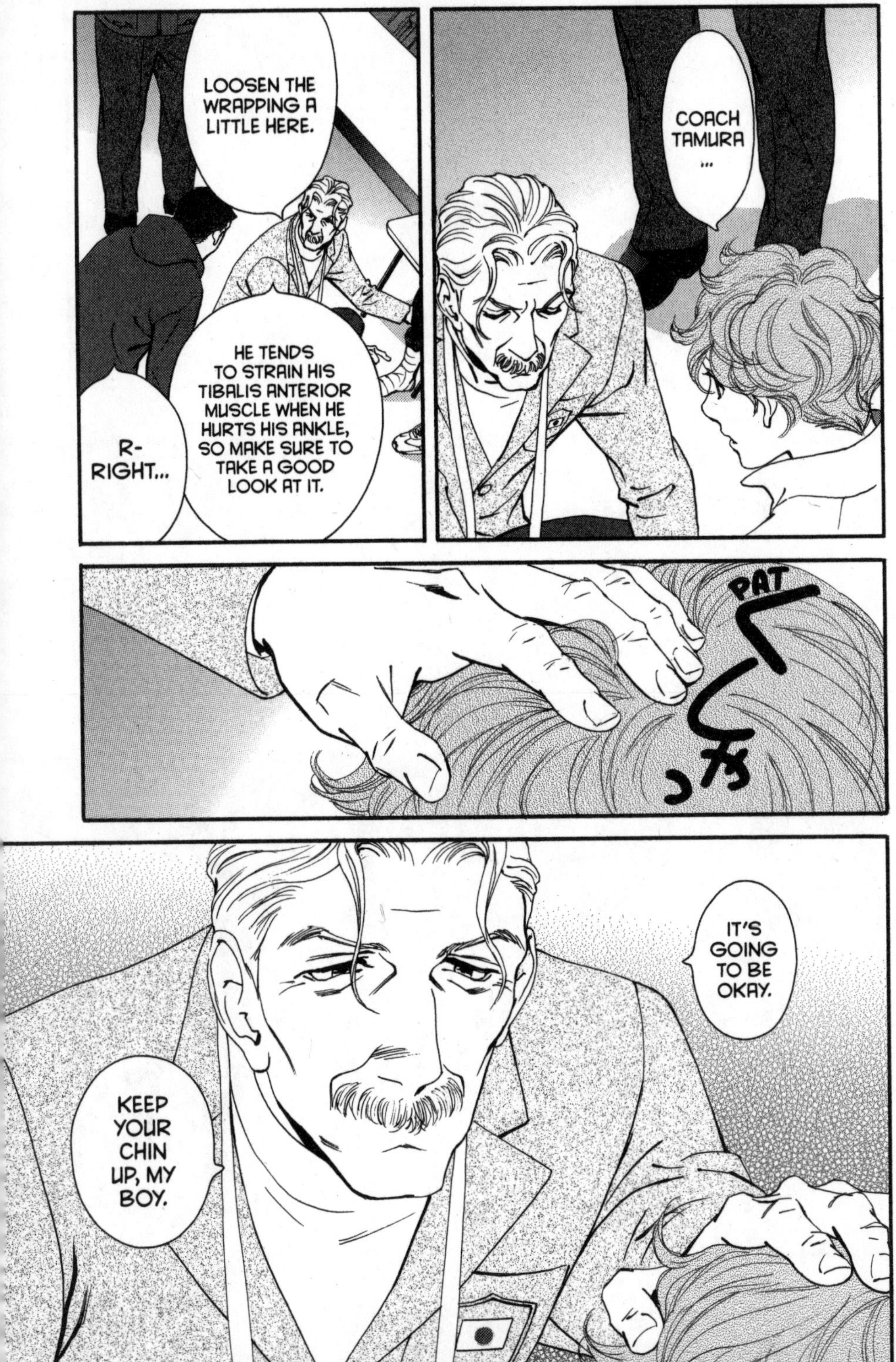
COACH TAMURA ...
LOOSEN THE WRAPPING A LITTLE HERE.
HE TENDS TO STRAIN HIS TIBALIS ANTERIOR MUSCLE WHEN HE HURTS HIS ANKLE, SO MAKE SURE TO TAKE A GOOD LOOK AT IT.
R-RIGHT...
PAT
IT'S GOING TO BE OKAY.
KEEP YOUR CHIN UP, MY BOY.

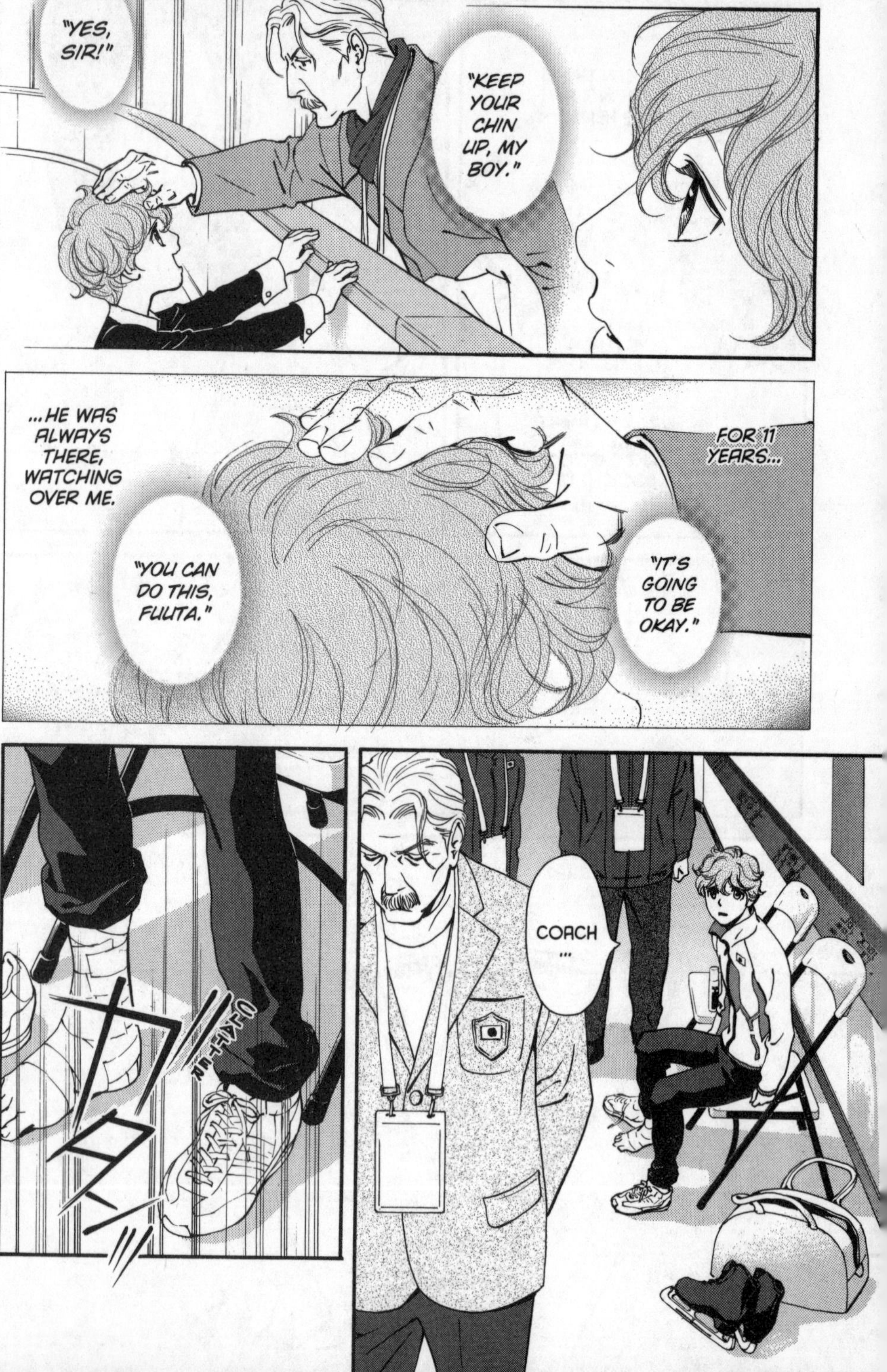
"KEEP YOUR CHIN UP, MY BOY."
"YES, SIR!"
FOR 11 YEARS...
"IT'S GOING TO BE OKAY."
"YOU CAN DO THIS, FUUTA."
...HE WAS ALWAYS THERE, WATCHING OVER ME.
COACH ...
CLATTER

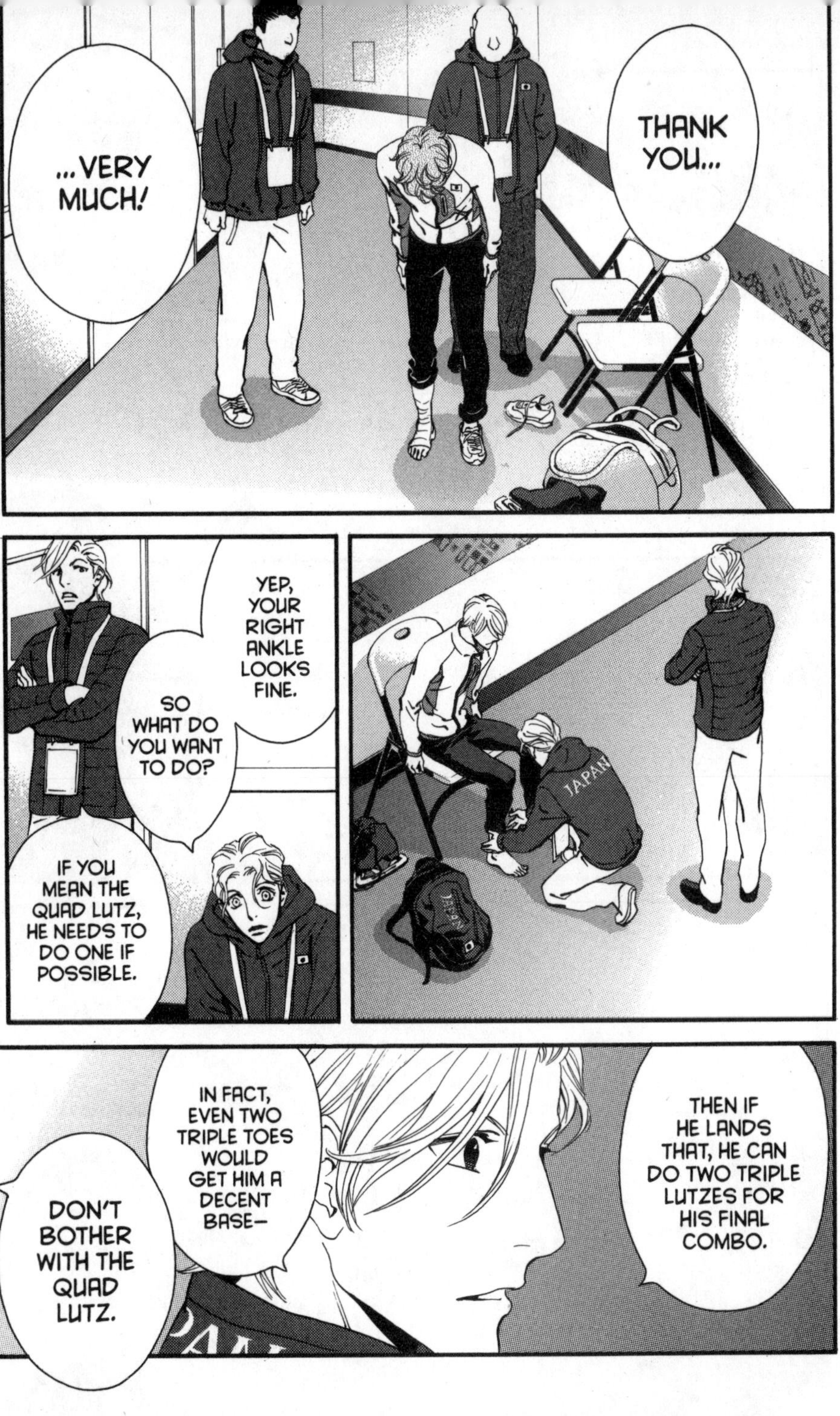
THANK YOU...
...VERY MUCH!
YEP, YOUR RIGHT ANKLE LOOKS FINE.
SO WHAT DO YOU WANT TO DO?
IF YOU MEAN THE QUAD LUTZ, HE NEEDS TO DO ONE IF POSSIBLE.
THEN IF HE LANDS THAT, HE CAN DO TWO TRIPLE LUTZES FOR HIS FINAL COMBO.
IN FACT, EVEN TWO TRIPLE TOES WOULD GET HIM A DECENT BASE—
DON'T BOTHER WITH THE QUAD LUTZ.

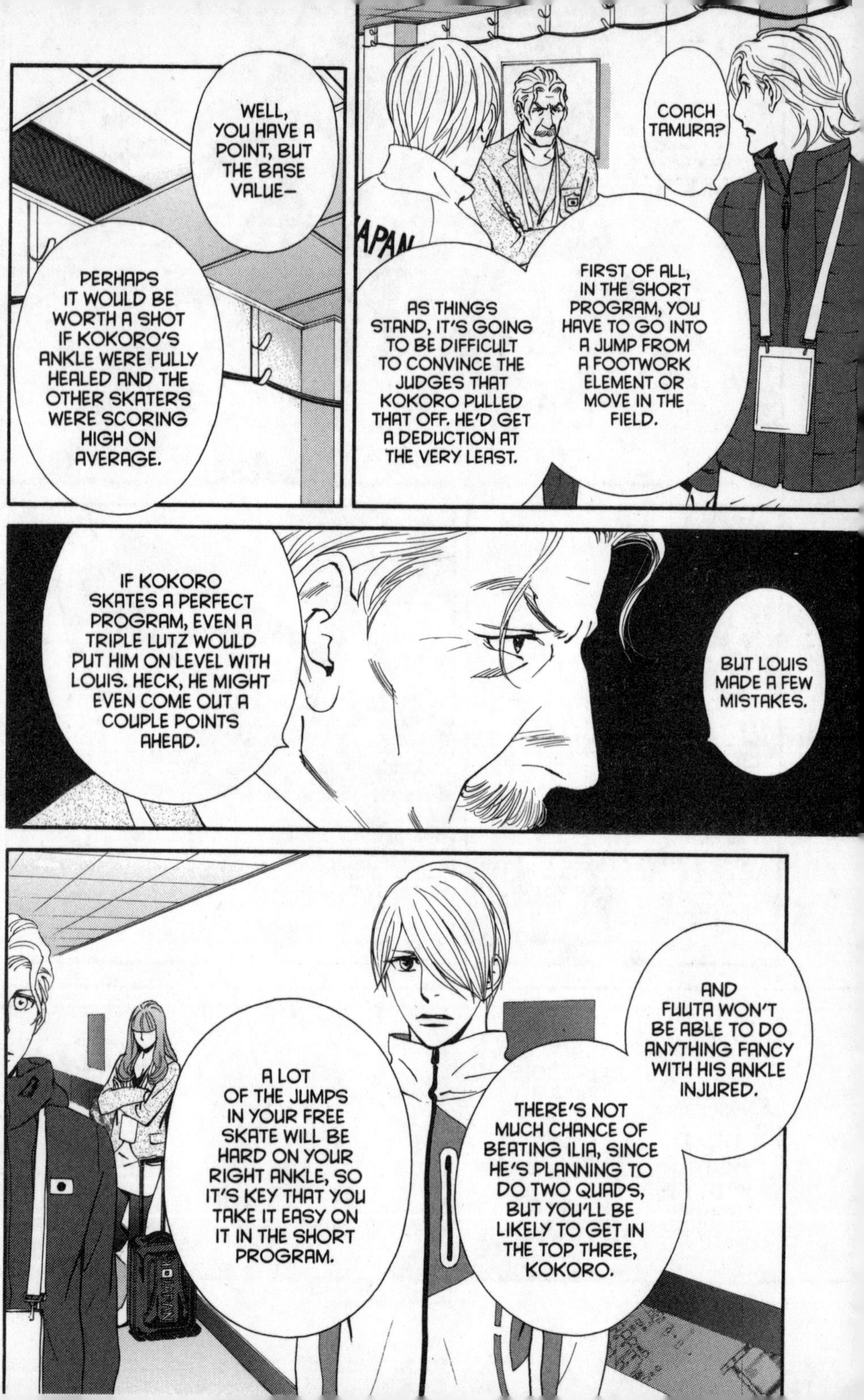
COACH TAMURA?
FIRST OF ALL, IN THE SHORT PROGRAM, YOU HAVE TO GO INTO A JUMP FROM A FOOTWORK ELEMENT OR MOVE IN THE FIELD.
AS THINGS STAND, IT'S GOING TO BE DIFFICULT TO CONVINCE THE JUDGES THAT KOKORO PULLED THAT OFF. HE'D GET A DEDUCTION AT THE VERY LEAST.
WELL, YOU HAVE A POINT, BUT THE BASE VALUE—
PERHAPS IT WOULD BE WORTH A SHOT IF KOKORO'S ANKLE WERE FULLY HEALED AND THE OTHER SKATERS WERE SCORING HIGH ON AVERAGE.
BUT LOUIS MADE A FEW MISTAKES.
IF KOKORO SKATES A PERFECT PROGRAM, EVEN A TRIPLE LUTZ WOULD PUT HIM ON LEVEL WITH LOUIS. HECK, HE MIGHT EVEN COME OUT A COUPLE POINTS AHEAD.
AND FUUTA WON'T BE ABLE TO DO ANYTHING FANCY WITH HIS ANKLE INJURED.
THERE'S NOT MUCH CHANCE OF BEATING ILIA, SINCE HE'S PLANNING TO DO TWO QUADS, BUT YOU'LL BE LIKELY TO GET IN THE TOP THREE, KOKORO.
A LOT OF THE JUMPS IN YOUR FREE SKATE WILL BE HARD ON YOUR RIGHT ANKLE, SO IT'S KEY THAT YOU TAKE IT EASY ON IT IN THE SHORT PROGRAM.

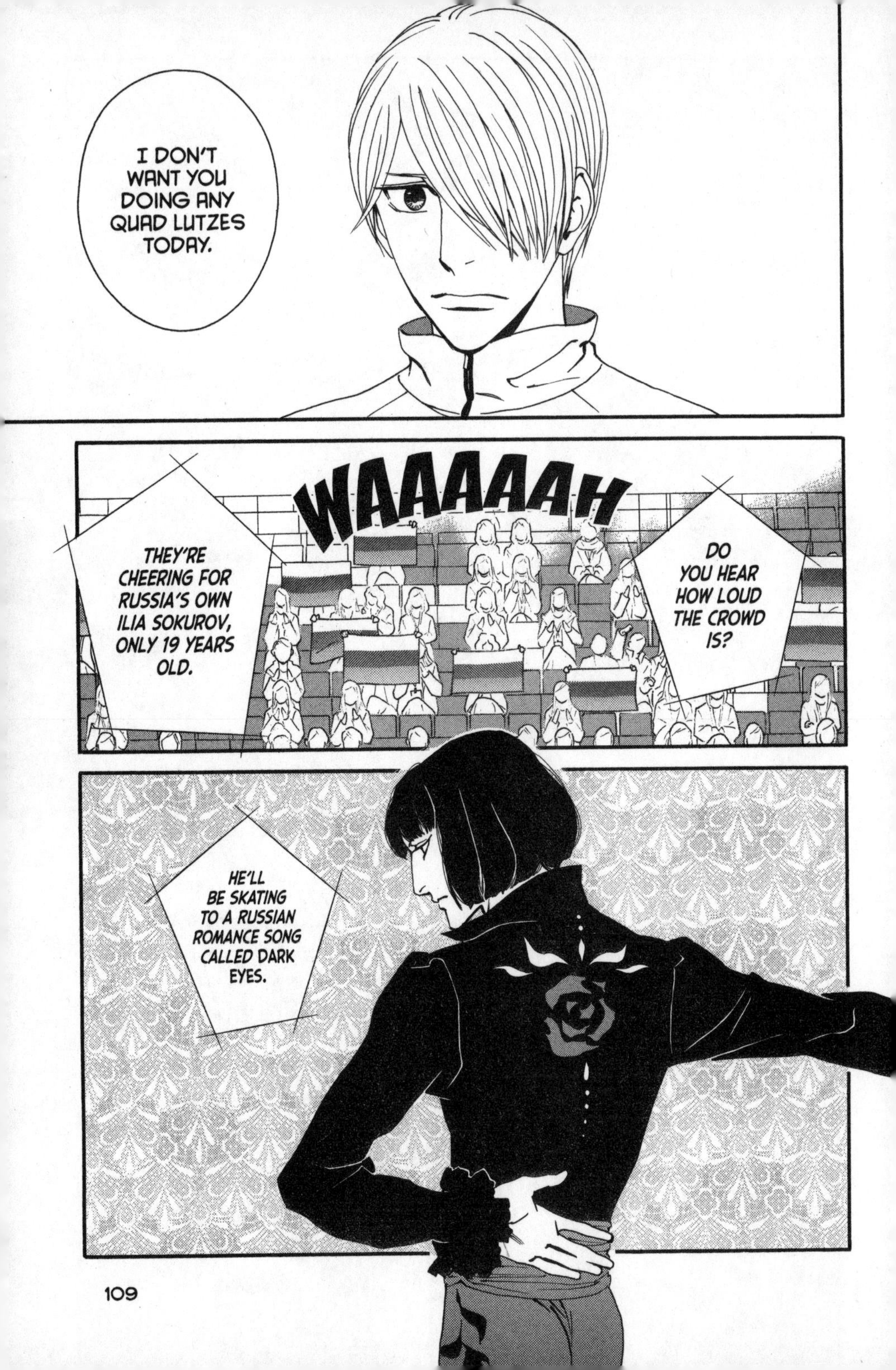

I DON'T WANT YOU DOING ANY QUAD LUTZES TODAY.
DO YOU HEAR HOW LOUD THE CROWD IS?
WAAAAAH
THEY'RE CHEERING FOR RUSSIA'S OWN ILIA SOKUROV, ONLY 19 YEARS OLD.
HE'LL BE SKATING TO A RUSSIAN ROMANCE SONG CALLED DARK EYES.

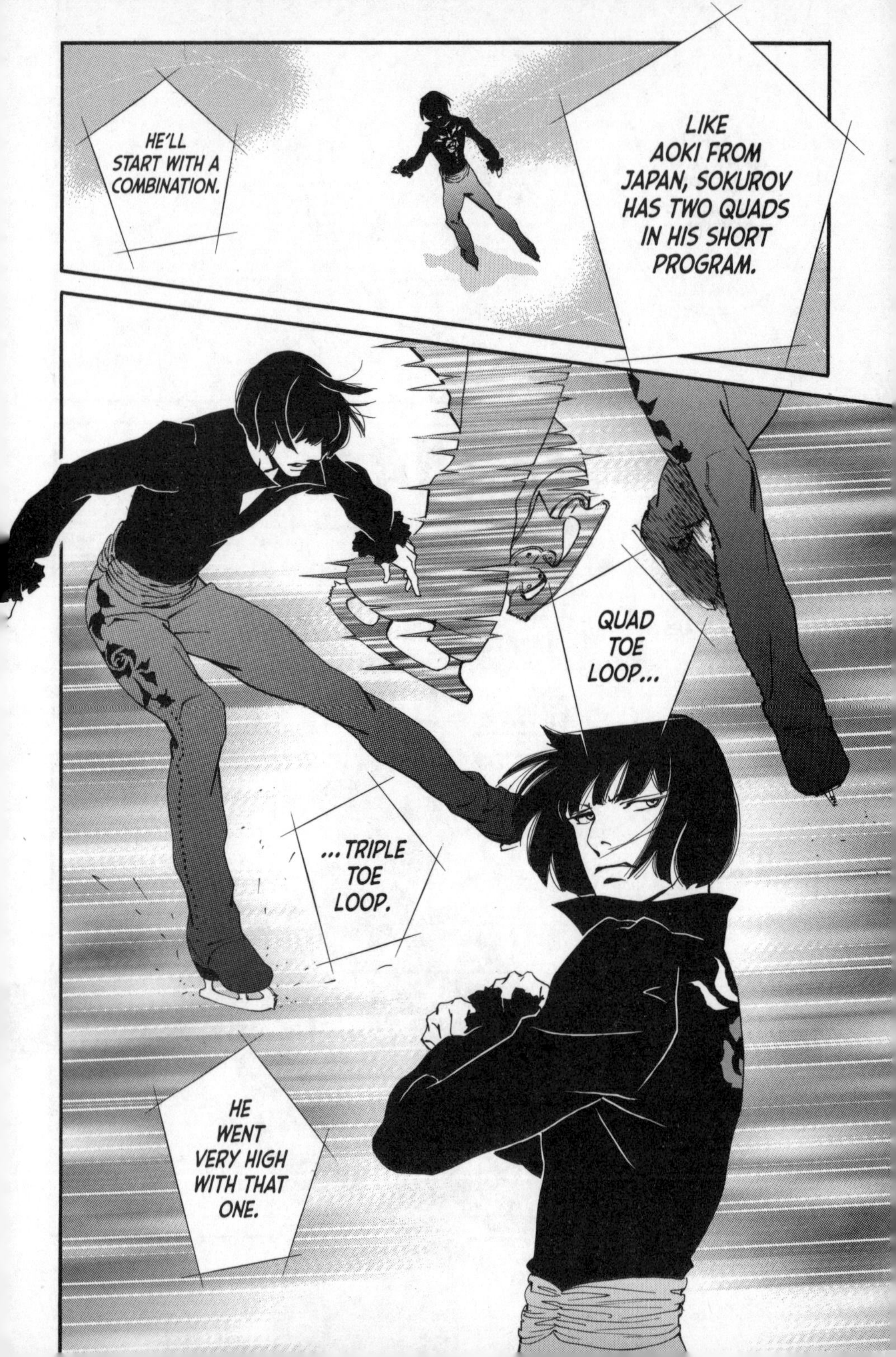
LIKE AOKI FROM JAPAN, SOKUROV HAS TWO QUADS IN HIS SHORT PROGRAM.
HE'LL START WITH A COMBINATION.
QUAD TOE LOOP...
...TRIPLE TOE LOOP.
HE WENT VERY HIGH WITH THAT ONE.

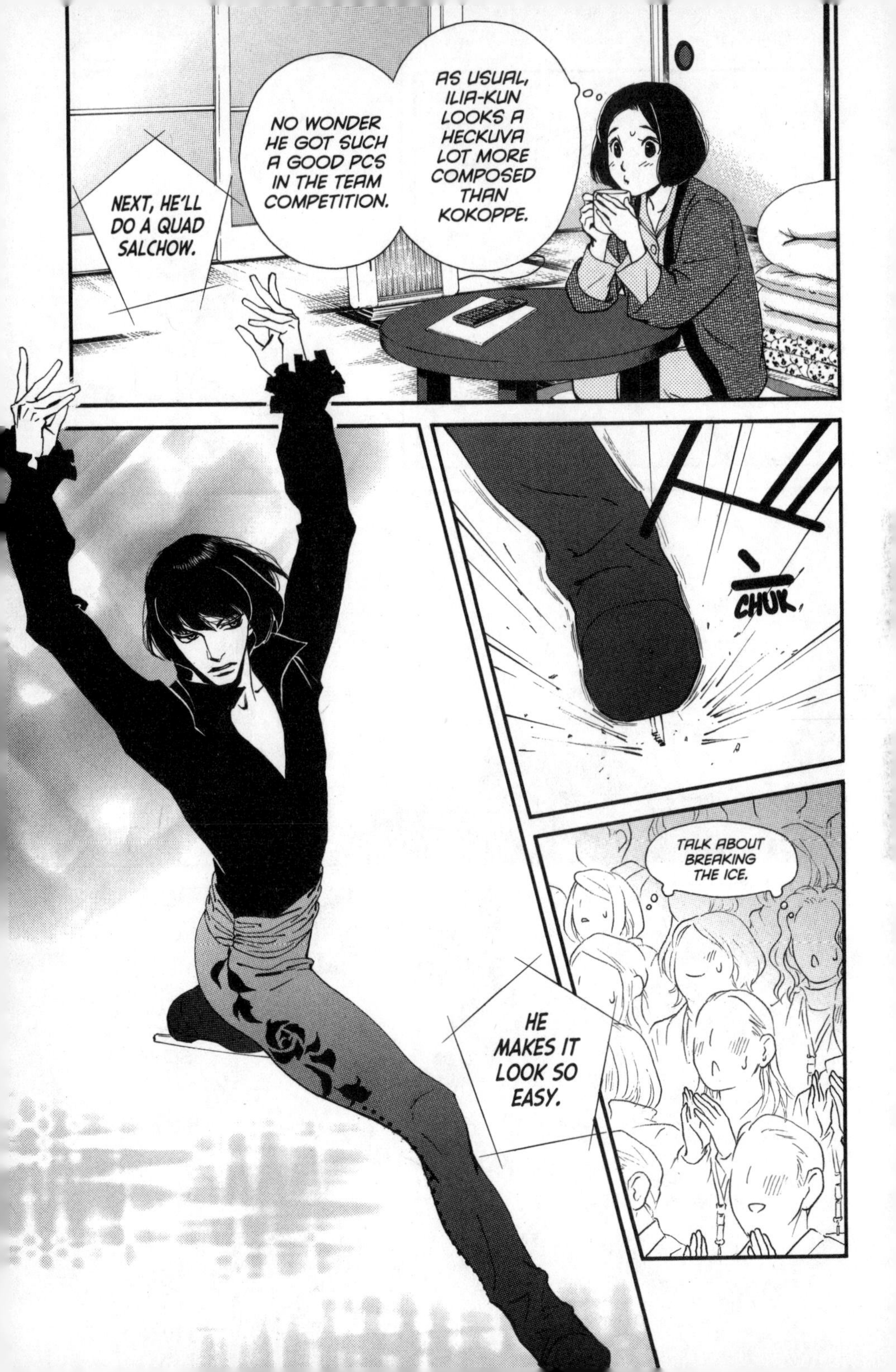

AS USUAL, ILIA-KUN LOOKS A HECKUVA LOT MORE COMPOSED THAN KOKOPPE.
NO WONDER HE GOT SUCH A GOOD PCS IN THE TEAM COMPETITION.
NEXT, HE'LL DO A QUAD SALCHOW.
CHUK
TALK ABOUT BREAKING THE ICE.
HE MAKES IT LOOK SO EASY.

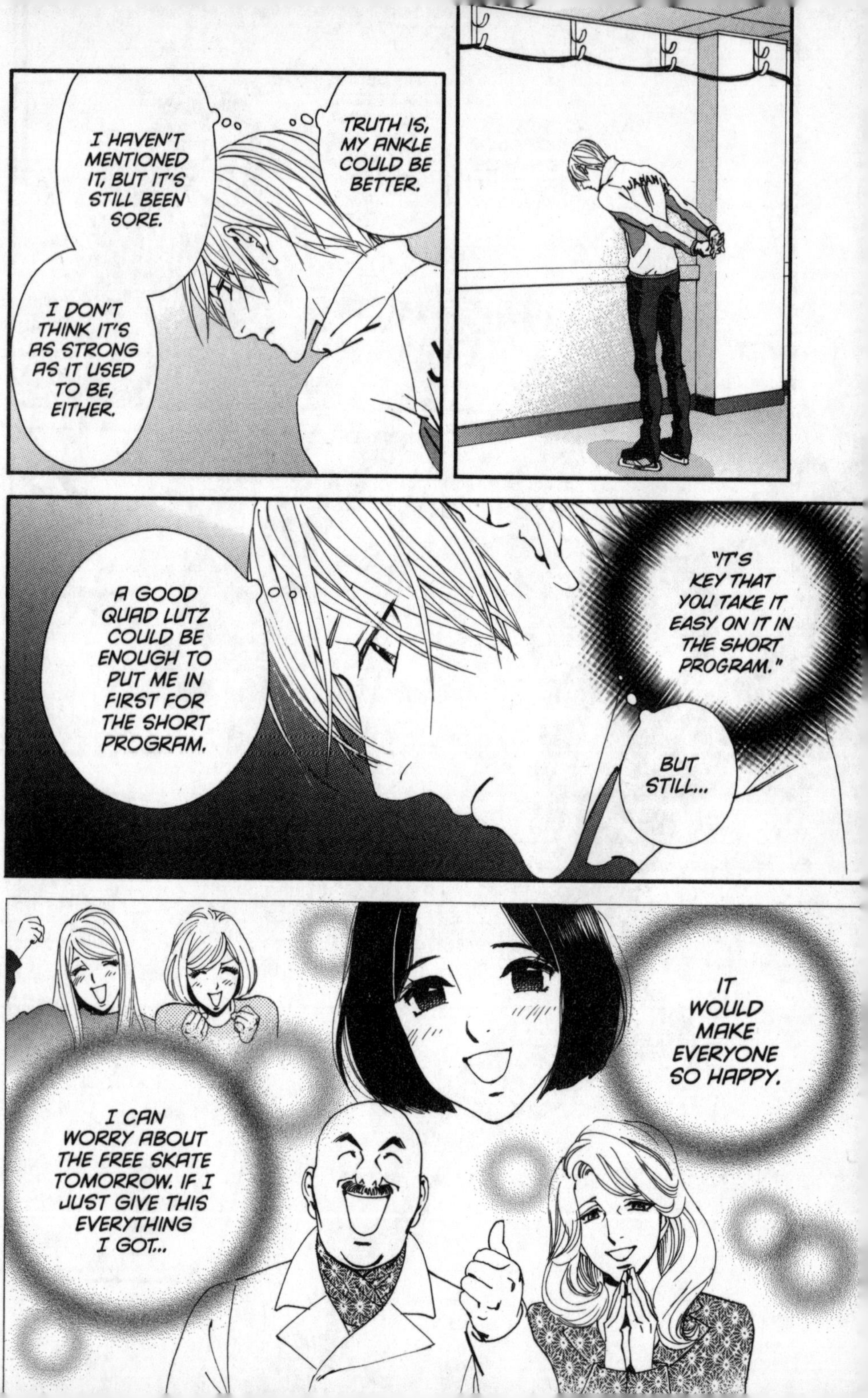
TRUTH IS, MY ANKLE COULD BE BETTER.
I HAVEN'T MENTIONED IT, BUT IT'S STILL BEEN SORE.
I DON'T THINK IT'S AS STRONG AS IT USED TO BE, EITHER.
JAPAN
"IT'S KEY THAT YOU TAKE IT EASY ON IT IN THE SHORT PROGRAM."
BUT STILL...
A GOOD QUAD LUTZ COULD BE ENOUGH TO PUT ME IN FIRST FOR THE SHORT PROGRAM.
IT WOULD MAKE EVERYONE SO HAPPY.
I CAN WORRY ABOUT THE FREE SKATE TOMORROW. IF I JUST GIVE THIS EVERYTHING I GOT...

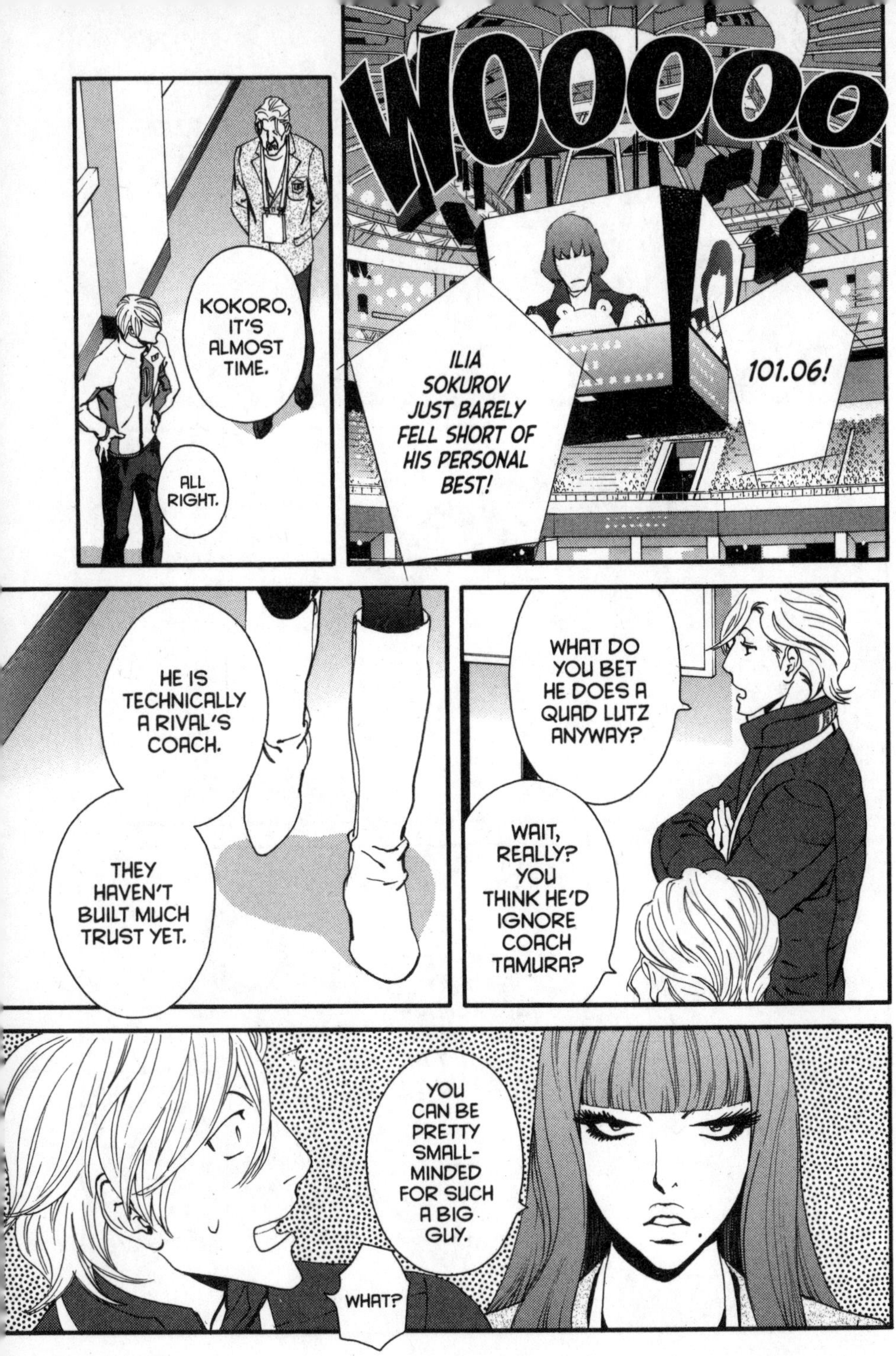
WOOOOO
ILIA SOKUROV JUST BARELY FELL SHORT OF HIS PERSONAL BEST!
101.06!
KOKORO, IT'S ALMOST TIME.
ALL RIGHT.
WHAT DO YOU BET HE DOES A QUAD LUTZ ANYWAY?
WAIT, REALLY? YOU THINK HE'D IGNORE COACH TAMURA?
HE IS TECHNICALLY A RIVAL'S COACH.
THEY HAVEN'T BUILT MUCH TRUST YET.
YOU CAN BE PRETTY SMALL-MINDED FOR SUCH A BIG GUY.
WHAT?

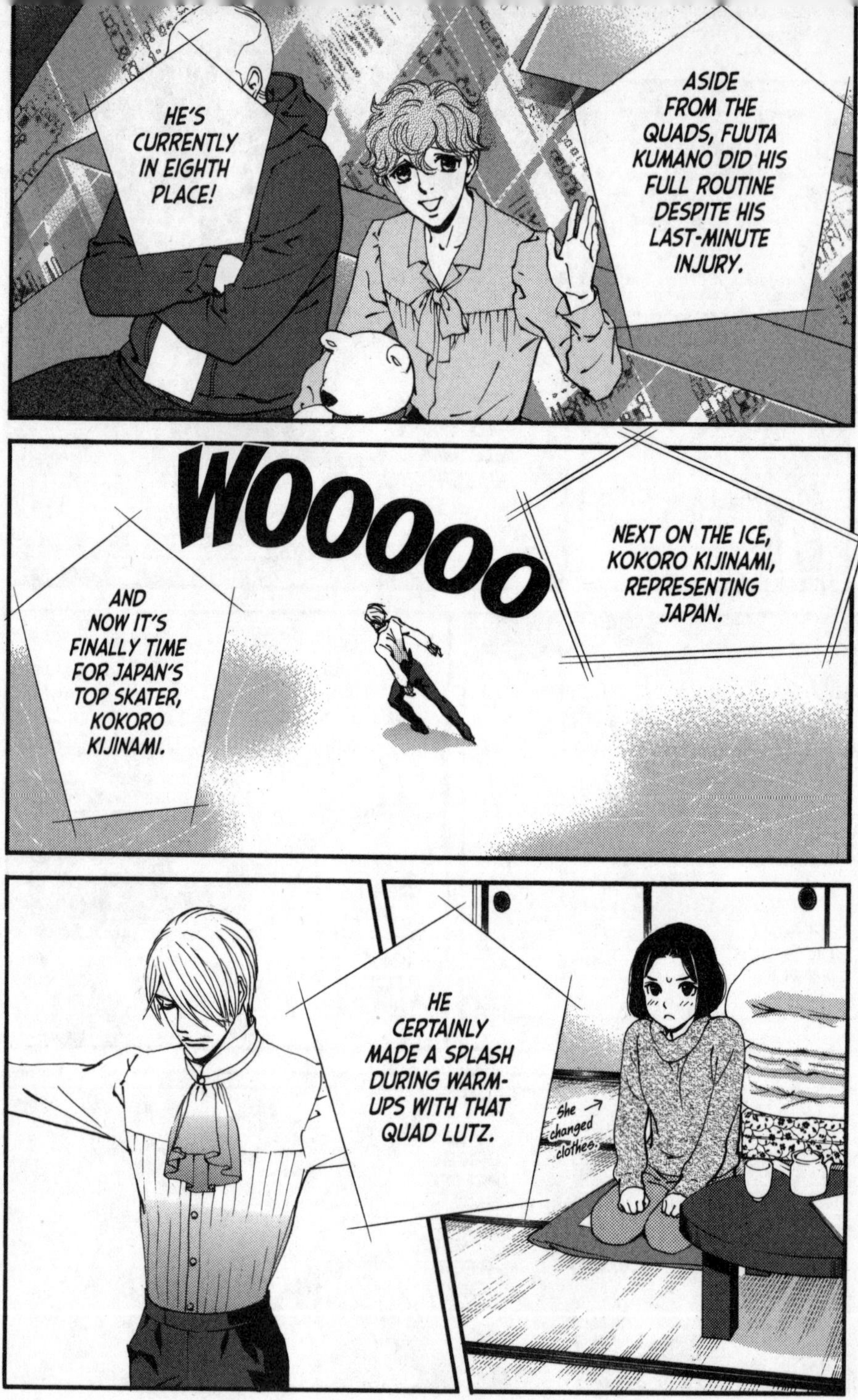
ASIDE FROM THE QUADS, FUUTA KUMANO DID HIS FULL ROUTINE DESPITE HIS LAST-MINUTE INJURY.
HE'S CURRENTLY IN EIGHTH PLACE!
NEXT ON THE ICE, KOKORO KIJINAMI, REPRESENTING JAPAN.
WOOOOO
AND NOW IT'S FINALLY TIME FOR JAPAN'S TOP SKATER, KOKORO KIJINAMI.
She changed clothes.
HE CERTAINLY MADE A SPLASH DURING WARM-UPS WITH THAT QUAD LUTZ.

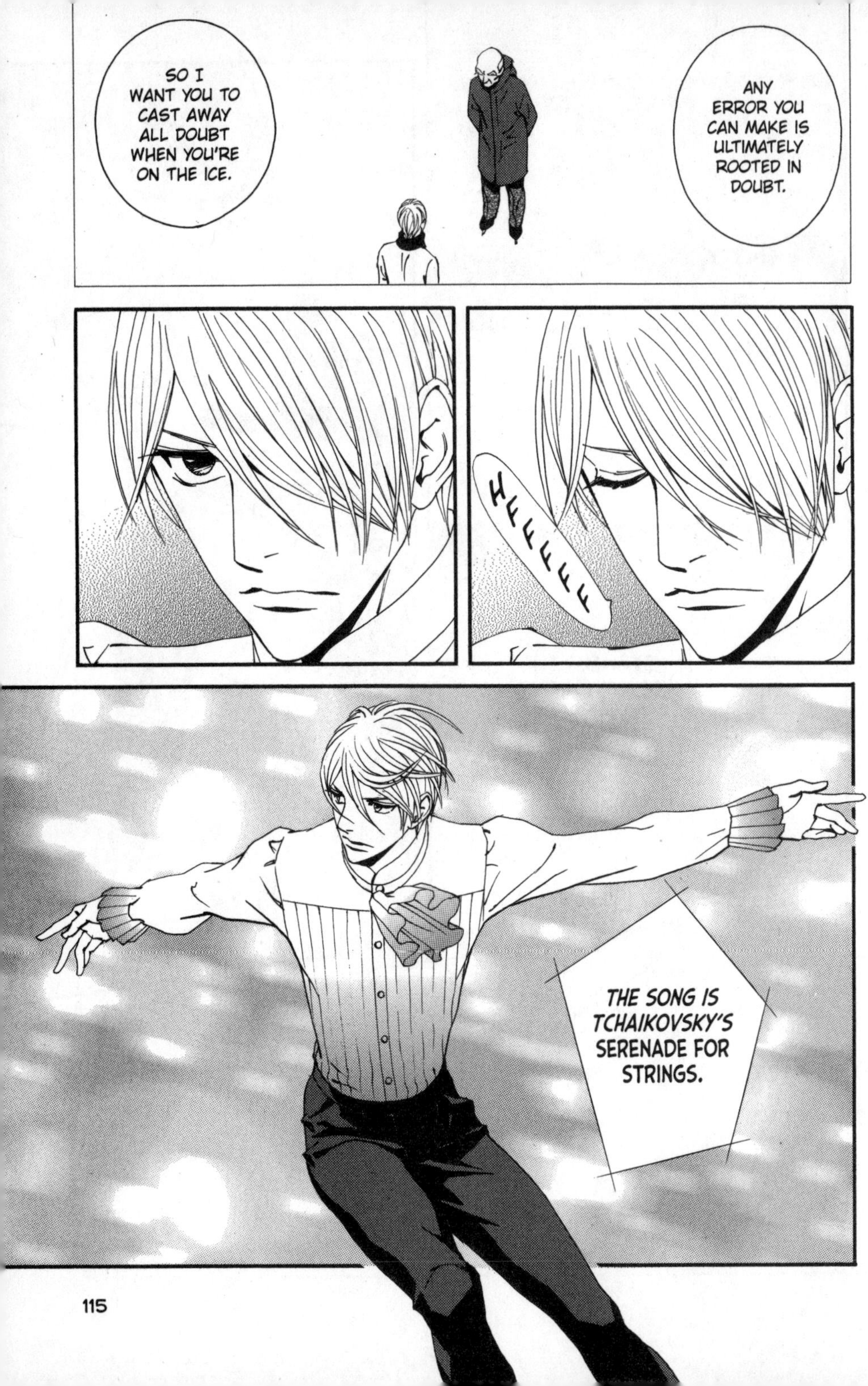
ANY ERROR YOU CAN MAKE IS ULTIMATELY ROOTED IN DOUBT.
SO I WANT YOU TO CAST AWAY ALL DOUBT WHEN YOU'RE ON THE ICE.
HFFFFFF
THE SONG IS TCHAIKOVSKY'S SERENADE FOR STRINGS.

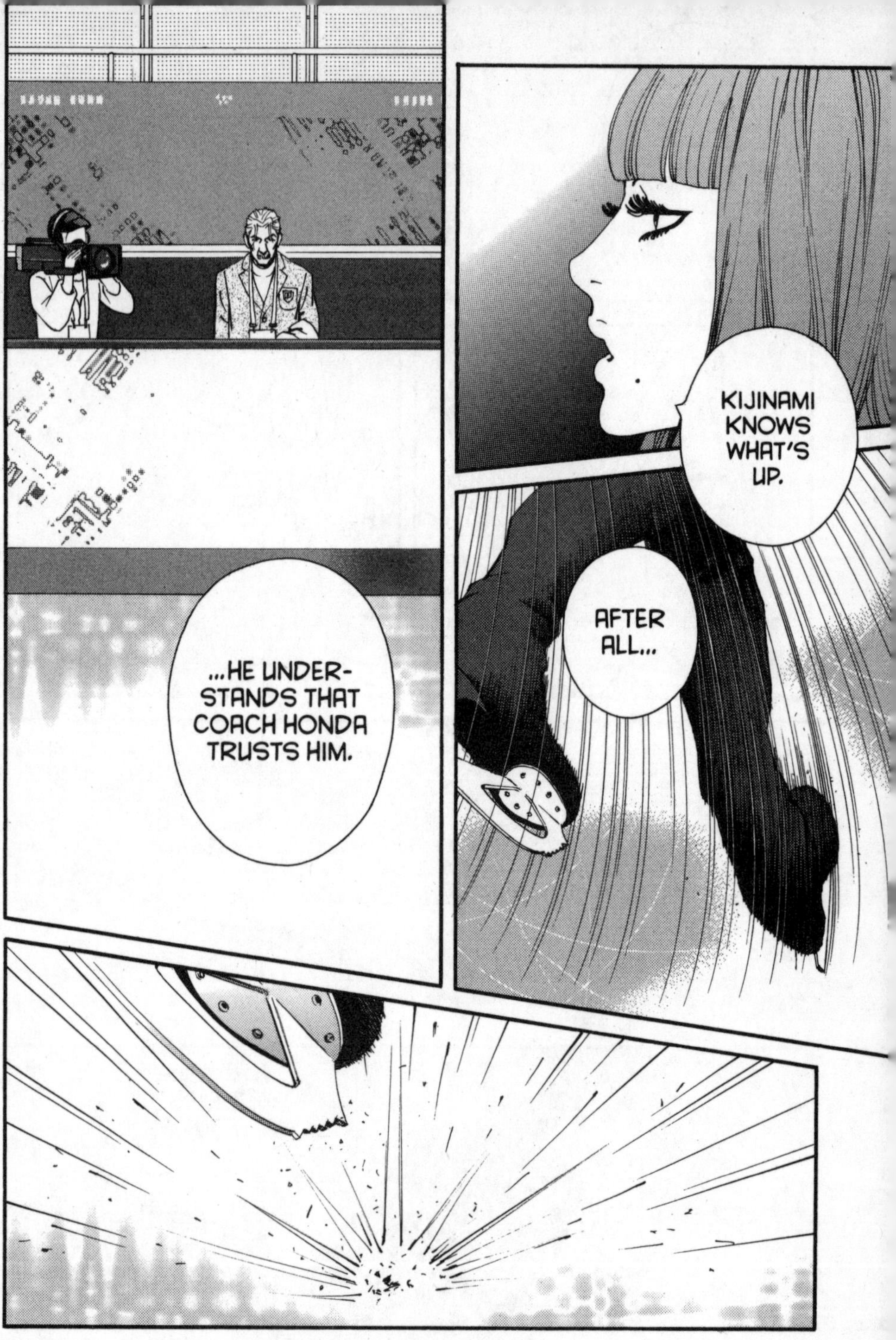
KIJINAMI KNOWS WHAT'S UP.
AFTER ALL...
...HE UNDER-STANDS THAT COACH HONDA TRUSTS HIM.

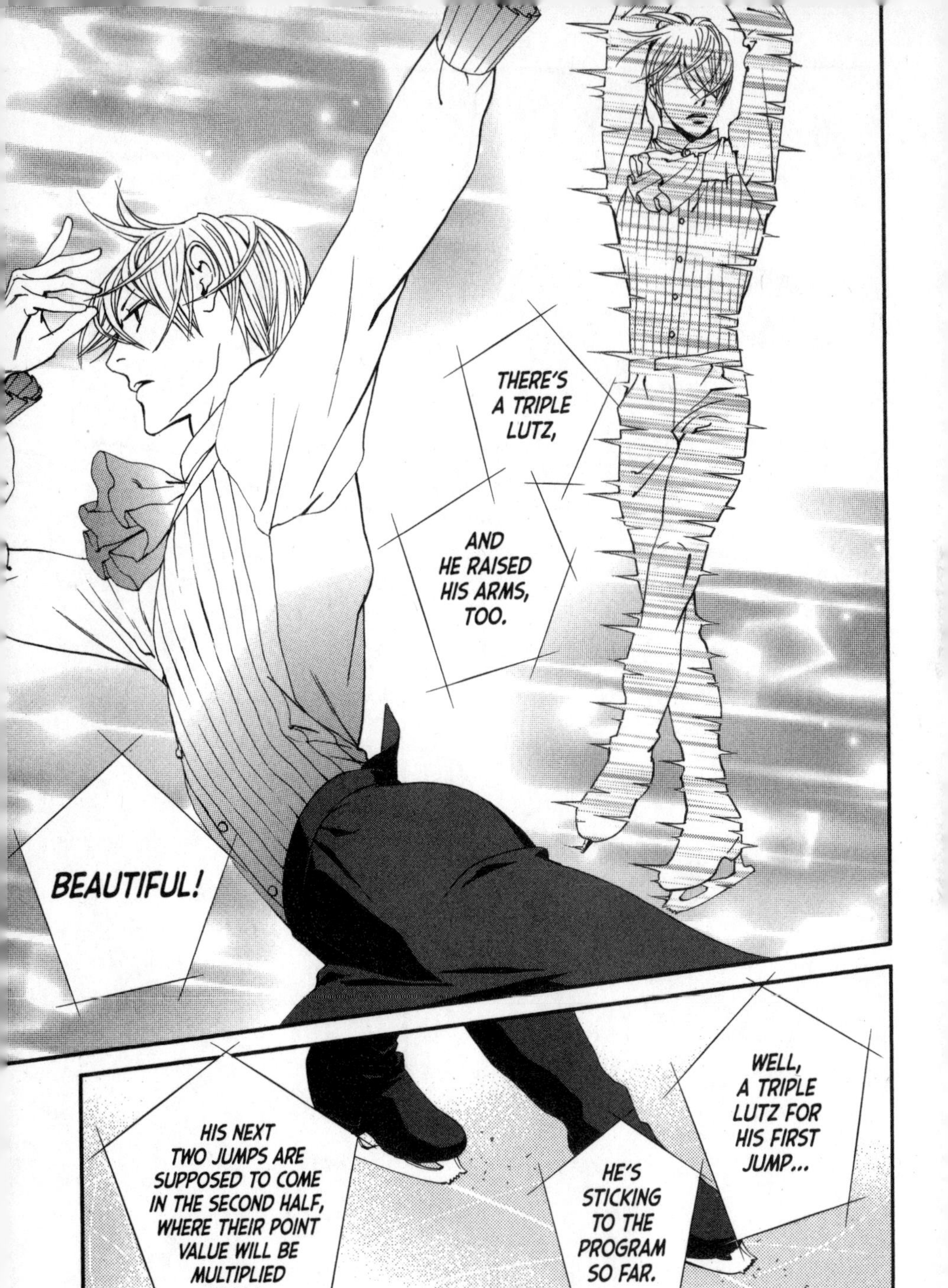
THERE'S A TRIPLE LUTZ,
AND HE RAISED HIS ARMS, TOO.
BEAUTIFUL!
WELL, A TRIPLE LUTZ FOR HIS FIRST JUMP...
HE'S STICKING TO THE PROGRAM SO FAR.
HIS NEXT TWO JUMPS ARE SUPPOSED TO COME IN THE SECOND HALF, WHERE THEIR POINT VALUE WILL BE MULTIPLIED BY 1.1.

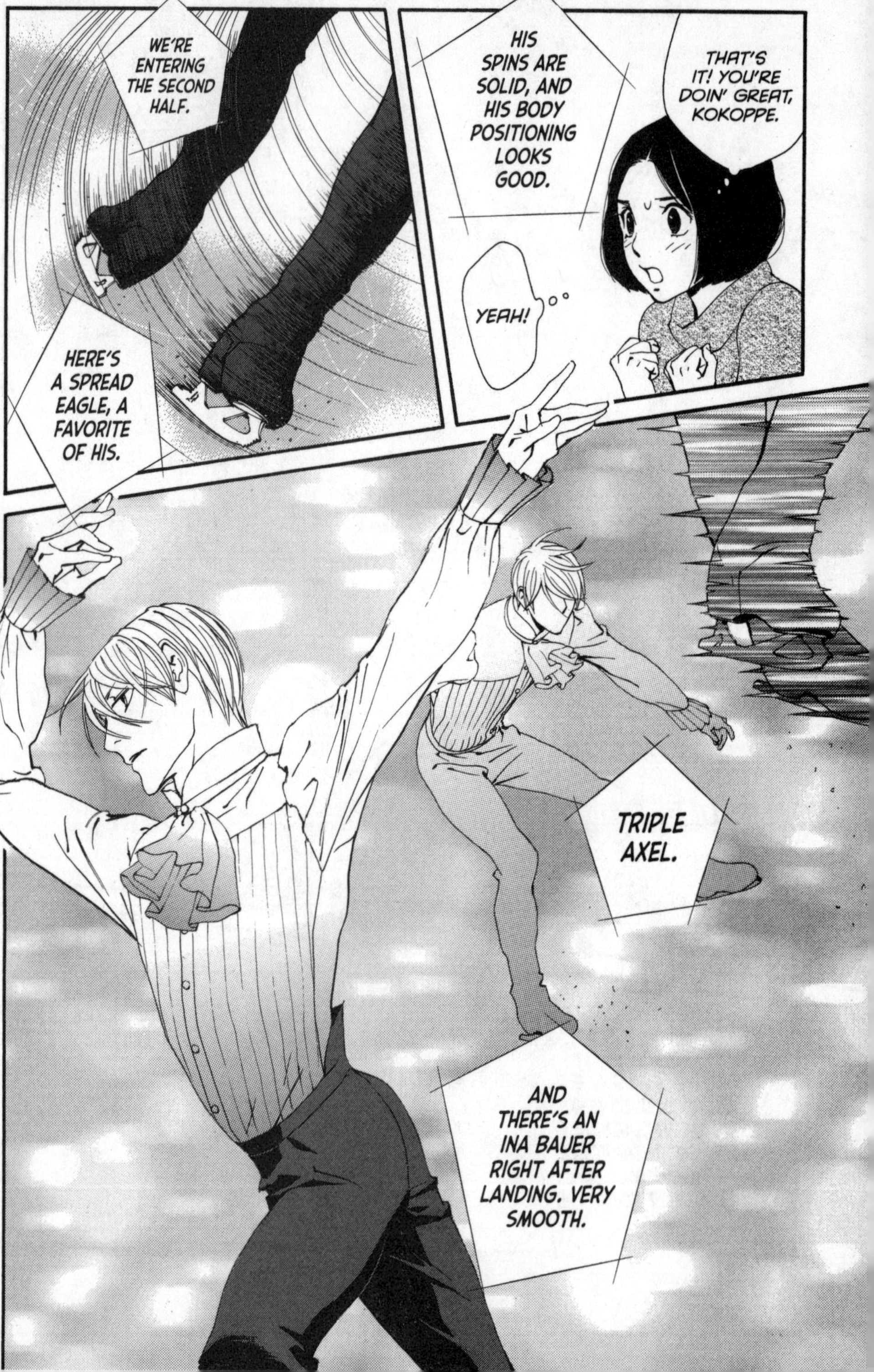
THAT'S IT! YOU'RE DOIN' GREAT, KOKOPPE.
HIS SPINS ARE SOLID, AND HIS BODY POSITIONING LOOKS GOOD.
YEAH!
WE'RE ENTERING THE SECOND HALF.
HERE'S A SPREAD EAGLE, A FAVORITE OF HIS.
TRIPLE AXEL.
AND THERE'S AN INA BAUER RIGHT AFTER LANDING. VERY SMOOTH.

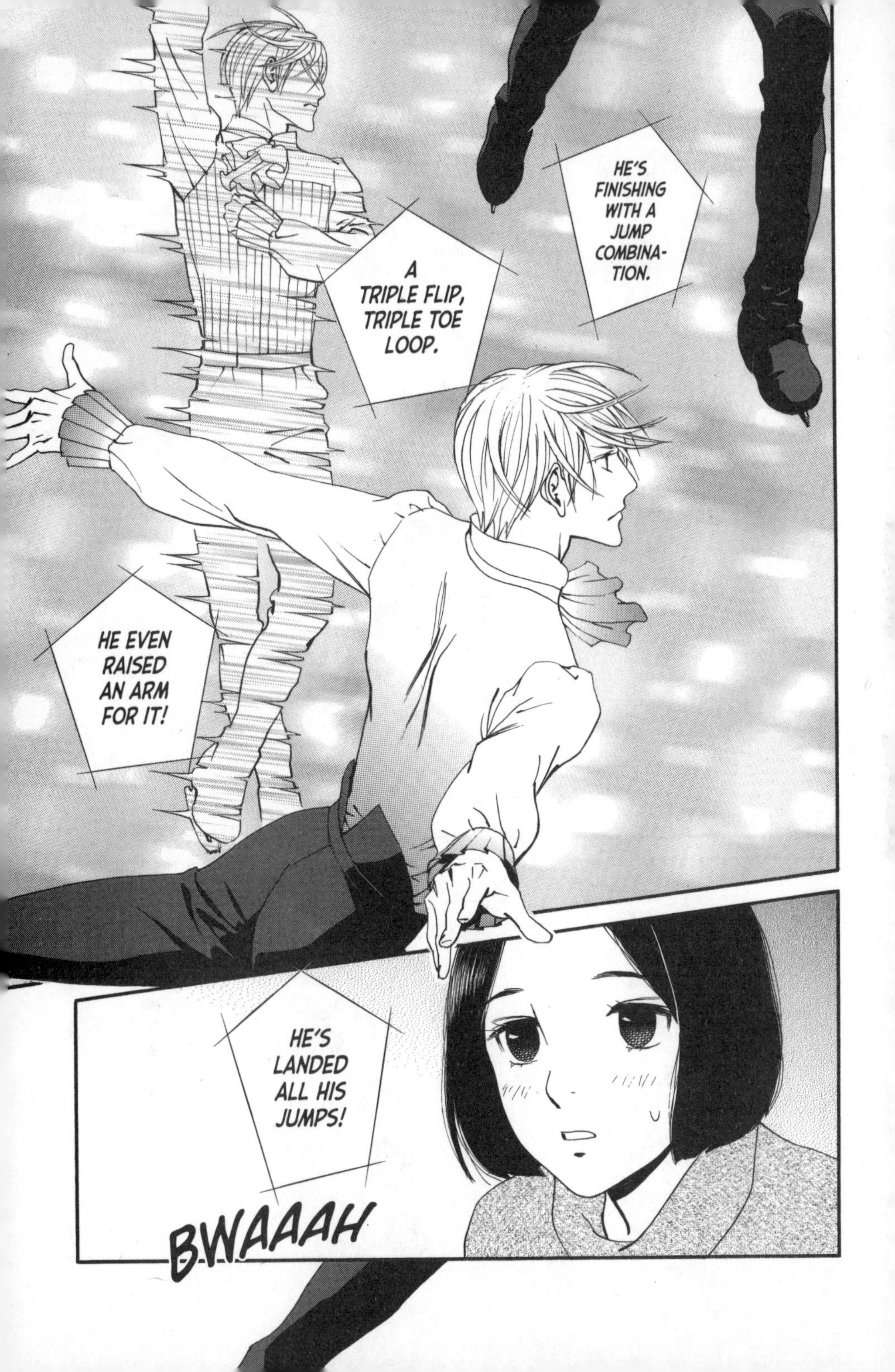
HE'S FINISHING WITH A JUMP COMBINATION.
A TRIPLE FLIP, TRIPLE TOE LOOP.
HE EVEN RAISED AN ARM FOR IT!
HE'S LANDED ALL HIS JUMPS!
BWAAAH

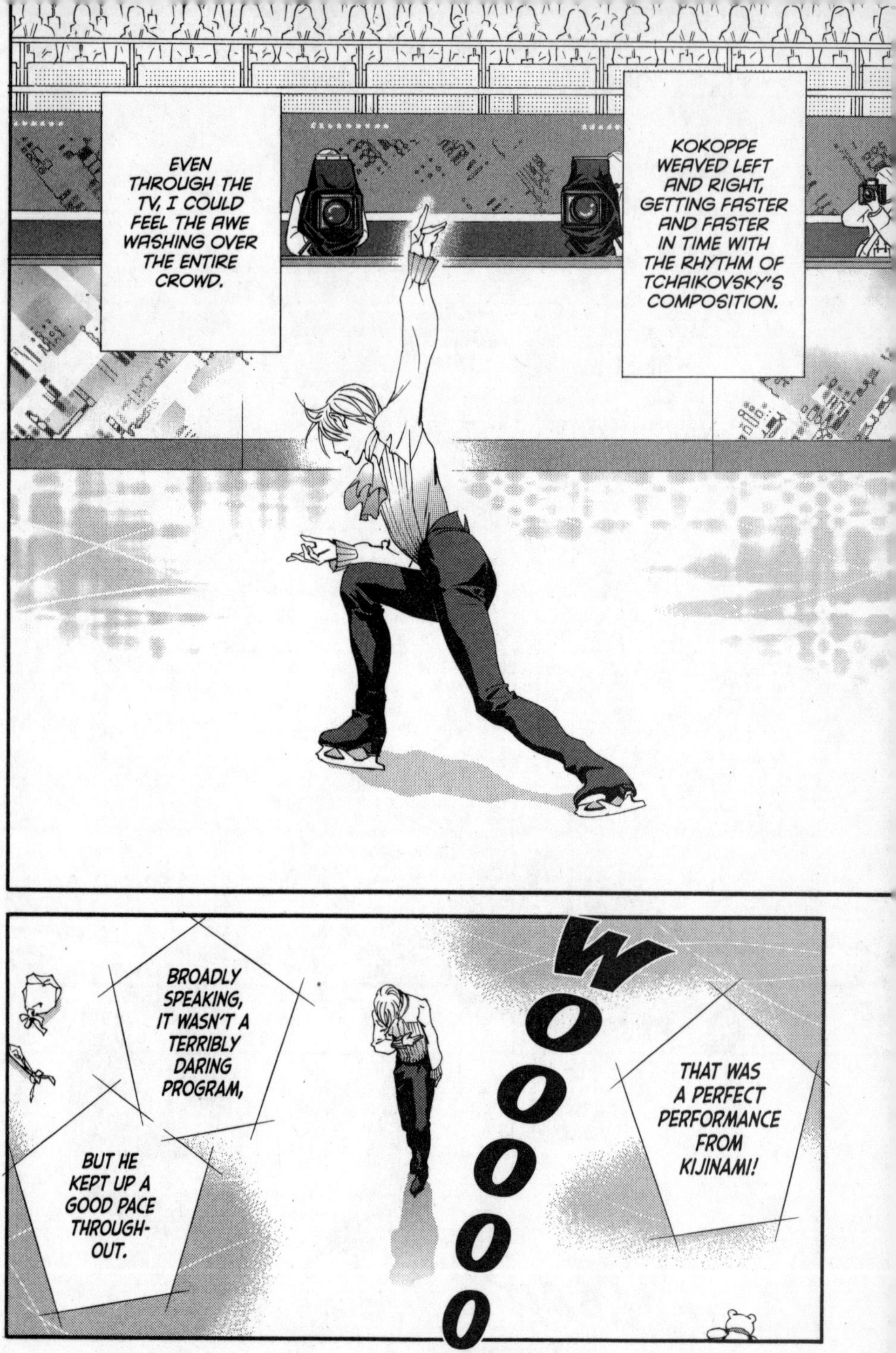
KOKOPPE WEAVED LEFT AND RIGHT, GETTING FASTER AND FASTER IN TIME WITH THE RHYTHM OF TCHAIKOVSKY'S COMPOSITION.
EVEN THROUGH THE TV, I COULD FEEL THE AWE WASHING OVER THE ENTIRE CROWD.
THAT WAS A PERFECT PERFORMANCE FROM KIJINAMI!
WOOOOOO
BROADLY SPEAKING, IT WASN'T A TERRIBLY DARING PROGRAM,
BUT HE KEPT UP A GOOD PACE THROUGH-OUT.

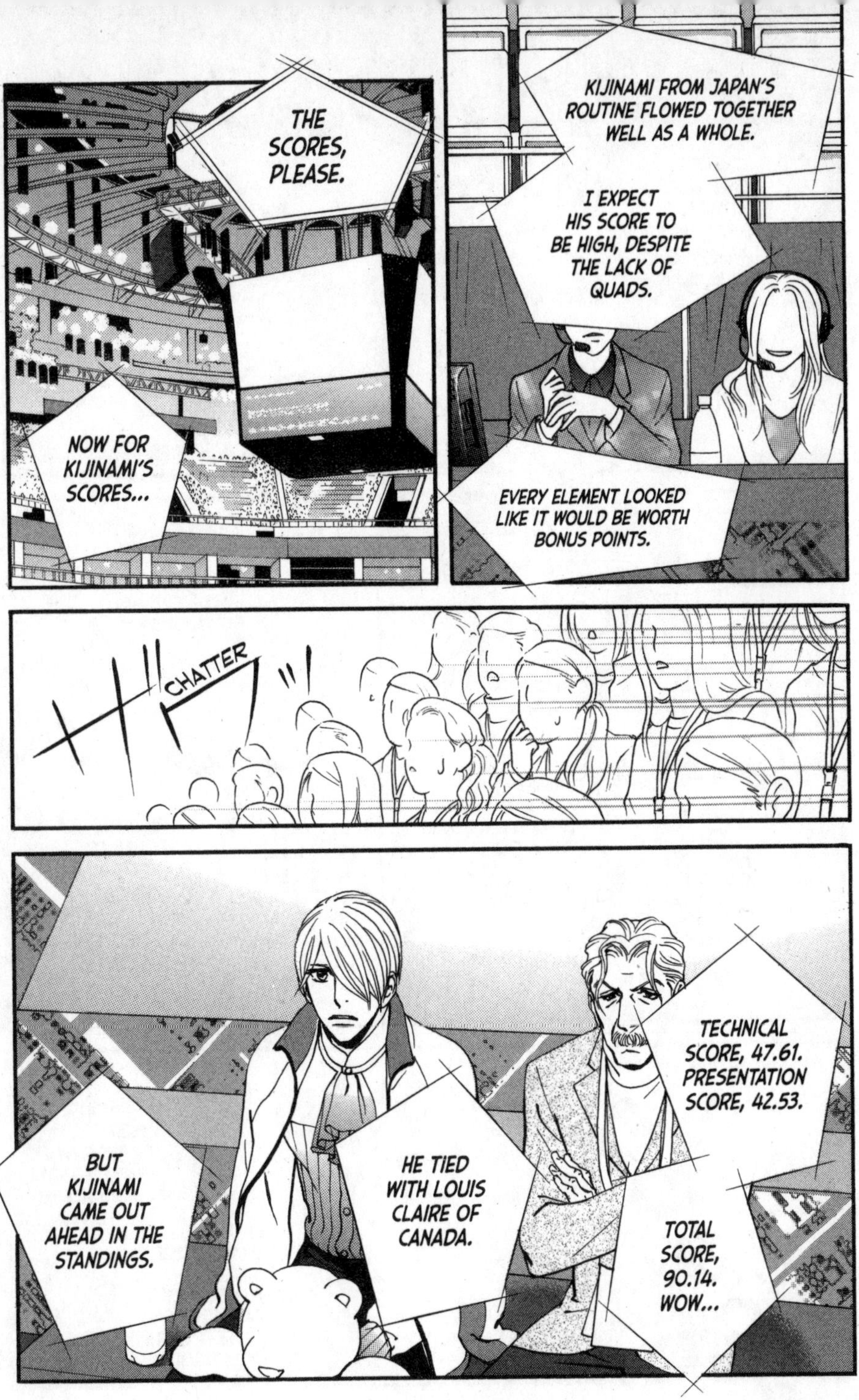
KIJINAMI FROM JAPAN'S ROUTINE FLOWED TOGETHER WELL AS A WHOLE.
I EXPECT HIS SCORE TO BE HIGH, DESPITE THE LACK OF QUADS.
EVERY ELEMENT LOOKED LIKE IT WOULD BE WORTH BONUS POINTS.
THE SCORES, PLEASE.
NOW FOR KIJINAMI'S SCORES...
CHATTER
TECHNICAL SCORE, 47.61. PRESENTATION SCORE, 42.53.
TOTAL SCORE, 90.14. WOW...
HE TIED WITH LOUIS CLAIRE OF CANADA.
BUT KIJINAMI CAME OUT AHEAD IN THE STANDINGS.

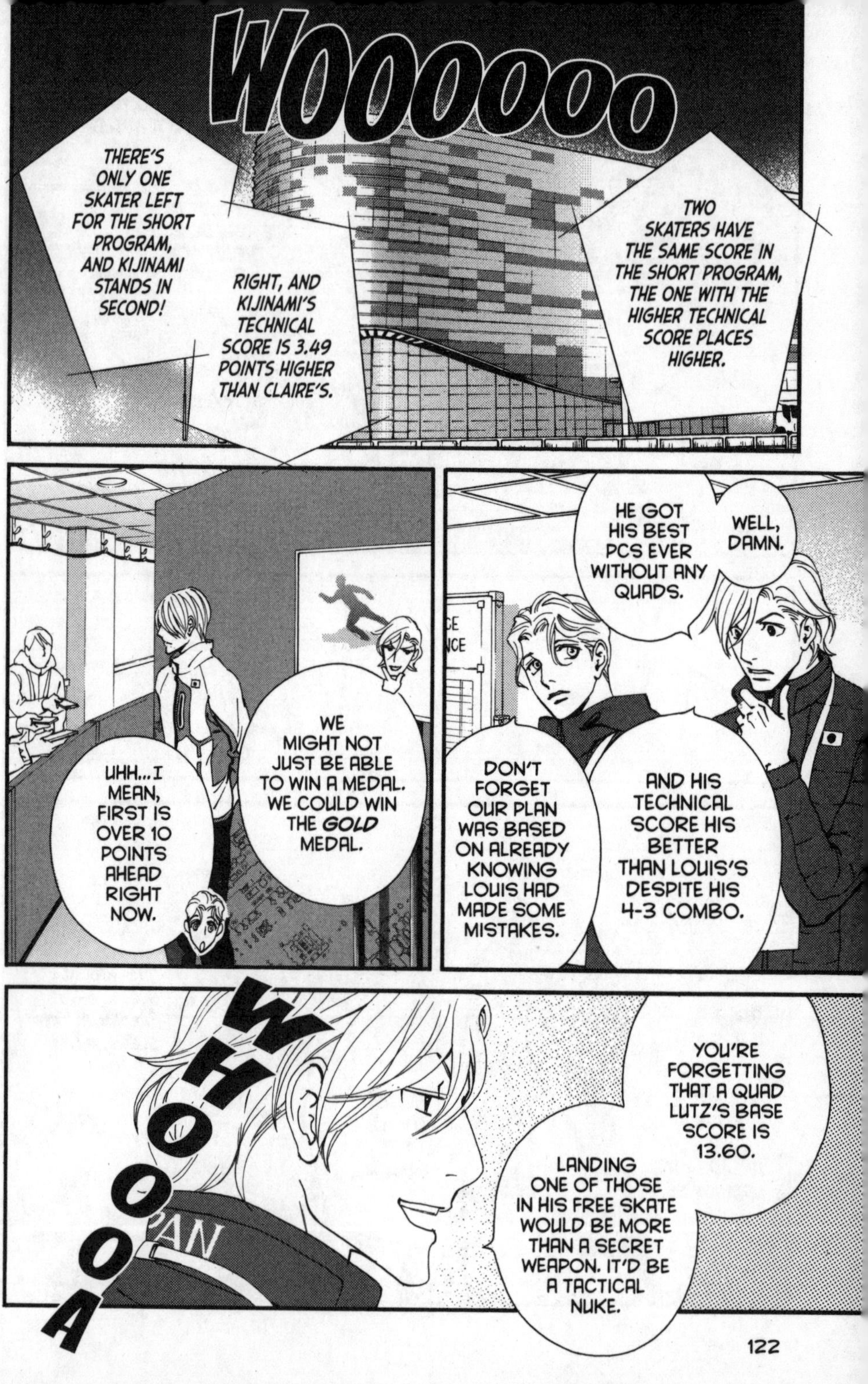
WOOOOOO
TWO SKATERS HAVE THE SAME SCORE IN THE SHORT PROGRAM, THE ONE WITH THE HIGHER TECHNICAL SCORE PLACES HIGHER.
RIGHT, AND KIJINAMI'S TECHNICAL SCORE IS 3.49 POINTS HIGHER THAN CLAIRE'S.
THERE'S ONLY ONE SKATER LEFT FOR THE SHORT PROGRAM, AND KIJINAMI STANDS IN SECOND!
WELL, DAMN.
HE GOT HIS BEST PCS EVER WITHOUT ANY QUADS.
AND HIS TECHNICAL SCORE HIS BETTER THAN LOUIS'S DESPITE HIS 4-3 COMBO.
DON'T FORGET OUR PLAN WAS BASED ON ALREADY KNOWING LOUIS HAD MADE SOME MISTAKES.
WE MIGHT NOT JUST BE ABLE TO WIN A MEDAL. WE COULD WIN THE *GOLD* MEDAL.
UHH...I MEAN, FIRST IS OVER 10 POINTS AHEAD RIGHT NOW.
WHOOOOA
YOU'RE FORGETTING THAT A QUAD LUTZ'S BASE SCORE IS 13.60.
LANDING ONE OF THOSE IN HIS FREE SKATE WOULD BE MORE THAN A SECRET WEAPON. IT'D BE A TACTICAL NUKE.

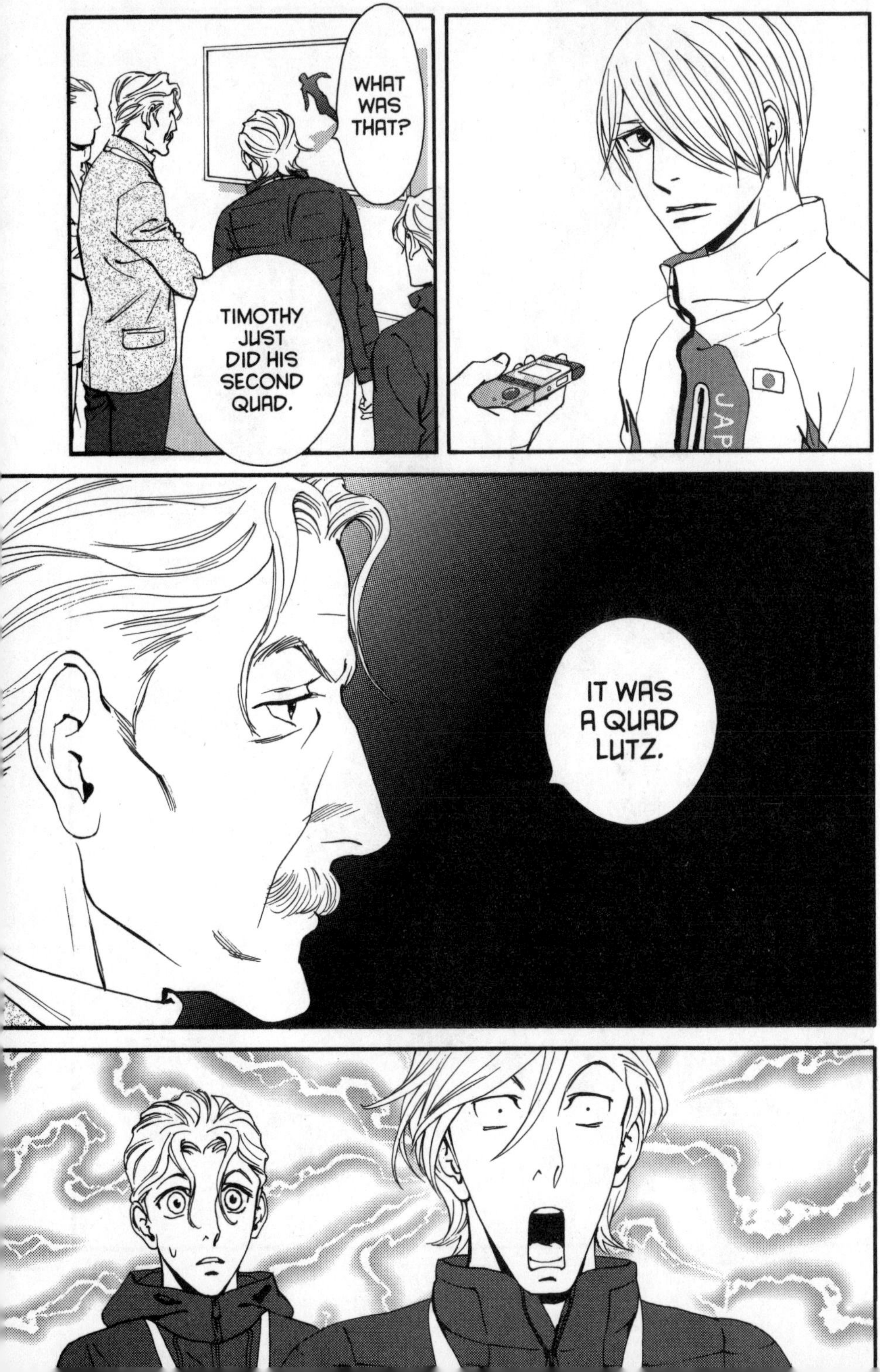
WHAT WAS THAT?
TIMOTHY JUST DID HIS SECOND QUAD.
IT WAS A QUAD LUTZ.

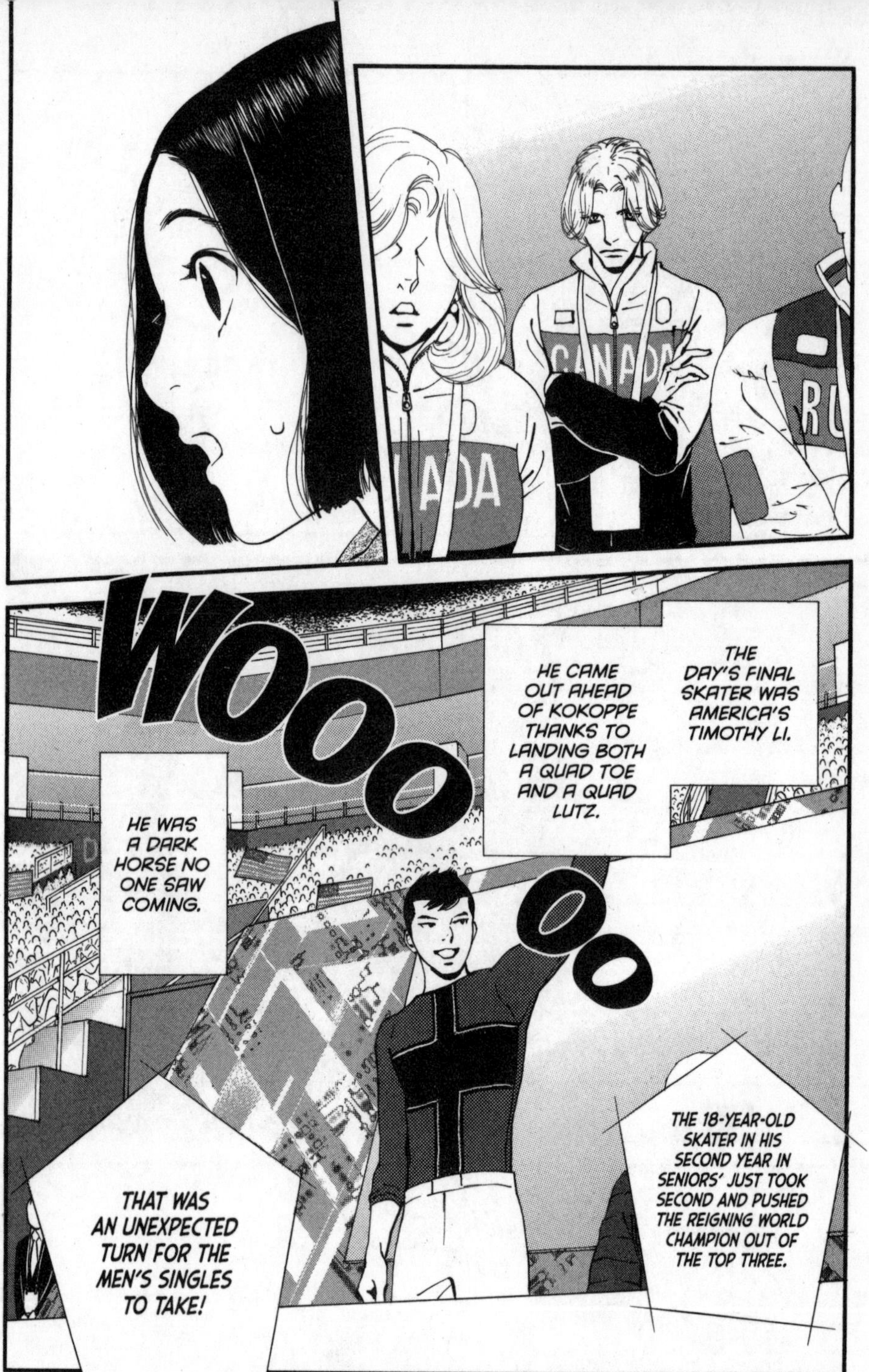
CANADA
THE DAY'S FINAL SKATER WAS AMERICA'S TIMOTHY LI.
HE CAME OUT AHEAD OF KOKOPPE THANKS TO LANDING BOTH A QUAD TOE AND A QUAD LUTZ.
WOOOOOO
HE WAS A DARK HORSE NO ONE SAW COMING.
THE 18-YEAR-OLD SKATER IN HIS SECOND YEAR IN SENIORS' JUST TOOK SECOND AND PUSHED THE REIGNING WORLD CHAMPION OUT OF THE TOP THREE.
THAT WAS AN UNEXPECTED TURN FOR THE MEN'S SINGLES TO TAKE!

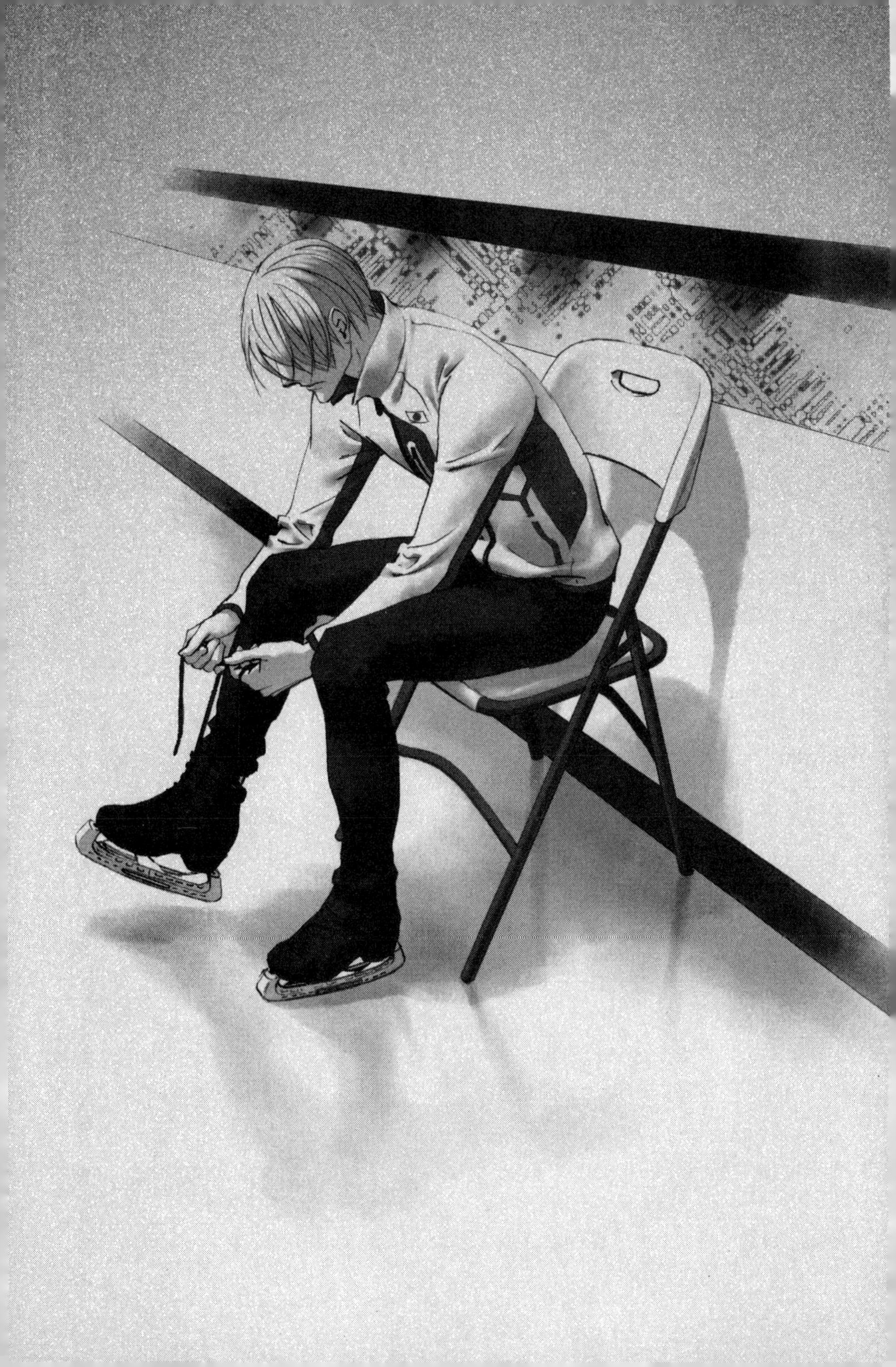

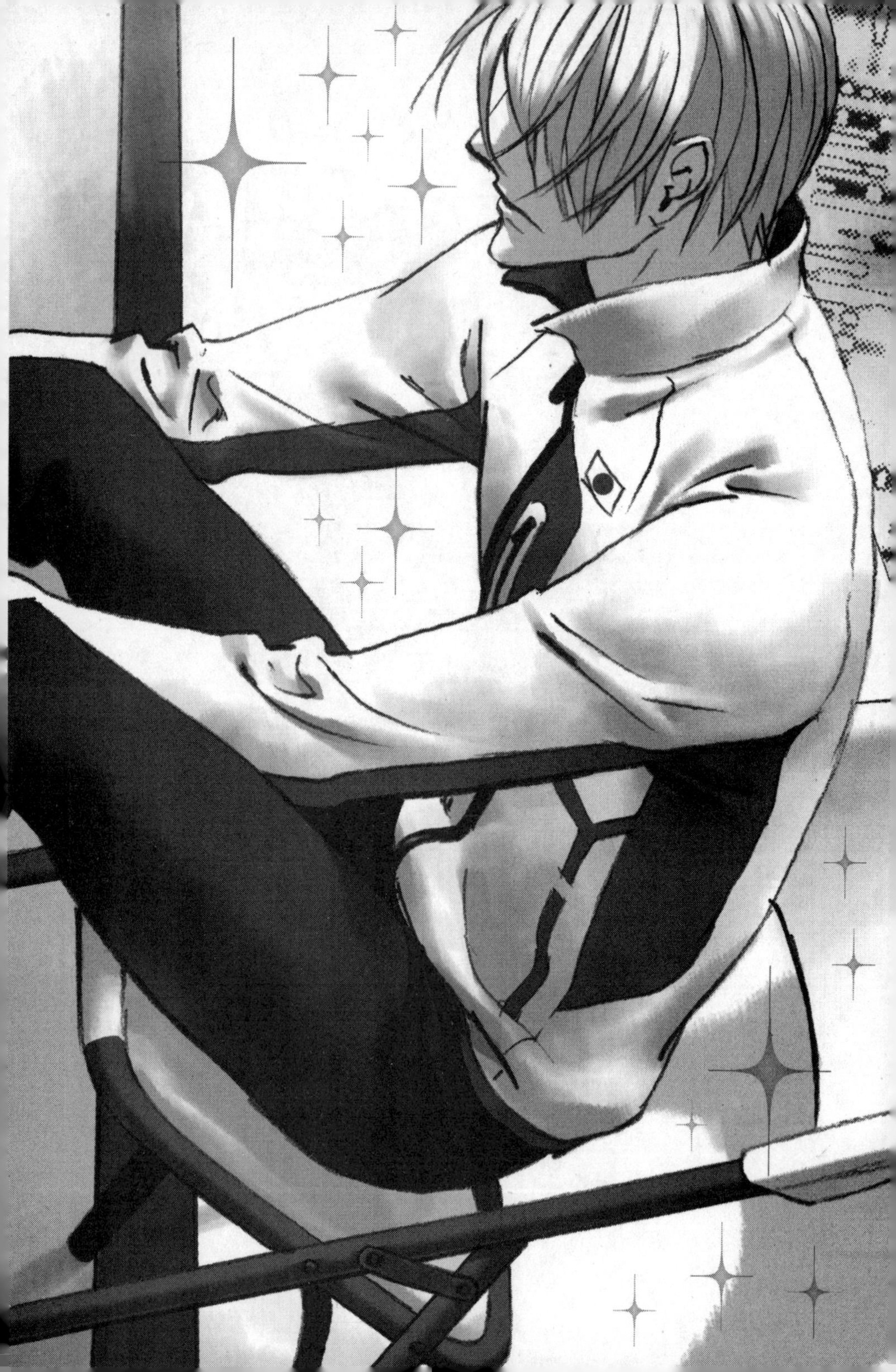

Spell 51
The Courage You Gave Me

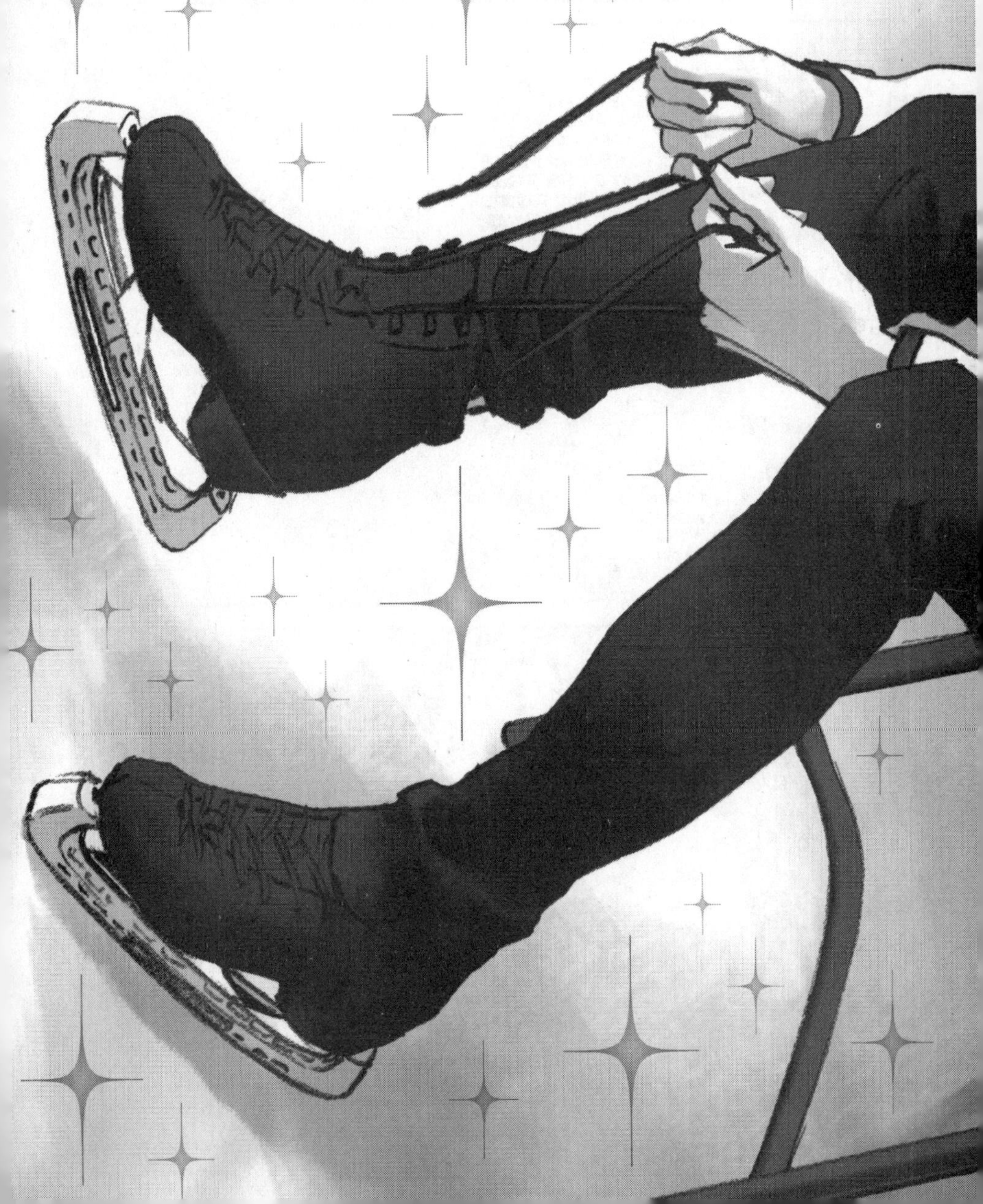

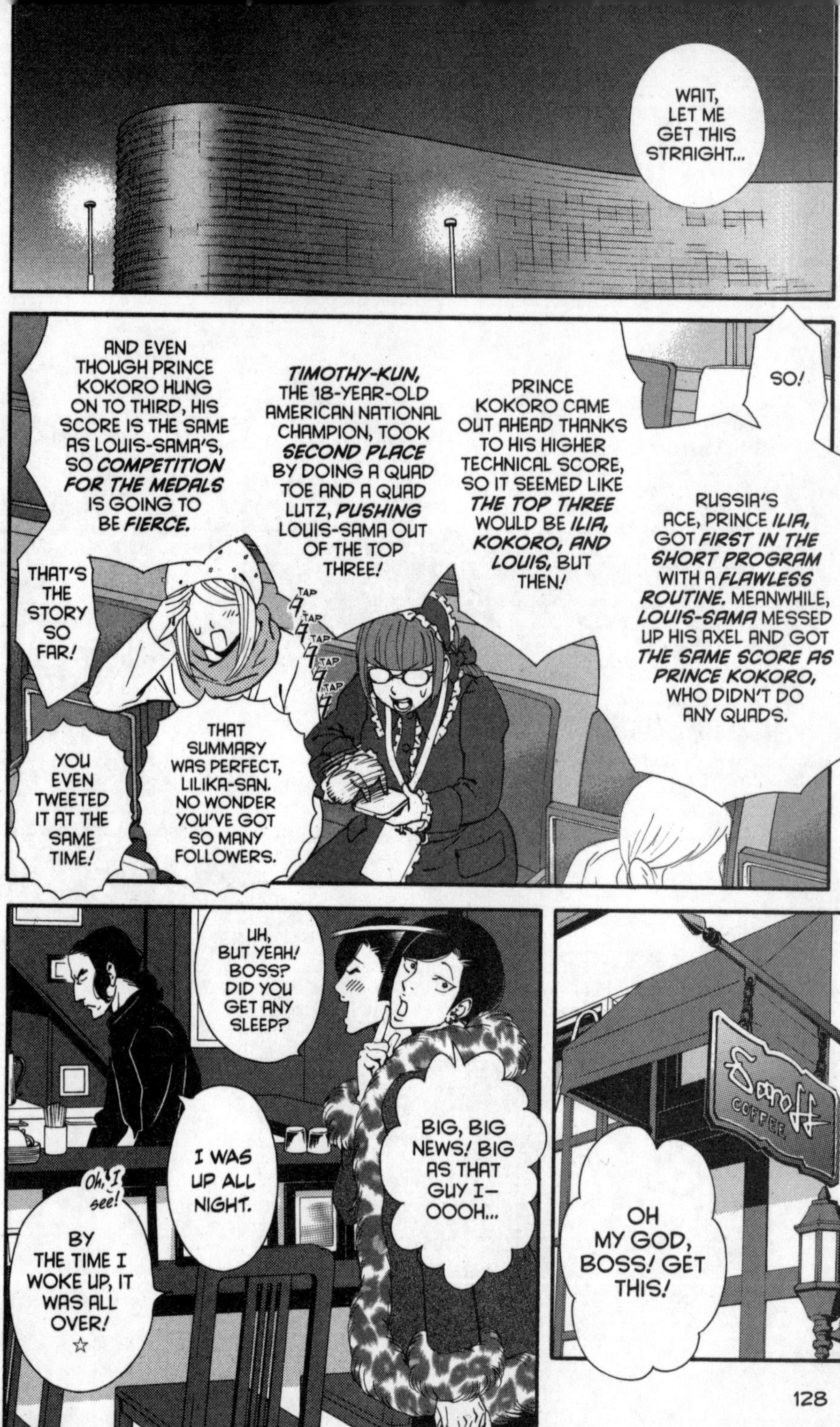
WAIT, LET ME GET THIS STRAIGHT...
SO!
RUSSIA'S ACE, PRINCE ILIA, GOT FIRST IN THE SHORT PROGRAM WITH A FLAWLESS ROUTINE. MEANWHILE, LOUIS-SAMA MESSED UP HIS AXEL AND GOT THE SAME SCORE AS PRINCE KOKORO, WHO DIDN'T DO ANY QUADS.
PRINCE KOKORO CAME OUT AHEAD THANKS TO HIS HIGHER TECHNICAL SCORE, SO IT SEEMED LIKE THE TOP THREE WOULD BE ILIA, KOKORO, AND LOUIS, BUT THEN!
TIMOTHY-KUN, THE 18-YEAR-OLD AMERICAN NATIONAL CHAMPION, TOOK SECOND PLACE BY DOING A QUAD TOE AND A QUAD LUTZ, PUSHING LOUIS-SAMA OUT OF THE TOP THREE!
TAP TAP TAP TAP
AND EVEN THOUGH PRINCE KOKORO HUNG ON TO THIRD, HIS SCORE IS THE SAME AS LOUIS-SAMA'S, SO COMPETITION FOR THE MEDALS IS GOING TO BE FIERCE.
THAT'S THE STORY SO FAR!
THAT SUMMARY WAS PERFECT, LILIKA-SAN. NO WONDER YOU'VE GOT SO MANY FOLLOWERS.
YOU EVEN TWEETED IT AT THE SAME TIME!
COFFEE
OH MY GOD, BOSS! GET THIS!
BIG, BIG NEWS! BIG AS THAT GUY I— OOOH...
UH, BUT YEAH! BOSS? DID YOU GET ANY SLEEP?
I WAS UP ALL NIGHT.
Oh, I see!
BY THE TIME I WOKE UP, IT WAS ALL OVER! ☆

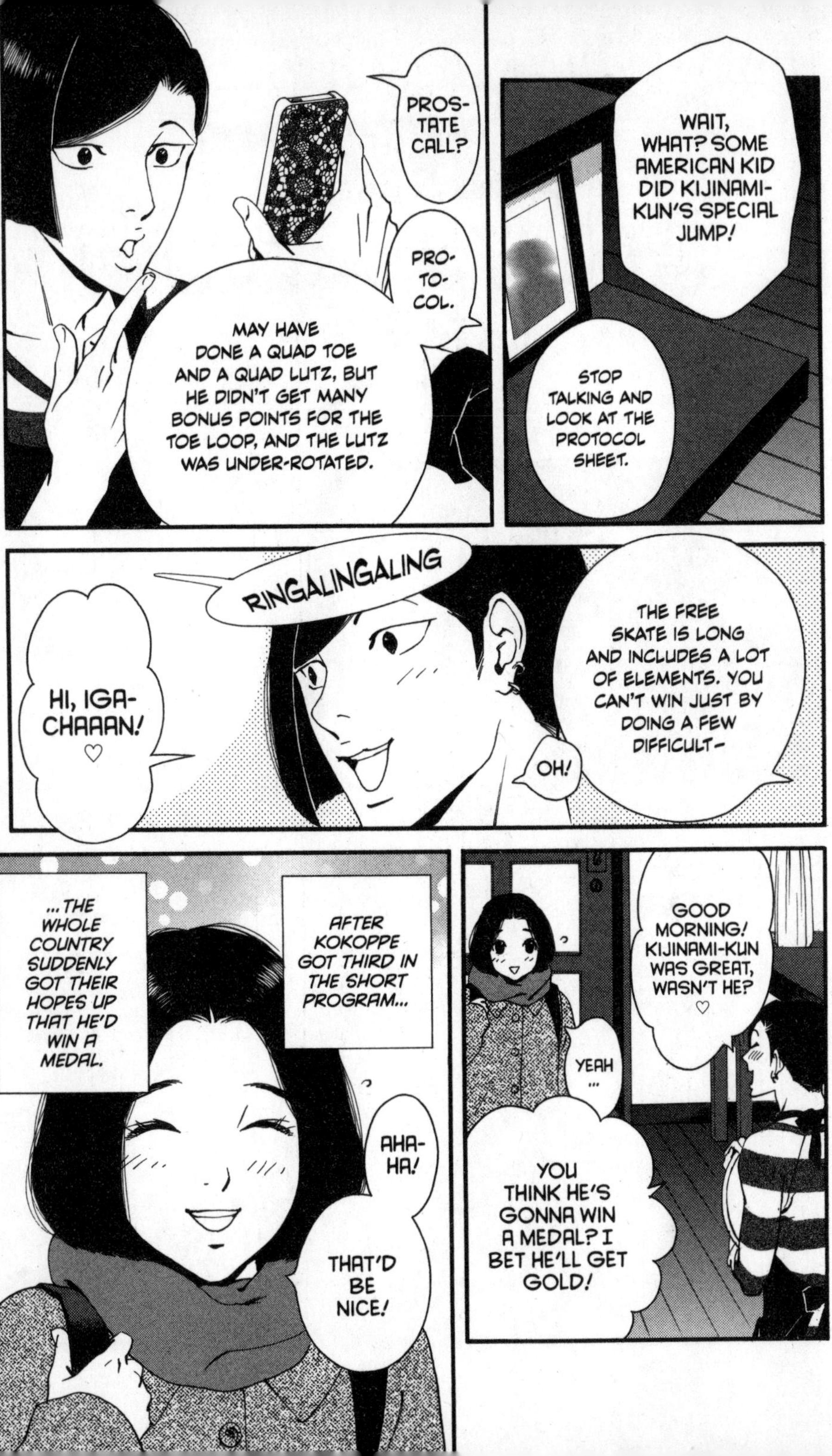
WAIT, WHAT? SOME AMERICAN KID DID KIJINAMI-KUN'S SPECIAL JUMP!
STOP TALKING AND LOOK AT THE PROTOCOL SHEET.
PROS-TATE CALL?
PRO-TO-COL.
MAY HAVE DONE A QUAD TOE AND A QUAD LUTZ, BUT HE DIDN'T GET MANY BONUS POINTS FOR THE TOE LOOP, AND THE LUTZ WAS UNDER-ROTATED.
THE FREE SKATE IS LONG AND INCLUDES A LOT OF ELEMENTS. YOU CAN'T WIN JUST BY DOING A FEW DIFFICULT-
OH!
RINGALINGALING
HI, IGA-CHAAAN! ♡
GOOD MORNING! KIJINAMI-KUN WAS GREAT, WASN'T HE? ♡
YEAH ...
YOU THINK HE'S GONNA WIN A MEDAL? I BET HE'LL GET GOLD!
AFTER KOKOPPE GOT THIRD IN THE SHORT PROGRAM...
...THE WHOLE COUNTRY SUDDENLY GOT THEIR HOPES UP THAT HE'D WIN A MEDAL.
AHA-HA!
THAT'D BE NICE!

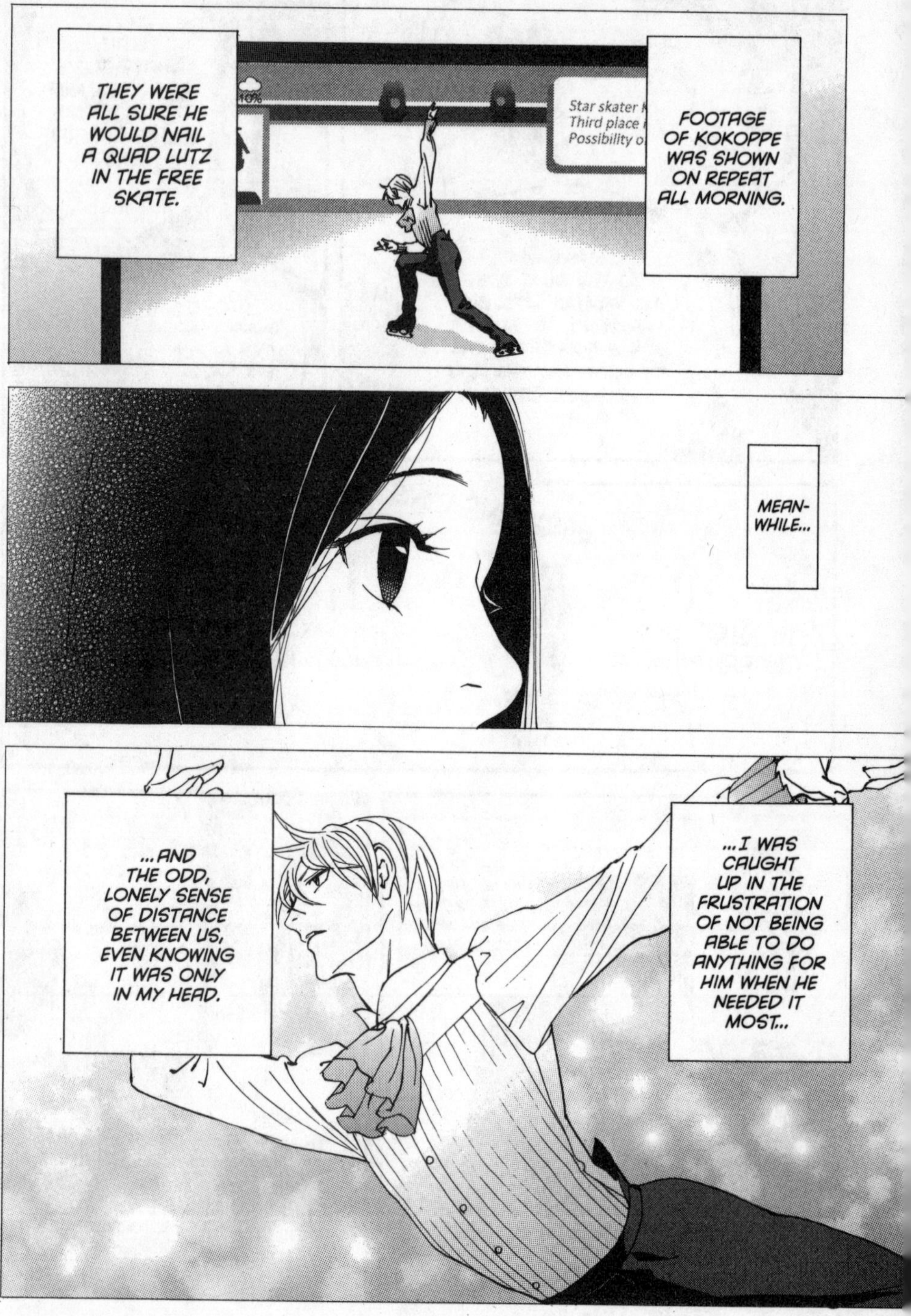
FOOTAGE OF KOKOPPE WAS SHOWN ON REPEAT ALL MORNING.
THEY WERE ALL SURE HE WOULD NAIL A QUAD LUTZ IN THE FREE SKATE.
MEAN-WHILE...
...I WAS CAUGHT UP IN THE FRUSTRATION OF NOT BEING ABLE TO DO ANYTHING FOR HIM WHEN HE NEEDED IT MOST...
...AND THE ODD, LONELY SENSE OF DISTANCE BETWEEN US, EVEN KNOWING IT WAS ONLY IN MY HEAD.

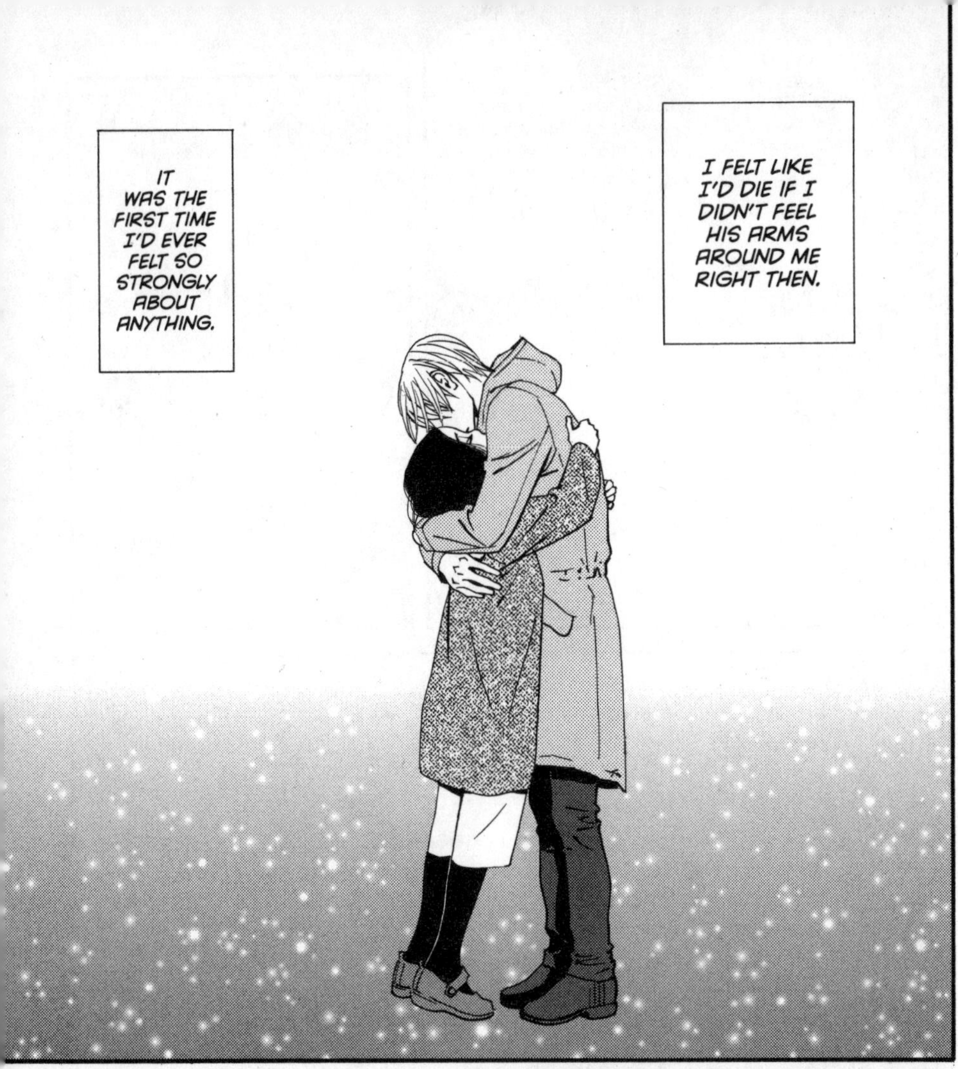
I FELT LIKE I'D DIE IF I DIDN'T FEEL HIS ARMS AROUND ME RIGHT THEN.
IT WAS THE FIRST TIME I'D EVER FELT SO STRONGLY ABOUT ANYTHING.

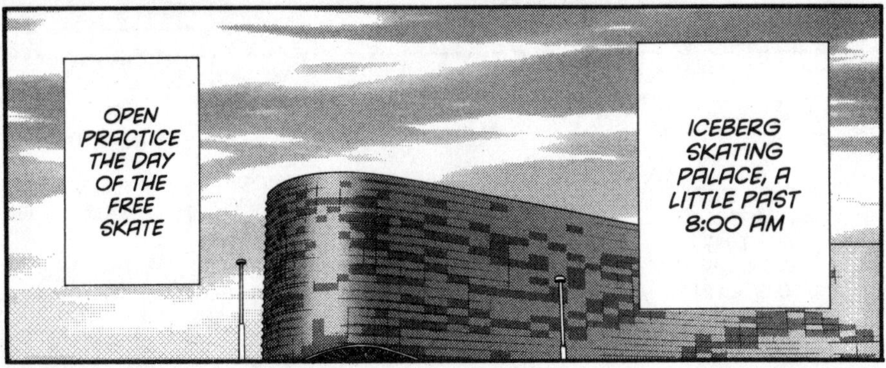
ICEBERG SKATING PALACE, A LITTLE PAST 8:00 AM
OPEN PRACTICE THE DAY OF THE FREE SKATE

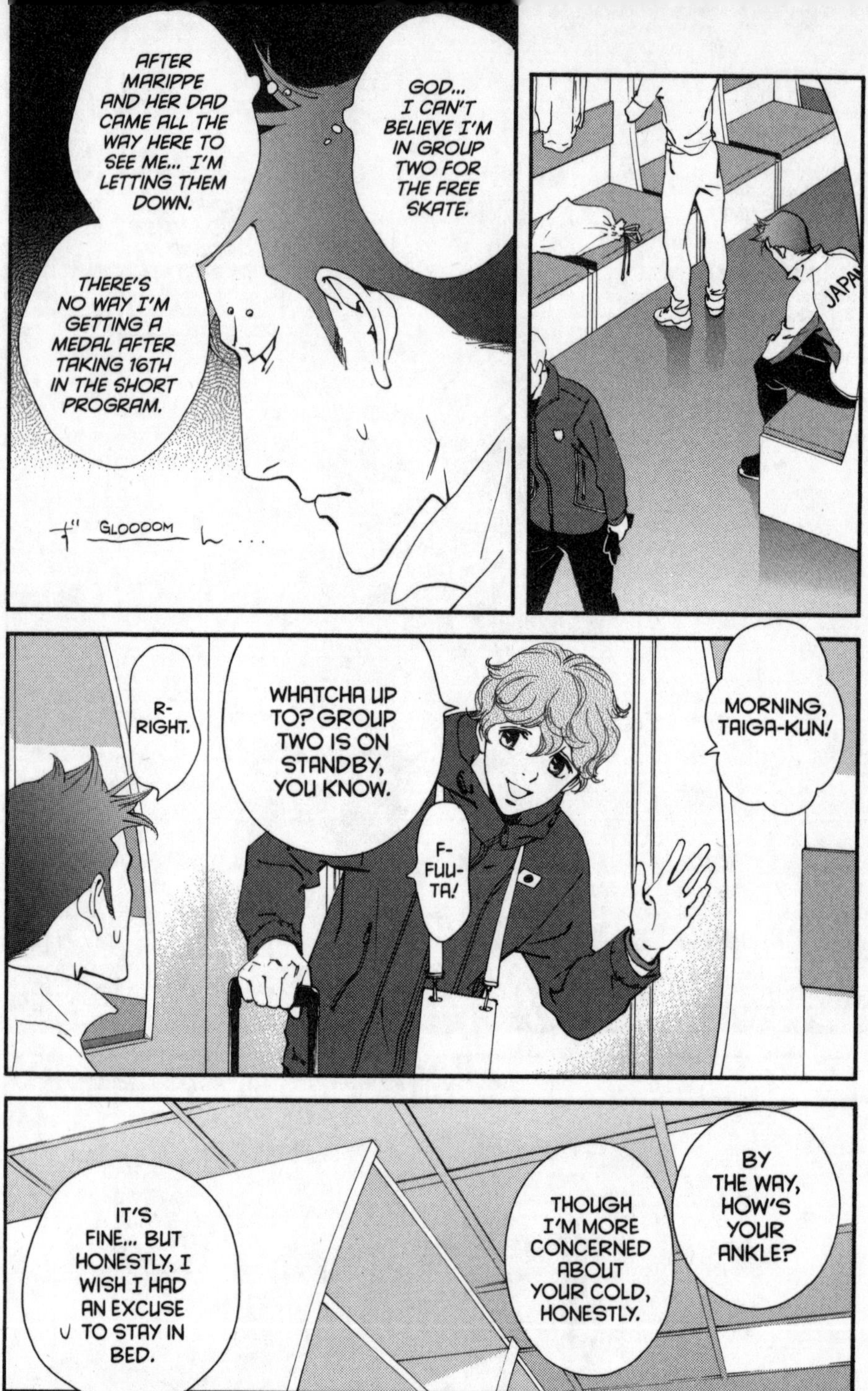
JAPAN
GOD... I CAN'T BELIEVE I'M IN GROUP TWO FOR THE FREE SKATE.
AFTER MARIPPE AND HER DAD CAME ALL THE WAY HERE TO SEE ME... I'M LETTING THEM DOWN.
THERE'S NO WAY I'M GETTING A MEDAL AFTER TAKING 16TH IN THE SHORT PROGRAM.
GLOOOOM
MORNING, TAIGA-KUN!
WHATCHA UP TO? GROUP TWO IS ON STANDBY, YOU KNOW.
F-FUU-TA!
R-RIGHT.
BY THE WAY, HOW'S YOUR ANKLE?
THOUGH I'M MORE CONCERNED ABOUT YOUR COLD, HONESTLY.
IT'S FINE... BUT HONESTLY, I WISH I HAD AN EXCUSE TO STAY IN BED.

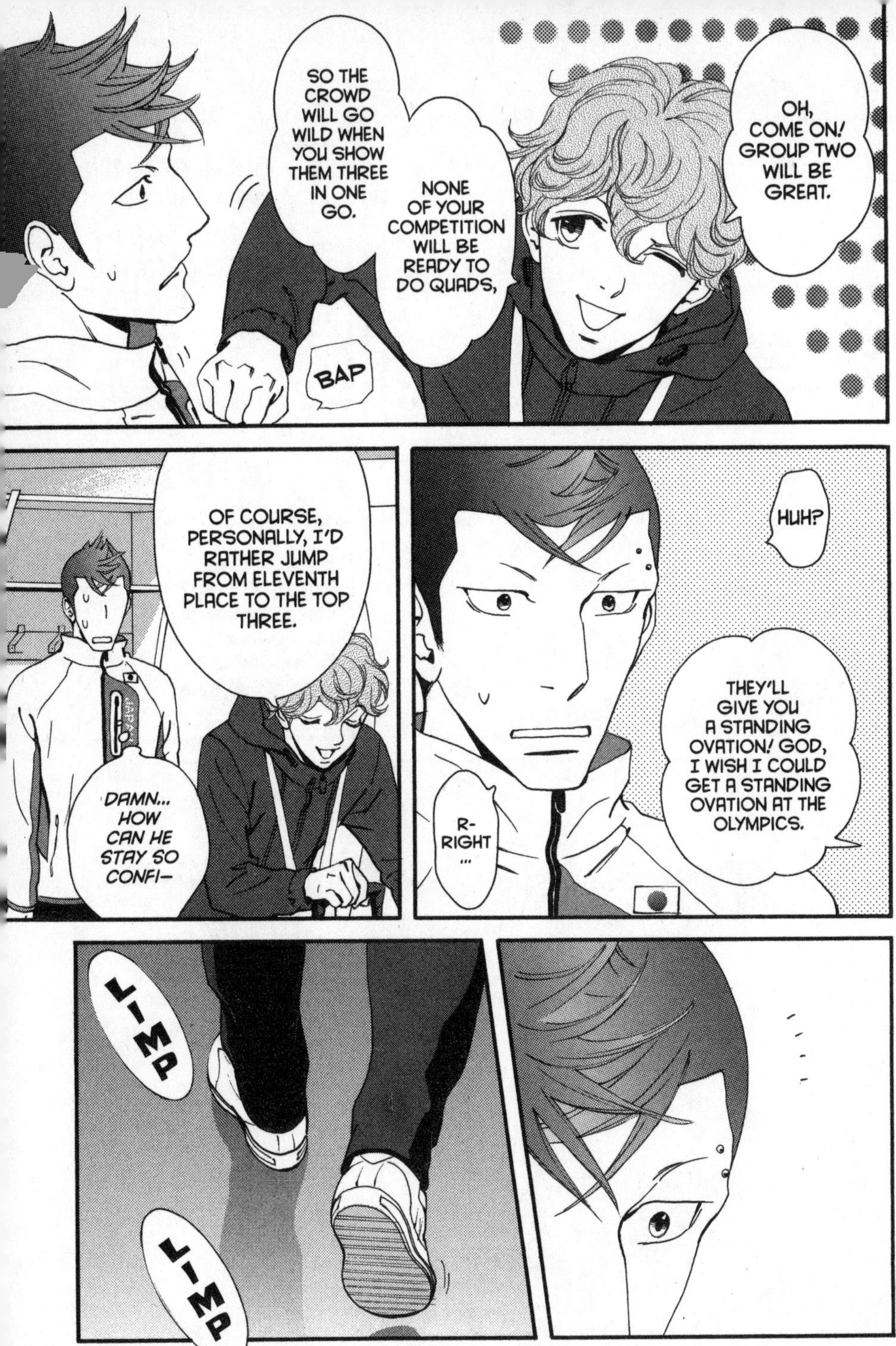
OH, COME ON! GROUP TWO WILL BE GREAT.
NONE OF YOUR COMPETITION WILL BE READY TO DO QUADS,
SO THE CROWD WILL GO WILD WHEN YOU SHOW THEM THREE IN ONE GO.
BAP
HUH?
THEY'LL GIVE YOU A STANDING OVATION! GOD, I WISH I COULD GET A STANDING OVATION AT THE OLYMPICS.
R-RIGHT...
OF COURSE, PERSONALLY, I'D RATHER JUMP FROM ELEVENTH PLACE TO THE TOP THREE.
DAMN... HOW CAN HE STAY SO CONFI-
LIMP
LIMP

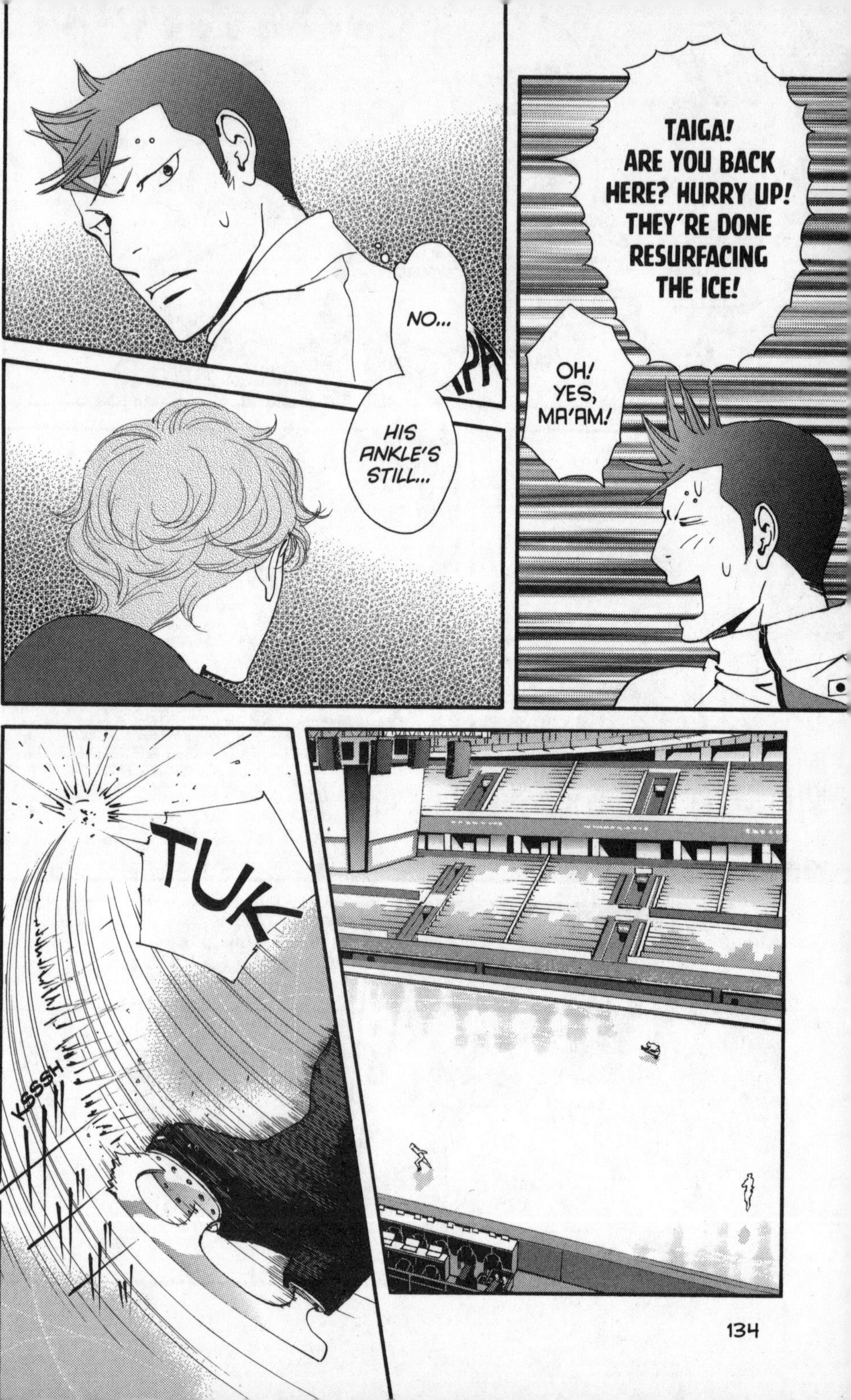
TAIGA! ARE YOU BACK HERE? HURRY UP! THEY'RE DONE RESURFACING THE ICE!
OH! YES, MA'AM!
NO...
HIS ANKLE'S STILL...
TUK
KSSSH

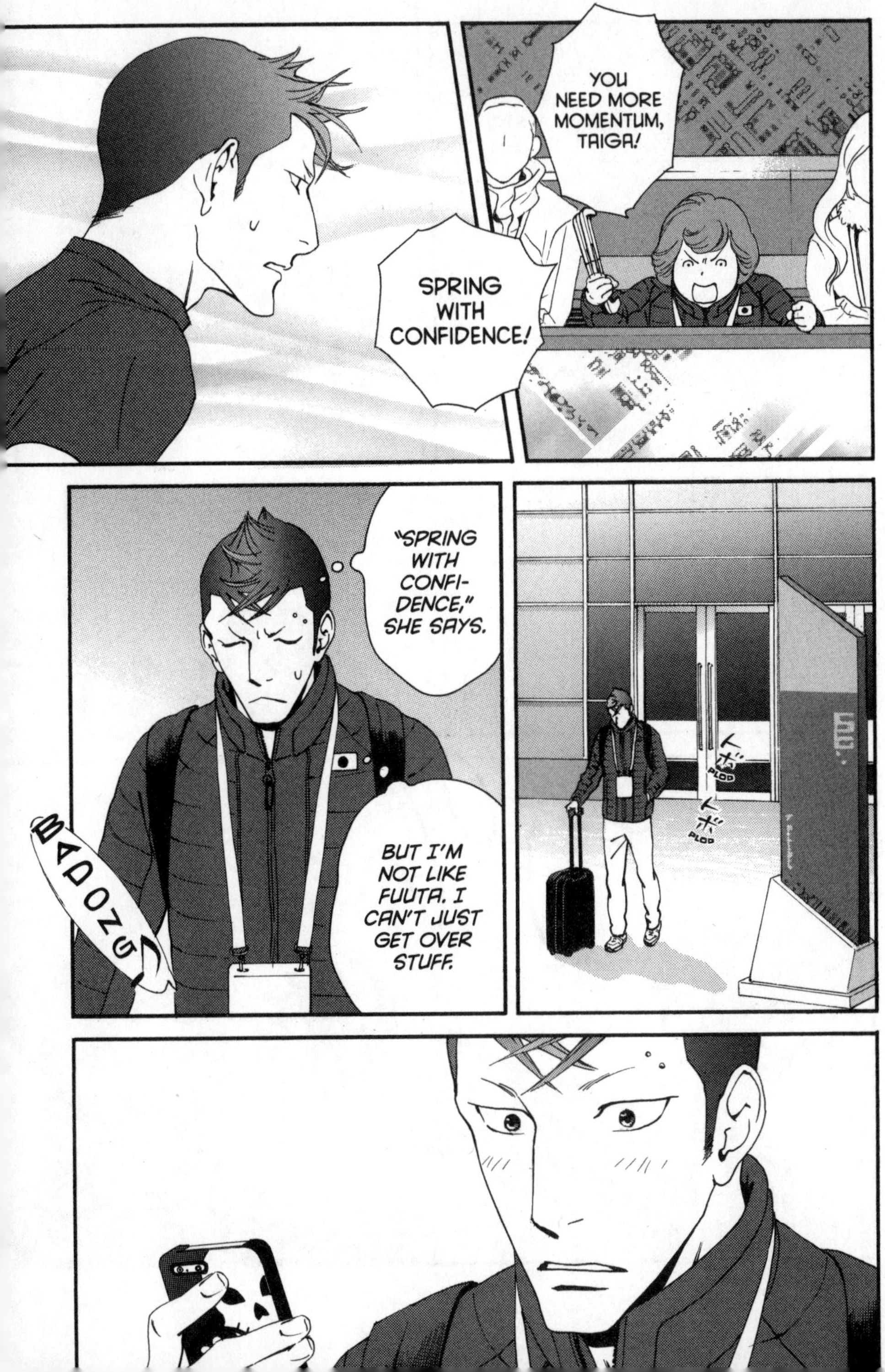
YOU NEED MORE MOMENTUM, TAIGA!
SPRING WITH CONFIDENCE!
トボ PLOD
トボ PLOD
"SPRING WITH CONFIDENCE," SHE SAYS.
BUT I'M NOT LIKE FUUTA. I CAN'T JUST GET OVER STUFF.
BADONG

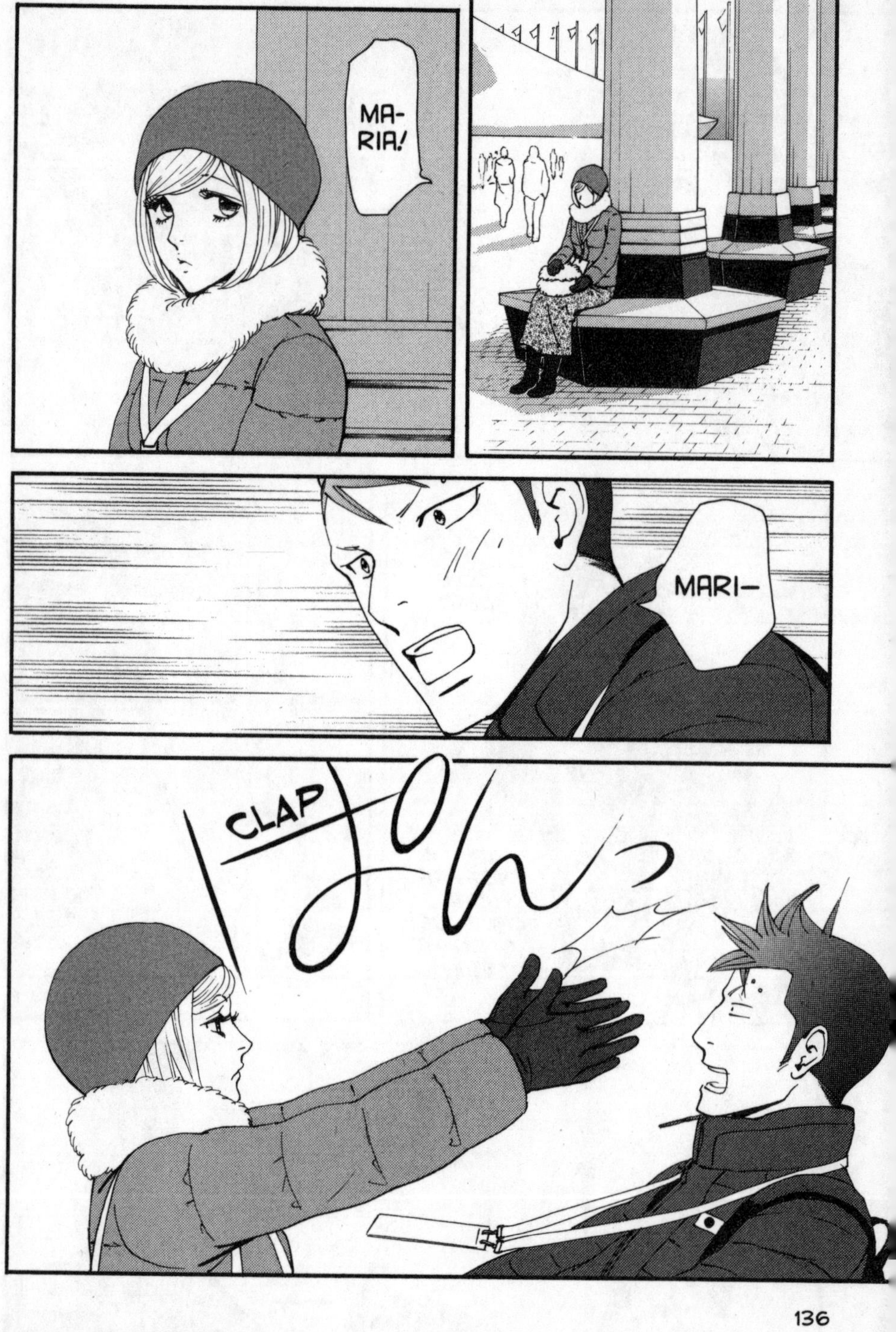
MA-
RIA!
MARI—
CLAP

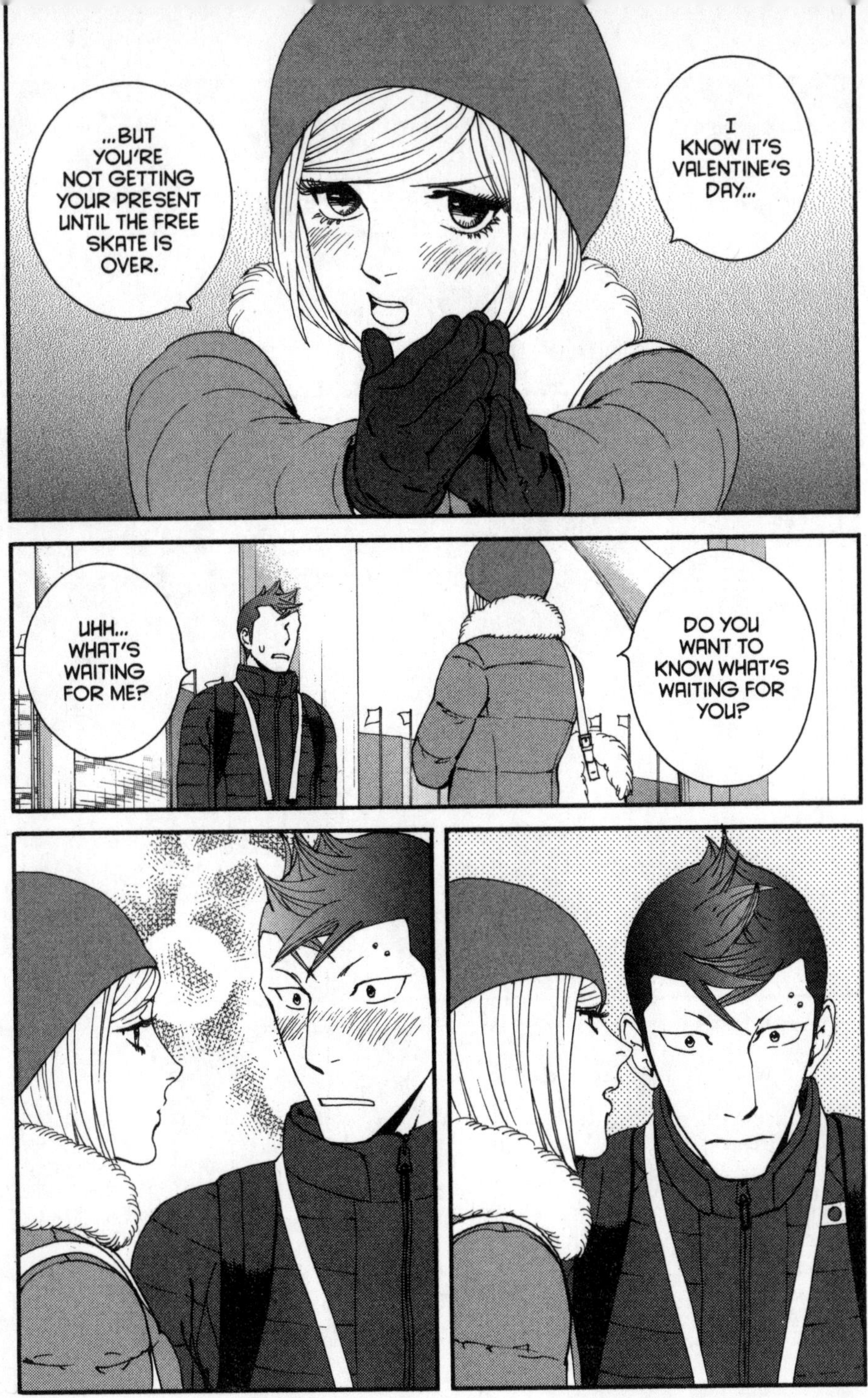
I KNOW IT'S VALENTINE'S DAY...
...BUT YOU'RE NOT GETTING YOUR PRESENT UNTIL THE FREE SKATE IS OVER.
DO YOU WANT TO KNOW WHAT'S WAITING FOR YOU?
UHH... WHAT'S WAITING FOR ME?

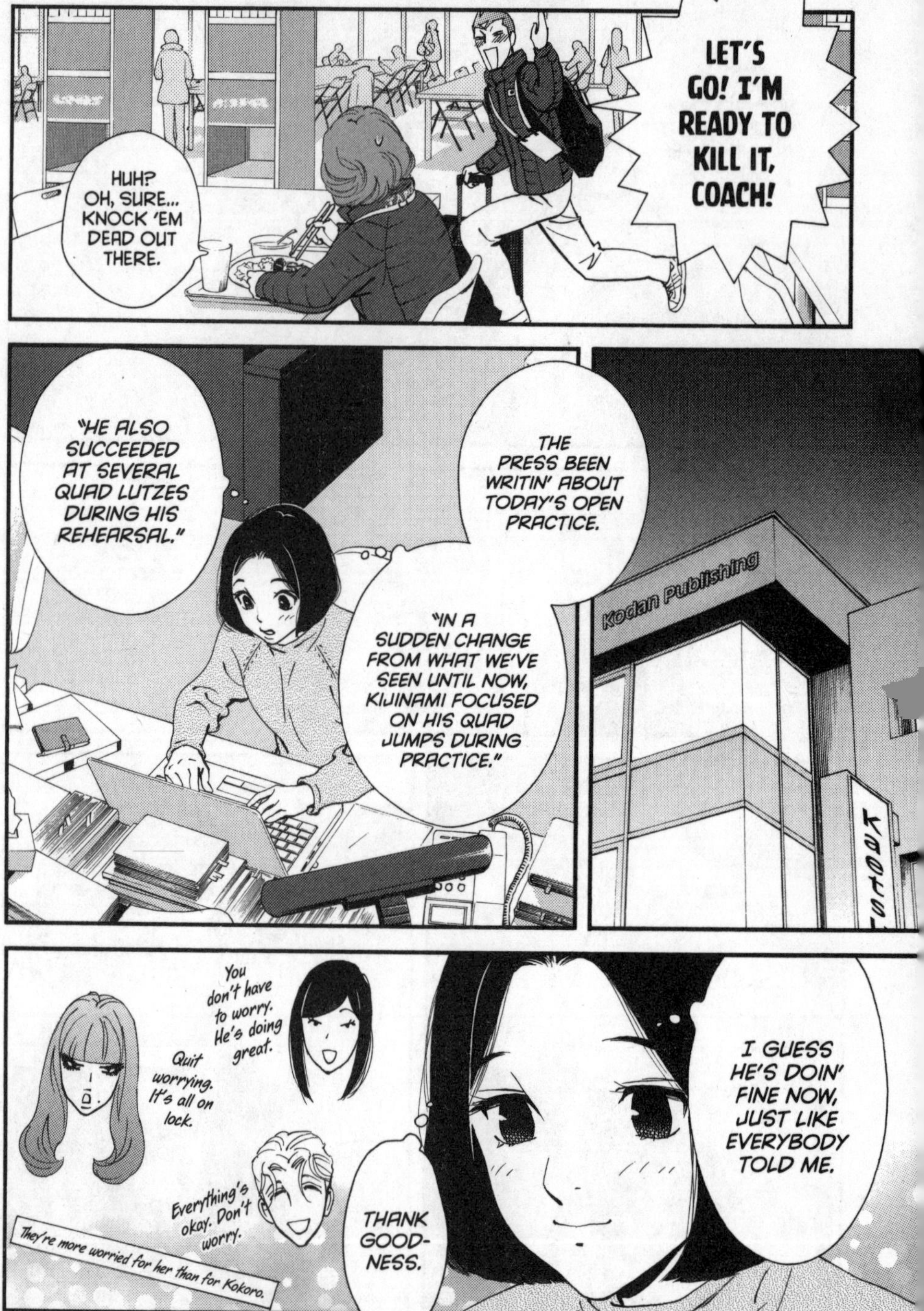
LET'S GO! I'M READY TO KILL IT, COACH!
HUH? OH, SURE... KNOCK 'EM DEAD OUT THERE.
Kodan Publishing
THE PRESS BEEN WRITIN' ABOUT TODAY'S OPEN PRACTICE.
"IN A SUDDEN CHANGE FROM WHAT WE'VE SEEN UNTIL NOW, KIJINAMI FOCUSED ON HIS QUAD JUMPS DURING PRACTICE."
"HE ALSO SUCCEEDED AT SEVERAL QUAD LUTZES DURING HIS REHEARSAL."
I GUESS HE'S DOIN' FINE NOW, JUST LIKE EVERYBODY TOLD ME.
THANK GOODNESS.
You don't have to worry. He's doing great.
Quit worrying. It's all on lock.
Everything's okay. Don't worry.
They're more worried for her than for Kokoro.

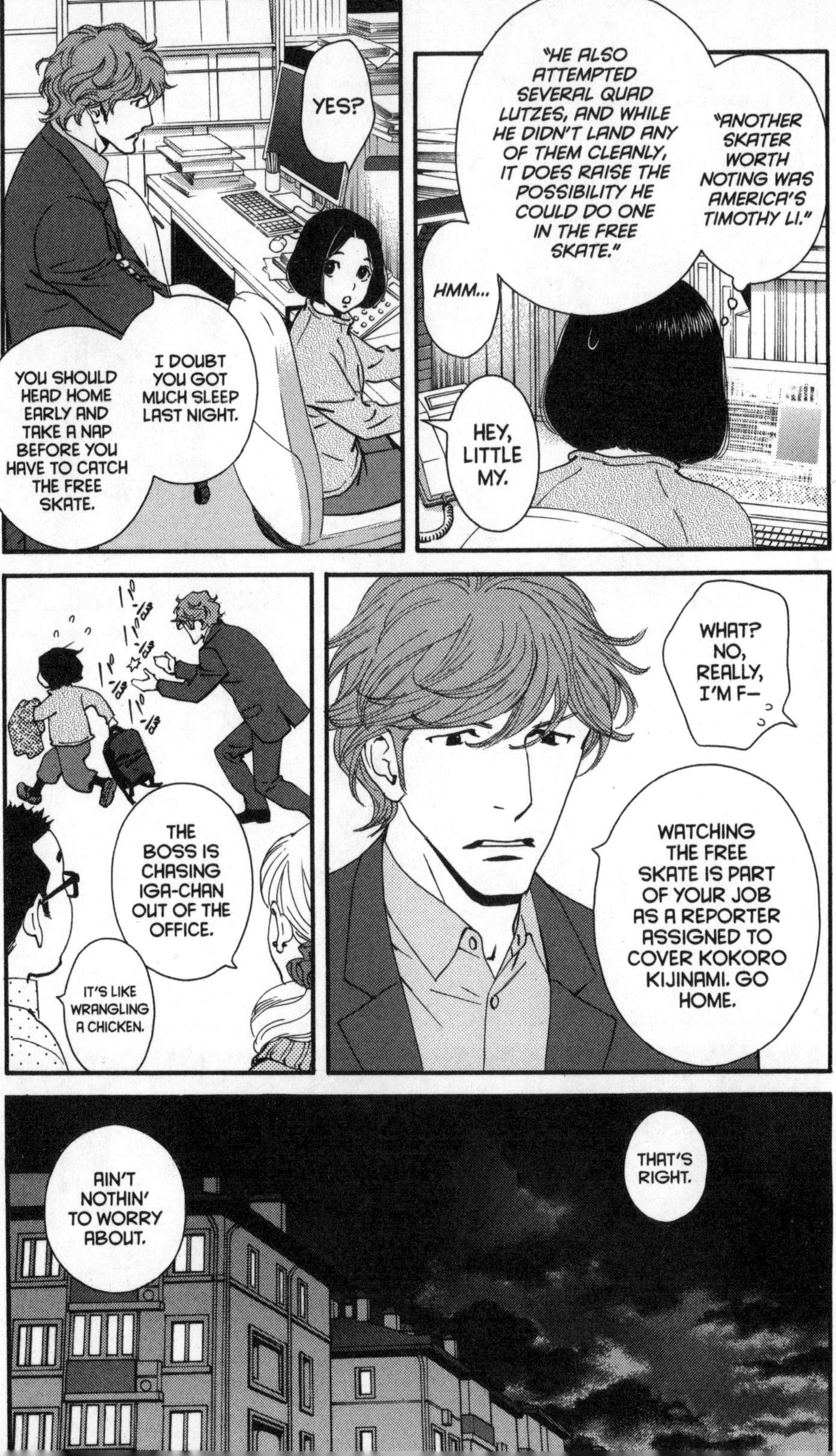
"ANOTHER SKATER WORTH NOTING WAS AMERICA'S TIMOTHY LI."
"HE ALSO ATTEMPTED SEVERAL QUAD LUTZES, AND WHILE HE DIDN'T LAND ANY OF THEM CLEANLY, IT DOES RAISE THE POSSIBILITY HE COULD DO ONE IN THE FREE SKATE."
HMM...
HEY, LITTLE MY.
YES?
I DOUBT YOU GOT MUCH SLEEP LAST NIGHT.
YOU SHOULD HEAD HOME EARLY AND TAKE A NAP BEFORE YOU HAVE TO CATCH THE FREE SKATE.
WHAT? NO, REALLY, I'M F—
WATCHING THE FREE SKATE IS PART OF YOUR JOB AS A REPORTER ASSIGNED TO COVER KOKORO KIJINAMI. GO HOME.
THE BOSS IS CHASING IGA-CHAN OUT OF THE OFFICE.
IT'S LIKE WRANGLING A CHICKEN.
THAT'S RIGHT.
AIN'T NOTHIN' TO WORRY ABOUT.

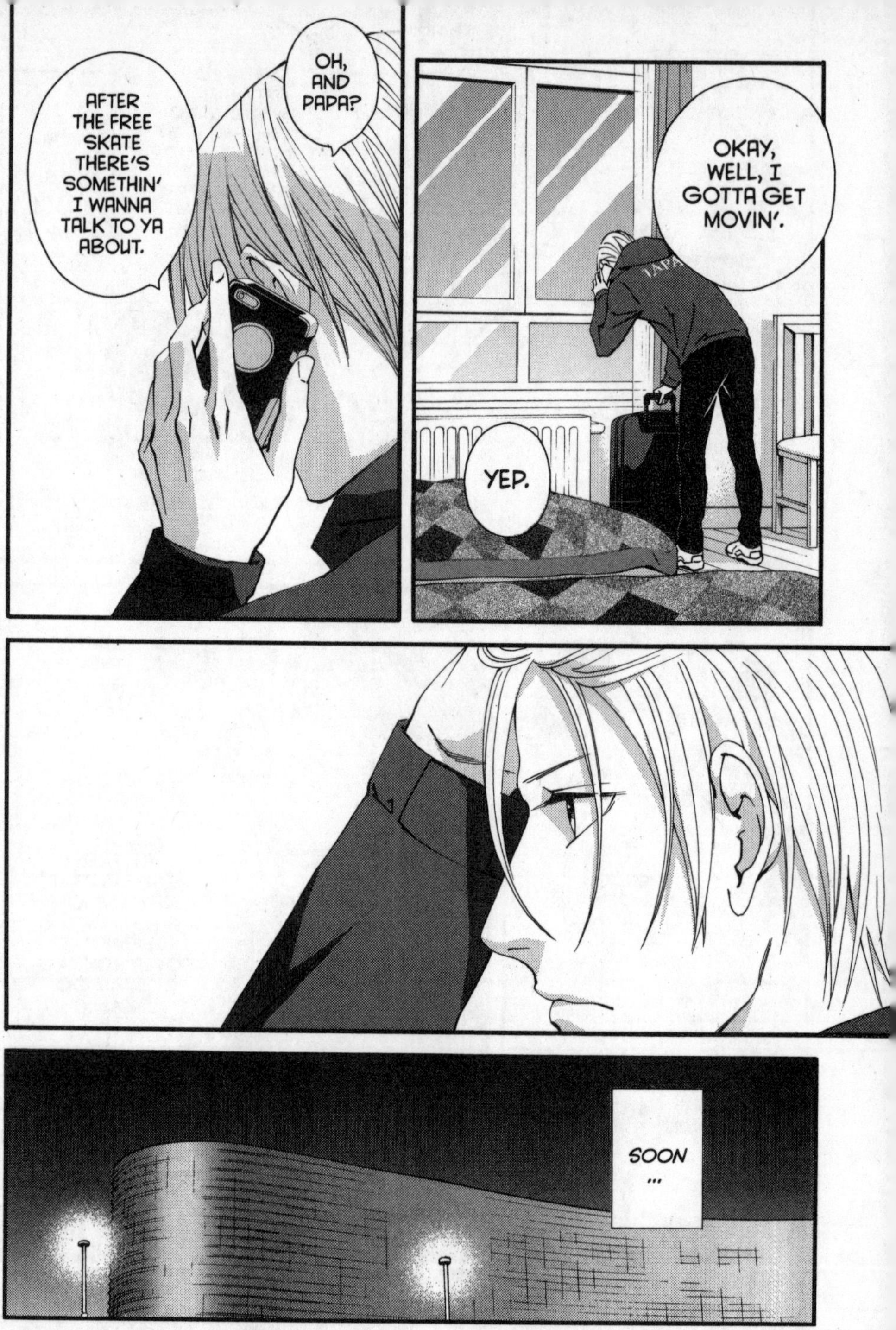
OKAY, WELL, I GOTTA GET MOVIN'.
YEP.
OH, AND PAPA?
AFTER THE FREE SKATE THERE'S SOMETHIN' I WANNA TALK TO YA ABOUT.
SOON ...

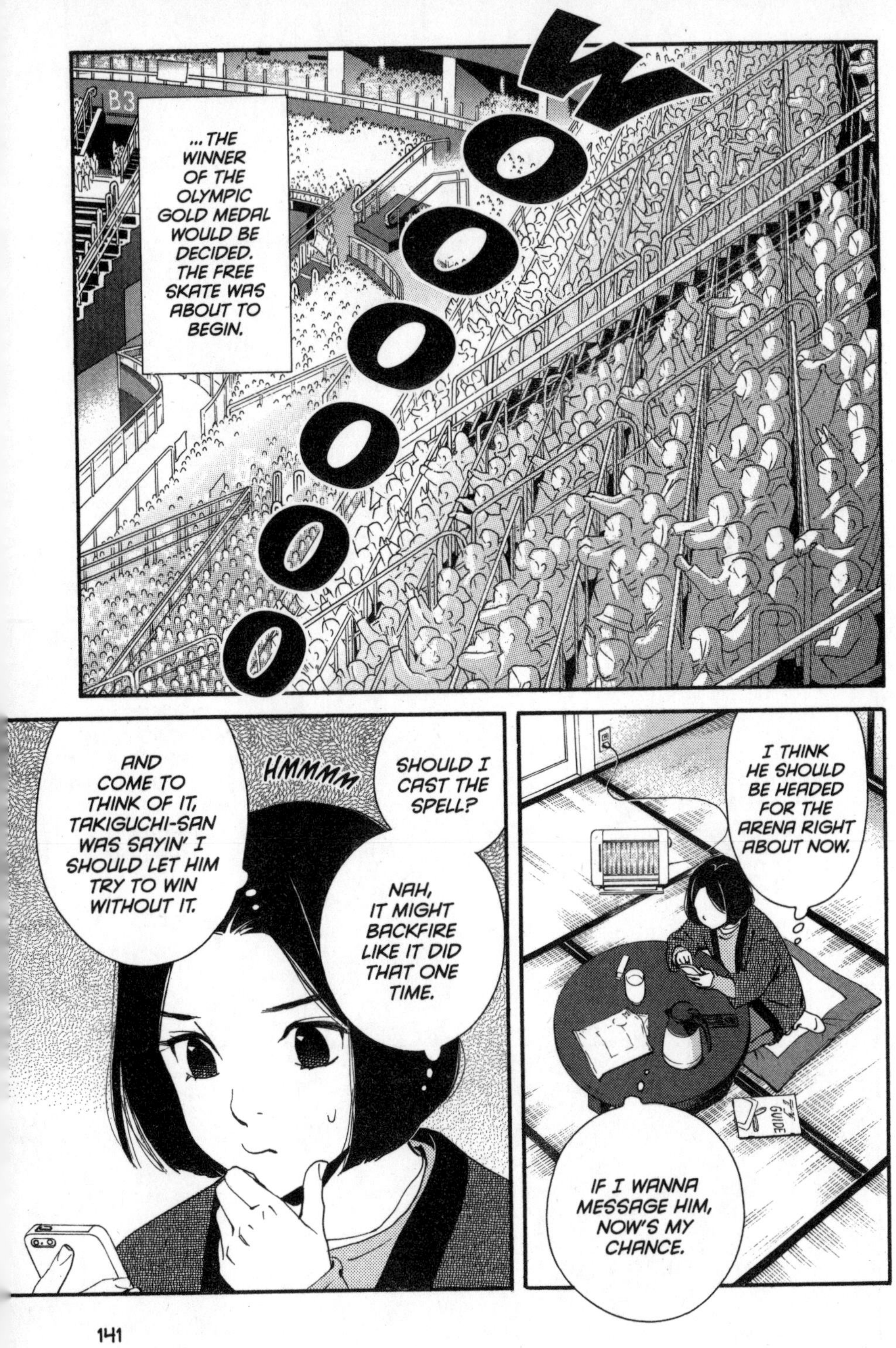
...THE WINNER OF THE OLYMPIC GOLD MEDAL WOULD BE DECIDED. THE FREE SKATE WAS ABOUT TO BEGIN.
WOOOOOO
I THINK HE SHOULD BE HEADED FOR THE ARENA RIGHT ABOUT NOW.
IF I WANNA MESSAGE HIM, NOW'S MY CHANCE.
SHOULD I CAST THE SPELL?
HMMMM
NAH, IT MIGHT BACKFIRE LIKE IT DID THAT ONE TIME.
AND COME TO THINK OF IT, TAKIGUCHI-SAN WAS SAYIN' I SHOULD LET HIM TRY TO WIN WITHOUT IT.

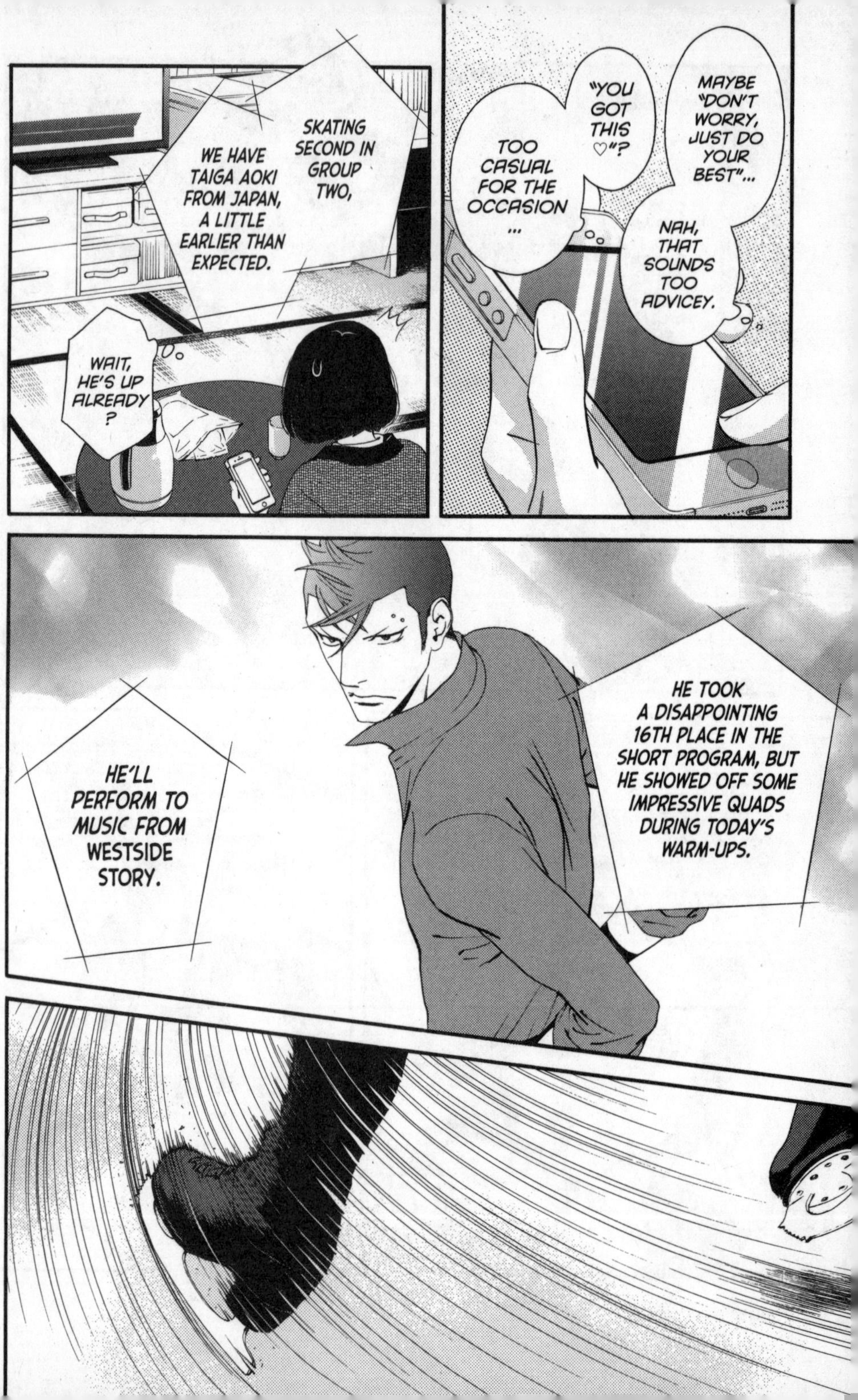
MAYBE "DON'T WORRY, JUST DO YOUR BEST"...
NAH, THAT SOUNDS TOO ADVICEY.
"YOU GOT THIS ♡"?
TOO CASUAL FOR THE OCCASION ...
SKATING SECOND IN GROUP TWO,
WE HAVE TAIGA AOKI FROM JAPAN, A LITTLE EARLIER THAN EXPECTED.
WAIT, HE'S UP ALREADY ?
HE TOOK A DISAPPOINTING 16TH PLACE IN THE SHORT PROGRAM, BUT HE SHOWED OFF SOME IMPRESSIVE QUADS DURING TODAY'S WARM-UPS.
HE'LL PERFORM TO MUSIC FROM WESTSIDE STORY.

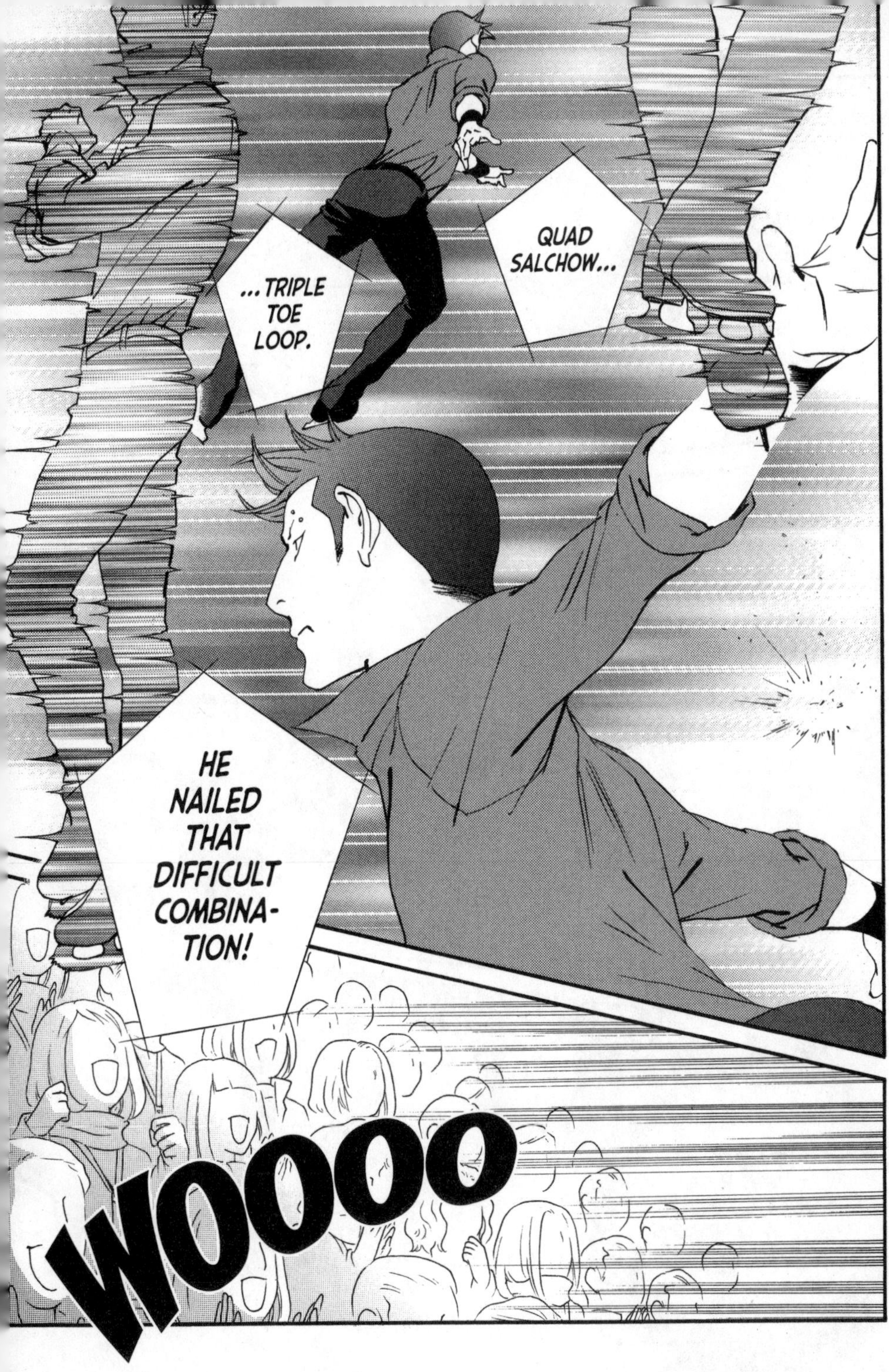
QUAD SALCHOW...
...TRIPLE TOE LOOP.
HE NAILED THAT DIFFICULT COMBINATION!
WOOOOO

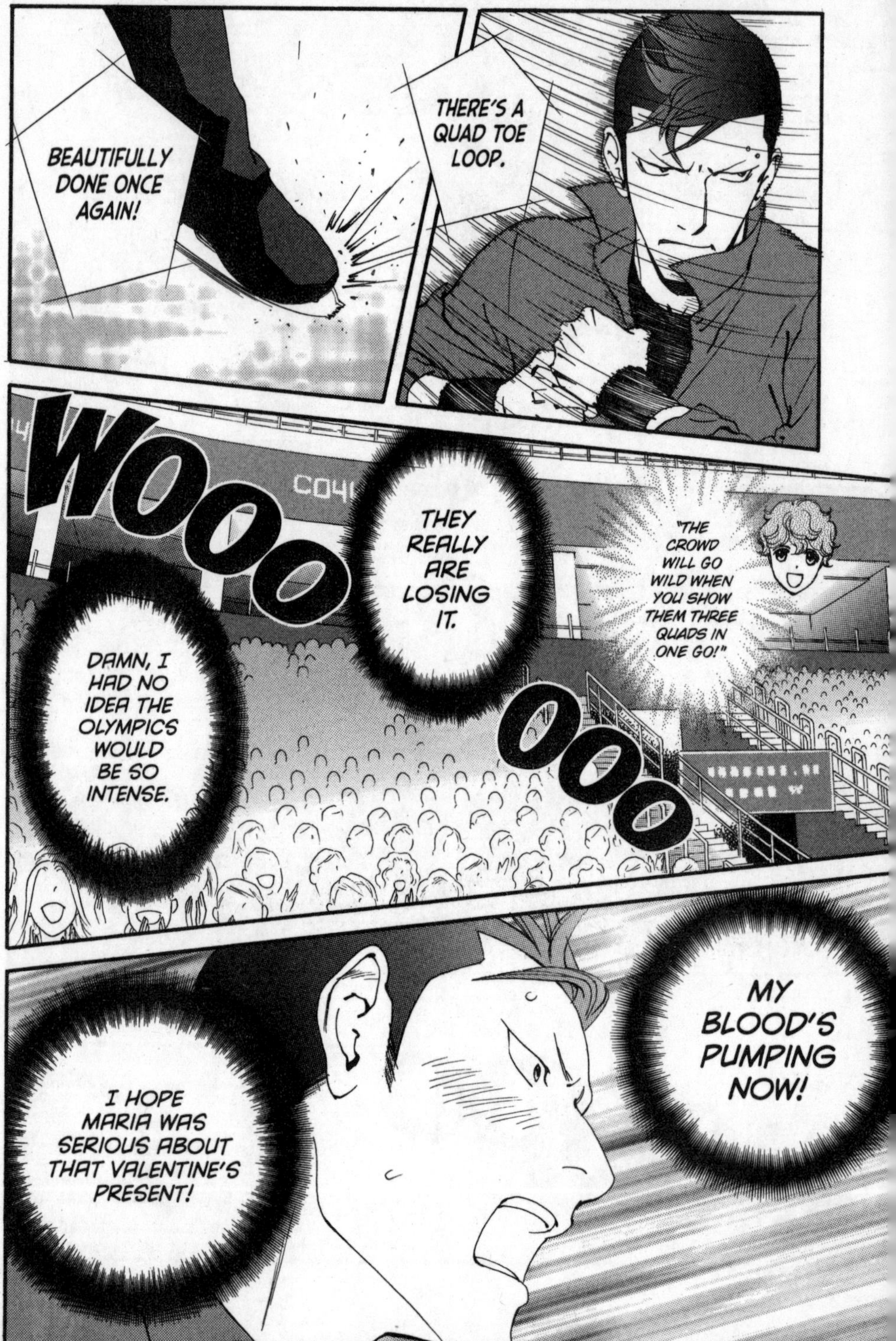
THERE'S A QUAD TOE LOOP.
BEAUTIFULLY DONE ONCE AGAIN!
"THE CROWD WILL GO WILD WHEN YOU SHOW THEM THREE QUADS IN ONE GO!"
THEY REALLY ARE LOSING IT.
WOOOOOOO
DAMN, I HAD NO IDEA THE OLYMPICS WOULD BE SO INTENSE.
MY BLOOD'S PUMPING NOW!
I HOPE MARIA WAS SERIOUS ABOUT THAT VALENTINE'S PRESENT!

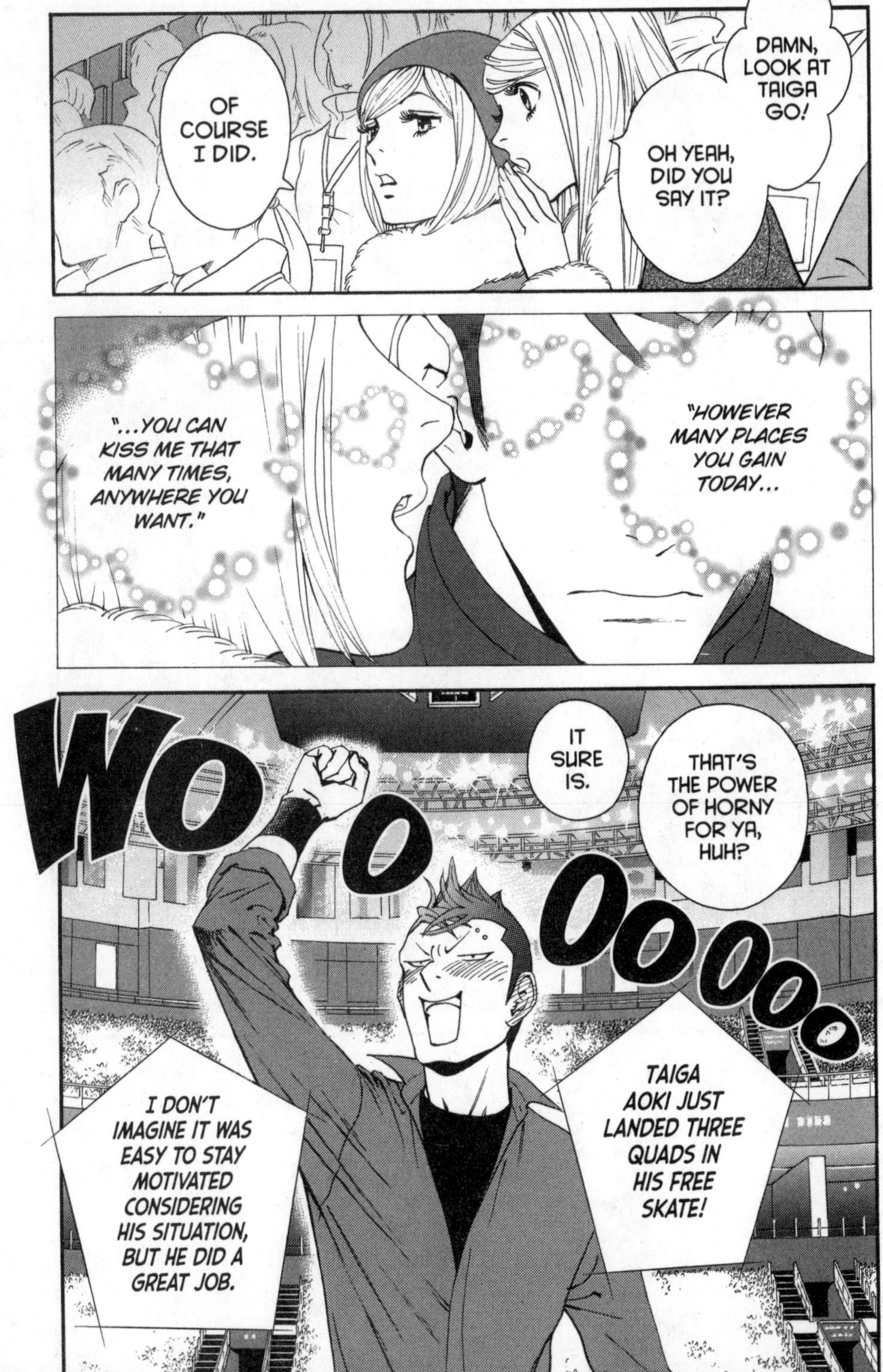
DAMN, LOOK AT TAIGA GO!
OH YEAH, DID YOU SAY IT?
OF COURSE I DID.
"HOWEVER MANY PLACES YOU GAIN TODAY...
"...YOU CAN KISS ME THAT MANY TIMES, ANYWHERE YOU WANT."
WOOOOOOOO
THAT'S THE POWER OF HORNY FOR YA, HUH?
IT SURE IS.
TAIGA AOKI JUST LANDED THREE QUADS IN HIS FREE SKATE!
I DON'T IMAGINE IT WAS EASY TO STAY MOTIVATED CONSIDERING HIS SITUATION, BUT HE DID A GREAT JOB.

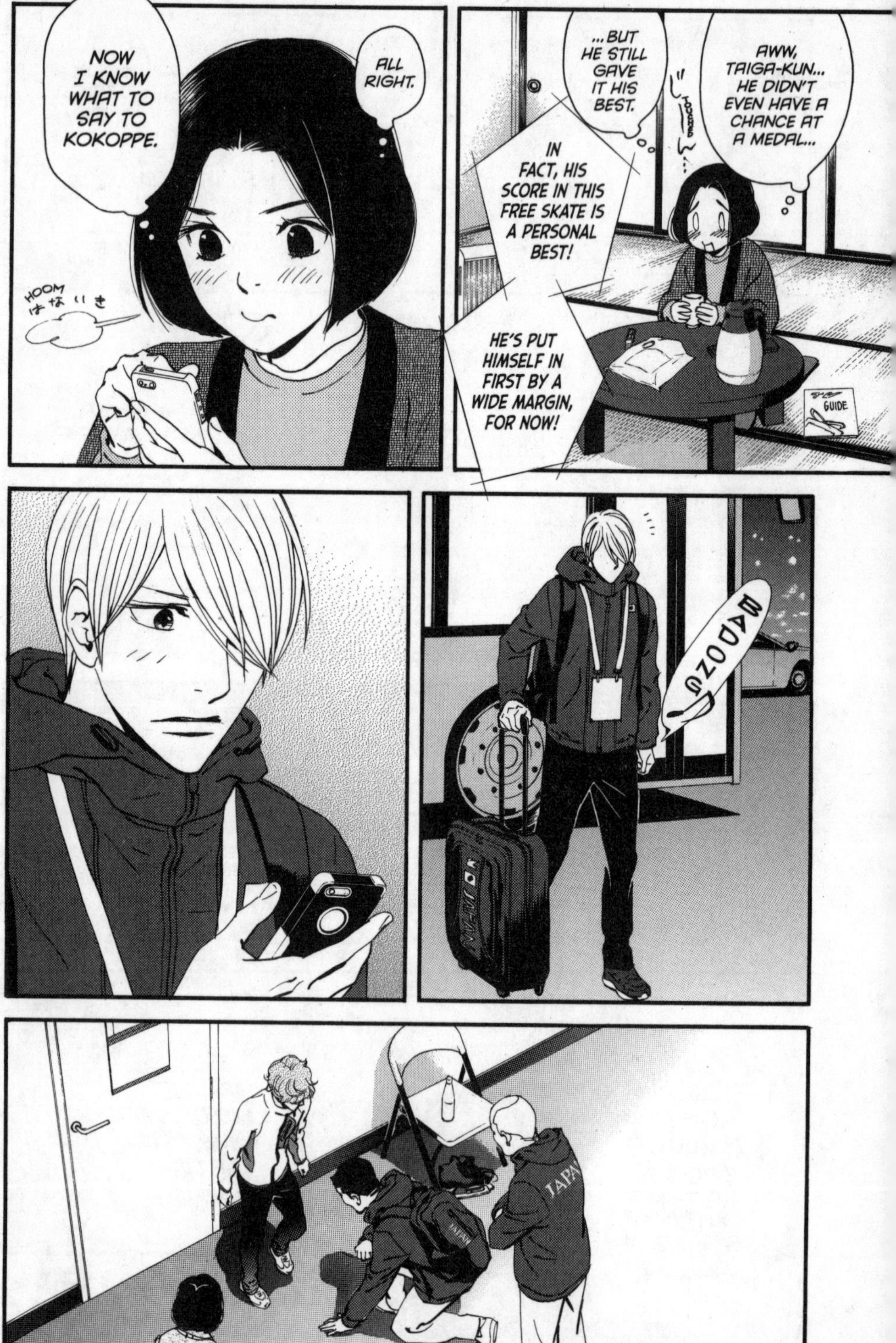
AWW, TAIGA-KUN... HE DIDN'T EVEN HAVE A CHANCE AT A MEDAL...
...BUT HE STILL GAVE IT HIS BEST.
IN FACT, HIS SCORE IN THIS FREE SKATE IS A PERSONAL BEST!
HE'S PUT HIMSELF IN FIRST BY A WIDE MARGIN, FOR NOW!
GUIDE
ALL RIGHT.
NOW I KNOW WHAT TO SAY TO KOKOPPE.
HOOM
はないき
BADONG
JAPAN

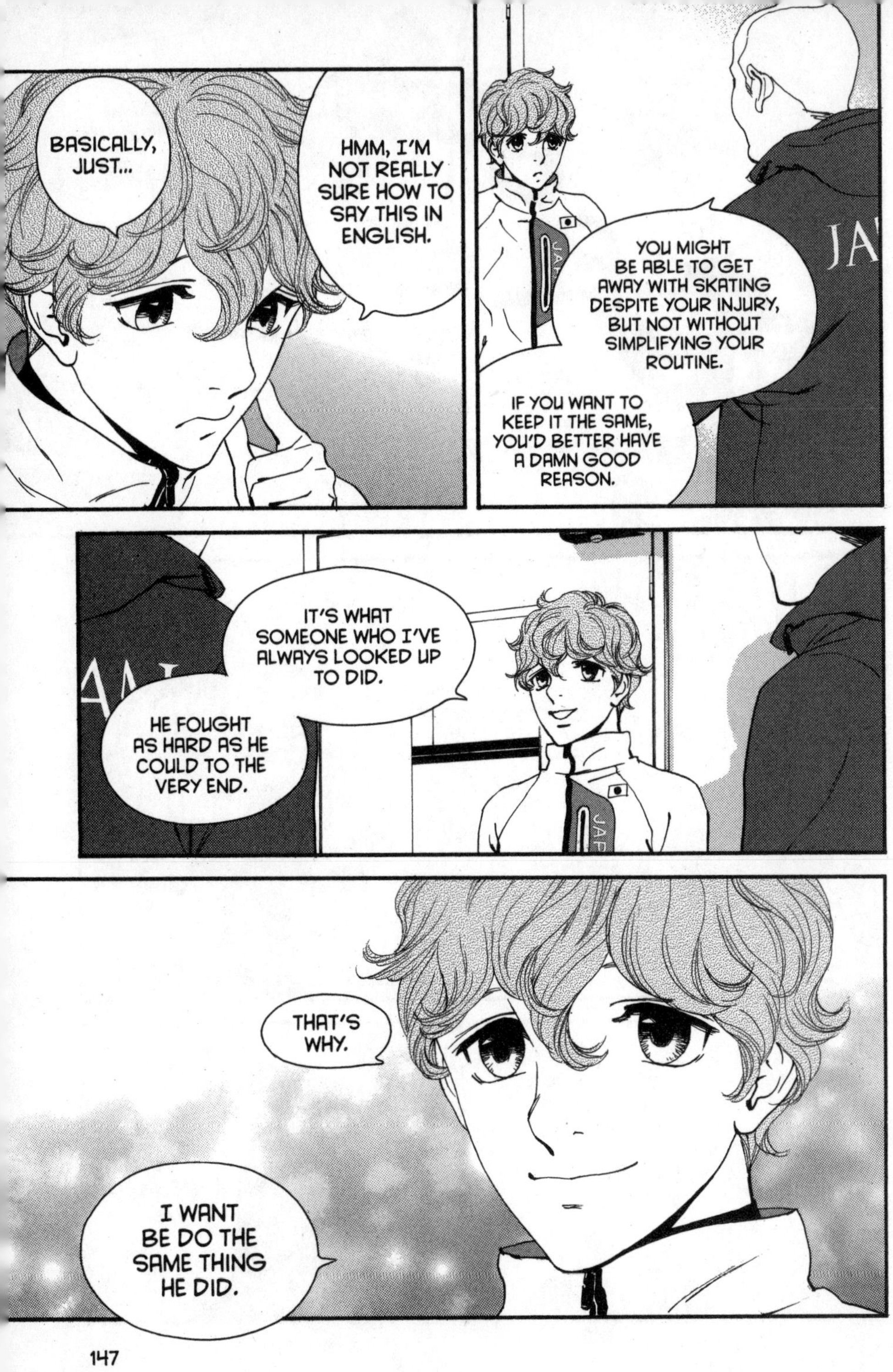
YOU MIGHT BE ABLE TO GET AWAY WITH SKATING DESPITE YOUR INJURY, BUT NOT WITHOUT SIMPLIFYING YOUR ROUTINE.
IF YOU WANT TO KEEP IT THE SAME, YOU'D BETTER HAVE A DAMN GOOD REASON.
HMM, I'M NOT REALLY SURE HOW TO SAY THIS IN ENGLISH.
BASICALLY, JUST...
JA
IT'S WHAT SOMEONE WHO I'VE ALWAYS LOOKED UP TO DID.
HE FOUGHT AS HARD AS HE COULD TO THE VERY END.
THAT'S WHY.
I WANT BE DO THE SAME THING HE DID.

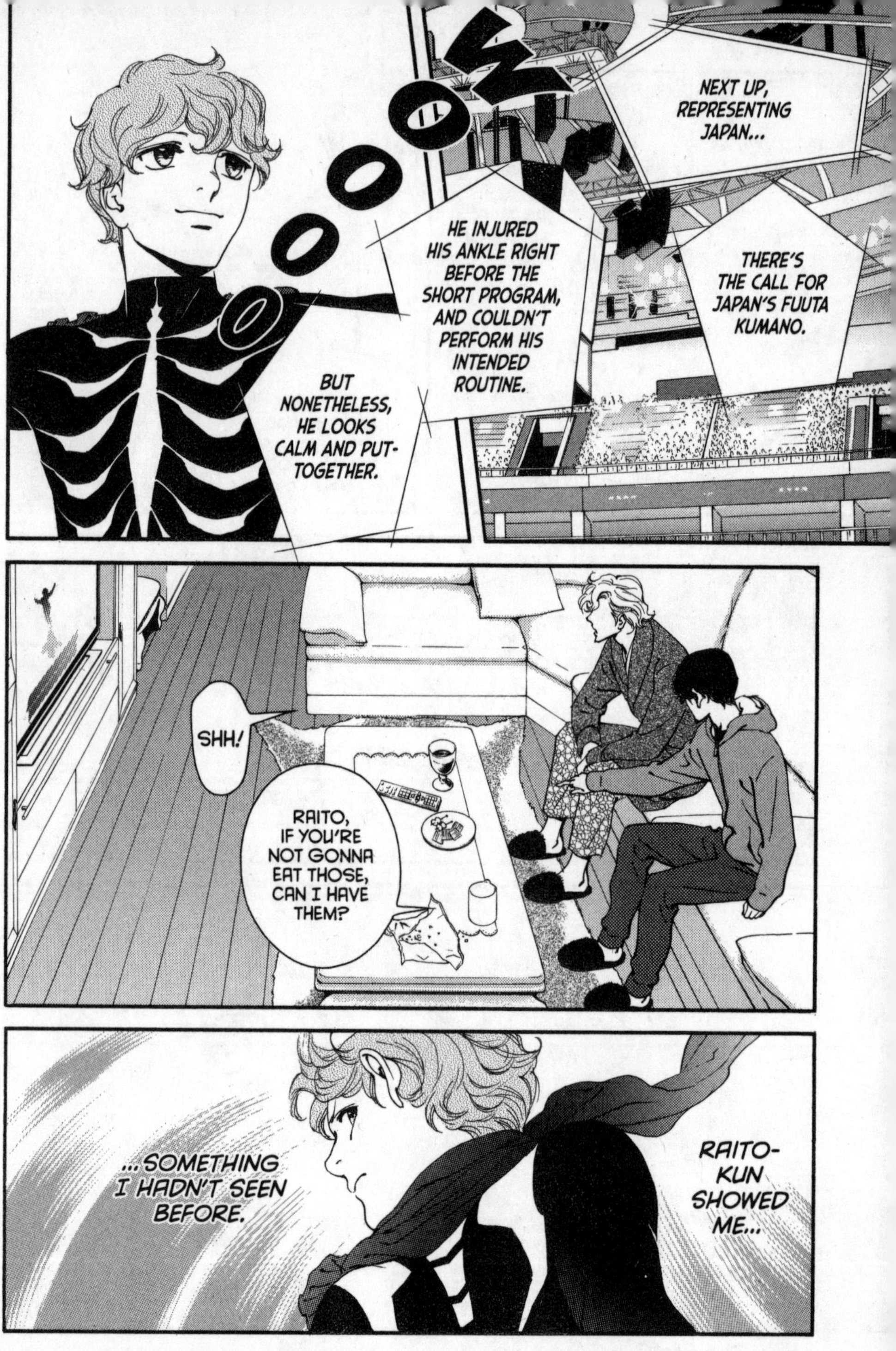
WOOOOO
NEXT UP, REPRESENTING JAPAN...
THERE'S THE CALL FOR JAPAN'S FUUTA KUMANO.
HE INJURED HIS ANKLE RIGHT BEFORE THE SHORT PROGRAM, AND COULDN'T PERFORM HIS INTENDED ROUTINE.
BUT NONETHELESS, HE LOOKS CALM AND PUT-TOGETHER.
RAITO, IF YOU'RE NOT GONNA EAT THOSE, CAN I HAVE THEM?
SHH!
RAITO-KUN SHOWED ME...
...SOMETHING I HADN'T SEEN BEFORE.

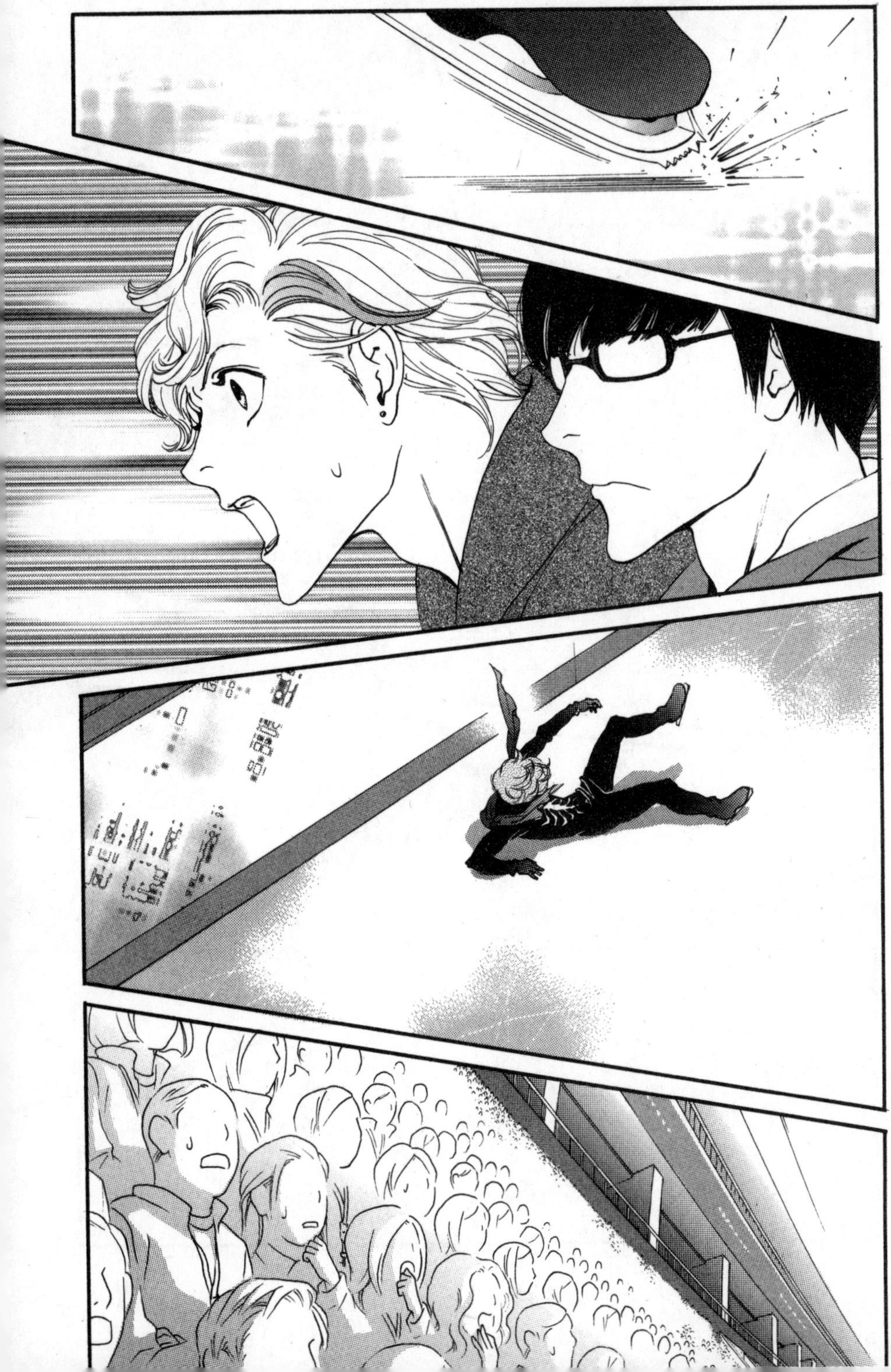

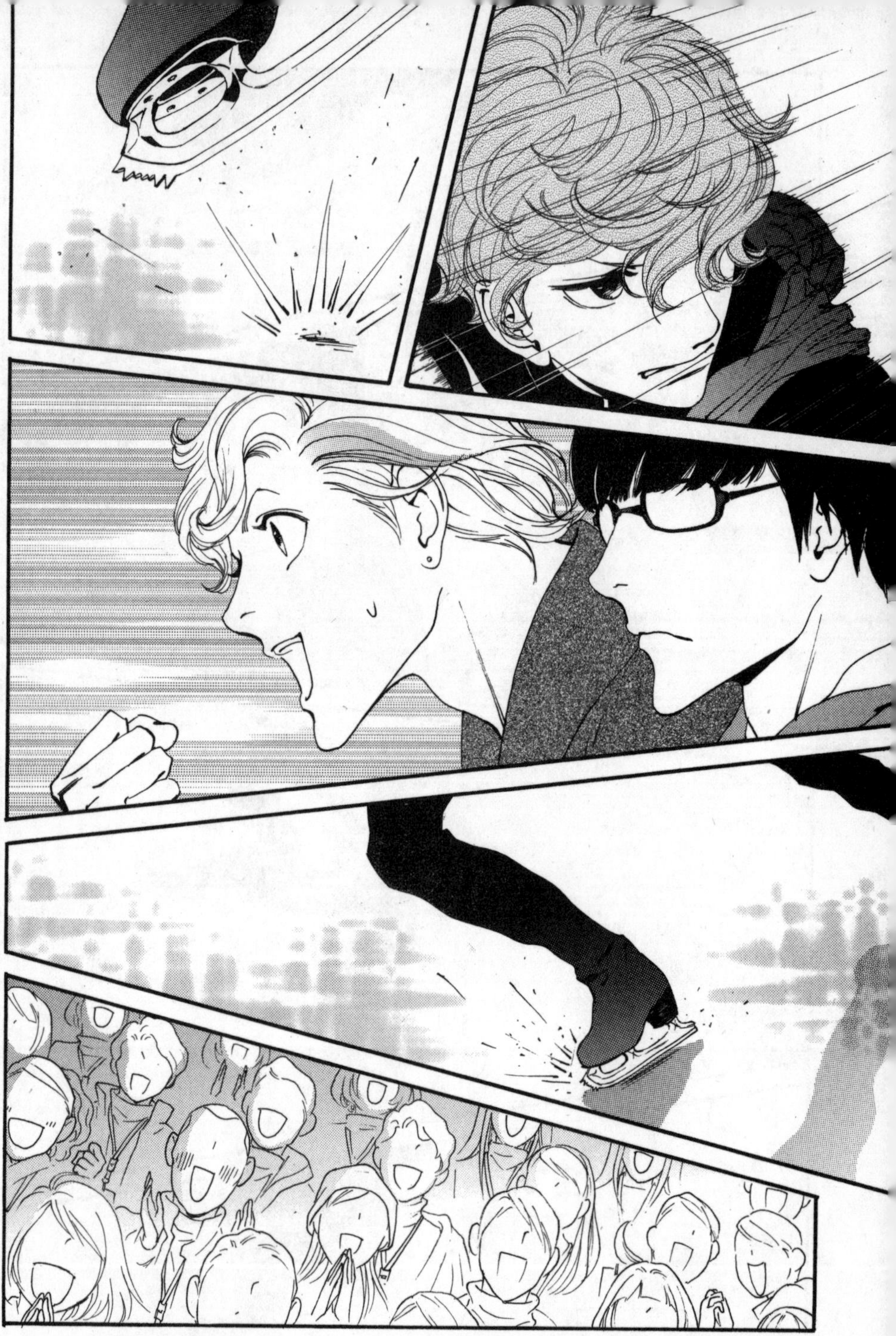

THERE'S GLORY IN REFUSING TO GIVE UP.

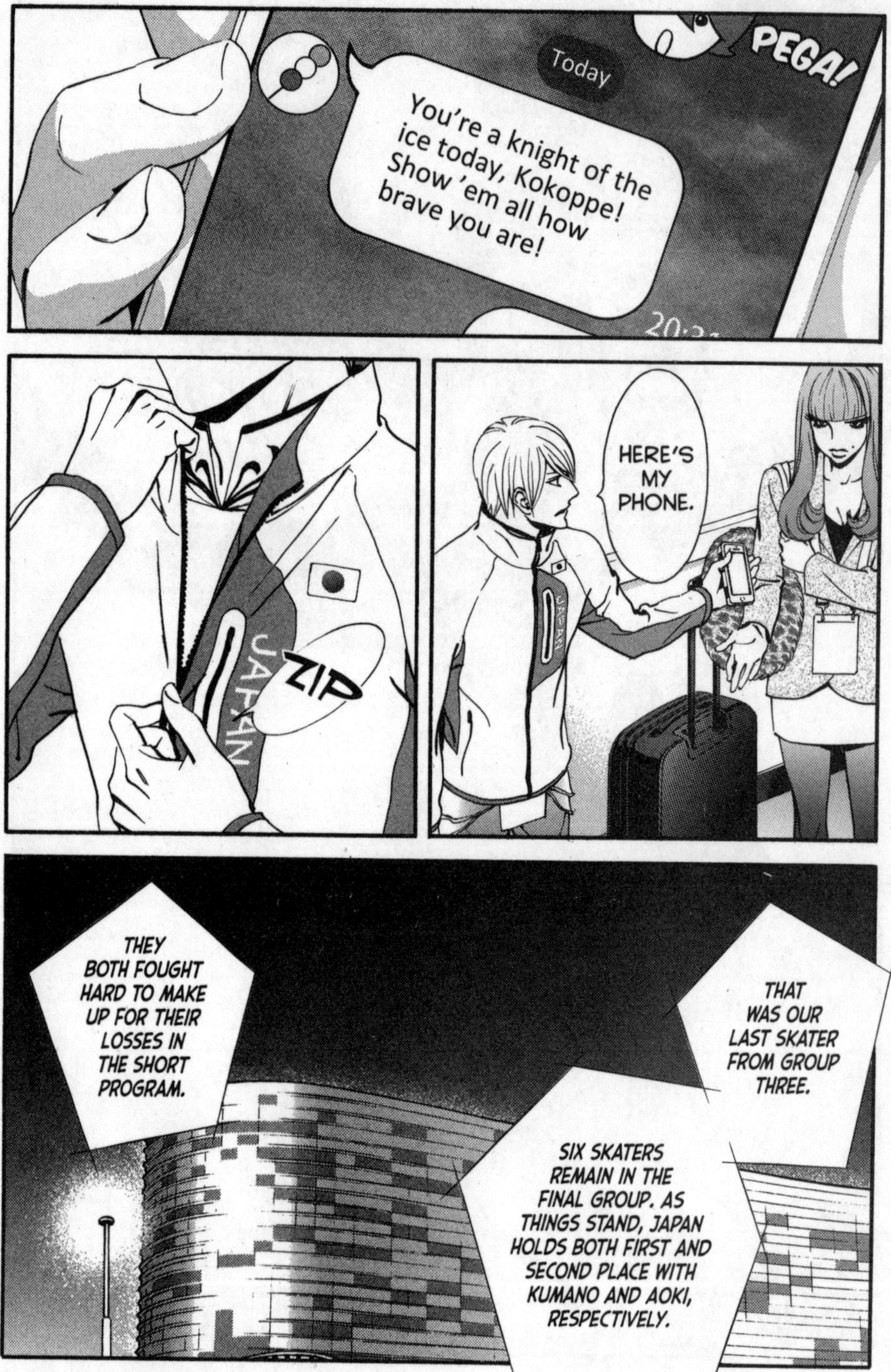
PEGA!
Today
You're a knight of the ice today, Kokoppe! Show 'em all how brave you are!
20:3
HERE'S MY PHONE.
ZIP
JAPAN
THAT WAS OUR LAST SKATER FROM GROUP THREE.
SIX SKATERS REMAIN IN THE FINAL GROUP. AS THINGS STAND, JAPAN HOLDS BOTH FIRST AND SECOND PLACE WITH KUMANO AND AOKI, RESPECTIVELY.
THEY BOTH FOUGHT HARD TO MAKE UP FOR THEIR LOSSES IN THE SHORT PROGRAM.

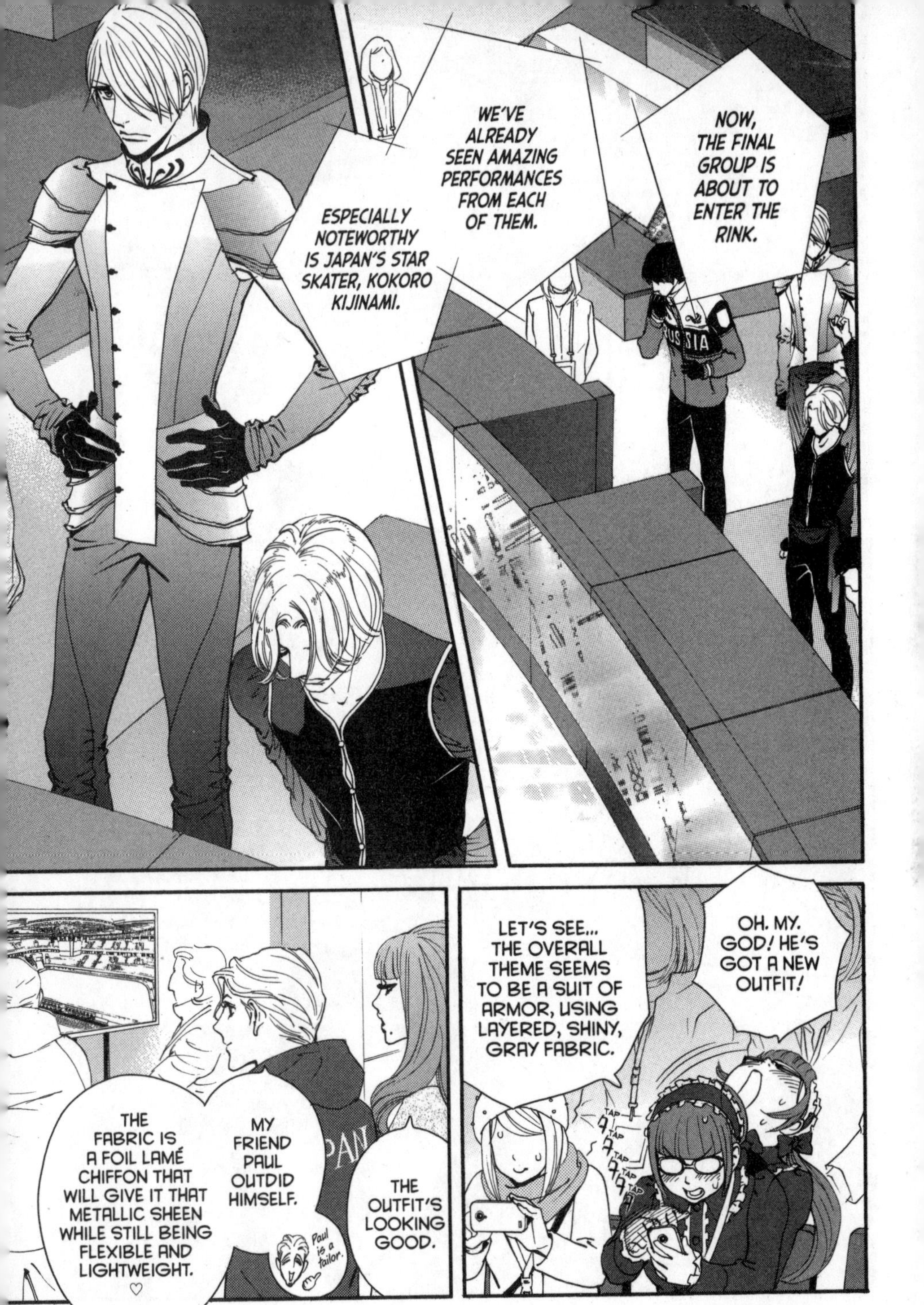
NOW, THE FINAL GROUP IS ABOUT TO ENTER THE RINK.
WE'VE ALREADY SEEN AMAZING PERFORMANCES FROM EACH OF THEM.
ESPECIALLY NOTEWORTHY IS JAPAN'S STAR SKATER, KOKORO KIJINAMI.
RUSSIA
OH. MY. GOD! HE'S GOT A NEW OUTFIT!
LET'S SEE... THE OVERALL THEME SEEMS TO BE A SUIT OF ARMOR, USING LAYERED, SHINY, GRAY FABRIC.
TAP TAP TAP TAP
THE OUTFIT'S LOOKING GOOD.
MY FRIEND PAUL OUTDID HIMSELF.
Paul is a tailor.
THE FABRIC IS A FOIL LAMÉ CHIFFON THAT WILL GIVE IT THAT METALLIC SHEEN WHILE STILL BEING FLEXIBLE AND LIGHTWEIGHT. ♡

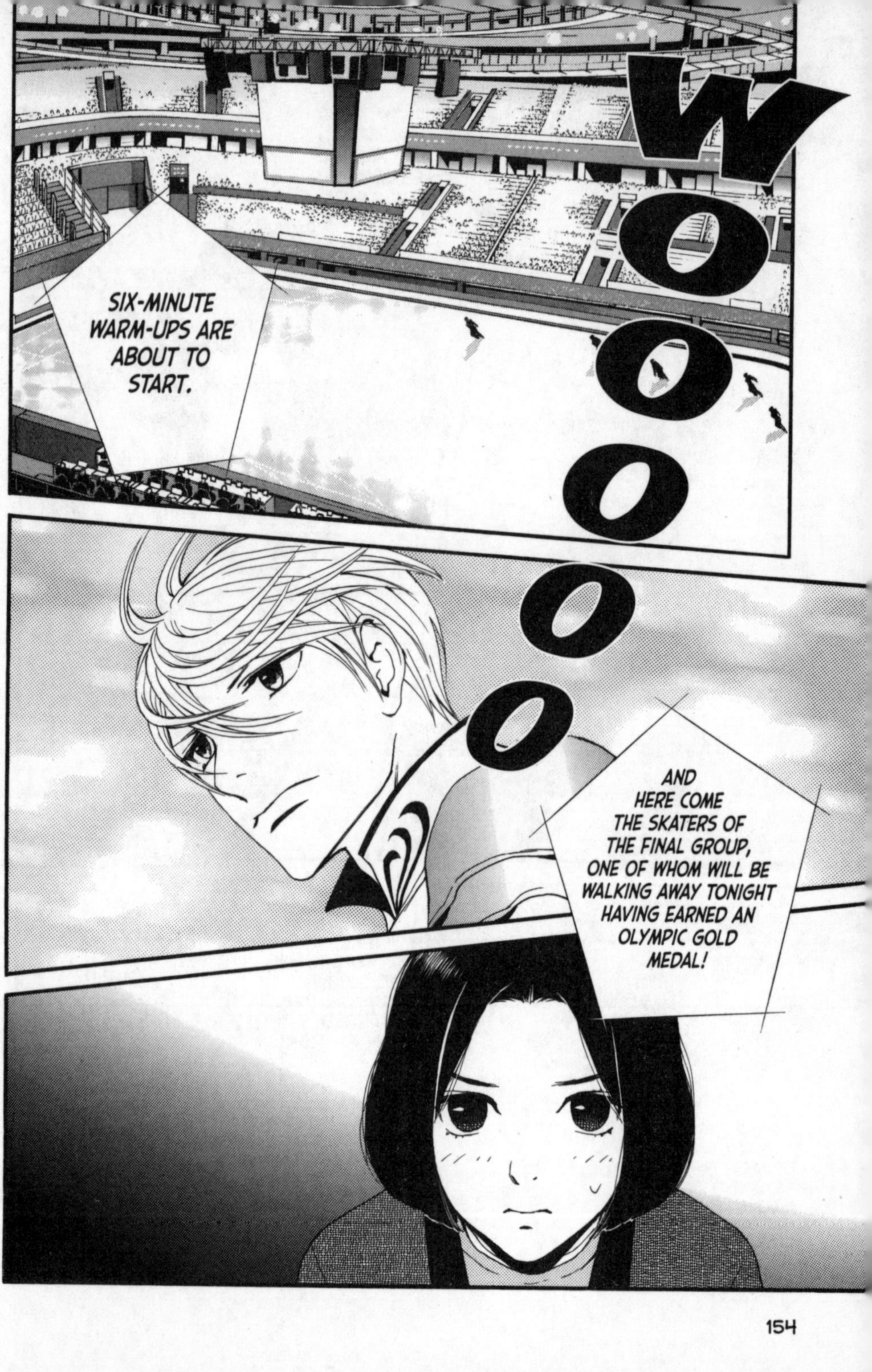

WOOOOO
SIX-MINUTE WARM-UPS ARE ABOUT TO START.
AND HERE COME THE SKATERS OF THE FINAL GROUP, ONE OF WHOM WILL BE WALKING AWAY TONIGHT HAVING EARNED AN OLYMPIC GOLD MEDAL!

To be continued...

TRANSLATION NOTES

DUEL AT HIGH NOON, PAGE 39

In Japanese, Moriyama references the duel of Musashi and Kojiro, two 17th-century samurai who were very influential in the development of Japanese sword fighting styles. They were both very skilled, but Musashi won through the use of psychological tactics, such as showing up three hours late on purpose.

Knight of the ICE

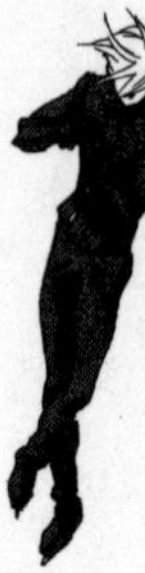

Glossary by Coach Akiyuki Kido

(based on January 2015 rules)

Trainer (page 11)
A trainer works to improve a skater's condition and make them more competitive by providing support and guidance to improve their physical fitness, psychological resilience, and overall health.

Russian Figure Skating Championships (page 12)
Canada, the United States, Japan, and various other countries hold national championships to where their best skaters compete for the title. The results of these competitions largely determine who will represent Japan at the Olympics and World Championships.

Short Program (page 13)
The short program is a segment in which the skaters have up to two minutes and fifty seconds to perform eight predetermined elements, such as jumps, spins, or steps.

Free skate (page 13)
In the free skating competition, skaters get to choose what elements and moves to use. Still, to ensure a well-rounded program, there are rules about what jumps, spins, and steps are required, as well as restrictions on the number of them allowed. In women's singles, this segment lasts four minutes, and in men's singles, it lasts four minutes and thirty seconds.

Triple Axel (3A) (page 13)
There are six different jumps in figure skating. An Axel is the only one that begins with the skater facing directly forward (on the forward outside edge). It's the most difficult jump, and a triple Axel requires three and a half midair rotations. Midori Ito was the first woman in Japan to successfully execute this jump.

Jumps in a program (page 13)
The six jumps in figure skating are the toe loop, Salchow, loop, flip, Lutz, and Axel. In the short program, the following jumps are required: 1) a triple-triple or triple-double jump combination, 2) a triple jump following a step, and 3) a double or triple Axel. In the free skate, the skater may perform up to eight jumps, one of which must be an Axel. No more than three jump combinations are allowed, and only one of those can consist of three jumps.

Quadruple Salchow (4S) (page 14)
A Salchow with four rotations. This jump is executed from the left foot's back inside edge by lifting the right foot forward and to the left. The way both feet face outward just before takeoff is a unique feature of the Salchow jump. It is typically considered an easy jump because its entrance from the back-inside edge makes rotating less difficult. Still, although they are rare, there do exist skaters who consider this their most difficult jump, often owing to personal difficulty skating on the back inside edge. It was named after the Swedish skater Ulrich Salchow.

Senior (page 15)
There are three age divisions in figure skating: novice, junior, and senior. The senior division includes skaters 15 or older, the junior division includes skaters ages 13 to 18, and the novice division is for skaters ages 10 to 13 (or sometimes 14). These ranges are based on their age on June 30th before the competition.

World Championships (page 20)
The World Figure Skating Championships, also known as Worlds, is the biggest event of the skating season. The winner earns the title of world champion for that season.

Team competition (page 31)
Each country is represented by two skaters from men's singles, two from women's singles, one team from pairs, and one ice-dancing pair in this free skate-only competition.

Coach (page 33)
Most coaches belong to the Figure Skating Instructor Association and teach at an ice rink. To work as a professional coach, even talented skaters are typically required to start by helping to teach beginners in a club or classroom setting.

Layback spin (page 33)
To do a layback spin, the spinner leans back and uses one leg to balance themselves while spinning in an upright position.

Spot (Olympic entries) (page 40)
A country can have at most three entries in figure skating competitions. Each country's number of entries is determined by the placements of their skaters at the World Championships the previous year. Each placement has a point value. Places 1 through 15 are worth a number of points equal to the placement, places 16 through 24 are each worth 16 points, and places from 25 and on are worth 18 points. A country's number of entries for the next year is based on these points and their number of entries for the current year in the following manner:
- Three entries: Three entries if the combined placement score of their two top-performing skaters is 13 or less, or two entries if it's 28 or less.
- Two entries: Three entries if the combined placement score is 13 or less, or two entries if it's 28 or less.
- One entry: Three entries if their placement score is 2 or less, or two entries if it's 10 or less.

The multiple entries are distributed automatically, and the remaining countries get the leftover entries in order of placement. A country that fails to get any entries for the Olympics by this means can get one entry by placing well in a designated Olympic qualifying event (such as the German Nebelhorn Trophy for the Sochi Olympics).

Ice Dancing (page 41)
Alongside singles and pairs, ice dancing is a category of figure skating competition. Skaters participate in teams of one man and one woman. This unique style of skating that was inspired by ballroom dancing. Rhythm, musicality, and footwork are given priority in ice dancing, and there are those who argue that it requires the most skill of any kind of figure skating competition.

Season (page 45)
Each year's skating season begins in July and ends in June of the next year.

Open Practice (page 54)
Open practice is typically held on the day before, or the day of, a competition. It's the skaters' last chance to polish their routines, and they're free to participate or not at their discretion. The technical panel—which consists of a technical specialist, an assistant technical specialist, and a technical controller—is required to watch and familiarize themselves with the skaters' programs.

Quad Lutz (4Lz) (page 56)
A Lutz with four rotations. The Lutz is considered the second hardest jump after the Axel. It is named after the Austrian skater Alois Lutz, the first person to perform this jump. To perform this jump, a skater uses their right toe pick (the front of the skate's blade where it has teeth) to launch themselves into the air from their left skate's back outside edge. Because of the difficulty of skating on this edge, many skaters make an edge error. Note that the roles of each foot are reversed for skaters who spin clockwise.

Triple Flip (page 80)

A flip with three rotations. To perform this jump, the skater rides the back inside edge of their left skate and uses their right toe to launch themself into the air. It is sometimes called the toe Salchow. Due to the relative difficulty of maintaining a vertical axis, this jump's base value is almost as high as that of the Lutz. Note that the roles of each foot are reversed for skaters who spin clockwise.

Triple Toe Loop (3T) (page 80)

A toe loop with three rotations. The toe loop is considered the easiest jump. The skater uses their left toe to launch themself into the air from their right skate's back outside edge. To date, no one has managed to execute this jump with more than four revolutions, and only a select few skaters can do even that.

Jump Combination (page 80)

A jump combination is when a skater performs a jump and then immediately performs another from the foot they land on. Since jumps are landed on the right skate's back outside edge (or the left skate's if you're spinning clockwise), all jumps after the first in a combination are limited to either the toe loop or the loop jump. If the skater weaves footwork between their jumps, it's called a jump sequence instead.

Six-minute warm-ups (page 84)

At the beginning of a competition, each group gets six minutes on the ice to practice.

Grand Prix Final (page 90)

The six highest-ranking skaters in the ISU Grand Prix go on to compete for first in the Final. The ISU Grand Prix is a series of six competitions held between October and December, including Skate America, Skate Canada, the Cup of China, the Trophée Eric Bompard (France), the Rostelecom Cup (Russia), and the NHK Trophy (Japan). The order they're held in varies by year.

Grade of execution (GOE) (page 101)

A skater's execution of each element is assigned a score modifier of between negative and positive three.

Deduction (page 101)

Each element—such as a jump, spin, step sequence, or spiral sequence—has a base value for use in scoring. The judges assign a modifier with one of seven values between negative and positive three to this base value, resulting in either a deduction or bonus points. Today, these deductions and bonuses are clearly defined in the rules, and there is a checklist of features that will earn one or the other (e.g., particularly high or low jumps, the overall flow, and speed).

Level (page 101)

Elements such as lifts, steps, twizzles, and dance spins are categorized into levels on the basis of certain features. An element with a higher level has a higher base value in scoring, and the highest level is four. World-class skaters perform most elements at level four.

Moves in the field (page 108)

Moves in the field are elements such as Ina Bauers which earn no points on their own but can affect the score of elements such as jumps and spins when used to transition in or out of them.

Base value (page 108)
Each element—such as a step, a spin, or a jump—has a base value. Three people—the technical specialist, the assistant technical specialist, and the technical controller—work together to do things like identify elements, count jump rotations, and distinguish the level and type of each spin or step. These determinations result in the assignment of a base score.

Program components score (PCS or presentation score) (page 111)
For this score, skaters are evaluated on the basis of five program components: skating skills, transitions, performance, composition, and interpretation. A skater's final score is the total of their program components score (PCS) and their technical score.

Spread eagle (page 118)
The spread eagle is a move in which the skater keeps both skates on the ice with the toes of each foot facing straight out to the sides.

Ina Bauer (page 118)
To do an Ina Bauer, the skater bends one leg out in front while stretching the other straight out behind them to skate sideways with their toes pointed out in opposite directions. It is most impressive when performed by skaters such as Shizuka Arakawa, gold medalist at the Turin Olympics, who are able to bend far back while doing it.

Raising an arm (page 119)
Doing this can earn a skater bonus points, as it's more difficult than executing a jump with one's arms crossed in front of their chest.

Technical score (page 121)
The technical score is determined by the technical elements included in the program and their quality. Jumps, spins, steps, and other elements each have a base value, which is modified by a grade of execution (GOE) to get the technical score. The GOE is the average of the modifiers assigned by the judges, excluding the highest and lowest. These modifiers have one of seven values between negative and positive three.

Under-rotate (page 129)
Under-rotation is the failure to include the necessary number of revolutions in a jump. A jump that's under-rotated by half a revolution or more is downgraded and has the base value of a jump with one fewer revolutions.

Akiyuki Kido was born on August 28th, 1975. He represented Japan in ice dancing at the 2006 winter Olympics in Turin, Italy. He took fifteenth place, the highest Japan had ever placed in ice dancing at the time. Today, he works as a coach at the Shin-Yokohama Skate Center.

Knight of the Ice Skater Profile 10

10	Timothy Li

Height:

170 cm

Blood type:

O

Birthday:

August 1st

Place of origin:

Chicago

Strongest element:

Jumps

Strongest jump:

Lutz

Most difficult jump performed to date:

Quad toe loop

Strength:

His speed and long jumping distance

Weakness:

Has difficulty focusing after a fall

Hobby:

Cycling

Talent:

Ice hockey

Family composition:

His parents, grandparents, and older brother

Favorite food:

Chinese steamed buns

Least favorite food:

Nothing in particular

Notes:

He may soon add the Quad Lutz to his repertoire...

Divided Opinion

⑨

Surely They Were Empty

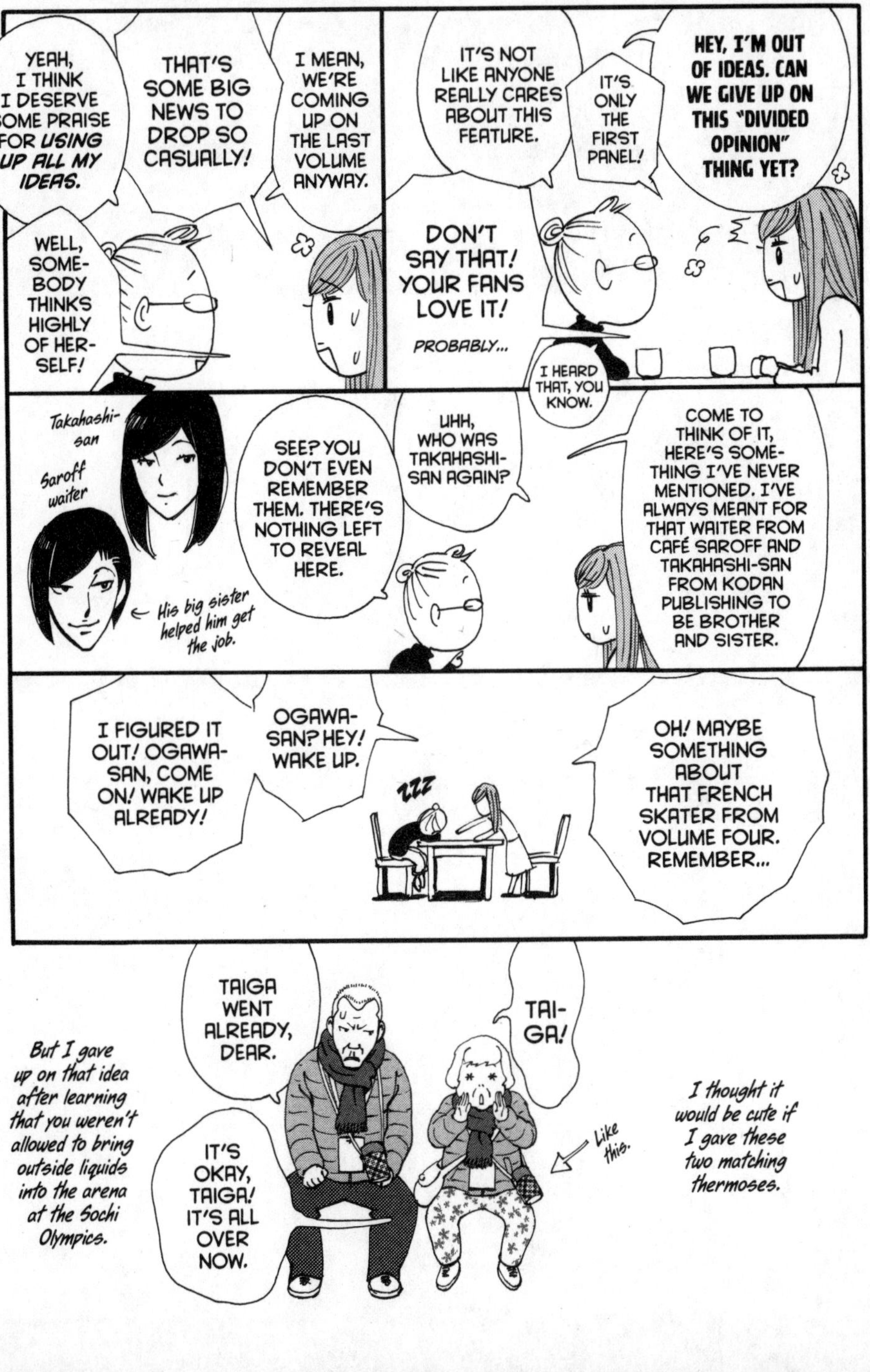
HEY, I'M OUT OF IDEAS. CAN WE GIVE UP ON THIS "DIVIDED OPINION" THING YET?
IT'S ONLY THE FIRST PANEL!
IT'S NOT LIKE ANYONE REALLY CARES ABOUT THIS FEATURE.
DON'T SAY THAT! YOUR FANS LOVE IT!
PROBABLY...
I HEARD THAT, YOU KNOW.
I MEAN, WE'RE COMING UP ON THE LAST VOLUME ANYWAY.
THAT'S SOME BIG NEWS TO DROP SO CASUALLY!
YEAH, I THINK I DESERVE SOME PRAISE FOR USING UP ALL MY IDEAS.
WELL, SOMEBODY THINKS HIGHLY OF HERSELF!
COME TO THINK OF IT, HERE'S SOMETHING I'VE NEVER MENTIONED. I'VE ALWAYS MEANT FOR THAT WAITER FROM CAFÉ SAROFF AND TAKAHASHI-SAN FROM KODAN PUBLISHING TO BE BROTHER AND SISTER.
UHH, WHO WAS TAKAHASHI-SAN AGAIN?
SEE? YOU DON'T EVEN REMEMBER THEM. THERE'S NOTHING LEFT TO REVEAL HERE.
Takahashi-san
Saroff waiter
His big sister helped him get the job.
OH! MAYBE SOMETHING ABOUT THAT FRENCH SKATER FROM VOLUME FOUR. REMEMBER...
ZZZ
OGAWA-SAN? HEY! WAKE UP.
I FIGURED IT OUT! OGAWA-SAN, COME ON! WAKE UP ALREADY!
I thought it would be cute if I gave these two matching thermoses.
Like this.
TAI-GA!
TAIGA WENT ALREADY, DEAR.
IT'S OKAY, TAIGA! IT'S ALL OVER NOW.
But I gave up on that idea after learning that you weren't allowed to bring outside liquids into the arena at the Sochi Olympics.

Who will take home the gold medal?
As blade meets ice, our story reaches its climax!

Knight of the Ice vol. 11
Coming soon!

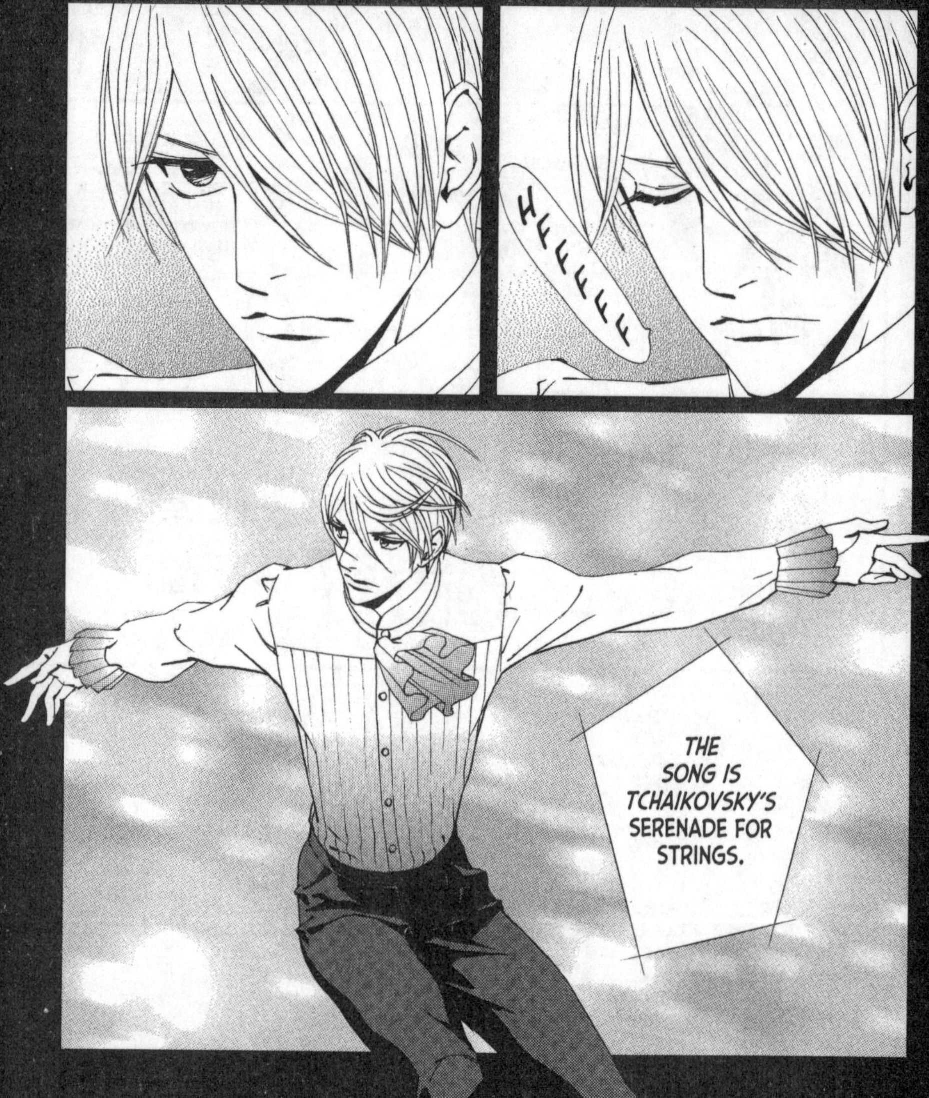
HFFFFFF
THE SONG IS TCHAIKOVSKY'S SERENADE FOR STRINGS.

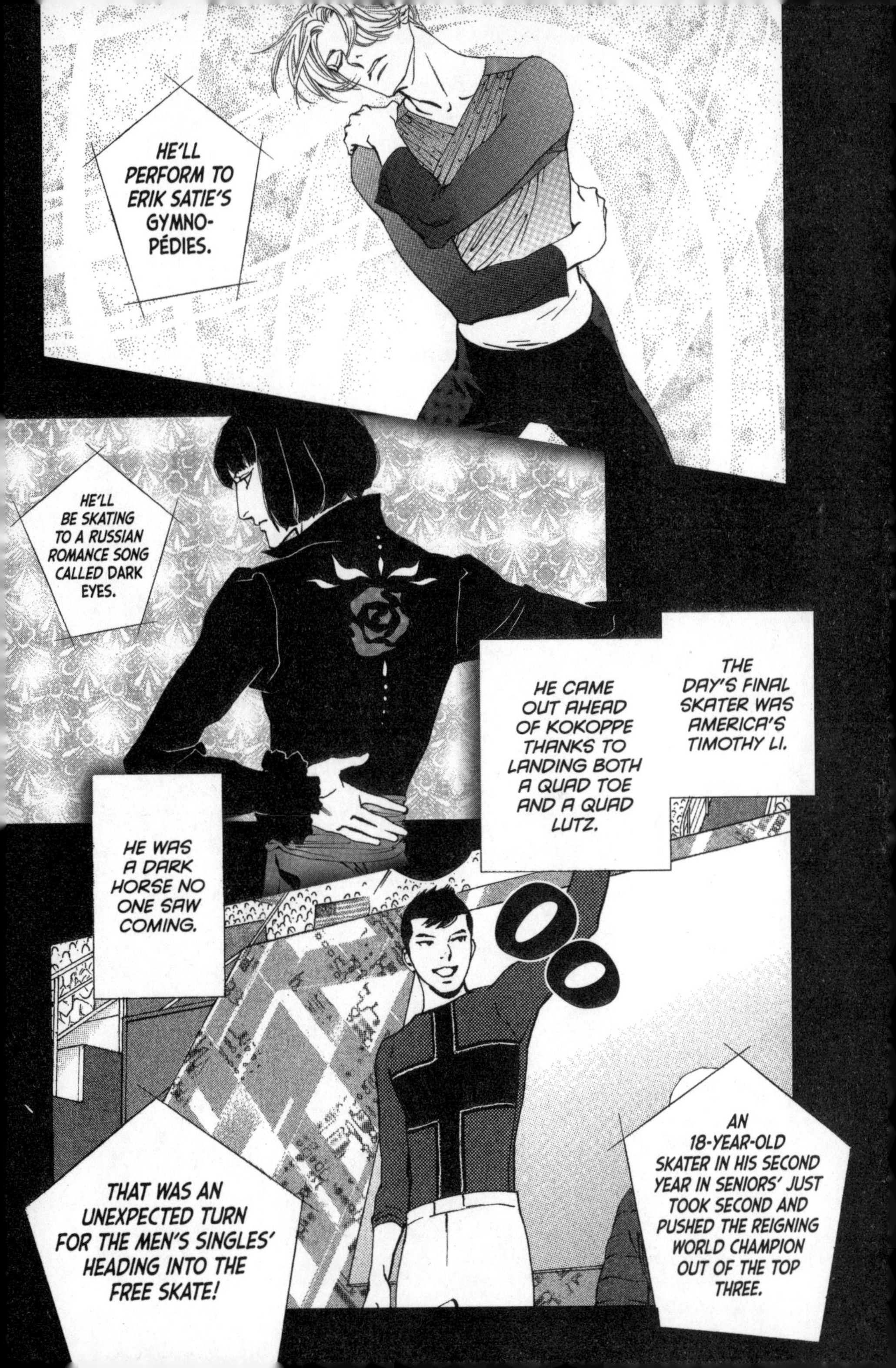
HE'LL PERFORM TO ERIK SATIE'S GYMNOPÉDIES.
HE'LL BE SKATING TO A RUSSIAN ROMANCE SONG CALLED DARK EYES.
THE DAY'S FINAL SKATER WAS AMERICA'S TIMOTHY LI.
HE CAME OUT AHEAD OF KOKOPPE THANKS TO LANDING BOTH A QUAD TOE AND A QUAD LUTZ.
HE WAS A DARK HORSE NO ONE SAW COMING.
AN 18-YEAR-OLD SKATER IN HIS SECOND YEAR IN SENIORS' JUST TOOK SECOND AND PUSHED THE REIGNING WORLD CHAMPION OUT OF THE TOP THREE.
THAT WAS AN UNEXPECTED TURN FOR THE MEN'S SINGLES' HEADING INTO THE FREE SKATE!

A SMART, NEW ROMANTIC COMEDY FOR FANS OF *SHORTCAKE CAKE* AND *TERRACE HOUSE!*

A romance manga starring high school girl Meeko, who learns to live on her own in a boarding house whose living room is home to the odd (but handsome) Matsunaga-san. She begins to adjust to her new life away from her parents, but Meeko soon learns that no matter how far away from home she is, she's still a young girl at heart — especially when she finds herself falling for Matsunaga-san.

The adorable new odd-couple cat comedy manga from the creator of the beloved *Chi's Sweet Home*, in full color!

Praise for Chi's Sweet Home

"Nearly impossible to turn away... a true all-ages title that anyone, young or old, cat lover or not, will enjoy. The stories will bring a smile to your face and warm your heart."

—School Library Journal

Sue & Tai-chan

Konami Kanata

Sue is an aging housecat who's looking forward to living out her life in peace... but her plans change when the mischievous black tomcat Tai-chan enters the picture! Hey! Sue never signed up to be a catsitter! *Sue & Tai-chan* is the latest from the reigning meow-narch of cute kitty comics, Konami Kanata.

Young characters and steampunk setting, like *Howl's Moving Castle* and *Battle Angel Alita*

Beyond the Clouds © 2018 Nicke / Ki-oon

A boy with a talent for machines and a mysterious girl whose wings he's fixed will take you beyond the clouds! In the tradition of the high-flying, resonant adventure stories of Studio Ghibli comes a gorgeous tale about the longing of young hearts for adventure and friendship!

PERFECT WORLD

Rie Aruga

A TOUCHING NEW SERIES ABOUT LOVE AND COPING WITH DISABILITY

An office party reunites Tsugumi with her high school crush Itsuki. He's realized his dream of becoming an architect, but along the way, he experienced a spinal injury that put him in a wheelchair. Now Tsugumi's rekindled feelings will butt up against prejudices she never considered — and Itsuki will have to decide if he's ready to let someone into his heart...

"Depicts with great delicacy and courage the difficulties some with disabilities experience getting involved in romantic relationships... Rie Aruga refuses to romanticize, pushing her heroine to face the reality of disability. She invites her readers to the same tasks of empathy, knowledge and recognition."
—Slate.fr

"An important entry [in manga romance]... The emotional core of both plot and characters indicates thoughtfulness... [Aruga's] research is readily apparent in the text and artwork, making this feel like a real story."
—Anime News Network

KC
KODANSHA
COMICS

Something's Wrong With Us

NATSUMI ANDO

The dark, psychological, sexy shojo series readers have been waiting for!

A spine-chilling and steamy romance between a Japanese sweets maker and the man who framed her mother for murder!

Following in her mother's footsteps, Nao became a traditional Japanese sweets maker, and with unparalleled artistry and a bright attitude, she gets an offer to work at a world-class confectionary company. But when she meets the young, handsome owner, she recognizes his cold stare...

KODANSHA COMICS

THE SWEET SCENT OF LOVE IS IN THE AIR! FOR FANS OF OFFBEAT ROMANCES LIKE *WOTAKOI*

Sweat and Soap © Kintetsu Yamada / Kodansha Ltd.

In an office romance, there's a fine line between sexy and awkward... and that line is where Asako — a woman who sweats copiously — meets Koutarou — a perfume developer who can't get enough of Asako's, er, scent. Don't miss a romcom manga like no other!

Saiyuki

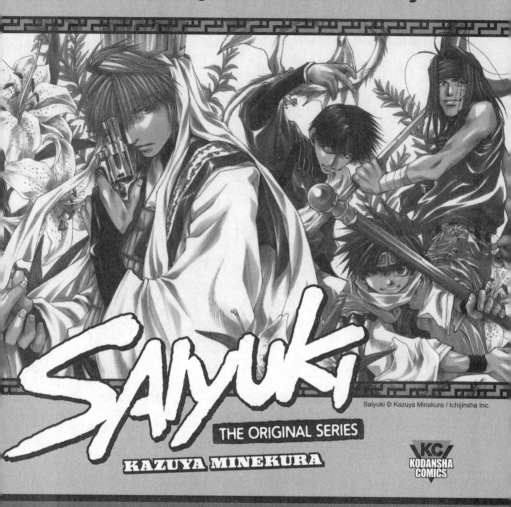

Poor college student Hideki is down on his luck. All he wants is a good job, a girlfriend, and his very own "persocom"—the latest and greatest in humanoid computer technology. Hideki's luck changes one night when he finds Chi—a persocom thrown out in a pile of trash. But Hideki soon discovers that there's much more to his cute new persocom than meets the eye.

KC
KODANSHA
COMICS

THE WORLD OF CLAMP!

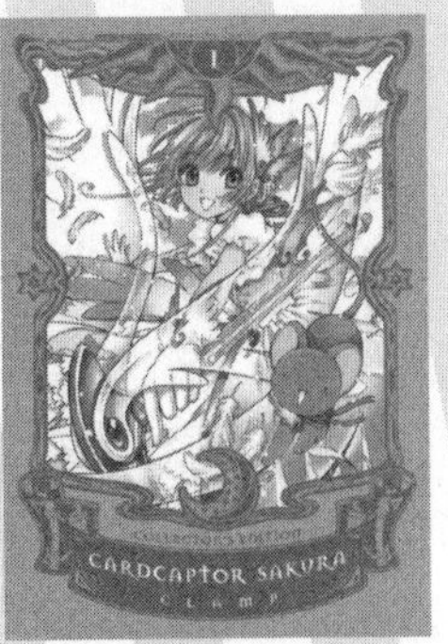
CARDCAPTOR SAKURA
CLAMP

Cardcaptor Sakura
Collector's Edition

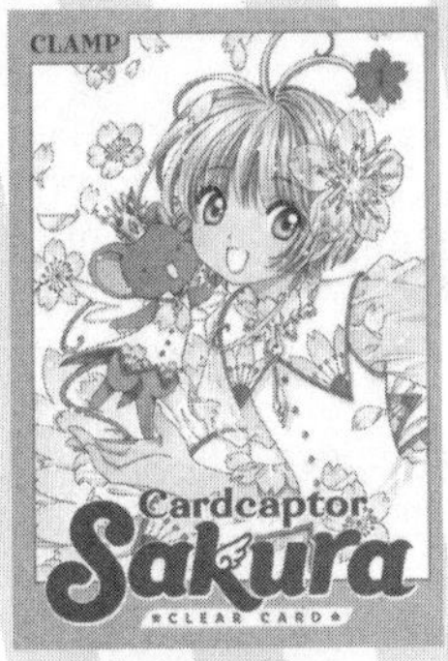
CLAMP
Cardcaptor
Sakura
CLEAR CARD

Cardcaptor Sakura:
Clear Card

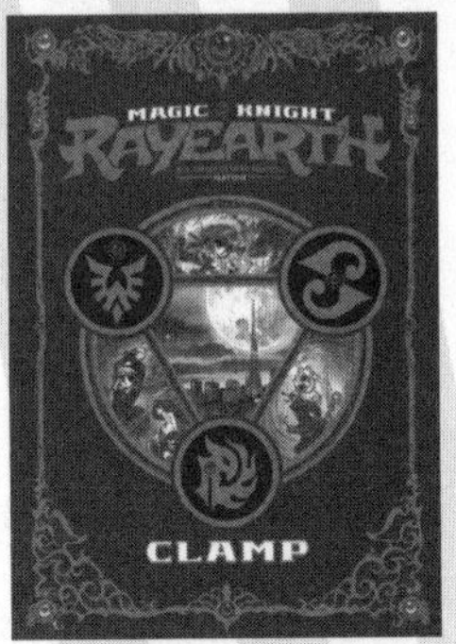
MAGIC KNIGHT
RAYEARTH
CLAMP

Magic Knight Rayearth
25th Anniversary Box Set

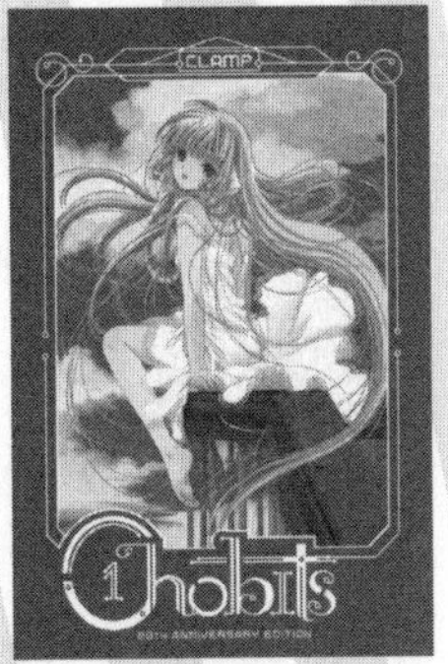
CLAMP
1
Chobits

Chobits

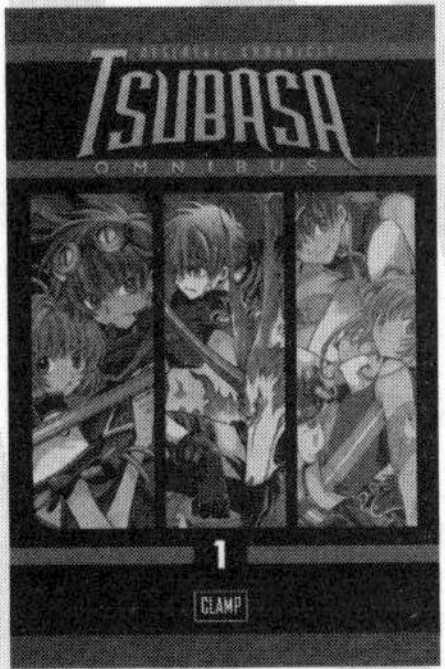
TSUBASA
1
CLAMP

TSUBASA Omnibus

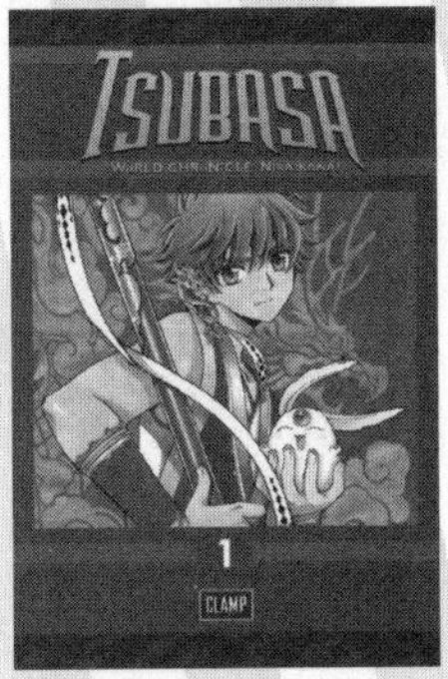
TSUBASA
1
CLAMP

TSUBASA WoRLD CHRoNiCLE

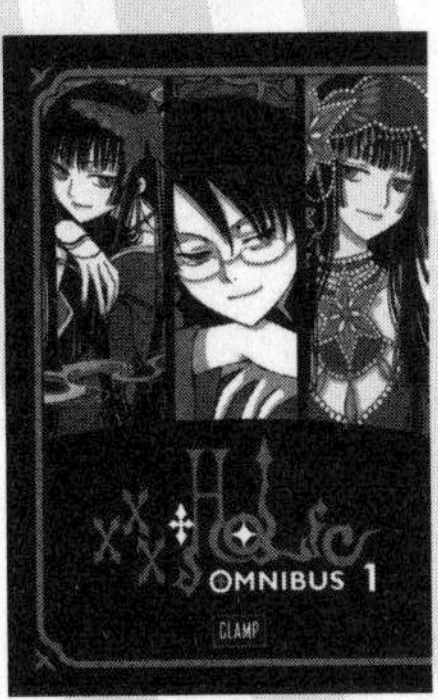
xxxHOLiC
OMNIBUS 1
CLAMP

xxxHOLiC Omnibus

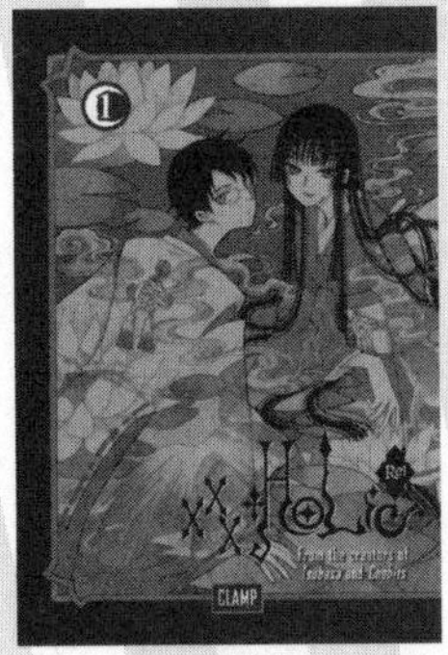
1
xxxHOLiC
CLAMP

xxxHOLiC Rei

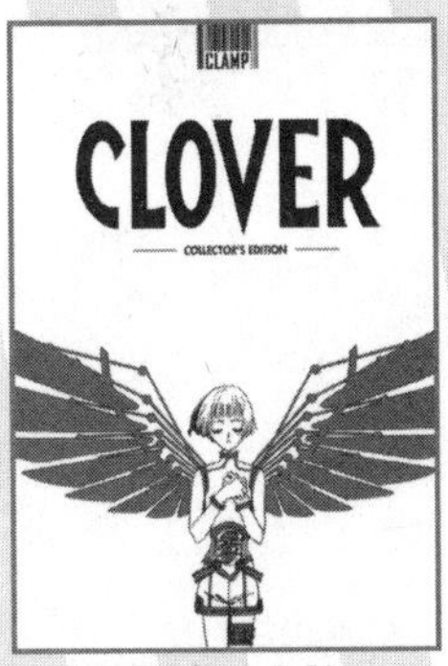
CLAMP
CLOVER
COLLECTOR'S EDITION

CLOVER Collector's Edition

KC
KODANSHA
COMICS

Kodansha Comics welcomes you to explore the expansive world of CLAMP, the all-female artist collective that has produced some of the most acclaimed manga of the century. Our growing catalog includes icons like *Cardcaptor Sakura* and *Magic Knight Rayearth*, each crafted with CLAMP's one-of-a-kind style and characters!

A Kodansha Comics Trade Paperback Original
Knight of the Ice 10 copyright © 2017 Yayoi Ogawa
English translation copyright © 2022 Yayoi Ogawa

All rights reserved.

Published in the United States by Kodansha Comics, an imprint of Kodansha USA Publishing, LLC, New York.

Publication rights for this English edition arranged through Kodansha Ltd., Tokyo.

First published in Japan in 2017 by Kodansha Ltd., Tokyo as *Ginban kishi*, volume 10.

ISBN 978-1-64651-087-0

Printed in the United States of America.

www.kodansha.us

1st Printing
Translation: Rose Padgett
Lettering: Jennifer Skarupa
Editing: Aimee Zink
Kodansha Comics edition cover design by Phil Balsman

Publisher: Kiichiro Sugawara

Director of publishing services: Ben Applegate
Associate director of operations: Stephen Pakula
Publishing services managing editors: Alanna Ruse, Madison Salters
Production managers: Emi Lotto, Angela Zurlo